Contributions to Management Science

The series *Contributions to Management Science* contains research publications in all fields of business and management science. These publications are primarily monographs and multiple author works containing new research results, and also feature selected conference-based publications are also considered. The focus of the series lies in presenting the development of latest theoretical and empirical research across different viewpoints.

This book series is indexed in Scopus.

More information about this series at http://www.springer.com/series/1505

Sonja A. Sackmann

Culture in Organizations

Development, Impact and Culture-Mindful Leadership

Springer

Sonja A. Sackmann
Universität der Bundeswehr
Munich, Germany

ISSN 1431-1941 ISSN 2197-716X (electronic)
Contributions to Management Science
ISBN 978-3-030-86079-0 ISBN 978-3-030-86080-6 (eBook)
https://doi.org/10.1007/978-3-030-86080-6

This Springer imprint is published by the registered company Springer Nature Switzerland AG.
The registered company address is: Gewerbestrasse 11, 6330 Cham, Switzerland

Preface

Organizational or corporate culture has become an important topic in business and gained its place in academia. Many business leaders consider culture vital for their firm's performance and survival—especially in today's VUCA business environment characterized by volatility, uncertainty, complexity, and ambiguity. Even leaders in not-for-profit organizations talk about their corporate culture and consider it a decisive factor for the satisfaction of their employees and the efficient and effective operations of their organization. Employees may thrive in particular organizational cultures, while others suffer from burnout or bore-out in other types of cultures. For young qualified people and professionals, an organization's culture has become crucial for their employer's choice. What is the secret behind organizational cultures that make people either excel or sick? What is culture in organizations all about?

These questions triggered my interest in the topic many years ago. As a student, I experienced academic and business settings whose people gave me twenty reasons why I could not do what I proposed. Others responded to my ideas, only asking, "Why not?" I also wondered why people, who had just returned from their vacation, started to plan their next vacation. Given the time that most of us spend at work, I asked how organizations could look like people felt encouraged, joy, and their time and efforts worthwhile spent?

At that time, I could hardly find any literature on the topic. Hence, I ventured out to study culture in organizational settings, develop the concept further, and test my ideas in organizations in both researcher and consultant roles. In the 1980s, culture was still the core concept in anthropology. Therefore, organizational scholars used anthropologists' conceptions of culture and introduced them into the corporate and management domain, including their underlying assumptions. Research including my work suggested that some of these assumptions needed adjustment, given that culture turned out to be less homogenous in organizational settings than assumed.

Since the 1980s, organizational or corporate culture has received several waves of attention from both organizational researchers and practitioners. Despite the challenges in studying this multifaceted phenomenon, scholars have further developed the concept with more elaborate research and knowledge from sociology and social and cognitive psychology. These efforts resulted in more insights into culture, its various facets, and its role and impact on organizations. The initial euphoria of practitioners trying to fix their culture has mostly given way to a more realistic idea regarding the challenges that an organization's culture poses and the benefits that it may have for organizations, their members and leaders.

Globalization, new waves of mergers and acquisitions, several fraudulent business practices, and the COVID-19 pandemic gave culture in organizations a new impetus. Globalization, among others, focused the attention on multicultural workforces within the boundaries of one organization and the impact of venturing into new markets for a company and its culture. The demise of several well-known companies like Enron, WorldCom, or Wirecard and the Dieselgate scandal raised questions about organizations' cultures and how they could drift unnoticed—at least to outsiders. When people had to work from home from one day to the next in many countries during the pandemic, leaders and managers started to worry about their culture and the potential impact of virtual work. Hence, organizational culture has gained its place both in practice and in research.

This book aims to provide a research-based, practice-oriented, and current overview of the topic of culture in the context of organizations and how to deal with it—also against the backdrop of a VUCA environment. It addresses leaders, managers, and consultants interested in a solid understanding of culture in organizations, its characteristics, functions and impact on organizational life and performance, and how it can be assessed, maintained, developed, or changed. The book is also of interest to scholars and students, who want to get a current and detailed understanding of the concept of culture in the context of organizations with its history, different facets, development and implications for organizational members and performance, and how it can be studied, understood, and further developed.

The book's ten chapters address the concept itself, and culture's impact on and implications for organizations, its members, managers, and leaders. Chapters 1–5 provide insights into the concept of culture to better understand this hard-to-grasp phenomenon. Chapter 1 informs about the concept's development and its place in management. The characteristics of organizational culture, its functions, and some myths about culture are subject of Chap. 2. Chapter 3 addresses its emergence and development in an organization's life cycle, including subcultures. Chapter 4 explores culture's effect on the different facets of organizational life, and Chap. 5 reports its various impacts on the performance of organizations.

Chapters 6–10 address more practical issues and implications of culture. Even though culture is always vital for organizations, it needs special attention in particular situations. Chapter 6 explores several of those with a focus on strategic alliances (joint ventures and mergers and acquisitions) and social value changes. Chapter 7 addresses how to analyze and evaluate the quality of an existing culture. What to do about culture regarding its development or change is the topic of Chap. 8. Given that many organizations face a VUCA environment, Chap. 9 explores those cultural characteristics that support an organization's viability in such a VUCA environment. Since culture development or change is eventually a journey, Chap. 10 points to the vital role of leaders and managers in paying conscious attention to their culture as culture-mindful leaders. Culture-mindful management and leadership may also help avoid unintended culture drifts.

Even though the chapters build on each other and refer to topics discussed in more depth in other chapters, each chapter stands on its own with its respective subject. Hence, if readers are interested in a particular topic such as culture assessment (Chap. 7), the concept of culture (Chap. 2), what happens when acquiring an organization (Chap. 6), or developing an organization's culture (Chap. 8), they can directly read that chapter without having read the prior ones, even though an understanding of the concept of culture in organizations may be helpful (Chap. 2). In addition, each chapter contains references for exploring different aspects of a topic further.

Given my background both in the academic and in practitioner's worlds, I illustrate my arguments with practical examples and include several short cases. My perspective of culture is rooted in a systemic and social constructivist perspective. I take the view of culture being negotiated by its members, and once they have created culture, it influences their behavior and all aspects of organizational life. I primarily use the term *organizational* instead of corporate culture since organizational culture applies to for-profit and not-for-profit organizations. I frequently use organizations as actors. Even though people are the actors of organizations, my use of the active term implies the collective nature of culture in organizations. It is the collective that acts rather than a single individual. In addition, I use the term *organizational members* when I refer to all people in an organization, including genders, leaders, and managers. When addressing hierarchical differences, I use employees (followers) and both terms *leaders* and *managers* since not all managers may be leaders.

With this book, I hope to contribute to further demystify, unravel, and better understand this multifaceted and hard-to-grasp phenomenon with its real implications for organizations' functioning and performance, and for organizational members' well-being. Furthermore, I hope that some of my questions stimulate more research on the topic and that my suggestions of culture-mindful management and leadership will help managers and leaders deal more consciously and mindfully with their organization's culture, thus embarking on their culture's journey.

Munich, Germany Sonja A. Sackmann

Acknowledgments

This book stands on many shoulders. On my culture journey, I had the opportunity to discuss and test my ideas in many exchanges with colleagues, students, and practitioners. Above all, I was fortunate to meet and work with managers and leaders interested in a better understanding of their organization's culture, its development and change, and a more mindful approach to it. These conversations and projects have sharpened my ideas and thoughts, expanded them, and enriched them with examples. I want to take this opportunity to thank them for these learning opportunities.

Several people have supported me in preparing and finishing this book. Some of them I want to acknowledge personally. First and foremost, I want to thank Silke Agricola, my long-time collaborator. She has formatted the text and checked all references and inconsistencies. She gave the figures a final touch and reviewed and cleaned up the manuscript with her energy, creativity, and above all, patience. My research assistant and doctoral student at the time, Regina Palmer, provided essential support in researching, cleaning up, and compiling the literature chapter by chapter. Many thanks for your contribution. I want to thank Rocio Torregrosa from Springer Nature, who accepted the book idea, Parthiban Gujilan Kannan, Springer Nature's project coordinator, and Nancey Biswas, Springer project manager. They were patient with me in turning in the manuscript later than promised. Thank you for your cooperation and patience.

Since preparing the manuscript took time at the expense of my family, I want to thank my two daughters, Julia and Angela, for accepting their working mommy and my husband, Wolfgang, for accepting me the way I am.

Contents

List of Figures

List of Tables

Chapter 1
Introduction

Culture has become a frequently used term in connection with organizations. Several scholarly and practitioner-oriented publications suggest that it may be a panacea for organizations in dealing with their tasks and challenges. Surviving in today's turbulent and competitive environment requires an *agile* culture (AOE, 2020; Jurisic et al., 2020). The challenges of unprecedented change can be mastered with a good *risk* culture that "is a critical element to institutional resilience in the face of any challenge" (Higgins et al., 2020). A *strong* corporate culture seems to be helpful in a pandemic (Li et al., 2021), while working from home requires a *specific* culture (Westfall, 2020) characterized by trust (Sackmann, 2020; Bissels et al., 2006).

Given these proclamations, expectations, hopes and findings, one may wonder what culture in organizations is all about. What does culture entail? How does culture come about in organizations? How does it develop? What kind of functions does it serve? Why is it important for organizations? Can it be changed, and if so, how? Which roles do leaders play regarding an organization's culture? These are some of the questions that this book will address, thus providing a thorough understanding of the concept of organizational culture. This introductory chapter provides an overview of the emergence and development of the concept of culture in the fields of organization theory and management and it explores some of the reasons behind the interest in organizational culture. The chapter closes with an overview of the remaining nine book chapters.

The first traces of the concept of culture applied to organizations go back to the 1930s, 1950s, and 1960s. It was, however, not until the late 1970s and early 1980s that the concept received increasing attention from both managers and organizational scholars who started to explore and research organizational culture more systematically. Since that time, organizational or corporate culture[1] has gained a firm place in

[1] *Organizational culture* is the broader term incorporating both cultures within for-profit as well as not-for-profit organizations. *Hence, corporate culture* is a subset of organizational culture, referring to culture within incorporated firms. In this book, I will primarily use the broader term or an organization's culture.

S. A. Sackmann, *Culture in Organizations*, Contributions to Management Science,
https://doi.org/10.1007/978-3-030-86080-6_1

the management literature, organization theory, research, and practice—although with varying attention and changing interests over the decades. At the beginning of this millennium, the concept of culture in organizations gained new impetus due to several business fraud cases, increasing competition, and the developing knowledge society in which human capital is increasingly important.

The following sections describe how the concept of culture became introduced in the fields of organizational theory and managerial practice, how it developed over the years, and why it is increasingly important for organizations.

1.1 The Emergence of the Culture Concept in Management and Organizational Research

The first traces of the concept of culture applied to organizations appeared in the 1930s in Chester Barnard's (1938) work. He argued that large organizations could only function because of their informal systems. The sociologist Talcott Parsons (1951) explored the problem of order in organizations and processes of institutionalization, stating that the structure of organizations consists of patterns of institutionalized values. Organizations turn into cultural systems when organizational members internalize these patterns of values that in turn influence their orientation and actions. The organizational sociologist Philip Selznick (1957) explored how organizations turn into institutions when the leader infuses them with values. In the late 1960s, researchers interested in large systems' change became interested in organizational culture, and they considered it critical for accomplishing sustained change (e.g., Bennis, 1969). Their work implied that change processes were only be sustainable if an organization's culture changed.

In all of these works, culture was mentioned but not really discussed and further investigated. Even though culture was considered a critical phenomenon for organizational actions and outcomes, scholars did not explore the concept on its own. It was not until the beginning of the 1980s that the organizational culture concept received increased attention, first in the United States and a few years later also in Europe. This interest was funneled by economic challenges that U.S. firms could not manage well or solve satisfyingly with then-existing business practices. These economic challenges started in the U.S. at the end of the 1970s. U.S. firms faced increasingly foreign competition, and especially foreign products entered their domestic market. This phenomenon was new to the U.S. economy and U.S. firms. While World War II had weakened or even destroyed most industrialized nations, the United States emerged and prospered as a world economy. At that time, the U.S. contributed 75 percent to the world's Gross National Product (Thurow, 1988). After World War II, the United States dominated the world economy (Servan-Schreiber, 1968), U.S. firms started to expand worldwide (Vernon, 1971), and the American management doctrine and related practices spread all over the world (Boyacigiller et al., 2009).

The increasing range of foreign products provided U.S. consumers with a broader choice. Being able to buy foreign products at a better price and getting better value for their money, U.S. consumers started to buy more foreign products. As a result, U.S. firms lost market share to foreign competitors, which was unfamiliar to them. The changes in U.S. consumers' buying patterns also uncovered several underlying problems of many U.S. firms relating to quality, productivity, and lack of innovation.

The automobile industry illustrates these problems. In the 1940s, it was considered the industry of all industries (Drucker, 1946), and in the 1980s, it still represented the largest industry sector in the U.S., with 50 million newly produced cars per year. Being confronted with foreign competition and especially with competition from Japanese firms, U.S. companies had increasing problems selling their products in their domestic markets. From 1955 to 1988, American-owned automobile manufacturers lost about 25 percent market share (Womack et al., 1990) while the market share of Japanese car manufacturers increased as shown in Fig. 1.1 for the years 1965–2016.

In addition, Japanese firms managed to shorten the product life cycle from customary eight to nine years to about five years, partially because of technological innovations. When U.S. firms tried to reduce their product life cycles, the problems mentioned above emerged related to quality, productivity, and a lack of innovation.

Faced with these challenges, the initial reaction of many U.S. firms' management was to intensify their well-known production and management methods, thus

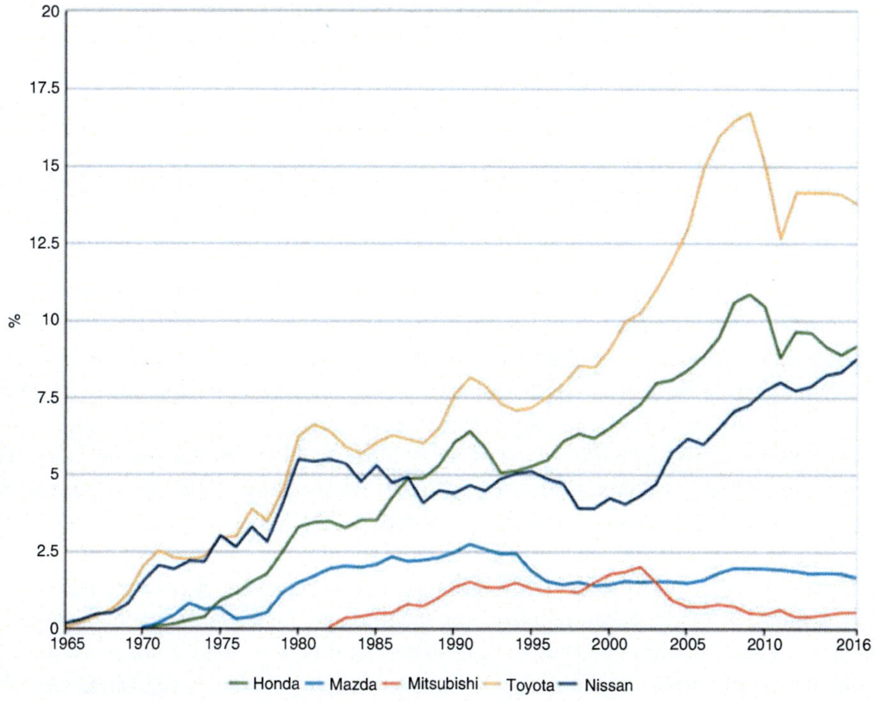

Fig. 1.1 Market share of Japanese automobile manufacturers 1965–2016 (Niedermeyer, 2018)

spending more time and effort doing more of the same things. These efforts, however, were not effective. Well-proven tools, established working and production methods, and management practices no longer resulted in the expected and desired outcomes. Hence, the success of Japanese car manufacturers made leaders of U.S. firms increasingly curious about Japanese production and management methods. Given that the care sector was the most important industry at that time, this interest had a significant impact on other sectors.

1.2 Japanese Management Practices

Pascale and Athos (1981) conducted one of the first systematic studies of successful Japanese firms and their production and management methods. The main results of their research characterized Japanese management practices as follows:

Practices of Successful Japanese Firms (Pascale & Athos, 1981)

- Innovation in technology and production methods.
- Emphasis on quality and performance.
- Specific human resources management practices, i.e.,
  - long tenure of employees with their employing firm,
  - decision making based on consensus,
  - responsibility based on the group (instead of individuals),
  - slow promotion based on loyalty,
  - horizontal career moves,
  - large span of control, and
  - high identification of organizational members with their employing organization.

These Japanese management practices resulted in increased productivity of 200–300 percent higher than US-American companies. The researchers attributed this productivity increase mainly to the specific management practices developed in Japan after World War II out of necessity. Japanese management practices contradicted the U.S. American experience and their practices. After World War II, Japanese firms had to invest in new technology and new production methods. The war had almost completely destroyed their infrastructure. Japanese firms faced a shortage of skilled labor, and they served only a small domestic market. Due to the specific societal values that emphasized a long-term perspective, quality, and collective effort (e.g., Hofstede, 2001; Nakane, 1970), Japanese firms' high quality and performance standards resulted from the specific way Japanese people had learned to think and work. These societal culture patterns influenced their work behavior and, in turn, all aspects of human resource management that contrasted with

U.S. American cultural patterns. Since Japanese culture considered firms extended family, employment contracts were usually life-long at the time and rather comprehensive. They included aspects that might otherwise be considered part of private life, such as arranging marriages. These strong ties between Japanese employees and their employing company led to a high level of organizational members' identification with their employing firm.

Because of the strong collective orientation, Japanese managers delegated responsibility to the group rather than a single person. Management did not consider individual performance criteria the only criteria for promotion. Instead, employees' contribution to the organization and especially their loyalty and tenure with the firm were critical components for promotion. The concept of a career was quite different when compared to the U.S. A horizontal move was also considered a career enhancement in Japan since it provided the person with increased experience, additional qualifications, or it implied a new learning opportunity. In addition, the traditional span of control of seven plus/minus two widely spread in U.S. firms was not part of Japanese firms' practices. Their supervisory span of control was higher due to their team-based management approach and the widely spread and strong collective orientation that influenced employees' thinking and actions.

These observed management practices that differed from U.S. managerial practices at the time were considered the major contributors to Japanese firms' success. Hence, many U.S.-American managers tried to copy the above-mentioned Japanese management practices. Some even traveled to Japan to study Samurai techniques and implement them back in the U.S. hoping to improve the results of their firms. The top executives of a U.S. company even renamed one of their meeting rooms after a famous Japanese Samurai. The name should demonstrate that meetings in this room implied positive fights among participants to develop the best solutions due to their open and critical debate and fight for the best decision (Pelton et al., 1990).

However, because of the differences in cultural values, the transfer of supposedly successful Japanese management practices to U.S. firms was ineffective. Expected results did not materialize. The lack of inter-and cross-cultural sensitivity blinded U.S. leaders to the fact that management practices that were successful within the context of Japanese firms in Japan may not have the same effects in another cultural context, such as U.S. firms operating in the U.S.

1.3 The Culture Concept's Rise and Set-Back

The lack of positive outcomes motivated another research team to focus their research efforts on studying practices of successful U.S. firms operating in the U.S. The results of such a study could be easier copied and implemented within the same national culture context. Tom Peters, a researcher at Stanford University and consultant at McKinsey, and Robert Waterman, a consultant at McKinsey, published the results of their study in the book *In Search of Excellence* in 1982. This book turned out to become a best-selling management book and propelled the idea of corporate or organizational culture as the most critical variable for a firm's success. According to Peters and Waterman (1982), successful U.S. firms were characterized by the following values and related practices:

- orientation toward action,
- close to the customer,
- autonomy and entrepreneurship,
- productivity through people,
- hands-on—value-driven,
- stick to your knitting (a focus on core competencies),
- simple structure—lean administration,
- large degrees of freedom at strong levels of social control.

The researchers included 62 firms in their study. They collected their data with structured interviews and a literature review covering 25 years. The companies represented the following industries:

- high-technology (e.g., Hewlett-Packard, IBM, Intel, Texas Instruments),
- consumer goods (e.g., Procter & Gamble, Johnson & Johnson),
- industrial production (e.g., Caterpillar, 3 M),
- service-based industry (e.g., Delta Airlines, McDonald's, Disney Productions),
- project management firms (e.g., Bechtel, Fluor),
- resource-based firms (e.g., Atlantic-Richfield [Arco], Dow Chemical, Exxon).

Since the 13 European-based firms initially included in the study did not constitute a representative sample, the researchers excluded them from presenting and discussing their results.[2]

In general, the results of this study can be considered the American answer to the perceived management crisis in the U.S. at that time. The researched firms did not lose time in time-consuming analyses and discussions. Instead, their management tried to decide and implement the next steps once an issue had been analyzed and discussed. They monitored their actions and obtained results, and adjusted them if needed. All of the included firms showed a high level of customer orientation. In addition, the firms included in the study also practiced a specific kind of human resource management comparable to the one found in Pascale and Athos' (1981) research about Japanese management practices. They provided a context in which their employees could act like entrepreneurs with a high level of self-organization, freedom to take initiatives, and the willingness to take responsibilities. Organizations and their leaders treated their employees as partners who acted responsibly. They showed respect, trusted them, and gave them large latitudes of freedom.

The studied companies focused on their core competencies regarding their strategy, even though this strategic concept was not yet propagated and widely spread.

[2]During a personal conversation, Tom Peters explained that the results of the European companies didn't fit with the pattern of the American firms. This observation was in and of itself an interesting finding that was unfortunately not addressed in their publication.

Although the idiom *stick with your knitting* is well-known, the U.S.-American economy still suffered from the acquisition wave of the 1960s at that time. Only years later, Prahalad and Hamel (1990) introduced the concept of core competencies into strategic management that was then widely adopted by practitioners.

"Hands-On—Values-Driven" implied that the firms had introduced or developed a value system important to them. This value system guided the organizations' selection processes and their organizational members' thinking and actions during daily work practices.

The researched companies kept their organizational structures simple to facilitate rather than hinder employees in their daily work. In addition, a loose-tight quality characterized the firms. On the one hand, they granted large latitudes of freedom to each employee while, on the other hand, the strong value orientation acted as a social control mechanism. These values guided employees' selection and hiring process and their promotion within the company. The large degrees of freedom for action were possible because organizational members had internalized the firms' value orientation that guided them in their daily work behaviors.

The researchers discuss the importance of corporate culture in one of the chapters:

> And the excellent companies are among the most fiscally sound of all. But their value set *integrates* the notions of economic health, serving customers, and making meanings down the line.... Yet it's surprising how little is said about the shaping of values in current management theories—particularly how little is said about companies as cultures (Peters & Waterman, 1982, p. 103).

This close link of values with companies as cultures may have led to the widespread focus on values when addressing or researching an organization's culture and even equating an organization's culture with its values.

After its publication, *In Search of Excellence* became a bestseller and significantly raised people's interest in organizational or corporate culture. The time had come to add a more human-oriented and emotional component to existing management theories and practices still dominated by rational thought. Until the mid-1960s, the ideas of behaviorism (Skinner, 1938, 1948)[3] and scientific management (Taylor, 1947) had primarily influenced organizations, their management, and their production methods. For example, Henry Ford implemented and perfected the principles of scientific management into industrial production with the so-called Fordism. Behaviorism and scientific management treated human beings predominantly as a "black box" production factor. In the late 1960s, this started to change within the social sciences[4] and the organizational and management sciences. In practice, the ideas of

[3]Burrhus Frederic Skinner (1904–1990) was a radical representative of human conditioning, which was considered a tool to turn people and their actions into anything they thought of.

[4]For example, Pondy and Boje (1980) argued to "bring mind back in" and include critical reflections as part of organizational life. Within psychology, the late 1970s and early 1980s were called the time of cognitive turn.

the Human Relations School[5] and humanistic psychology[6] found more resonance. With the publication of *In Search of Excellence,* the concept of culture had become an inherent part of organizational theory, management research, and management education and practice.

The growing interest in culture among managers was and is still grounded in the hope and assumption to gain an additional tool to ensure a firm's success. Besides Peters and Waterman (1982), several other scholars have nurtured this hope in the past. Silverzweig and Allen (1976) observed that changes in culture increased performance in six out of eight firms. The research by Ouchi and Jaeger (1978) and Ouchi (1980) suggested that a unitary vision, a focus on humanistic values with a concern for people, and consensual decision-making promote financial success. Barney (1986) argued on theoretical grounds that corporate culture—depending on its specific characteristics—can be the most important source of sustained competitive advantage (e.g., Barney, 1986, 2002). The idea behind this argument was that an organization's culture is difficult if not impossible to imitate by other firms.

However, it soon became apparent to researchers and practitioners that an organization's culture cannot be studied and managed as easily as initially assumed. In practice, the promised and expected success did frequently not materialize from so-called culture interventions because decision-makers hesitated to provide time and data needed for thorough culture analysis. Empirical studies of organizational culture proved complicated and required more time than many researchers were willing to invest, and interventions turned out to be difficult. A CEO, who had attended a talk on corporate culture, announced to his employees the following Monday that he wanted the company to have a corporate culture by the end of the week. Book titles such as *Gaining Control of the Corporate Culture* (Kilmann et al., 1985) supported such a mechanistic treatment of culture. Since such mechanistic approaches to culture did not work, practitioners lost interest in culture and turned to the concept of reengineering.

1.4 Resurged Interest in Organizational Culture

In the 1990s, organizational culture regained increasing attention in the context of reengineering projects since many of them failed. According to a study by Scott-Morgan (1994), about 70–75 percent did not achieve the desired results. The author attributed this high failure rate to the change programs' insufficient consideration of the *secret rules* of the respective organizations, thus pointing to the lack of attention to culture. In addition, the increasing number of strategic alliances and acquisitions

[5]Early representatives of the Human Relation School were Elton Mayo (1880–1949) and Fritz Jules Roethlisberger (1898–1974). Both were professors at Harvard University.

[6]Well-known representatives and co-founders of Humanistic Psychology are Carl Rogers (1902–1987), Abraham H. Maslow (1908–1970) and Charlotte Bühler (1893–1973).

around the turn of the millennium gave organizational culture a renewed impetus and highlighted its significant role for organizations, their functioning and performance. Integration processes proved to be more difficult than assumed due to different corporate cultures. They contributed to the failure of several acquisitions, mergers, and joint ventures. Vivid examples are General Motor's acquisition of EDS, and the mergers Daimler and Chrysler or BMW and Rover that were both unsuccessful and burnt many human and financial resources.

At the beginning of the millennium, scandals and fraudulent business behaviors that led to insolvencies and even bankruptcies also spurred new interest in the topic of organizational culture and especially its contribution to ethical or unethical behavior (Ardichvili et al., 2009). A well-known example is the collapse of Barings Bank, where a culture drift in the managerial control system allowed behavior that eventually caused the collapse of the 150-year-old company (Pike, 2020). Other examples are the falsifications of balance sheets at Enron, Parmalat, and Worldcom that led to significant financial losses and made many people jobless. The more recent discussion about *Dieselgate*, the exhaust fumes scandal at VW, has further increased interest in corporate culture. How could an organization and its culture allow a systematic deception of customers and authorities? Here again, researchers and practitioners suggested that the organization's culture played a significant role (e.g., Ahbab & Yu, 2019; Belcher, 2018; Judd, 2019).

Kotter and Heskett's study (1992) sparked renewed interest in the success factor corporate culture. They compared 207 companies from 22 industries over eleven years. Their results showed that firms whose managers acted as leaders and focused simultaneously on their customers, employees, and shareholders, increased their revenue on average by 682 percent, the number of employees by 282 percent, their shareholder value by 901 percent, and their net income by 756 percent (Kotter & Heskett, 1992, p. 11). These amazing results triggered the question how to tap sustainably into this powerful potential of an organization's culture.

Several more recent studies show that culture has regained attention among practitioners. They consider it increasingly important for the short- and long-term financial success of a firm. Top and middle managers rated culture's current and future importance for their company's success even higher than the H.R. managers (see Fig. 1.2).

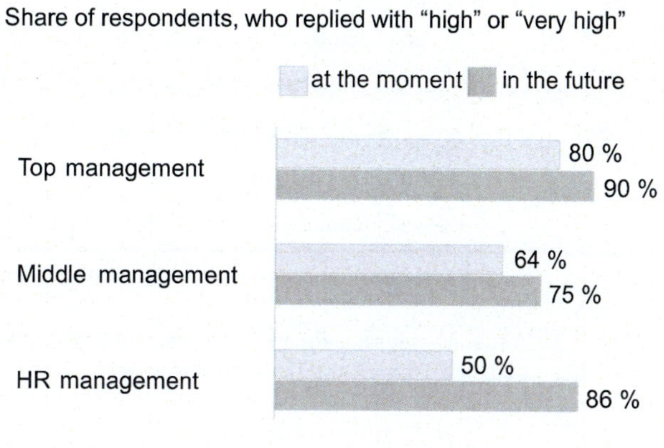

Fig. 1.2 Assessment of the **importance of corporate culture for financial success** (at the moment/in the future) (Source: Leitl et al., 2011, p. 13)

In addition, all three groups reported that their employees' interest in corporate culture is currently high or even very high and that this interest will increase in the future (see Fig. 1.3).

A recent survey on organizational purpose that is part of an organization's culture supports these earlier results (Leape et al., 2020). 82 percent of 1214 managers and front-line employees responded that it is important for organizations to have a purpose. Furthermore, the topic of corporate culture ranked first among the most important H.R. topics and fields of action in the Hays HR Report, 2015/2016 (see Fig. 1.4).

In addition, a study surveying 1348 corporate executives in North America and in-depth interviews of an additional 18 business leaders highlight the importance of

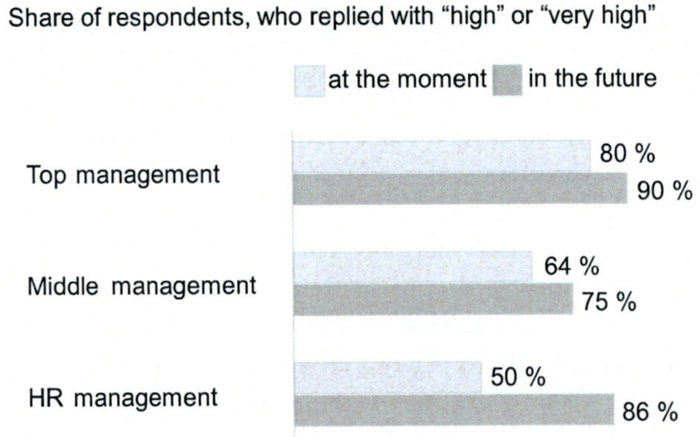

Fig. 1.3 Assessment of organizational members' interest in corporate culture (currently/in the future) (Source: Leitl et al., 2011, p. 14; translated by the author)

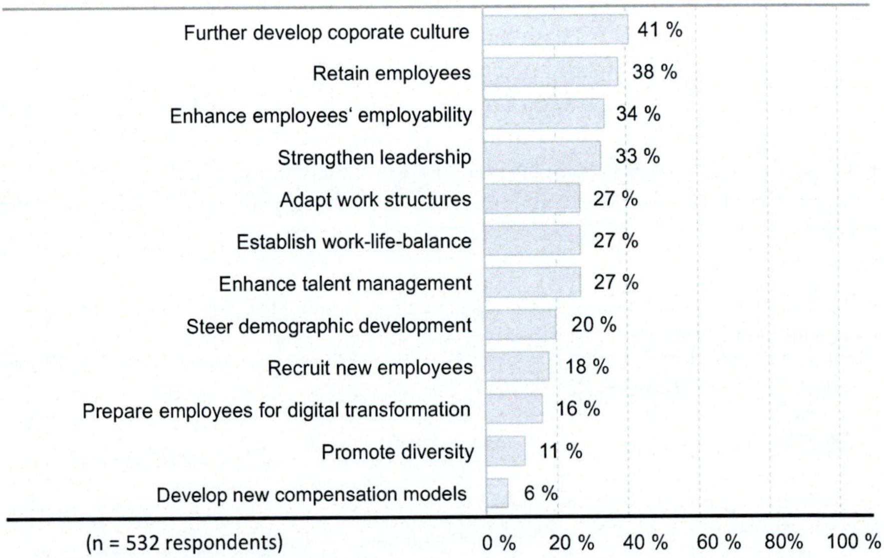

Fig. 1.4 Corporate culture is the most important theme and field of action (Source: Hays, 2016: HR-Report 2015/2016, p. 9; translated by the author)

the topic to business leaders. 92 percent of respondents believed that improving their organization's culture would increase the value of their company. However, only 16 percent of these executives reported that their own firm's culture is where it needs to be (Graham et al., 2021).

Since the 1990s, many theoretical and empirical studies have contributed to further differentiate the concept of culture in the context of organizations, including its link to performance. For example, Hartnell et al. (2011) report more than 4600 publications concerning organizational culture. More refined research designs and research methods that went beyond correlational analysis between dimensions of organizational culture and performance indicators provided more information on the impact of culture. Longitudinal research, as well as cross-cultural studies focusing on different industries, divisions, and issues, yielded additional information about the influence and potential effects of organizational culture.

These research results evidence that the concept of culture in organizational settings has gained a significant place within both organization and management research and practice. In addition, the research involving practitioners suggests that it is worthwhile for leaders to spend time and effort trying to understand their organization's culture—especially if they want to better leverage its potential for their organization.

This book wants to contribute to a thorough understanding of culture and mindfully dealing with culture in the context of organizations. Such an understanding includes information about the concept itself, culture's characteristics, functions, and impact that it may have on organizational life and an organization's effectiveness and performance. In addition, the book provides information about how to develop an understanding of an organization's culture and how to assess if an existing culture is helpful or hindering an organization's functioning. Finally, it discusses characteristics of culture that enable an organization's viability in turbulent environments and the role of leaders in maintaining a given and desired culture, thus avoiding unintended culture drift.

The following section provides a glimpse into the content of the following nine book chapters.

1.5 Overview of the Book Chapters

Chapter 2 provides the theoretical background for the concept of culture in the context of organizations. First, it discusses three different perspectives of culture that exist in the organization and management literature and practice. This discussion includes the different assumptions, interests, and expectations that undergird these three perspectives and their implications for handling culture in organizations. Second, the chapter explains the dynamic construct perspective of culture on which this book is based. Third, the chapter defines organizational culture with its various functions and characteristics. Subsequently, organizational culture is compared to related concepts such as organizational identity, organizational climate, image, reputation, and branding and linked to related concepts of corporate strategy, organizational design, and leadership systems. Furthermore, this chapter points out what the concept of organizational culture does not entail. Finally, the chapter closes with a discussion of an organization's cultural context consisting of culture at different levels: the regional, national, supranational, and industry levels.

Chapter 3 addresses the emergence and development of culture in organizations, including its subcultures. The discussion focuses on three major development phases: the founding, developing, and mature phases. The chapter explores the characteristics of each phase, their challenges for organizations, and their culture. The discussion includes the emergence of subcultures and their implications for organizations, the emergence of cultural knowledge, and the impact of increasing overdetermined behavior. The latter may eventually result in a crisis. If it is handled properly, the organization's culture may become rejuvenated. Otherwise, an organization's demise will follow.

How does an organization's culture influence organizational life, and what exactly does it influence? An exploration of these questions is the focus of **Chap. 4.** First, the chapter explains how an organization's culture exerts its influence. Subsequently, the chapter discusses the various influences of an organization's culture on its strategy and strategy development process, the choice of an organization's design, management systems and instruments. Subsequently culture's influence an organization's leaders, leadership, and employees is addressed.

Chapter 5 explores the relationship between an organization's culture and organizational performance. The chapter addresses the different ways used to measure both culture and organizational performance or effectiveness. Given that both concepts are multifaceted and thus multidimensional, few studies can be directly compared due to the different indicators used for measuring culture and performance. The discussion of existing studies and their results regarding the link between culture and performance uses five categories: research that investigated a direct link between the two concepts; studies that explored the effects of different kinds of culture on performance; research revealing an indirect link; and studies pointing to a non-linear and reciprocal relationship. The chapter closes by addressing the notion if strong cultures may be better for performance.

Chapter 6 discusses several situations requiring special attention to culture. These may originate from an organization's internal or external environment. Internal situations discussed are fast growth, stagnation, strategic alliances, and entering new markets. Given their importance, the focus of discussion lies in two types of strategic partnerships: joint ventures and mergers and acquisitions. The chapter explores the cultural challenges involved when different cultures meet in mergers and acquisitions and the resulting impact on culture. External situations discussed include societal changes, technological changes in terms of digitization, and politics. The focus of exploration concentrates on societal changes in terms of values, their evolution over time, the value pattern of different generations, and those represented in today›s increasingly diverse workforce.

How can one understand a given culture and evaluate if it supports or impedes an organization's functioning? Based on the particular characteristics of culture, **Chap.**

7 discusses different ways and methods for analyzing an organization's culture, including the methods' strengths and challenges. The chapter also provides standards that are helpful for evaluating the quality of a given culture. Finally, two examples of a culture assessment in practice are described.

Chapter 8 explores an organization's planned development and change. First, it points to some of the specifics of human systems that impact development- and change efforts. Second, it explains assessing the risk associated with a culture change. Third, the chapter explores two different planned change strategies: evolutionary and revolutionary change. I also addresses the peculiarities when moving through a change process and people's different ways of dealing with change. The discussion of change interventions focuses on evolutionary change and explores several methods that focus either on people or the context.

Given the increasingly volatile, uncertain, complex, and ambiguous (VUCA) environment in which organizations need to compete and survive, **Chap** 9 explores those cultural characteristics that support an organization's viability in such a VUCA context. Even though every organization's culture is unique, the chapter discusses ten generic content-related culture characteristics for supporting an organization's viability in such a dynamics environment. In addition, three quality criteria help to assess a culture's condition.

Chapter 10 addresses the role of managers and leaders in paying conscious attention to culture, mindfully maintaining a given culture, and developing or changing it to avoid an unintended culture drift. The discussion includes exploring the characteristics of culture-mindful leadership and management and the characteristics of culture-mindful leaders.

References

Ahbab, A., & Yu, M. (2019). *An inquiry into how company culture influenced the Volkswagen 2015 emissions scandal. Student works*. The University of Texas at Austin. https://doi.org/10.26153/tsw/7627

AOE. (2020). *Agile corporate culture*. Online platform (Company). Accessed Jan 29, 2021, from www.aoe.com/en/company/agile-culture.html

Ardichvili, A., Mitchell, J. A., & Jondle, D. (2009). Characteristics of ethical business cultures. *Journal of Business Ethics, 85*(4), 445–451. https://doi.org/10.1007/s10551-008-9782-4

Barnard, C. I. (1938). *The functions of the executive*. Harvard University Press.

Barney, J. B. (1986). Organizational culture: Can it be a source of sustained competitive advantage? *Academy of Management Review, 11*(3), 656–665.

Barney, J. B. (2002). *Gaining and sustaining competitive advantage* (2nd ed.). Prentice-Hall.

Belcher, A. (2018). Corporate culture: Changing board responsibilities and changing governance rhetoric. *RAIS Conference Proceedings*, November 19–20. Accessed Jun 17, 2021, from http://rais.education/wp-content/uploads/2018/11/01AB.pdf

Bennis, W. W. (1969). *Organization development: Its nature, origins, and perspectives*. Addison-Wesley.

Bissels, T., Sackmann, S., & Bissels, S. (2006). Die Arbeitssituation von Selbständigen: Eine beschreibende Studie zu Belastungen, individuellen Bewältigungsstrategien/–kompetenzen und den Konsequenzen in Erleben und Arbeit. *Zeitschrift für Arbeitswissenschaften, 60*(2), 97–106.

Boyacigiller, N. A., Kleinberg, M. J., Phillips, M. E., & Sackmann, S. A. (2009). Conceptualizing culture: Elucidating the streams of research in international cross-cultural management. In T. G. Andrews & R. Mead (Eds.), *Handbook of cross-cultural management* (pp. 371–380). Routledge.

Drucker, P. F. (1946). *Concept of the corporation*. Transaction.

Graham, J. R., Grennan, J., Campbell, R. H., & Rajgopal, S. (2021). Corporate culture: Evidence from the field. *27th Annual Conference on Financial Economics and Accounting,* May 17. Columbia Business School Research Paper No. 16–49, Duke I&E Research Paper No. 2016–33. https://doi.org/10.2139/ssrn.2805602.

Hartnell, C. A., Ou, A. Y., & Kinicki, A. J. (2011). Organizational culture and effectiveness: A meta-analytic investigation of the competing values Framework's (CVF) theoretical supposition. *Journal of Applied Psychology, 96*(4), 677–694.

Hays. (2016). *HR-Report 2015/2016: Schwerpunkt Unternehmenskultur*. Mannheim: Hays. Accessed Jun 17, 2021, from www.hays.de/documents/10192/118775/hays-studie-hr-report-2015-2016.pdf

Higgins, R., Liou, G., Maurenbrecher, S., Poppensieker, T., & White, O. (2020). Strengthening institutional risk and integrity culture. *McKinsey & Company Online*, November 2. Accessed Jun 17, 2021, from www.mckinsey.com/business-functions/risk/our-insights/strengthening-institutional-risk-and-integrity-culture

Hofstede, G. (2001). *Cultural consequences: Comparing values, behaviors, institutions and organizations across nations* (2nd ed.). Sage.

Judd, R. (2019). Lessons learned about culture from VW Dieselgate. *CEOWorld Magazine Online,* November 12. Accessed Jun 17, 2021, from https://ceoworld.biz/2019/11/12/lessons-learned-about-culture-from-vw-dieselgate/

Jurisic, N., Lurie, M., Risch, P., & Salo, O. (2020). Doing vs. being: Practical lessons on building an agile culture. *McKinsey & Company Online*, August 4. Accessed Jun 17, 2021, from www.mckinsey.com/business-functions/organization/our-insights/doing-vs-being-practical-lessons-on-building-an-agile-culture

Kilmann, R. H., Saxton, M. J., & Serpa, R. (1985). *Gaining control of the corporate culture*. Jossey-Bass.

Kotter, J. P., & Heskett, J. L. (1992). *Corporate culture and performance*. Free Press.

Leape, S., Zou, J., Loadwick, O., Nuttall, R., Stone, M. & Simpson, B. (2020). More than a mission statement: How the 5Ps embed purpose to deliver value. *McKinsey & Company online*. Accessed Feb 9, 2021, from www.mckinsey.com/business-functions/strategy-and-corporate-finance/our-insights/more-than-a-mission-statement-how-the-5ps-embed-purpose-to-deliver-value

Leitl, M., Meifert, M., & Sackmann, S. (2011). *Unternehmenskultur: Ihre Rolle und Bedeutung. Studie 2011*. In Kienbaum Management Consultants (Ed.), In cooperation with the Harvard Business Manager and Sonja Sackmann/Institute for Developing Viable Organizations. Gummersbach: Kienbaum Management Consultants.

Li, K., Liu, X., Mai, F., & Zhang, T. (2021). *The role of corporate culture in bad times: Evidence from the COVID-19 pandemic (May 6, 2021).* European Corporate Governance Institute–Finance Working Paper No. 726/2021. DOI: https://doi.org/10.2139/ssrn.3632395.

Nakane, C. (1970). *Japanese society*. University of California Press.

Niedermeyer, P. (2018). Chairside classics: U.S. market share by manufacturer–1961-2016. *Curbside classic Online*, Blog, April 10. Accessed Jun 17, 2021, from www.curbsideclassic.com/blog/history/chartside-classics-us-market-share-by-manufacturer-1961-2016

Ouchi, W. G. (1980). Markets, bureaucracies, and clans. *Administrative Science Quarterly, 25*(1), 129–141.

Ouchi, W. G., & Jaeger, A. M. (1978). Type Z organization: Stability in the midst of mobility. *Academy of Management Review, 3*(2), 305–314.

Parsons, T. (1951). *The social system*. Free Press.
Pascale, R. T., & Athos, A. G. (1981). The art of Japanese management. In *New York*. Warner.
Pelton, W., Sackmann, S. A., & Boguslaw, R. (1990). *Tough choices: The decision making styles of America's top 50 CEOs*. Dow Jones-Irwin.
Peters, T. J., & Waterman, R. H. (1982). *In search of excellence*. Harper & Row.
Pike, M. (2020, September 9). Lessons from Barings Bank: Have we emerged from cultural decline? *LinkedIn Online*. Accessed Sep 21, 2021, from www.linkedin.com/pulse/lessons-from-barings-bank-have-we-emerged-cultural-decline-mike-park
Pondy, L. R., & Boje, D. M. (1980). Bringing mind back in. In W. M. Evan (Ed.), *Frontiers in organization and management* (pp. 83–101). John Wiley.
Prahalad, C. K., & Hamel, G. (1990). The core competence of the corporation. *Harvard Business Review, 68*(3), 79–91.
Scott-Morgan, P. (1994). *The unwritten rules of the game*. McGraw-Hill.
Sackmann, S. (2020, September 8). Arbeiten im Homeoffice–Chance und Herausforderung zugleich. *Universität der Bundeswehr München Online*. Accessed Sep 20, 2021, from www.unibw.de/home/news-rund-um-corona/homeoffice-chance-und-herausforderung
Selznick, P. (1957). *Leadership in administration: A sociological interpretation*. Row Peterson.
Servan-Schreiber, J. J. (1968). *The American challenge*. Atheneum.
Silverzweig, S., & Allen, R. F. (1976). Changing the corporate culture. *Sloan Management Review, 17*(3), 33–50.
Skinner, B. F. (1938). *The behavior of organisms: An experimental analysis*. Appleton-Century.
Skinner, B. F. (1948). 'Superstition' in the pigeon. *Journal of Experimental Psychology, 38*(2), 168–172.
Taylor, F. W. (1947). *Scientific management*. Harper & Brothers.
Thurow, L. (1988). *Keynote address*. Western Academy of Management.
Vernon, R. (1971). *Sovereignty at bay: The multinational spread of U.S. enterprises*. Basic Books.
Westfall, C. (2020, May 21). How organizations can create a working from home culture and embrace the remote workforce. *Forbes Online*. Accessed Sep 27, 2021, from www.forbes.com/sites/chriswestfall/2020/05/21/how-organizations-can-create-awork-from-home-culture-and-embrace-the-remote-workforce
Womack, J. P., Jones, D. T., & Roos, D. (1990). *The machine that changed the world*. Macmillan.

Chapter 2
What Is Culture in the Context of Organizations?

The concept of culture evokes differing associations. Anthropology is the original and central domain of culture. Since the end of the eighteenth century, anthropologists have been investigating culture as their basic and central concept. Malinowski (1939) and Chase (1948) have gone so far to suggest that it is the foundation and the most central problem of all social sciences. Anthropologists have, therefore, exerted a significant influence on the concept's meanings. In addition, culture has also received attention from sociology and social psychology before it found its way into the fields of management and organizational theory in the early 1980s, where Peters (1984) considered it to be the *most important stuff around*. Since that time, publications around organizational or corporate culture have soared with different hopes attached to the concept and projected into it.

Although anthropologists, sociologists, organizational scholars, and managers use the same term and similar definitions, the meanings that they associate with *culture* are not always the same—not even within the same discipline. These various understandings are due to the different contexts and assumptions associated with these contexts and projected onto culture. These meanings are related to differing interests regarding culture. They lead to different expectations about what the concept can accomplish. Hence different lenses have been used to explore the theoretical base of culture, explain its impact, study it, and apply it to organizations.

This chapter provides the theoretical background of culture in organizations. Three different perspectives of and approaches to the concept of culture in the context of organizations are discussed, including their implications for practice. They are based on different interests and expectations rearding the concept of culture. In this book, culture is defined based on the dynamic construct perspective, which is explained with its implications for dealing and working with culture in organizations. The various functions that culture may serve are described in this chapter and illustrated with examples. The concept of culture is then compared to and distinguished from related concepts such as organizational identity, organizational climate, image and reputation, and branding. Finally, culture exists at different levels that also have an influence on organizations and their culture. These are

S. A. Sackmann, *Culture in Organizations*, Contributions to Management Science,
https://doi.org/10.1007/978-3-030-86080-6_2

cultures at the regional, national as well as industry level. This chapter ends with a summary of the central characteristics of culture in the context of organizations.

2.1 The Concept of Culture Applied to Organizations

If one asks practitioners about their understanding of organizational's culture, they may give the following answers: Culture is

- "our glue—what holds us together."
- "what we stand for."
- "how we do things around here."

These short characterizations may typify essential features of culture, but they are not well suited for really understanding what culture is. Such an understanding requires a more differentiated approach.

In anthropology, several perspectives exist regarding the concept of culture that relates to different schools of thought. Examples are evolutionary, functionalist, particularistic, materialistic, cognitive, structuralist, holistic, and symbolic.[1] These different perspectives also made their way into the fields of management and organization theory, as demonstrated by the following list of culture definitions in the context of organizations:

- Shared values (Peters & Waterman, 1982).
- Shared values and expectations (Silverzweig & Allen, 1976).
- The collective programming of the human mind (Hofstede, 1978).
- A system of meanings that accompanies the various behaviors and methods considered unique (Jelinek et al., 1983).
- The interconnected sets of relatively stable beliefs, values, expectations, and goals are shared and promoted by a central person of an organization (Sathe, 1985).
- The entire set of opinions, norms and values developed over time that affects leader and employee behavior (Pümpin, 1984).
- The entire set of values, beliefs, mindsets, and norms affecting employees' behavior on all levels and hence the company's image (Frey et al., 1984).
- The general constellation of beliefs, mores, customs, value systems, behavioral norms, and ways of doing business that are unique to each corporation, that set a pattern for corporate activities and actions, and that describe the implicit and emergent patterns of behavior and emotions characterizing life in the organization (Tunstall, 1983).
- The pattern of basic assumptions that a group has invented, discovered or developed in learning to cope with its problems of external adaptation and

[1] The interested reader finds more detailed information in Sackmann (1991, p. 7-16).

internal integration and that has worked well enough to be considered valid, and, therefore, to be taught to new members as the correct way to perceive, think, and feel concerning those problems (Schein, 1985, 2010).
- The game whose rules are taken for granted that are applied unconsciously, and that only get noticed when being violated (Simon, 2004).
- The number of routines in which a company distinguishes itself from its environment (Berner, 2012).
- The personality or character of an organization (Berner, 2012; Wilkins, 1989).

These definitions of organizational culture are partly based on different assumptions about culture and expectations regarding what the concept can do in and for organizations. In the management and organization literature, researchers distinguish three perspectives rooted in different disciplines and associated with other interests in the concept of culture in organizational settings. The three perspectives are (Sackmann, 1989a)[2]:

- Culture as a variable,
- Culture as a metaphor,
- Culture is a dynamic construct.

The following sections further explain these three perspectives. This discussion also includes their central assumptions and implications for management practice.

2.1.1 Culture as an Organizational Variable

The *variable perspective* is prevalent in the management literature. It is based on the social-factist paradigm[3] and focuses on expressions and manifestations of culture. This perspective treats culture as a tangible, concrete phenomenon that managers can influence, shape, and change to pursue the organization's goals and their achievement. Within the framework of the social-factist paradigm, organizational culture is considered another variable in addition to an organization's structure, size, or technology that managers and leaders can manipulate in a deterministic manner. As a result, every organization *has a culture*. Next to an organization's products and services, it also develops a culture. This culture product may consist of various partial products that manifest themselves in tangible objects such as buildings, documents, written values, and visible collective verbal and non-verbal practices.

[2] The discussion does not include the three perspectives by Martin (1992) and the five perspectives by Smircich (1983).

[3] A paradigm is comparable with a worldview that influences the choice of questions that researchers explore and the methodology and methods they consider most appropriate for investigating their research questions. Within the social-factist paradigm, the social world consists of facts that are objectively given.

Together, these partial products constitute the overall product organizational culture that is considered a homogenous, integrated entity.

Within this perspective, the focus of interest lies in the visible manifestations of an organization's culture, its functions, and how it can be managed. Organizational culture is often defined in terms of observable behavioral patterns, for example, "the way we do things around here." Visible artifacts such as language, jargon, written values, rules, and standards are viewed as tangible and factual culture products without considering their underlying meanings. Referring to the sociologist Talcott Parsons (1951), organizational culture may serve the two functions that are considered within the variable perspective:

- external adaptation and
- internal integration, including coordination.

Adaptation to external changes is necessary to stay viable as an organization. Organizational members need to recognize changes in the relevant environment, including their opportunities and threats. In addition, an organization needs specific skills to react to those changes appropriately so that it can focus on the opportunities and use them to the company's advantage.

Collectively shared values and norms pervasive in an organization develop and foster internal integration across departments and divisional boundaries, and hierarchical levels. These pervasive norms and values promote a group feeling that connects and unites organizational members. This property of culture has also been labeled as "internal glue".

The function of coordination is linked to internal integration. To work toward common goals, organizational members need to engage in mutual coordination and adjustment. An organization's culture provides a common language that enables coordination and coordinated efforts toward the common goal.

Within the variable perspective, these two functions of culture are treated factually with a normative claim. A *good* organizational culture is homogenous, rich in manifestations, and strong. Strong implies that culture is pervasive within and across all units of an organization. It is based on a consensus among all organizational members and gives an organization its unique imprint. According to this perspective, top management creates organizational culture. Top leaders are responsible for the culture's management regarding maintaining, manipulating, and changing it if necessary to reach the organization's goals. The variable perspective assumes that one can directly infer the underlying norms and values from the visible manifestations usually codified in some way and no longer questioned once codified. Collecting and analyzing the manifestations of culture will suffice for getting an understanding of an organization's culture. If it does not fit with the organization's goals, managers change it with its products in a deterministic way. The overall goal is to improve effectiveness and performance using the variable culture.

2.1.2 Culture as a Metaphor

The *metaphor perspective* is a counter-position of the variable perspective. Its representatives postulate that an organization *is* a culture. From this perspective, organizations are seen and researched as cultures whose members create and negotiate the cultural reality in their daily interactions. Based on an interpretative paradigm, organizations are considered human systems whose sense-making and sense-giving structures are essential. Consequently, this perspective does not focus on culture's products but rather on their underlying meanings attributed by organizational members and created and changed in their interactions. The promoters of the metaphor perspective are not interested in the cultural manifestations themselves, such as buildings, language, documents, or rituals. Instead, they focus on their underlying, partly symbolic meanings and their specific interpretations, patterns, and meaning attributions by the actors within a given organizational context. The primary goal of this perspective is to gain new insights into a given organization as a living and dynamic system, including its specific functioning. The latter may include processes that lead to effective or ineffective outcomes.

Hence, a culture's core consists of ideational aspects such as cognitive maps, cognitions, underlying assumptions, sense- and symbolism-creating aspects. Particularly interesting are the specific *mindsets*, the *collectively organized knowledge* of organizational members, their collective perception, their particular way of information processing, and their interpretation patterns. They are used to interpret external and internal events and constellations to initiate culturally adequate actions.

Representatives of this perspective define organizational culture as shared understandings, collectively held meanings, underlying commonly-held assumptions or beliefs (Phillips, 1994; Schein, 1985), or the "collective programming of the human mind" (Hofstede, 1978). Sharing occurs among the members of a group and not necessarily within the entire organization. Consequently, an organization's culture can consist of several subcultures that may differ and do not necessarily act in a coordinated way.

Within the metaphor perspective, managers and leaders are less important. All organizational members are culture carriers and may influence the development and characteristics of an organization's culture and its subcultures. These characteristics develop when organizational members try to deal with internal tasks and problems, and challenges imposed by its external environment (Schein, 2010).

The planned development and design of organizations as cultures play a subordinate role within the metaphor perspective. Since each organizational member may influence culture, cultural awareness and sensitivity may be an issue. However, the primary goal and interest are to better understanding organizations as a cultural system.

Both the variable and the metaphor perspectives attempt to conceptualize culture in organizations and better understand and grasp this complex phenomenon. Both views have specific strengths and weaknesses regarding the understanding and clarification of the organizational culture concept. Whereas the variable perspective is dominant in management and especially among practitioners, the metaphor perspective is more common in organization science, sociology, and anthropology. However, neither the variable nor the metaphor perspective alone can explain the multifaceted nature of this complex phenomenon culture in organizations with all of its characteristics, functions, dynamics, and impact. In the context of organizations, they provide, to some extent, complementary insights.

2.1.3 Organizational Culture as a Dynamic Construct

At first sight, the perspective of organizational culture as a dynamic construct seems to combines the variable and the metaphor perspectives. Representatives of the dynamic construct perspective conceptualize culture as something that emerges through organizational members' social interactions. During these interactions, they create, negotiate, and attribute meaning to their actions. Hence, culture may also develop and change over time. This conceptualization is based on system theory and a social-constructivist paradigm and, therefore, close to the metaphor perspective. In addition to their sense-making activities, organizational members' interactions over time result in manifestations such as products, services, organizational structures, processes, rules, regulations, or documents. Once these manifestations are created and repeatedly used, they achieve a factual character which in return starts to influence organizational members' behavior. Hence, within the dynamic construct perspective, organizations ***are*** cultures and ***have*** culture in the sense of cultural manifestations that their members have created over time. The term *construct* indicates that culture is a complex and dynamic phenomenon actively created by its culture carriers.

Contrarily to the variable perspective, the dynamic construct perspective is not interested in cultural manifestations as factual givens but rather in their underlying meanings assigned by organizational members. These meanings are not directly accessible and may also have lost their original sense over time. As in the metaphor perspective, culture provides meaning for organizational members and constitutes their cultural reality. Culture offers orientation within a given organization and helps reduce complexity in everyday work life. In addition to the metaphor perspective, an organization's culture develops a factual side over time due to its continuous use by organizational members, who create artifacts in the course of their interactions. Once in existence, these manifestations achieve realist features in their regular use. Hence, they start to influence the organizational members' behavior and the success or failure resulting from their actions and interactions that evenutally impact the organization's performance.

Like the metaphor perspective, every organizational member can influence, develop and thus change the cultural context of an organization. Because of existing power structures, people in higher hierarchical positions tend to have a more influential role in doing so. Yet, due to the probabilistic nature of organizations and their culture, leaders or managers cannot create, design, manage or change an organization's culture in a mechanistic way. In the dynamic construct perspective, leaders and managers can only create conditions that may increase or decrease the probability of certain behaviors occurring. This difference in underlying assumptions of determinism vs. probabilism is the significant difference between the variable and the dynamic construct perspective.

Table 2.1 summarizes the major characteristics of the three perspectives regarding their assumptions, their underlying paradigm, the functions that culture is assumed to fulfill, the source for culture development, and potential normative recommendations for potentially managing an organization's culture.

In the next section, organizational culture is defined and characterized, including its potential functions. The following descriptions and explanations are based on the dynamic culture perspective rooted in the social-constructivist paradigm and modern system theory.

2.2 Definition and Characteristics of Culture in the Context of Organizations

Based on the discussion above, the definition of culture is offered from a dynamic construct perspective:

> *Organizational culture consists of a set of basic beliefs commonly-held by the members of a group. This set is typical for the group* and
>
> – influences the group members' perceptions, thinking, actions, and feelings,
> – may become manifest in the group members' actions and their artifacts,
> – evolved from the experiences of the group members and may further develop in their interactions,
> – is learned and passed on to new members of the group,
> – drops out of awareness over time.

This definition, which has many commonalities with the definition by Edgar Schein (2010), has several implications for understanding culture in organizational settings. These include its central components, functioning and impact, its analysis, and its conscious development, maintenance, and change. The following section discusses the main terms of the definition given above in more detail.

2.2.1 Culture Is the Property of a Group

Culture is the property of a group. Hence, it is a **collective** phenomenon. Culture typifies the essence of a group and is never the property of a single organizational

Table 2.1 An Overview and comparison of the three perspectives of culture

	Variable Perspective	**Metaphor Perspective**	**Dynamic Construct Perspective**
Assumptions	Culture = Variable; organizations have a culture that consists of different parts forming a homogenous whole; fulfills important functions; can be managed	Culture = Metaphor; organizations are cultures that are socially constructed and negotiaged; provides a cognitive map for its carriers' orientation	Culture = Multiple Dynamic Construct; culture is socially constructed and negotiated; as such, organizations are cultures and its carriers develop culture manifestations in their social interactions; provides cognitive maps and scripts for its carriers that guide them in their perseptions, thinking and behavior
Core Interest	Control, management, change	Understanding and characterization	Understanding, characterization and conscious maintenance or development
Underlying Paradigm	Social facist / functional (rational-mechanistic)	Interpretative	Pluralistic: Multiple Paradigms
Methods for Analysis	Questionnaires	Ethnographic methods	Multiple methods
Functions	Serves internal intergration and coordination as well as external adaptation	Sense-making and complexity reduction	Sense-making, complexity reduction, orientation; may be helpful or obstructive
Source of Culture	Founder, top leader(s)	Every organizational member	Potentially every organizational member with people in power having more influence incl. founder(s) and leaders
Normative Assumptionist	The culture good for performance is strong, homogenous, consistent and pervasive	—	Should enable and facilitate goal achievement
Source for Adaption and Change	Top leaders	Every organizational member; evolutionary development as a result of social interactions and negotiations	Every organizational member; Evolutionäre and consciuos development
Change Strategies	Planned change of components of culture with direct and indirect measures	Offering new interpretation patterns	Culture-sensitive maintenance and development; symbolic management; offering new interpretation patterns

member. This collective nature has significant implications for understanding and developing culture in organizations. When analyzing an organization's culture, one cannot rely on information and data obtained from one individual since this may only reflect the view of that particular person. His or her viewpoint may diverge from the group's perspective. Only if several people within an organization hold the same basic beliefs, are they likely part of the set of basic cultural beliefs of that particular group. Hence, data must be collected horizontally and vertically within and across different organizational units during a culture analysis.

Since culture is anchored in a group, the collectively-held basic beliefs define that group's cultural identity and boundaries. The beliefs determine group membership. They specify who is a member of the in-group and who is a member of an *out-group*. The commonly-held basic beliefs help the group develop a group identity and differentiate itself from other groups, who may think and act differently.

Depending on the range of commonly-held basic beliefs, these may be typical for an entire organization or limited to a subgroup within that organization. The larger the organization is in terms of members, the higher the probability of emerging subcultures (Van Maanen & Barley, 1985). Hence, the larger an organization, the more likely subcultures exist. In general, the existence of several subcultures is not necessarily good nor bad. Depending on their specific interrelations, existing subcultures may be neutral, functional, or dysfunctional for the organization. In any case, they are an essential characteristic of the fabric of the cultural context of that particular organization. Potentially, these subcultures can differ significantly from one another and thus act independently of each other. They may complement each other or even conflict with each other. Chap. 3 discusses the potential relationship among subcultures and the implications for an organization's culture and its performance in more detail.

This collective aspect of culture also has implications for developing an organization's culture or changing it. A planned culture change process can only succeed if the members of the relevant group(s) have developed or changed accordingly. A single member's change is not sufficient for such an endeavor.

2.2.2 Culture Consists of Basic Beliefs and Manifestations

Culture in organizations consists of both visible manifestations as well as non-visible, collectively-held basic beliefs. Especially older organizations may have accumulated over time a large number of visible manifestations. Nevertheless, their basic beliefs constitute their culture's cognitive core which is mental rather than material. The collective mindset of organizational members is characteristic of an organization's culture and essential for its understanding, less so the visible, directly observable culture manifestations.

An iceberg metaphor can explain this characteristic of culture. The most significant part of an iceberg lies underneath the water surface and is invisible. Likewise, the essential component of an organization's culture is also hidden and thus below

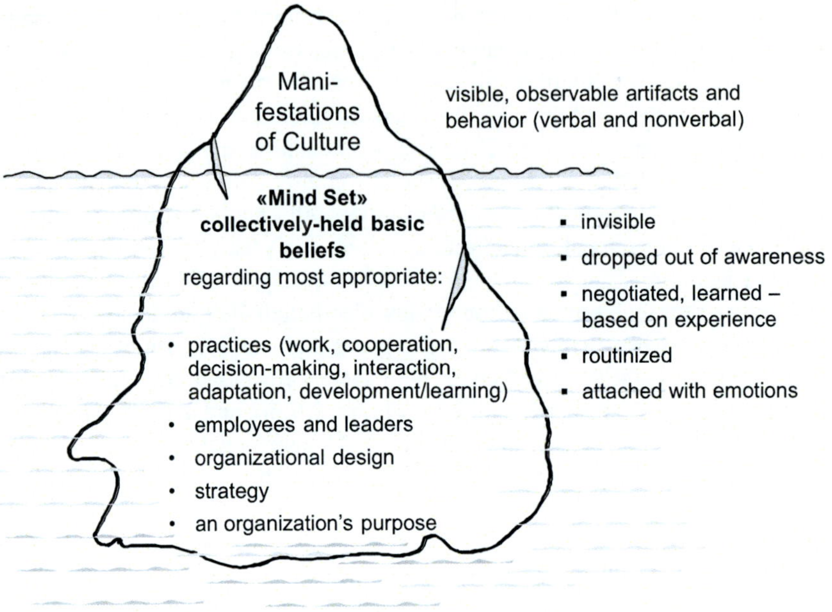

Fig. 2.1 Organizational culture compared with the image of an iceberg

the surface. Even though the manifestations of a particular organizational culture may by far outnumber its underlying set of basic beliefs, this set of basic beliefs constitutes the sense-making mechanisms of that culture. They need to be surfaced and addressed for understanding the specific meanings of the visible culture manifestations and the behavior of organizational members. However, over time, the visible manifestations can develop a life of their own and thus influence the behavior of organizational members in unintended ways. Hence, one needs to regularly examine an organization's culture to avoid such unintended effects.

As depicted in Fig. 2.1, visible manifestations of culture above the surface level may consist of artifacts including verbal and nonverbal behavior. **Artifacts** are all things made by humans, such as buildings, furniture, pictures on the walls, documents, or products. **Verbal behavior** refers to the spoken *language,* such as the specific *jargon* used in a given organization, the type of *humor*, the *stories, legends*, and *myths* that organizational members share among each other. **Non-verbal behavior** consists of *body language*. Examples are gestures and facial expressions, but also *rites and rituals*, *celebrations,* and *ceremonies*.

Artifacts

Artifacts are person-made objects. They comprise a building's architecture, its floorplan, the size and location of offices, the interior design with the type of furniture, the artwork on the walls, or the allocation of rooms. Are people working in individual offices or open spaces? Who has a separate office and on which floor? How large is the office, and what kind of view does it have? What kind of products and services does the organization deliver in what type of packaging? What does the

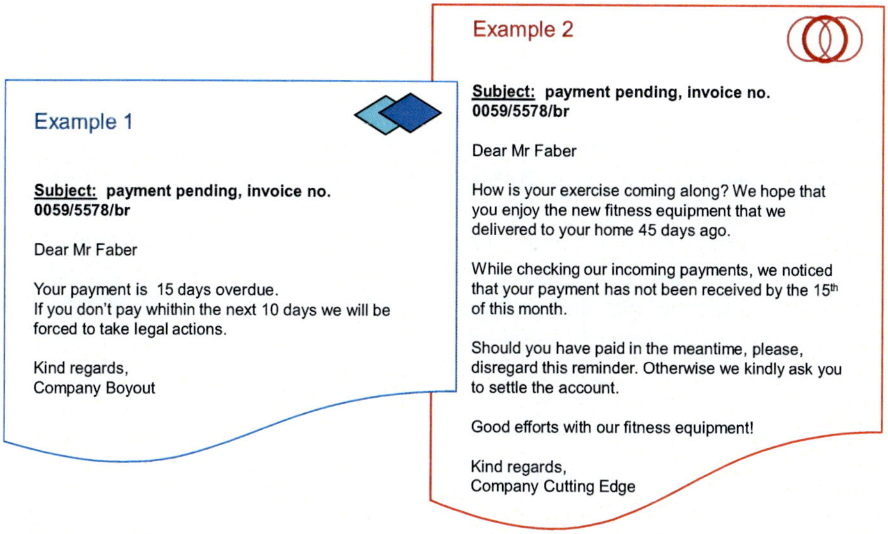

Example 1

Subject: payment pending, invoice no. 0059/5578/br

Dear Mr Faber

Your payment is 15 days overdue.
If you don't pay whithin the next 10 days we will be forced to take legal actions.

Kind regards,
Company Boyout

Example 2

Subject: payment pending, invoice no. 0059/5578/br

Dear Mr Faber

How is your exercise coming along? We hope that you enjoy the new fitness equipment that we delivered to your home 45 days ago.

While checking our incoming payments, we noticed that your payment has not been received by the 15th of this month.

Should you have paid in the meantime, please, disregard this reminder. Otherwise we kindly ask you to settle the account.

Good efforts with our fitness equipment!

Kind regards,
Company Cutting Edge

Fig. 2.2 Two examples of a payment reminder

marketing look like for these products and services? How are jobs advertised? What kind of internal and external documents do exist, and how do they look like? These may be internal reports, budgets, memos, organizational charts, financial statements, or regular surveys. Figure 2.2 shows two different kinds of late payment reminders. They contain both the same facts, but these are expressed quite differently and thus will most likely provoke different reactions.

Jargon

Jargon refers to the specific language and vocabulary used by a group. Research has shown that new organizational members learn the most critical jargon of a particular organization within a short period. Knowing the specific language of a specific industry, firm, and workgroup is essential for accomplishing everyday work and communicating effectively with colleagues, co-workers, and superiors. Hence, knowing the particular jargon is crucial for daily work and one's potential survival in an organization. The following examples show that the specific context influences the type of jargon. Hence, knowing this context helps in decoding the jargons' particulars meaning as, for example, industry culture may influence a particular jargon.

Examples

- How is our appendix doing today? (Context of a hospital.)
- *The liver goes to no. 15.* (Context of a restaurant: the food goes to the table no. 15.)
- The *marriage* happens in this area. (Context of a car assembly: it refers to connecting the motor block to the chassis.)
- The speaker *is torched.* (Meaning: He can no longer be used for this client.)

- We are in a *bullish market.* (The stock market is doing well.)
- Hand me the *16.* (Manufacturing context: *16* refers to a bottle opener.)

Humor

The specific type of humor observed in an organization may also be typical for its culture or subculture. In some organizations, organizational members neither laugh nor tell jokes. Those organizations have lost their sense of humor. Generally, culturally typical jokes and humor can take different forms. In some organizations, the humor is sarcastic, while in other organizations, people simply like to laugh. The following joke was told at a computer manufacturing firm and characterized the significance of the technical support:

> A technical service agent gets into a cab. The cab driver asks him where he wants to go. The technical service agent replies: 'It doesn't matter. I'm needed everywhere'.

The following joke addresses change processes:

> The chairman of the board, Jim, drives with his wife next to him. She asks him about the progress of his company's change process. Instead of answering, he stops, exits the car, and steps beneath the power line next to the road. A large number of birds sit on the power line. Jim claps his hands; all birds fly up and settle back on the power line after a while. Jim gets back in his car, turns to his wife, and says: 'This is my estimation of the progress being made in the change process.

Stories

The repeatedly told stories in a company may also be manifestations of its particular culture. Martin et al. (1983) have shown, for example, that the stories told in different Silicon Valley companies differed from each other while the core or the moral of the stories was identical across companies. The authors conclude that stories help answer and resolve critical questions and issues for employees. The stories that the authors found and analyzed dealt with the following six problems that organizational members faced:

- Is the "Big Boss" human?
- Can the little person rise to the top?
- Will I get fired?
- Will the organization help me when I have to move?
- How will the boss react to mistakes?
- How will the organization deal with obstacles?

Legends and Myths

Legends are historically based narratives repeatedly told in organizations, but their validity can no longer be proved. Myths are legends about the so-called heroes of an organization whose validity is highly doubtful. Nevertheless, one generation of organizational members tells the legends to the next. In this process, people enrich them with colorful details. Hence, over time the legends turn into myths.

Legends often revolve around outstanding people, such as the founder. The following example is a legend told about the founder of a computer firm later bought by Siemens. Several legends existed around this founder and his leadership behavior. It was told, for example, that he fired and re-hired the same employee several times the same day. Another legend about him dealt with his death allegedly caused by a typical problem of the organization:

> The company founder danced exuberantly with the daughter of one of the employees on the last night of the company's one-week onboarding event for new employees. While dancing, he got a heart attack. Since people attending the event had parked their cars chaotically around the building where the event took place, the ambulance needed about two hours to reach the founder for the first treatment. They took him to the hospital, where he passed away. Rumor says that he would have had a chance to survive if they had arrived earlier.

Ways of Addressing each Other

How organizational members address each other in organizations may be pretty different and reveals their degree of formality. In some organizations, employees may address each other formally despite knowing each other for a long time. They may use each other's last name and even titles like "Dr. Smith" or "Professor Miller". In other organizations, it may be customary to address each other only by the last name, not by mentioning their titles. In organizations characterized by an informal culture, people may address each other by their first names regardless of titles, tenure, or hierarchical level.

Even though culture at the national, industry and regional level partly influences the degree of formality of addressing each other, the specific way of addressing each other may still be affected by and an expression of the particular group's or organization's culture.

Example: Language as an Expression of Organizational Culture

Language influences perception and the sense-making of events and situations. A change in the choice of words may change the underlying meaning, as illustrated by the following examples:

Organizations are	Language in Disneyland
• Well-oiled machines	• Onstage and backstage
• Theatres	• Actors in costumes
• Political arenas	• Guests
• Open systems	• Casting department
• Social constructions	• Security hostesses

Each of these terms triggers different associations about organizations and places the focus on other issues in organizations.

Body Language

Body language may also be an expression of a particular organizational culture. It may also be partially influenced by one's personality as well as the professional, industry, national, and even regional culture. Before the COVID-19 pandemic with its physical distancing, body language could be well observed while greeting each other. How do colleagues greet each other? Do they pass one another in the hallway without saying anything or slightly nodding? Do they shake hands? Do they address each other with all titles, by their last name or by the first name? Do they shake hands, or do they greet each other the French way with kisses on both cheeks? How do employees behave when encountering their manager? Do they seem to be close or distant when they greet each other? When people from different hierarchical levels meet, does the body language reveal these hierarchical differences?

Rites and Rituals
Rites are standardized, reoccurring procedures. Rituals are recurring events with the purpose of sustaining the group. Rituals happen in a designated place, at a specific time, and with a fixed role allocation. Rites and rituals reinforce and reaffirm the existing social order with its hierarchy and power structure. Thus defined, specific assessment center procedures and Christmas parties classify as rituals. These events usually occur at the same place and the same time. The process and design are the same, and the speeches at Christmas parties are typically held by the same people and address the same topics (e.g., Kieser, 1988).

Some meetings may classify as rituals. Weekly or monthly meetings are usually held in the same place and at the same time. The agenda tends to contain the same topics. If the sequences in which people speak and arguments and counter-arguments are predictable, such a regular meeting classifies as a ritual. The organizers may well desire such a ritualistic nature. But if specific problems should be addressed and solved, such a ritualistic nature is counterproductive.

Several human resource management practices have also developed a ritualistic character, as Trice et al. (1969) discussed. Their findings are still relevant today. Some organizations rely on the results of assessment centers when hiring new organizational members or when promoting employees to a management position. Passing an assessment center or some kind of test may have the nature of a ritual. It demonstrates to the new employee or manager that they are worth joining a selected group. In addition, the group feels its elite status confirmed since one has to pass these tests before being able to join their group.

Celebrations
Celebrations function as emotional outlets in and for organizations. Planned and employed purposefully, they serve to vent emotional pressure and reaffirm the identification with the group or organization. Examples of such celebrations are an annual excursion, a barbecue, the annual Christmas party, or the annual celebration of top performers. An organization may celebrate the completed milestone in a project with a party or a soccer or football game played by teams of different hierarchical levels, departments, locations, or divisions. The timing and setting of a celebration are crucial for emotional catharsis. An organization's culture defines an appropriate celebration, timing, and setting for a specific occasion.

Examples for Celebrations
- Tandem's "Beer Busts" & "philosophy hour".
- Mary Kay's "Seminars".

- Hewlett-Packard's "Picnics".
- Bell Industries' annual manager meeting, Christmas party, picnics, trip to Disneyland, biannual collective lunch, and football game.
- The yearly top-level managers' meetings of many firms with a few external speakers in a nice location.
- McKinsey's annual meeting of consultants and their spouses for an attractive program at an attractive resort.

Ceremonies

Ceremonies are ritualized celebrations with a festive nature where attendees control their emotions. Like rituals, ceremonies occur at a designated time, in a designated place, and fixed roles. However, the ostentatiously festive nature of the celebration does not allow spontaneous expressions of emotions. Examples are award ceremonies of all kinds—be it the award ceremony of Bachelor or Master diplomas, for best quality, best design, best performance, outstanding leadership, or awarding the Nobel Prizes.

All the manifestations mentioned above are visible and therefore accessible to observation. Their underlying meanings are specific to a given organization's culture and become only apparent when the specific sense-making mechanisms are unraveled and understood. The same manifestations across groups or organizations can differ considerably in their attributed meanings. While one organization may introduce open-space offices to facilitate cooperation and interaction between employees, functions, and hierarchy levels, another organization may have adopted them for cost-saving reasons or lack of sufficient office space. In one organization, the widespread use of iPhones may be due to its excellent business relationship with the iPhone manufacturer that has offered them an excellent deal. In another company, iPhones may represent a status symbol that is only given to the top two levels of management while the other levels get less prestigious mobile phones. Over time and employee generations, the original meaning of artifacts may be forgotten or may have drifted. Commonly known examples for such drifts in a sense is the annual gift-giving at St Nicolas' Day or Christmas.

To understand the specific meanings that guide organizational members in their thinking, decision-making, and actions, one needs to go beneath the surface level of the cultural iceberg. The following section discusses a more differentiated levels model of culture.

2.2.3 The Different Levels of Culture

While the iceberg metaphor of culture distinguishes two levels above and below the surface, the concept of culture consists of more levels that allow for a more differentiated analysis and understanding. Some authors, such as Edgar Schein (1985, 2010), distinguish between three levels: artifacts, values, and basic

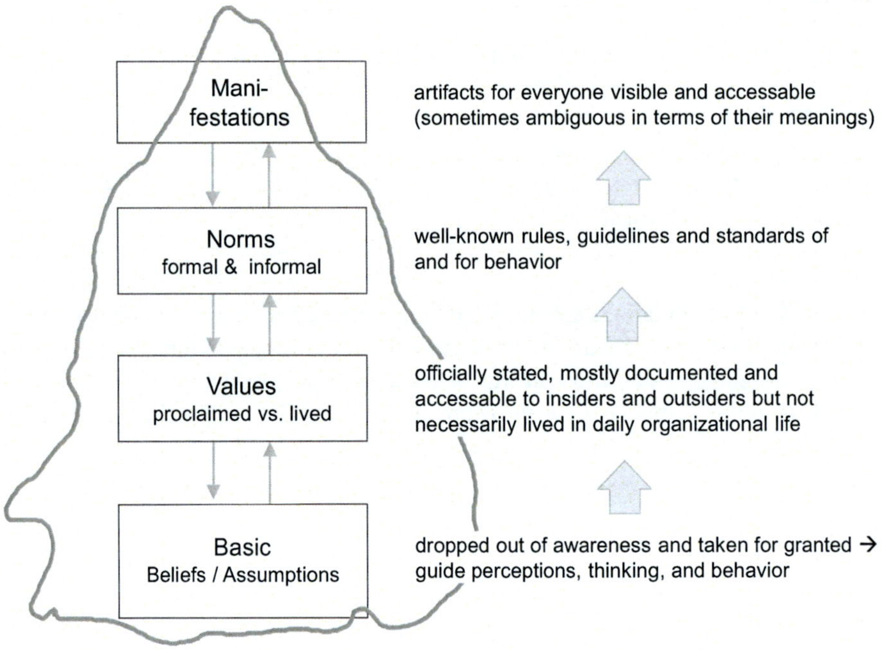

Fig. 2.3 The four levels of culture in organizations

assumptions. The model discussed in this section consists of four levels. Figure 2.3 depicts them with the iceberg model overlaid.

Artifacts constitute the uppermost and outermost layer of culture. Artifacts are manifestations of all kinds, as described above. They are visible to insiders and outsiders, but one needs to infer their underlying meaning from deeper levels of culture. The next level is *rules*, followed by *values. Basic beliefs* or *assumptions* constitute the deepest level or most inner level when using an onion metaphor.

Norms

Norms consist of rules and regulations, guidelines, and standards of all kinds and for all areas of an organization. These may be rules regarding what is considered appropriate travel expenses and how to handle them. Rules and regulations may exist regarding access to the organization, working time and place, and all kinds of internal resources such as parking spaces or office supplies. Norms exist regarding the quality of work, products, services, or security standards. In many organizations, these norms are formally expressed and documented in writing. As such, they are well-known guidelines for what is considered appropriate and expected behavior from organizational members.

In addition to these formalized norms, informal rules and standards may exist that are not written down. Instead, employees pass them on to others. An example may be how to go about acquiring a needed but scarce resource that would usually require a formal procedure and take several weeks. Another example may be how to convince a specific superior that project A or consultant A is better than project B or consultant B. This kind of informal knowledge is usually only passed on to people who are considered trusted insiders.

Values

Values are located on the next lower level. Values may be officially communicated and proclaimed but not necessarily lived in daily work. Proclaimed or declared values are written down and thus visible to insiders and most often also to outsiders. Examples are the official value statement of an organization written down and given to new organizational members. Most likely, they are also available to outsiders on the organization's website. Below are examples of the corporate values of Apple, the BMW Group, Tesla, IKEA, and Greenpeace. Frequently, these proclaimed values are part of the organization's mission, vision, and values statement.

Apple's Values[4]

- *Accessability.* Apple's products are designed so that everyone has access to them. ...
- *Education.* Since 2014, Apple has been on the forefront of providing education to schools across the United States. ...
- *Environment.* Apple focuses on taking care of the environment just as much as they are determined to come up with quality products. ...
- *Inclusion and diversity.* The company draws its greatest strength from the fact that people from all walks of life work here. ...
- *Privacy.* Apple products hold a lot of sensitive user information, and the company believes that privacy is a fundamental human right. ...
- *Supplier responsibility.* Apple holds its suppliers and partners responsible for creating quality products for its users, who always come first. ...

BMW: Our Core Values[5]

- *RESPONSIBILITY*

We take consistent decisions and commit to them personally. This allows us to work freely and more effectively.

- *APPRECIATION*

We reflect on our actions, respect each other, offer clear feedback and celebrate success.

(continued)

[4] https://mission-statement.com/apple/#:~:text=Apple%20core%20values%20include%20%E2%80%9Cinclusion,a%20technological%20and%20innovation%20leader. Retrieved: Sep 19, 2021

[5] www.bmwgroup.jobs/gb/en/culture.html. Retrieved: January 26, 2021.

- *TRANSPARENCY*

We acknowledge concerns and identify inconsistencies in a constructive way. We act with integrity.

- *TRUST*

We trust and rely on each other. This is essential if we are to act swiftly and achieve our goals.

- *OPENNESS*

We are excited by change and open to new opportunities. We learn from our mistakes.

Tesla: Core Values[6]

- *Always do your best*

We endeavor to apply the brightest minds and the best available technology to each and every new challenge. We do not cut corners and we do not settle.

- *No forecast is perfect, but try anyway*

We constantly strive to improve the accuracy of our forcasts as well as the reliability and service with which they are delivered.

- *Respect and encourage people*

We believe that our companies are only as successful as our clients and team members are successful. Treating them with respect and encouraging their success is the surest way to ensure the companies´ success.

- *Always be learning*

The world in which we live and the industry in which we operate are constantly changing. It is imperative to both personal and professional success that we understand those changes and adapt accordingly.

- *Respect the environment*

We believe that our efforts to help the energy industry achieve greater efficiencies help ease the strain that humans put on the environment.

(continued)

[6] www.teslaforecast.com/about-tesla/4. Retrieved: Sep 19, 2021.

IKEA: "Our Values"

- *Humbleness and willpower*

We respect each other, our customers and our suppliers. Using our willpower means we get things done.

- *Leadership by example*

Our managers try to set a good example and expect the same of IKEA co-workers.

- *Daring to be different*

We question old solutions and, if we have a better idea, we are willing to change.

- *Togetherness and enthusiasm*

Together, we have the power to solve seemingly unsolvable problems. We do it all the time.

- *Cost-consciousness*

Low prices are impossible without low costs, so we proudly achieve good results with small resources.

- *Constant desire for renewal*

Change is good. We know that adapting to customer demands with innovative solutions saves money and contributes to a better everyday life at home.

- *Accept and delegate responsibility.*

We promote co-workers with potential and stimulate them to surpass their expectations. Sure, people make mistakes. But they learn from them!

Greenpeace: Our Core Values[7]

- *Personal responsibility and nonviolence.*

We take action based on conscience. This means we are accountable for our actions and take personal responsibility. We are committed to peacefulness; everyone on a Greenpeace action is trained in nonviolence.

- *Independence.*

We do not accept money from governments, corporations, or political parties. Individual contributions, together with grants from foundations, are the only source of our funding.

(continued)

[7] www.greenpeace.org/international/explore/about/values. Retrieved: February 19, 2021.

- *Greenpeace has no permanent friends or foes.*

  If your government or company is willing to change, we will work with you to achieve your aims. Reverse course, and we will be back. What matters isn't words, but actions.

- *Promoting solutions.*

  It's not enough for us to point the finger; we develop, research and promote concrete steps towards a green and peaceful future for all of us.

These proclaimed values and value statements express what an organization strives for and what kind of behavior it expects from its members. Hence, proclaimed values have more the nature of aspirations how an organization wants to be and what type of behavior it expects from its leaders, managers, and employees. As such, value statements represent the ideal image of an organization. They do not tell us whether these proclaimed values are actually lived in everyday organizational life and thus guiding the daily actions and interactions of its employees, leaders, and the organization in general. The priorities that guide organizational members in their daily work behavior express lived values, including the posteriorities that result from the chosen priorities. The truly existing values guiding organizational members' behavior become manifest in their decisions and the kind of behavior they display during their daily work activities.

Popular management literature often equates organizational culture with the proclaimed values of an organization. Based on this level's perspective of culture, culture in organizations cannot and should not be reduced to its values since they only represent one of the several levels of culture. A comprehensive understanding of an organization's culture requires knowledge about all levels, including the most inner one.

Basic Beliefs/Assumptions

The set of basic beliefs or assumptions held by a group is the lowest level or the innermost core of an organization's culture. This set consists of several beliefs or assumptions that provide answers to the group's essential problems. They provide the sense-making mechanisms for organizational members and thus guide their behavior. Drawing on the anthropologists Kroeber and Kluckhohn (1952), Schein (1985, 2010) distinguishes five assumptions that he transferred to organizations. These are assumptions about the nature of human beings, the nature of human relationships, the nature of the environment, and the nature of time and space. Based on the works of Berger and Luckmann (1967), my research in the context of organizations has shown that the following basic beliefs are essential for understanding culture in the context of today's organizations. These are beliefs about

- an organization's purpose: Why does the organization exist?
- an organization's strategy: Where do we want to go?
- an organization's design: How do we best organize ourselves?

- organizational members: What kind of people fit (the culture of) the organization (and who does not fit)?

These four set the boundaries for

- the collective (work and interaction) practices, routines, and processes considered appropriate in an organization, and the
- causal logic: Why do things happen the way they do?

These collectively-held beliefs are interconnected and together form a set in a given organization. Figure 2.4 illustrates that the organizational purpose, strategy, design, and type of organizational members act as framing parameters for the relevant organizational practices. Practices are the way of working, adapting and changing, interacting with insiders and outsiders, and the way of learning that are considered appropriate by an organization and the right way of doing things. Across this set of beliefs run the priorities of an organization's culture: What is considered important (and what unimportant)?

The set of basic beliefs have the following characteristics: Since they locate at the deepest level of culture, they are not directly accessible or observable. They constitute the meaning system of an organization and need to be inferred. Once organizational members have learned and internalized this set of basic beliefs, they are no longer aware of them. The beliefs have dropped out of awareness. Due to their repeated use, they become habits of thoughts and actions and attached to positive emotions because they have worked well and are well known. These particular characteristics are further discussed with their implications in Chap. 4. Over time, a cultural knowledge system develops that is composed of four different kinds of knowledge, as shown in Table 2.2: dictionary knowledge, directory knowledge, recipe knowledge, and axiomatic knowledge.

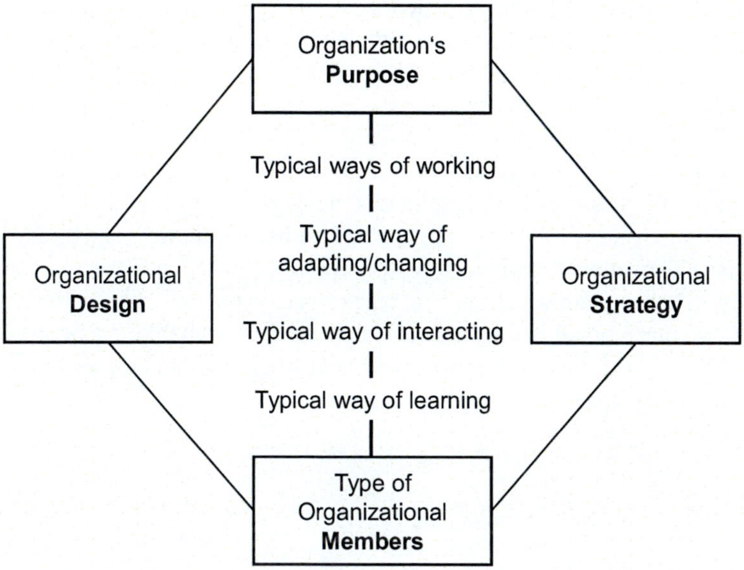

Fig. 2.4 Relevant areas that affect the specific content of culture in organizations

Table 2.2 An overview over the developing cultural knowledge system

Priorities (*what* is important?)	→ dictionary knowledge
Practices (*how* do people behave/work?)	→ directory knowledge
Recommendations (*what should* be done?)	→ recipe knowledge
Axioms (*why* do we behave like this?)	→ axiomatic knowledge

Sackmann (1991) provides a more detailed discussion of these different kinds of cultural knowledge

Priorities express what is important to an organization or a group. What do organizational members need to pay attention to, and what is less or not at all important? Priorities affect all tasks and behaviors in an organization. They accumulated as *dictionary knowledge*. While in one company, revenue, control, shareholder value, and growth may have the highest priority, another company can see profitable growth, a balance between employees, customers, shareholders, and innovation as its main priorities.

Practices concern all collective behavior and routines, such as work processes and human interactions. They accumulate over time as directory knowledge. This stock of knowledge is about the *how*—how things are one in a culturally adequate manner within a group or organization. Directory knowledge entails the entire work-related behavior typical for an organization or group and is considered the *right* way of doing things. Directory knowledge includes information about how an organization makes decisions and the culturally adequate treatment of and interaction with colleagues, employees, supervisors, and externals such as customers, suppliers, and investors. Directory knowledge defines the specific way of how to do one's work *right* as defined by the organization or the group. At the same time, the existing directory knowledge also indicates what is left out, what is not part of the culture.

Basic beliefs concerning **improvements** have a normative character and refer to recommendations about what to do to improve the organization's functioning. This **recipe knowledge** contains experience-based, concentrated recommendations of how to handle a particular topic or problem best. Over time, so-called recipes of success and failure develop. Success recipes refer to knowledge about what has worked well in the past, whereas failure recipes refer to knowledge about what has not led to the desired results and should be avoided.

Axioms, like in mathematics, are basic assumptions once set a priori. They cannot be argued. They almost have a religious character. They explain *why* a particular organization exists, why it acts in its specific, idiosyncratic way, and finally, why it is as it is. As mentioned earlier, these axioms refer to the particular organization's purpose. They explain why a specific type of person fits the organization best, why a specific organizational design is considered the most suitable for the organization, which strategy is the most promising one, and what kind of practices are considered best and most appropriate for the organization. In many instances, only those individuals who once had set or negotiated the axioms know them. Most organizational members, however, act based on these axioms without being aware of them.

2.2.4 Culture Influences Organizational Members' Perception, Thinking, Behaviors, and Emotions

Once a specific culture exists with its basic beliefs, these collectively-held basic beliefs function like a lens or a magnifying glass. They influence the attention of their carriers, what they perceive (and what not), how they process the perceived data, and how they transform the data into information. They influence organizational members' actions based on their evaluations and how they feel about the entire process, from perceiving to processing information and taking actions. The basic beliefs define for their carriers what is important in a certain situation and what is unimportant. They help evaluate what organizational members consider as *good* and *bad*, appropriate and inappropriate, including characterizations of *good* employees or managers and how they differ from those considered *bad*. These collectively held beliefs also specify what expectations about a *good* leader. In this way, culture with its commonly-held basic beliefs influences and controls organizational members' perception, thinking, and actions.

The specific set of commonly-held basic beliefs and their characterization of culturally appropriate behavior become attached with positive emotions over time. The repeated use creates familiarity and thus also security. This influencing and mutually reinforcing process between basic beliefs, verbal- and nonverbal behavior, artifacts, and emotions is illustrated in Fig. 2.5.

Once the link is established between basic beliefs and verbal- as well as nonverbal behavior, with artifacts and emotions, it becomes very difficult to change any of these components because all four components are interconnected with their respective manifestations and peculiarities. In addition, they reinforce each other over time. Figure 2.6 shows several examples for each of the individual components of culture.

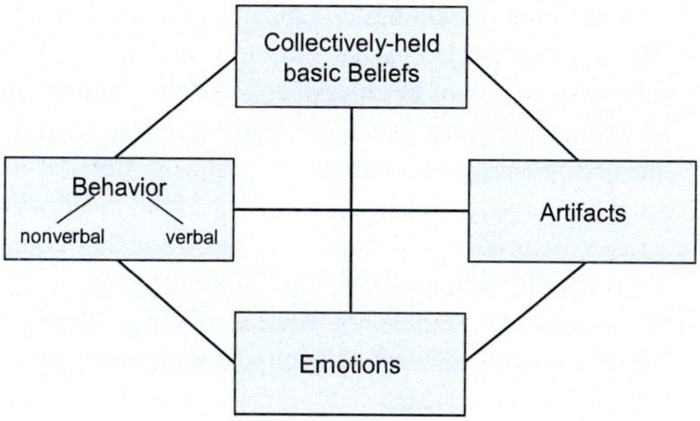

Fig. 2.5 The interconnected system of components of organizational culture

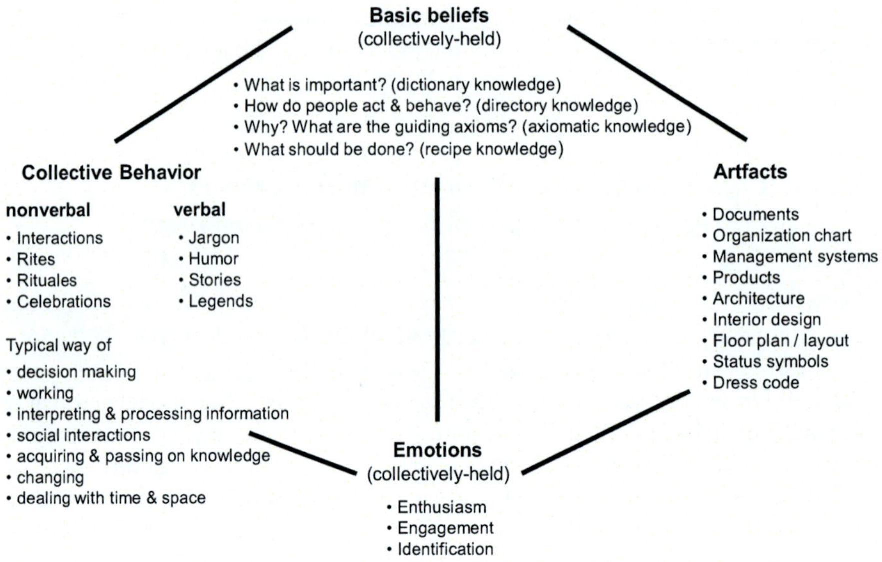

Fig. 2.6 Network of components of organizational culture with examples

Specific metaphors used in an organization are a good example demonstrating the impact of this interconnection between behaviors, basic beliefs, artifacts, and emotions. Metaphors are verbal images that are, on the one hand, characterized by basic beliefs. On the other hand, they reinforce existing basic beliefs when used (Morgan, 2006). A study revealed how gardening metaphors such as sowing, weeding, and fertilizing expressed a distinctive aspect of an organization's culture, namely how the organization treated people. At the same time, these metaphors from gardening characterized the relationships among co-workers and, above all, between employees and managers (Sackmann, 1989b).

2.2.5 Culture Is Based on Experience and Learned

The collectively-held basic beliefs develop in solving problems concerning internal integration and external adaptation (Parsons, 1951; Schein, 2010). Several issues emerge in processes of internal collaboration and interaction between colleagues and between employees and their leaders. These refer to the specific way of acting, interacting, and collaborating. How is work best accomplished? Alone, as a team, or involving experts? These issues refer to the meaning and importance of power and status. The problems at hand need to be solved, requiring collaboration in a coordinated way for achieving results. Moreover, issues in the external environment call for appropriate actions—be it a customer problem, the development of new technology, existing or lacking regulatory requirements, or whether a new competitor has entered the market.

When dealing with regularly occurring problems such as recruiting and onboarding a new organizational member, routines develop over time. Orgnizational member continue to use those decisions and actions that have worked well and produced satisfying results. Over time, these decisions, procedures, and behavior that proved successful become the *right* and appropriate way of dealing with these specific or related problems. If certain decisions or behaviors do not lead to the desired outcomes or produce even worse than expected results, organizational members will most likely not repeat them. Hence, the basic beliefs regarding what works well and what kinds of behavior will lead to failure develop when dealing with specific problems. As such, they are learned, they are accumulated as dictionary and directory knowledge, and as recipes for success and failure.

2.2.6 Culture Drops out of Awareness

Once these collectively-held basic beliefs exist and manifest themselves in the different forms of cultural knowledge that guide organizational members' perceptions, thinking, and behavior on a daily basis, they become habituated and turn into routines. Routines are produced automatically without conscious thought or conscious reflection—they have become habits of thought and actions. Once internalized and habituated, organizational members use these habits of thought and action automatically in response to specific signals.

These routines may develop for all kinds of working areas and functions. To give two examples, once established, the budgeting process tends to be the same every year, as will be the recruiting, hiring, and onboarding process. New organizational members are often hired based on prevailing basic beliefs that help the organization choose the right type of person who fits best with the organization. Hence, basic beliefs guide unconscious processes of selective perception and decision-making.[8]

2.2.7 Culture Is Passed on to New Organizational Members

These basic beliefs, their corresponding practices, and routines are passed on to new group members as the *right* or *wrong* conduct in a certain situation. Organizations may deliberately design this passing-on process in an onboarding program that may include a seminar or workshop, an introduction to all of the relevant functions with explanations why things are done the way they are. In addition, a long-term organizational member and a good example of the organization's culture may act as an onboarding coach. In addition to such a planned enculturation process, culture

[8] In cognitive psychology, this influence in selection processes is known as unconscious bias (Ross, 2014).

is also passed on informally. Newcomers pick up cultural specifics during daily work by observing the behavior of colleagues, managers, and leaders, including the consequences of their behavior by getting feedback from colleagues and superiors. This formal and informal socialization and enculturation processes ensure that one generation of employees transfers the organization's culture to the next.

2.3 Functions of Culture in Organizations

Organizational culture serves several functions both for its members and the organization. These functions result from the cognitive map that culture provides for its members. As such, these functions are neither positive nor negative regarding their effects. Their specific design and content decide if they are helpful for organizational members and supporting an organization's performance or if they have adverse consequences both for employees and the organization.

In general, culture fulfills four primary and interdependent functions and four secondary functions associated with the primary ones. Table 2.3 gives an overview of these four primary and secondary functions.

2.3.1 *Order*

Every organizational culture entails rules for a specific order and thus provides a structure, which guides employees in their daily actions. However, newcomers need to learn first the particular order. One manifestation of the existing order is the organization chart: Who reports to whom? Who has authority over whom? Who is powerful and has what kind of status? The sort of interior design, descriptions of jobs and functions, access to specific information or areas are also an expression of this order function providing organizational members with a cognitive map of what and who is important in the organization.

Table 2.3 Primary and secondary functions of culture in the context of organizations

Primary function	Secondary function
• Order	• Reducing complexity
• Orientation	• Organizational adaptation
• Stabilization	• Internal coordination
• Meaning	• Motivation and identification

2.3.2 *Orientation*

In addition to the structure-providing cognitive map that also defines priorities, orientation has a dynamic component based on the directory knowledge. Providing orientation enables organizational members to behave in a culturally adequate manner in different situations as soon as they have internalized the directory knowledge. Directory knowledge informs them what they are supposed to do and how they are supposed to perform their actions. At the same time, it also includes what they should refrain from doing if they want to be considered a *good* organizational member.

Due to this orientation function, they also know what the organization's culture defines as *good* behavior and *good* work, and *bad* behavior and *bad* work. Furthermore, a given culture helps them set the *right* priorities and guides them in their daily work. It provides the stock of knowledge and routines in dealing appropriately with emerging problems and interactions with colleagues, superiors, subordinates, and external people, such as customers and vendors. The culture provides guidelines for the *right* attitude, how to express oneself appropriately as defined by the culture. It informs members of the organization about all the components illustrated in the culture iceberg model in Fig. 2.1. Hence, organizational members know how to behave *right* and appropriately in the spirit of their organization. In cognitive psychology, directory knowledge specific to a particular situation is also called a script, like the script of the role in a movie. An organization's repertoire usually comprises several scripts for different situations, functions, roles, and culture-adequate interpretation and enactment.

2.3.3 *Stabilization*

One of the critical roles of an organization's culture is its ability to provide the stability that gives an organization and its members continuity and a sense of security. One way of defining organizational culture is *the collective memory* of an organization. A company's historical development influences its culture. The passing on of culture from one generation to the next develops and maintains a particular tradition. It preserves an organization's essential beliefs and collective practices passed on to new employees and turned into organizational routines. Hence, culture provides stability, continuity, and a commonly-held basis for interpretation and communication spanning generations of employees. Manifestations of established stabilizing mechanisms are celebrations, rites, rituals, and ceremonies that enforce the existing order. Without culture, coordinated actions would not be possible, and organizations could not function well. However, the historical imprint and legacy of an organization's culture can also result in problems during times of change as discussed in Chap. 8.

2.3.4 *Meaning*

Another important yet often neglected function of organizational culture is its ability to provide sense-making mechanisms and thus meaning to organizational members. When referring to an organization's culture and its basic beliefs or assumptions, Edgar Schein (2010) also speaks about the *religion* of organizations. The culture explains the "raîson d'être" of an organization or a group. Why do we exist? What distinguishes us from the others? What makes us unique? What is the meaning of certain work? Do organizational members perform simply a job? Or do leaders convey how their job contributes to their unit's and the organization's performance? If and how managers and leaders use this potential culture function of providing meaning has a crucial impact on its member's motivation and, hence, their performance.

2.3.5 *Complexity Reduction*

These four primary functions of organizational culture lead to its secondary functions, one of them being *complexity reduction*. The primary functions of order, providing orientation, stability, and meaning, reduce the generally existing information overload and complexity in organizations for their members. Thus, culture serves as a kind of lens or magnifying glass that help identify relevant information and help distinguish important from unimportant information. This complexity-reducing function enables organizational members to act when confronted with the daily flood of data and information.

Once existing and internalized, organizational culture allows its members to quickly choose the *right* and thus the culturally good script that helps them appropriately assess a situation and react in a manner that is considered appropriate by the organization. When meeting with important clients, organizational members will choose another script in preparing for the meeting than when they meet informally with a colleague. The available culture scripts developed for various situations and roles allow organizational members to appropriately behave as defined by their organization's culture in these different situations and roles. However, if those scripts become over-generalized and people apply them to situations for which they were not designed, confusion and subsequent problems may emerge.

2.3.6 *Organizational Adaptation*

Organizational adaptation is another secondary function that results from the primary function *orientation*. It is essential for the long-term viability of organizations that they can adapt to their external environment and its changes, especially when they act in a dynamic environment. However, the question is whether the existing set of basic beliefs allows organizational members to recognize the need for development or change in time. Several studies in strategy research have found that organizational members may not recognize the need for change in time due to their culturally influenced selective perception. A well-known example is General Motors. GMs decision-makers at various levels did not take their Japanese and European competitors seriously for several years, and they recognized customers' desire for different car designs rather late. The same applies to many car manufacturers regarding the rise of electric mobility and Tesla as a car manufacturer. For several years, they did not consider Tesla as a serious competitor.

2.3.7 Internal Coordination

An organization's culture provides its members with a cognitive map and collective cultural knowledge that are commonly-held and allows them to see and evaluate different situations, events, and problems similarly. In addition, the directory knowledge provides a common language that enables organizational members to talk to each other in a meaningful way. A common language and shared understandings and sense-making mechanisms are prerequisites for mutual coordination, cooperation, and aligning the behavior of organizational members. How and to what extent such coordination will occur depends on the concrete specifications of an organization's culture.

2.3.8 Motivation and Identification

Depending on the specific characteristics of an organization's culture, it may enable and foster motivation and the identification with a group and the entire organization. The yearly surveys on the best companies to work for result in a list of organizations in which organizational members feel highly motivated to work next to their strong identification with their employer. Does the organization provide a purpose and overarching meaning that is worth putting in an extra effort? How strongly can and do organizational members identify with the purpose and the related superordinate goals? The more socially acceptable and desirable the overarching goals and the purpose of an organization are, the higher is the probability that organizational members will identify with these goals and purpose, and the stronger the resulting motivation will be. High motivation, in turn, may have positive effects on their performance and, ultimately, the company's performance. Do people feel that they are appreciated and treated fairly? Can they communicate openly and directly with colleagues and superiors within and across organizational boundaries and hierarchies? Do they feel trusted? These are some of the characteristics of high-performing organizations in which people are highly motivated.

On the other hand, many organizations exist with cultures that kill motivation and reduce employees' identification. Several factors may contribute to a loss in identification and motivation, such as the company's suffering reputation due to a scandal or bad leadership. If organizational members do not feel appreciated, if they don't have a sense of their role and the meaning of their work, they will most likely neither experience motivation nor feel a strong identification with the organization. The resulting consequences of such a cultural context may range from demotivation and working according to the book to high turnover and even sabotage.

Several concepts have emerged in recent years related to culture. These are discussed in the following Sect. 2.4.

2.4 Organizational Culture and Related Concepts

Several concepts exist in organization theory related to organizational culture, but they differ from it in several aspects. These include the concepts of *organizational climate*, *organizational identity*, image, reputation, and branding.

2.4.1 Organizational Culture Vs. Organizational Climate

Some authors and practitioners have equated the term organizational or work climate with organizational culture or used organizational culture instead of work climate. However, culture in organizations differs from its climate. These are two different concepts that refer to different aspects of organizational life and cannot be substituted for each other. Organizational culture is a long-term, collectively-held phenomenon that refers, among other things, to the organization's collective expectations of its organizational members. In contrast, organizational climate is individually anchored; it relates more to short-term sentiment and expresses an employee's satisfaction with some aspects of the organization. Organizational climate refers to the expectations of individual, organizational members toward their work organization. Their respective satisfaction or dissatisfaction results from the intersection of personal expectations and expectations fulfilled by the work organization. Organizational climate can therefore also be regarded as a mood barometer of an organization. Since climate is anchored in individuals, one can easier influence it than the culture of an organization. Single actions and events such as a big speech, a joint event, a celebration, and a critical event such as a sharp decline in sales figures, can have an immediate effect on the organizational climate both positively and negatively.

On the other hand, organizational culture is the context in which organizational life occurs, with the respective boundaries for expected and desired behavior. It contains the company's expectations of what it takes to qualify as a *good* or excellent employee. It thus defines an organization's range of adequate, desired, and undesired behavior, including the rules for conduct and the respective sanctioning mechanisms. As stated in the above definition, organizational culture is a collective phenomenon. It is part of a group and consists of the commonly-held basic beliefs of the group or an organization. Because of this collective anchoring and its transfer to other employees and newcomers, organizational culture is much more difficult to influence than organizational climate. One-time actions don't accomplish a culture change that usually takes a more extended period and a combination of interlocking interventions at all hierarchical levels.

2.4.2 Organizational Culture Vs. Organizational Identity

The concept of organizational identity has a shorter history in management and organization theory than organizational culture. The core of culture, the fundamental beliefs that provide guidelines for the behavior of organizational members, have dropped out of their awareness. Organizational members act on these basic beliefs routinely in their daily work. However, the concept of organizational identity is based on a conscious self-reflection (Kreiner, 2011; Ravasi & Schultz, 2006), often comparing other organizations. The formulation of an organizational identity results from conscious reflection on the question: who are we? It represents the internal self-image of an organization. This conscious reflection is usually carried out or initiated by top-level management in a strategy development process. They discuss and decide on the strategic positioning of a company vis-à-vis its competitors. The identity is then communicated to the members of the organization. Hence, the concept of organizational identity is part of the concept of culture in organizational settings. In contrast to an organization's culture, which refers to the very characteristic of an organization that guides employees` actions without being aware of this guidance, they are aware of the organizational identity, which is usually spelled out in writing and communicated internally and externally.

2.4.3 Organizational Culture Vs. Image, Reputation, and Branding

Organizational culture concerns and characterizes the inner life of an organization. Image, reputation, and branding are concepts directed at the external world of an organization. Image and reputation concern the generalized external image that the public and thus persons external to the organization, such as suppliers, customers, financiers, or former employees, have (Grey & Balmer, 1998). This external image does not necessarily correspond to the self-image of an organization, its organizational identity. In general, organizations deliberately try to influence their image and reputation through image brochures and image campaigns, and advertising or public relations measures to appear in a positive light.

An example is the public apology of sporting goods manufacturer Adidas' CEO, which the company published in the public media during the COVID-19 pandemic in March 2020. When it became known that CEO Kasper Rorsted had ordered a suspension of the April 2020 rent to many Adidas stores, the press coverage was very negative. Hence, a few days later, Rorsted publicly announced that they had paid the April rent, and he apologized for his behavior (Hofer, 2020).

Branding is a concept from marketing and, in its original meaning, refers to the external image of brands. It is, therefore, more specific than the organizational image and reputation of an organization. More recently, the branding concept has been differentiated into external and internal branding and applied to organizations as a whole. External branding refers to the conscious influencing of the external image of an organization by the organization itself. Thus, the term *employer branding* has been coined, and it is especially used when searching for potential employees. Internal branding refers to the conscious influencing of the behavior of organizational members in terms of the brand content of the organization (Eichel, 2018). Thus, internal branding is a small subset of organizational culture. Internal branding's content is also consciously reflected and formulated, similar to organizational identity. In contrast to organizational identity, however, internal branding focuses on deliberate influence.

Table 2.4 summarizes the central characteristics, similarities, and differences between the concepts of organizational culture, organizational identity, organizational climate, image and reputation, and branding.

2.5 Some Misconceptions about the Culture Concept Applied to Organizations

The more popular literature has promoted specific ideas about culture that are not correct, and they tend to have more the quality of myths. Some of them are addressed in this section, such as organizational culture

- is something that only some organizations have;
- is equated with the humanization of work;
- refers to civilization;
- is better when it is a strong and homogenous entity.

2.5.1 Myth 1: Not all Organizations Have a Culture

Parts of the popular literature promote a myth that only *good* firms possess a culture and others don't. Every organization develops a culture and potential subcultures

Table 2.4 Comparison of the concept of organizational culture with related concepts

	Organizational Culture	Organizational Identity	Organizational Climate	Image & Reputation	Branding
Core questions	What is typical for the organization?	Who are we?	How do I feel in this organization?	How are we seen?	How are our brands perceived?
Is result of	Learning processes in dealing with internal and external issues/problems	Conscious self-reflection process	Single actions either emergent or planned	Externally oriented/ visible behavior of the organization	Planned externally oriented brand communication
Collective vs. indivdual phenomenon	Collectively-held	Collectively-held	Individually held	Collectively-held	Collectively-held
Orientation	Internal	Internal	Internal	External	External
Manifestation	Internalized, dropped out of awareness, core is not visible visible manifestations may be misleading	Written down and communicated	Subjectively perceived, emotional, situational mood/ atmosphere	External image as reaction of organizational actions	Consious brand management by organization and/or designated members
Development/ Change	Long-term	Short-term	Short-term	Medium-term	Medium-term
Essence	Is the context in which organizational members act	Formulated text	Mood barometer	Formulated external image charged with emotional aspects	Planned, managed and control by organization

throughout its existence. Whether the developing culture is *good* or *bad* for an organization and its members depends on its specific content and the extent to which its underlying set of basic beliefs with its related routines supports or hinders an organization's functioning. The same applies to its member's perception of external changes and subsequent action taken, the internal work activities that require appropriate interactions and coordinated activities, and the level of engagement of its members. Hence, one can only assess a culture's quality as helpful or hindering for an organization by comparing it with the organization's strategy, its goals, and the degree of employee engagement and health. An organization's specific culture can also lead to several problems and contribute to its failure. Examples are the fast rise and fall of a Silicon Valley company (Schumacher, 1997), the demise of Enron, Barings Bank, and the reading society in Appenzell (Eberle, 1997), or the recent collapse of the financial service firm Wirecard.

2.5.2 *Myth 2: Organizational Culture Is Humanization of Work*

Another myth refers to linking organizational culture to the humanization of work, thus creating positive human workplaces. Misconceptions exist that an organization's culture automatically improves organizational climate and the internal work environment for its members. Unfortunately, this is not automatically the case. As mentioned above, every organization has and is a culture with its characteristics and potential subcultures. Whether or not a particular culture is beneficial for its organizational members and how they feel depends on the culture's specific features and content. Unfortunately, organizations exist with cultures or sub-cultures characterized by micro-political behavior, mobbing, and other detrimental behaviors occurring regularly. Other organizations exist that exploit human labor. For example, in the German warehouses of Amazon, workers have gone on strike because of the firm's working conditions.[9] Organizational culture defines a specific way of how to conduct one's work, how to deal with questions and problems, and how to cooperate efficiently. It can—but must not—result in positive outcomes for the company and its people and consequences associated with a decent, ethical or human workplace.

2.5.3 *Myth 3: Organizational Culture Refers to* Civilization

It is tempting to equate the term organizational culture with *civilization*. As discussed in this chapter, culture in organizations has little to do with fine arts,

[9] www.reuters.com/article/uk-amazon-com-germany-strike/amazon-workers-at-german-warehouse-to-strike-again-idUKKBN2890L6. Retrieved: February 4, 2021.

good wines, or sophisticated literature. These may be expressions of a specific culture. Still, the core of culture in organizational settings consists of the commonly-held basic beliefs that guide its members' thoughts, emotions, and behavior. No links exist between organizational culture and civilization. Civilization implies a hierarchy and a development from lower or less sophisticated standards toward higher or more refined standards. This kind of development is not a quality of culture.

2.5.4 Myth 4: A Stronger and Homogenous Culture Always Better

Another myth exists about the strength and homogeneity of an organization's culture. Early publications on the topic have implied that organizational culture is and should be a consistent, monolithic entity acting as a glue for its members. Early literature on culture promoted this idea by describing successful companies as having *strong* organizational cultures with consistent and pervasive values (e.g., Peters & Waterman, 1982). The characterization of culture as internal *glue* and data mainly collected from top leaders and top management enforced this belief.

In the meantime, several studies have refuted this belief (e.g., Ernst, 2003; Martin, 1992; Sackmann, 1991, 1997, 2011). A strong, homogenous organizational culture can be even worse for a company's or group's viability if it demonstrates or allows for little variety in its members' thinking and actions (Eberle, 1997; Janis, 1982). For example, a study on innovation revealed that a consistent organizational culture is only beneficial for organizations operating in a relatively technologically stable environment (Ernst, 2003). If an organization has to survive in a dynamic environment, which requires constant innovation, a *strong*, consistent, and homogenous culture is not helpful since organizational members may not recognize the ongoing changes in the environment. Hence, the organization does not act in time. Neither does a homogenous organization have the requisite variety needed for dealing with a wide range of challenges. In addition, its existing routines of thought and action may prevent people from thinking out of the box and develop new ideas and solutions.

2.6 The Cultural Context of an Organization

During its development, culture in organizations emerges and is influenced by several factors. This section explores the overall cultural context of organizations that affects them and their culture at the organizational level. Figure 2.7 gives an overview of this cultural context.[10] It consists of culture on different levels, namely

[10] Sackmann (1996, 1997) provides a detailed discussion of the complex cultural context of organizations.

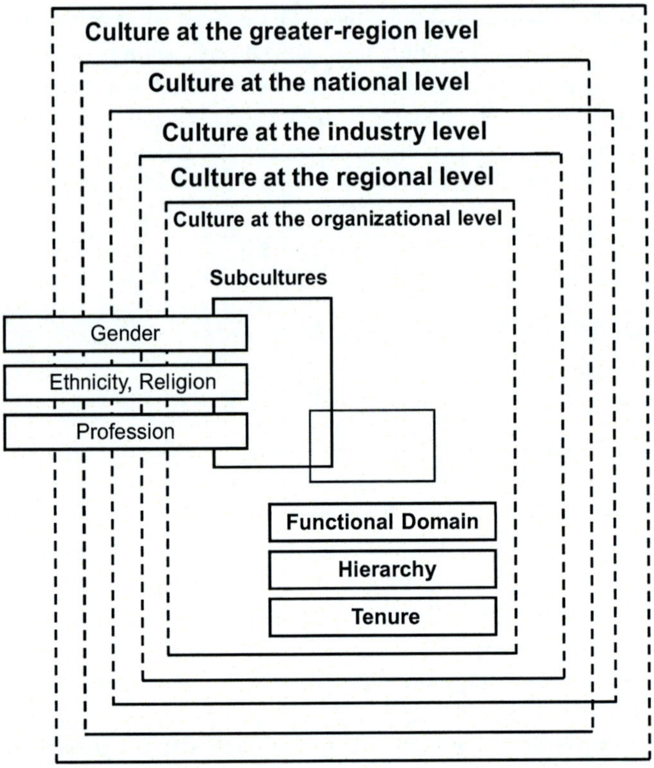

Fig. 2.7 The cultural context of organizations

the organizational, regional, national, supranational, transorganizational, and industry level.

Within a specific culture, several sub-cultures may exist, which may emerge regarding different issues or criteria. They can reflect the various organizational units, functions, hierarchical levels in an organization, and organizational members' tenure. Other ethnic groups may lead to subcultures and different professional orientations, or differences in tenure and gender. The potentially existing subcultures and their impact on organizations will be discussed in Chap. 3.

The founding of an organization happens within a specific region that influences the emerging organization—especially when its founder or founding team originates from this region.[11] The car manufacturer Daimler can be taken as an example. Its organizational culture still has a regional and especially Swabian imprint—despite its global presence, its investors from China and Saudi Arabia, its former merger with Chrysler, and its Swedish CEO. Many countries consist of regional differences between north and south, east and west. Examples are Germany with regional differences between the east and west, the north and south, and municipal influences

[11] One possible exception is the so-called born-global organizations that are not discussed.

by large cities such as Munich, Berlin, Hamburg, Düsseldorf, Cologne, and Frankfurt. Italy has a strong south and north divide; England with Scotland, Wales, and Ireland. Spain has regional differences between Madrid, Catalonia, and the Basque region. The U.S. consist of several different areas such as the East- and the Westcoast, the North, and the South. Virtually every country consists of various regions with specific local (sub-) cultures. These regional cultural influences affect business customs as well. For example, Weiss and Delbecy (1987) have shown how companies within the same industry differ culturally along the U.S. East and West coast due to regional influences.

Cultural differences at the national level (e.g., Hofstede, 2011; Trompenaars & Hampden-Turner, 1998) have become increasingly important with internationalization and globalization processes. These national differences are in part, however, superimposed by regional cultures. For instance, there is more cultural similarity among the neighboring countries at Lake Constance than between the cities within the same country, such as Friedrichshafen and Berlin, Lindau and Hamburg for Germany, Vorarlberg and Vienna in Austria, or between the east and the west of Switzerland. On a national level, specific institutions and jurisdictions influence organizations and their cultures. Corporate law affects the taxation of individual and corporate income, and labor law impacts the practices, the nature of work, and interactions between organizational members. Labor law determines, for example, the number of working days, the number of holidays and length of vacation, the regular working hours, and the role and rights of unions. It also regulates the extent of employee participation and the required documentation. All of these factors constitute a framework for people's behavior within organizations. Hence, these institutional factors at the national level influence, directly and indirectly, the thinking and acting of employees, organizations as a whole, and their culture. However, recent studies suggest that the impact of organizational culture is more important than national culture in multi-national organizations and mergers and acquisitions.

Culture on a continental-regional level refers to the differences between the big economic blocks such as Europe, the U.S.A., China, and the Asian region. But also supranational economic blocs such as the EU, EFTA, NAFTA, Mercosur, ASEAN, or CARICOM were founded to jointly work on topics, rules, and regulations that affect organizations in those regions and regulate collaborations across included nations. For example, in the European Union, increasingly more issues are discussed on the EU level formulating respective regulations and laws that subsequently have to be implemented by the individual member states. The purchase of Covid-19 vaccines of the EU compared to its member states is a recent example of the increasing influence of the supranational level.

Additionally, industry culture affects the culture of organizations within a specific industry or strategic business unit (Phillips, 1994). One crucial factor is the standard technologies an related work practices that an industry's organizations are using. Hence, culture at the industry level crosses regional and national borders and their respective cultural characteristics. For example, the typical way of building a car, producing wine, or conducting retail and investment banking can be similar across different regions and countries. Still, companies can differ in how they apply those technologies and thus distinguish themselves in terms of organizational culture from their competitors.

2.7 Summary of the most Central Characteristics of Culture

Chapter 2 has introduced the three different perspectives of culture in the context of organizations. Culture in the context of organizations was defined and characterized, including its functions. Finally, the chapter addressed the cultural context of organizations with the mutual influence on culture at the organizational level. The following listing summarizes the most central characteristics of culture at the organizational level:

Culture in the Context of Organizations . . .

- . . . is a collective phenomenon.
- . . . is based on collectively-held basic beliefs/assumptions.
- . . . emerges from dealing with recurring problems of external adaptation and internal integration.
- . . . is the result of collective negotiation and learning processes.
- . . . has an emotional component.
- . . . is passed on to new members, who learn and adopt the existing culture.
- . . . exists in every organization.
- . . . guides and thus influences the perception and behavior of organizational members.
- . . . consists of typical patterns of thought, emotions, and action that turn into routines due to their repeated use.
- . . . drops out of awareness once it is internalized and routinized.
- . . . becomes visible in its manifestations, such as behavior patterns that are typical for the group or organization. Examples of behavior patterns are work routines, rituals, symbolic actions, stories, and legends. Manifestations can be buildings, equipment, office design, and other artifacts.
- . . . evolves over time and hence has a history.
- . . . is influenced by the cultural context of the organization.

Chapter 3 explores the emergence of culture in the context of organizations and how it develops over time. It addresses how subcultures may emerge and evolve, including their implications for organizations.

References

Berger, P. L., & Luckmann, T. (1967). *The social construction of reality*. Anchor Books.

Berner, W. (2012). *Culture change*. Schäffer-Poeschel.

Chase, S. (1948). *The proper study of mankind*. Harper & Row.

Eberle, T. S. (1997). Cultural contrasts in a democratic nonprofit organization: The case of a Swiss reading society. In S. A. Sackmann (Ed.), *Cultural complexity in organizations: Inherent contrasts and contradictions* (pp. 133–159). Sage.

Eichel, V. (2018). *Einfluss der Diskrepanz zwischen externem und internem Branding auf das Organizational Citizenship Behavior*. Eul.

Ernst, H. (2003). Unternehmenskultur und Innovationserfolg: Eine empirische Analyse. *Zeitschrift für Betriebswirtschaftliche Forschung, 55*(2), 23–44.

Frey, A., Kobi, J.-M., Wissmann, P., & Wüthrich, H. A. (1984). Wie gestaltet man eine starke Unternehmenskultur? In Allgemeine Treuhand AG (ATAG) (Ed.), *Die Bedeutung der Unternehmenskultur für den künftigen Erfolg Ihres Unternehmens* (pp. 43–52). ATAG.

Grey, E. R., & Balmer, S. A. (1998). Managing corporate image and corporate reputation. *Long Range Planning, 31*(5), 695–702.

Hofer, J. (2020). Adidas-Chef Rorsted entschuldigt sich und zahlt doch Miete. *Handelsblatt online*, April 1, 2020. Accessed Feb 19, 2021, from www.handelsblatt.com/unternehmen/handel-konsumgueter/das-pr-debakel-eines-erfolgsmanagers-adidas-chef-rorsted-entschuldigt-sich-und-zahlt-doch-miete/25704442.html?ticket=ST-300130-F2fjRD7eNBSg2bj39NuR-ap5

Hofstede, G. (1978). Culture and organization: A literature review. *Journal of Enterprise Management, 1*, 127–135.

Hofstede, G. (2011). Dimensionalizing cultures: The Hofstede model in context. *Online Readings in Psychology and Culture, 2*(1). https://doi.org/10.9707/2307-0919.1014

Janis, I. L. (1982). Groupthink: Psychological studies of policy decisions and fiascos. Houghton-Mifflin.

Jelinek, M., Smircich, L., & Hirsch, P. (1983). Introduction: A code of many colors. *Administrative Science Quarterly, 28*(3), 331–338.

Kieser, A. (1988). Von der Morgensprache zum "gemeinsamen HP-Frühstück". Zur Funktion von Werten, Mythen, Ritualen und Symbolen –"Organisationskulturen"– in der Zunft im modernen Unternehmen. In E. Dülfer (Ed.), *Organisationskultur* (pp. 207–225). Poeschel.

Kreiner, G. E. (2011). Organizational identity. Culture's conceptual cousin. In N. M. Ashkanasy, C. P. M. Wilderom, & M. F. Peterson (Eds.), *The handbook of organizational culture and climate* (pp. 463–480). Sage.

Kroeber, A. L., & Kluckhohn, C. (1952). *Culture: A critical review of concepts and definitions*. The Museum.

Malinowski, B. (1939). Review of six essays on culture by Albert Blumenthal. *American Sociological Review, 4*(4), 588–592.

Martin, J. (1992). *Cultures in organizations: Three perspectives*. Oxford University Press.

Martin, J., Feldman, M. S., Hatch, M. J., & Sitkin, S. B. (1983). The uniqueness paradox in organizational stories. *Administrative Science Quarterly, 28*, 438–453.

Morgan, G. (2006). *Images of Organization* (Updated ed.). Sage.

Parsons, T. (1951). *The social system*. Free Press.

Peters, T. J. (1984). *In search of excellence: Lessons from American's best-run companies*. Presentation at the conference "Managing Corporate Cultures", Pittsburgh, October 24–27.

Peters, T. J., & Waterman, R. H. (1982). *In search of excellence*. Harper & Row.

Phillips, M. E. (1994). Industry mindsets: Exploring the cultures of two macro-organizational settings. *Organization science, 5*(3), 384–402. https://doi.org/10.1287/orsc.5.3.384

Pümpin, C. (1984). *Unternehmenskultur, Unternehmensstrategie und Unternehmenserfolg*. Presentation at the ATAG conference „Die Bedeutung der Unternehmenskultur für den künftigen Erfolg Ihres Unternehmens“, Zurich.

Ravasi, D., & Schultz, M. (2006). Responding to organizational identity threats: Exploring the role of organizational culture. *Academy of Management Journal, 49*(3), 433–458.
Ross, H. J. (2014). *Everyday bias: Identifying and navigating unconscious judgments in our daily lives*. Rowman & Littlefield.
Sackmann, S. A. (1989a). »Kulturmanagement«: Läßt sich Unternehmenskultur »machen«? In K. Sandner (Ed.), *Politische Prozesse in Unternehmen* (1st ed., pp. 157–184). Heidelberg: Physica. (2nd ed. 1992).
Sackmann, S. A. (1989b). The role of metaphors in "organizational transformation". *Human Relations, 42*(6), 463–485.
Sackmann, S. A. (1991). *Cultural knowledge in organizations. Exploring the collective mind*. Sage.
Sackmann, S. A. (1996). Erfassung und Analyse von National- und Organisationskultur: Eine kritische Betrachtung. In R. Lang (Ed.), *Wandel von Unternehmenskulturen in Ostdeutschland und Osteuropa* (pp. 55–64). Rainer Hampp.
Sackmann, S. A. (Ed.). (1997). *Cultural complexity in organizations: Inherent contrasts and contradictions*. Sage.
Sackmann, S. A. (2011). Culture and performance. In N. M. Ashkanasy, C. P. M. Wilderom, & M. F. Peterson (Eds.), *Handbook of organizational culture and climate* (2nd ed., pp. 188–224). Sage.
Sathe, V. (1985). *Culture and related corporate realities: Text, cases, and readings on organizational entry, establishment, and change*. Richard D Irwin.
Schein, E. H. (1985). *Organizational culture and leadership*. Wiley.
Schein, E. H. (2010). *Organizational culture and leadership* (4th ed.). Wiley & Sons.
Schumacher, T. (1997). West coast Camelot: The rise and fall of an organizational culture. In S. A. Sackmann (Ed.), *Cultural complexity in organizations: Inherent contrasts and contradictions* (pp. 105–132). Sage.
Silverzweig, S., & Allen, R. F. (1976). Changing the corporate culture. *Sloan Management Review, Spring, 17*(3), 33–50.
Simon, F. B. (2004). *Gemeinsam sind wir blöd? Die Intelligenz von Unternehmen, Managern und Märkten*. Heidelberg: Carl-Auer. (4th ed. 2013.)
Smircich, L. (1983). Concepts of culture and organizational analysis. *Administrative Science Quarterly, 28*(3), 339–358.
Trice, H. M., Belasco, J. E., & Allutto, J. A. (1969). The role of ceremonials in organization behavior. *Industrial & Labor Relations Review, 23*(1), 40–51.
Trompenaars, F., & Hampden-Turner, C. (1998). *Riding the waves of culture: Understanding cultural diversity in global business* (2nd. ed.). McGraw-Hill.
Tunstall, W. B. (1983). Cultural transition at AT&T. *Sloan Management Review, 25*(1), 15–26.
Van Maanen, J., & Barley, S. R. (1985). Culture organizations: Fragments of a theory. In L. R. Pondy, P. J. Frost, G. Morgan, & T. C. Dandridge (Eds.), *Organizational symbolism* (pp. 31–53). JAI Press.
Weiss, J., & Delbecq, A. (1987). High-technology cultures and management: Silicon Valley and route 128. *Group and Organization Studies, 12*(1), 39–54.
Wilkins, A. L. (1989). *Developing corporate character: How to successfully change an organization without destroying it*. Jossey-Bass.

Chapter 3
The Development of Culture and its Subcultures

How does culture emerge and further develop in organizations? What are its major development phases and what kind of characteristics and challenges do they entail for an organization's culture? When and how may subcultures emerge and what kind effect do they have for an organization? Chapter 3 discusses an organization's founding, developing and mature phase with its related culture an subculture development including cultural knowledge with its recipes of success and failure. The chapter addresses the impact of increasing over-determined behavior during the mature phase, which may lead to a crisis. Depending on the actions taken in the mature stage, rejuvenation or demise of an organization and its culture may follow.

As an organization develops, so does its culture. Both go through similar stages. These are

- the founding stage,
- the developing stage,
- the mature stage, which may lead to
- a potential crisis resulting in rejuvenation or
- the crisis resulting in demise.

Figure 3.1 illustrates these major stages in the development and life-cycle of culture in organizations including a potential crisis, rejuvination or demise.

This chapter explores each of these stages and their respective characteristics, including their inherent opportunities and challenges for organizations. Knowledge about these issues helps address each stage's challenges constructively ahead of time. Such early actions may avoid problems and a potential crisis.

S. A. Sackmann, *Culture in Organizations*, Contributions to Management Science,
https://doi.org/10.1007/978-3-030-86080-6_3

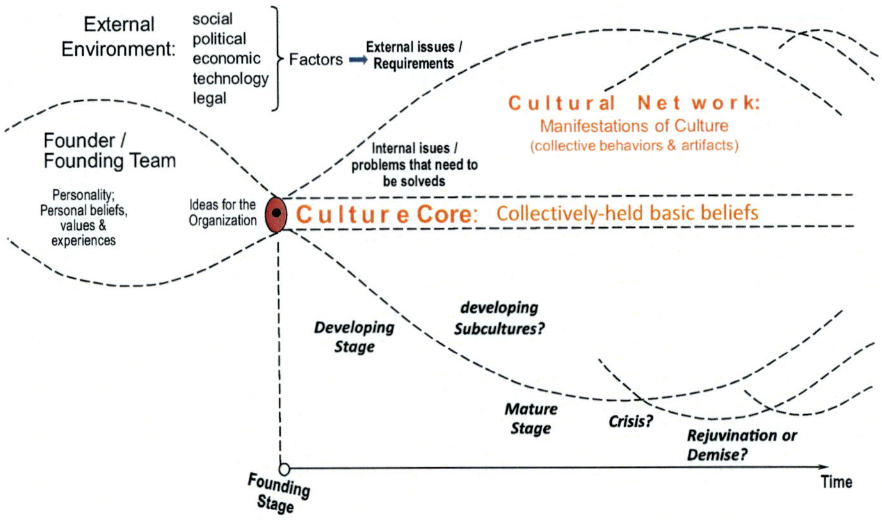

Fig. 3.1 Emergence and development of culture in organizations

3.1 The Founding Stage: Factors Influencing an Organization's Culture

How does culture come into existence? The culture of an organization emerges with the founding of the organization. The founder or the founding team have a business idea they believe in. They are convinced of their business idea and that it is going to work. They are confident that a market exists for their envisioned products or services, as shown in the following examples:

- **Apple Computer.** At the end of the 1970s, Steve Jobs and Steve Fary "Woz" Wozniak, the founders of Apple Computer, had the idea of reproducing a desktop on a PC's monitor. PCs should be as user-friendly as possible and easy to use for people who have never worked with a computer before. The two founders started in the garage of Steve Job's parents since they could not afford an office until they could spread their idea to others and expand (www.apple.com) (see also, Rogers & Larsen, 1984, pp. 1–24).
- **Facebook.** Mark Zuckerberg's idea was that Facebook would offer the possibility to get in contact with the people in their lives and share content with them. Facebook—an open and connected world.
- **Nixdorf Computers.** Heinz Nixdorf's idea was offering problem solutions to customers rather than selling the best hardware—an idea that was rather progressive at that time.
- **Scooters.** Their inventor, engineer Sieghart Straka, found a way to get from home or work to public transport more quickly (Küppers, 2000).

- **Jamba!** was founded in 2000 by the telecommunication corporation Debitel, the electronic chains Media Markt and Saturn, and the three Samwar brothers Alexander, Marc, and Oliver Samwar. The idea behind Jamba! was selling subscriptions to ringtones for mobile phones. After only six weeks, Jamba! reported 300,000 registered users and a growth of 4000 customers per day. After one year, the number had risen to 1,000,000 users. Jamba! was sold in 2004 to the U.S. corporation VeriSign for $ 270 million.
- The pay-to-surf start-up **CyberProfit**, founded in 1999 and declared insolvency only two years later in 2001, is one example of the many start-ups that do not survive the founding stage, often due to underfinancing despite their promising idea. The three young entrepreneurs recorded the most important milestones, moments of joy and despair during this founding stage in a diary. CyberProfit paid its customers for surfing the internet, financed through banner advertisement. Even though the journal focuses primarily on the founding stage, there is plenty of information about the business idea the entrepreneurs wanted to realize and about the first problems they confronted, including their handling of those. The diary also illustrates how passionate they were about founding their organization and how they looked for that same kind of passion in new organizational members—many times in vain. However, finding new people who are passionate about the business is significant in this stage, as illustrated in the following diary entry:

  > Every new employee wants to have the same financial stakes as the founders. I have the impression they are only interested in the money and not in the work, the fun, or the cash machine itself. We three love the cash-machine .... It is difficult for us to understand that other people don't think the same way. It makes a huge difference, whether you are welded together right from the start or whether you try to blend in later. We will discuss this openly tonight. The result: Our candidate says goodbye. Really a sad day. We had hoped to integrate a fourth leader. This hope is now definitely buried (WirtschaftsWoche 2000, p. 110).

- **ShelfSailor** was founded in 2014 in Hamburg by Miriam Bundle (director) and Stephan Creifelds (marketing). Their idea was to rent a private storage room to people nearby who need storage for a few months for their furniture, books, or old clothes. The website brings together both sides. Trust is the essential ingredient of the business model. Currently, the founding team wants to stay among themselves because they know and understand each other and complement each other with their expertise (www. shelfsailor.com).

Many business founding stories can be added to this list when looking at the start-up scene in various countries.

The prior experience that founders bring with them into the new organization influences their business ideas. Relevant influencing factors are their specific upbringing, their formal and informal education, their family and friends, their values, interests, motivation, and significant life events. All these factors shape their thinking and behavior. What influenced them when they grew up? What was the spirit of the times? What kind of technologies opened new avenues? Today's information technologies lead to very different business ideas when compared to those of the 1980s. The so-called FinTechs or social network companies would have almost been utopian from the technological perspective at that time. What has worked well for the founders in their lives concerning family, education, and occupation, and what has not? What has fascinated and inspired the founders in the course of their education or work so far? What kind of negative or demotivating experiences did they have? What motivated them in their work and regarding their business idea? Which work environment did they experience as stimulating and productive? For instance, a U.S. steel company's founder was influenced by a significant experience when he was a student. To afford his university studies, he worked part-time in a factory. After a short time, he realized that he could accomplish the assigned tasks for the day within two hours. The rest of the time, he immersed himself in the books for his studies. When his manager noticed his behavior, he told him that he should spread his tasks over the entire workday instead of reading books. The student was so appalled by this attitude that he swore to himself that one day he would have a company in which everybody could work as much or as little as they wanted for a matching salary. Several years later, he implemented this idea in his steel company.

These and similar experiences impact the founding of a new organization and give it its particular imprint. In addition, founders also have basic ideas and beliefs about the culture and the primary product or service concept. These ideas include the *good* or *right* way to organize their business and related tasks, lead people, inform, supervise and control them. These beliefs are usually implicit, guiding all their business-related behavior. They can only verbalize them when they are deliberately addressed or questioned. Furthermore, these beliefs affect the founders' ideas about whom to work with and what kind of people they need to develop their business further, as shown by CyberProfit's diary entry.

The following influences from the external environment also impact the founding stage, thus the development of an organization's culture. Figure 3.1 visualizes them:

- The spirit of the times.
- Socio-cultural values: Which values are essential in a specific context? Do homogeneous or pluralistic values characterize society? Are entrepreneurship and innovation appreciated in a given country or region, or considered unimportant?
- The economic situation: Is there an economic upturn or an economic recession? What kind of economic system exists in the country? Is it a social market economy like Germany, a free market economy like in the U.S., or a state-directed economy like in China and several Eastern European countries?
- The country's or region's legal system in which the organization operates: What kind of jurisdiction exists and what are the implications for founding and running a business in a specific country? What kind of opportunities and challenges does the specific jurisdiction present regarding, for example, founding requirements, labor law, taxation, and reporting?
- The standards, regulations, and growth stage and growth rate of the particular industry: What are the technological standards? How mature is the industry? Is it

saturated or a relatively young and developing industry with new market opportunities? How long are the standard product development period and product life cycle? What kind of time pressure does this impose for an organization of that particular industry?

A set of basic beliefs constitute the culture core of a gradually developing organization and its culture. These beliefs concern: What is important to us? What kind of people do we want and need? How can we treat people? How do we solve our work-related problems? During this start-up phase, relatively few cultural components and cultural knowledge exist since the organization is in emergence. In this phase, the organization's culture and the respective collective behavior are *underdetermined*. The founding group members need to make every decision for the first time; they have to solve every problem for the first time. They have not yet developed decision- and problem-solving patterns, and experience has not yet established proven paths. Experimenting behavior and the absence of routines is therefore characteristic for this founding phase. As a result, inefficiencies occur since every task requires time, a conscious effort, and energy from organizational members to be addressed and solved.

The literature provides many examples and illustrations of this exciting and challenging founding and early development stage of organizations and their culture, such as:

- Bosch company history (Herdt, 1986).
- Facebook (Mezrich, 2009).
- Google (Kilday, 2018).
- The HP Way (Packard, 1995).
- Hilton (Hilton, 1987).
- Mary Kay (Kay Ash, 1981).
- Sho Dog: A Memoir by the creator of NIKE (Knight, 2016).
- The Toyota Way (Liker, 2004).

3.2 The Developing Stage of Culture

In dealing with those day-to-day problems that emerge internally from daily work and the external business environment, requirements and issues to be tackled come up repeatedly. Patterns slowly emerge in handling the same issues and problems as well as in decision making. During this ongoing process of working, problem-solving, and learning, cultural knowledge develops regarding dictionary, directory, and recipe knowledge, including cultural manifestations typical for the organization (Sackmann, 1983). Figure 3.2 illustrates this cultural development process that goes hand in hand with the organization's development.

Figure 3.2 differs from Fig. 3.1 in that it includes the cultural network with its cultural manifestations regarding behavior and some of the cultural artifacts. This cultural network contains explicit rules and standards that have developed based on

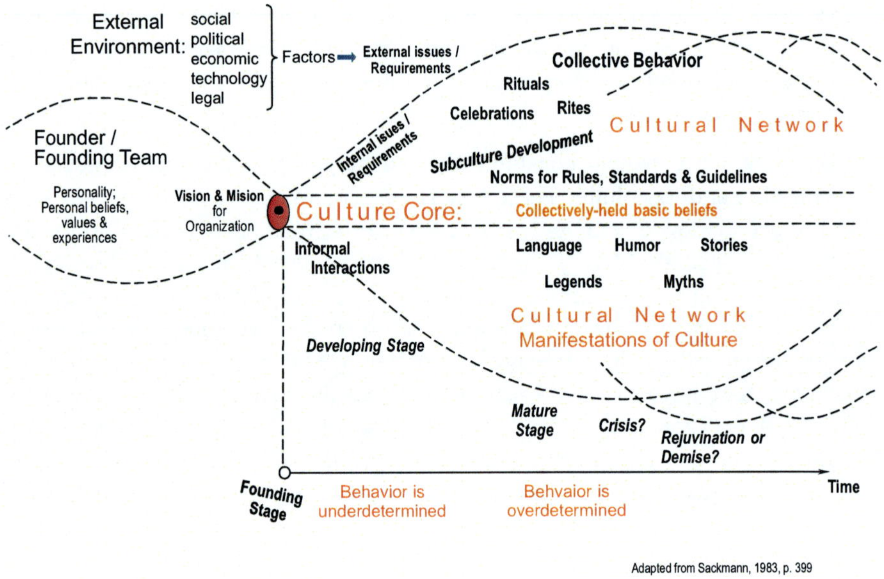

Fig. 3.2 Organizational culture: A development perspective

tackling recurring problems. In addition, rites, rituals, stories, celebrations, sagas, legends, and myths may have developed as part of the cultural network. The dotted curved lines illustrate the life-cycle and development stages that culture tends to follow parallel to the organization's life-cycle (e.g., Adizes, 1979). Depending on an organization's current stage, its cultural knowledge and cultural network are more or less developed, and stage-specific questions, problems, and challenges arise.

3.2.1 *Challenges Resulting from an Organization's Growth for Culture*

Once the founding team has overcome the turbulences of the founding stage and the business idea has proven successful, the organization is likely to face external market pressure to grow. However, the number of people they can develop from within and hire from the outside limit an organization's growth speed. When hiring new organizational members during this stage, technical knowledge, expertise, and experience are essential, including their fit with the organization's culture. New organizational members need to fit with the culture in their way of thinking, their typical behavior regarding working and dealing with people, and their enthusiasm for the organization and the business idea. The following example of *CyberProfit* demonstrates this challenge well:

> ... The third one is the new colleague we had been looking for so desperately ... That is a milestone in the history of CyberProfit ... The man knows what he does when it comes to advertising. He also has the 'spirit' that the other candidates were lacking. He is red-hot for our baby. Sure, he could earn more money elsewhere, but the Cash-Machine has him hooked. The chemistry is right between us. Now we're going to kick it up a notch (WirtschaftsWoche, 2000, p. 112).

If they can find qualified people with the appropriate mindset and *right chemistry* and hire them successfully, the next stage of problem-solving and related challenges emerge in daily operations. Even though organizational members have brought with them their prior experience, it does not necessarily fit the newly founded organization's tasks and challenges. Hence, they need to solve every issue needs for the first time since the organization's collectively-held cultural knowledge is just emerging. This cultural knowledge develops in dealing with recurring everyday problems of internal cooperation and coordination and tackling external challenges. It will take some time until organizational members can draw on a solid stock of cultural knowledge that enables them to act quickly.

3.2.2 The Development of Cultural Knowledge

According to the sociologist Parsons (1951), every social system has to solve four main tasks or problems. These are:

- *external adaptation*: recognizing the opportunities and challenges of the external business environment and adapting appropriately,
- *goal achievement*: the setting of goals and achieving them,
- *internal integration*: dealing with problems of coordination and communication within the organization, and
- *latency*: developing a culture, preserving or retaining it, and transferring it to the next generation of organizational members.

Organizational culture, cultural knowledge, and artifacts develop when its members deal with everyday problems in their day-to-day business. At the founding stage, directory knowledge does not yet exist. Hence, organizational members need to make every decision for the first time. They carry out every task for the first time and establish and maintain every customer contact for the first time. This initial stage of a young organization entails the challenge that behavior is under-determined. No established and proven problem solutions exist that organizational members could draw on for solving their daily problems, often resulting in duplicating efforts. They (re-) invent the wheel over and over again. Since everybody is so busy with their daily tasks, every upcoming issue and problem seems to be a new one at first glance, and they approached it with effort. Hence, organizational members waste time and energy dealing with and solving these issues since they have not yet recognized and addressed reoccurring patterns. Therefore, up to this point, behavior is under-determined in the organization.

Only when organizational members recognize that specific issues or problems come up repeatedly on a more or less regular basis can they develop standards and routines for dealing with them. These standards and routines prescribe how specific issues and problems are and should be handled *best* or most appropriately in the organization. Over time, so-called recipes of success and failure emerge based on the feedback and results of actions taken. According to learning theory, individuals will more likely repeat a specific behavior if it receives positive feedback. Achieving the desired outcome with actions taken is one form of positive feedback (Illeris, 2018). If, on the other hand, a particular work or problem-solving behavior leads to undesirable results or even failure, individuals will less likely repeat the specific behavior that led to such adverse outcomes.

When organizational members pass on these recipes of success and failure to other members and use them in their daily work, these recipes of success and failure start to become the organization's cultural knowledge—primarily in the form of directory knowledge. Once these routines have become established as part of the organization's culture and are available to organizational members for regular use, they help reduce complexity at work. These available routines enable employees to perform their tasks quickly and in a standardized way as defined by their culture's standards. Hence, these standardized routines require less attention and energy from people using them, and they have more time and energy for addressing new tasks and challenges (see also, Schein, 2010). This routinization process also implies that organizational members, who have internalized these behavior patterns, can no longer deliberately decide if they want to use the internalized routines. They become part of their behavioral repertoire and non-decidable decision premisses.

3.2.3 Development Stages and Related Challenges

In case a newly founded organization is successful, it will start to grow following its founding stage. Growth and the further elaboration of directory knowledge characterize the development stage. During this stage of evolutionary development, several growth-related issues emerge that need to be addressed (Flamholtz & Randle, 1990; Greiner, 1972). Figure 3.3 illustrates these issues and challenges.

In the process of evolutionary development, an organization regularly faces critical challenges that may have a revolutionary character. Organizational members need to overcome the difficulties of each growth stage to move to the next state and thus facilitate the organization's further development. According to Greiner (1972), growth through creativity characterizes *the innovative founding stage*. If the organization is successful, the founding team needs to hire more people, and the founders can no longer be all involved in handling the same issues. They need to solve the problems of responsibility, accountability, and leadership. If not adequately addressed, the organization will encounter a leadership challenge. In the process of further growth, strong leadership in terms of concentration of decision making in one or a few people may become a bottleneck, thus leading to challenging autonomy.

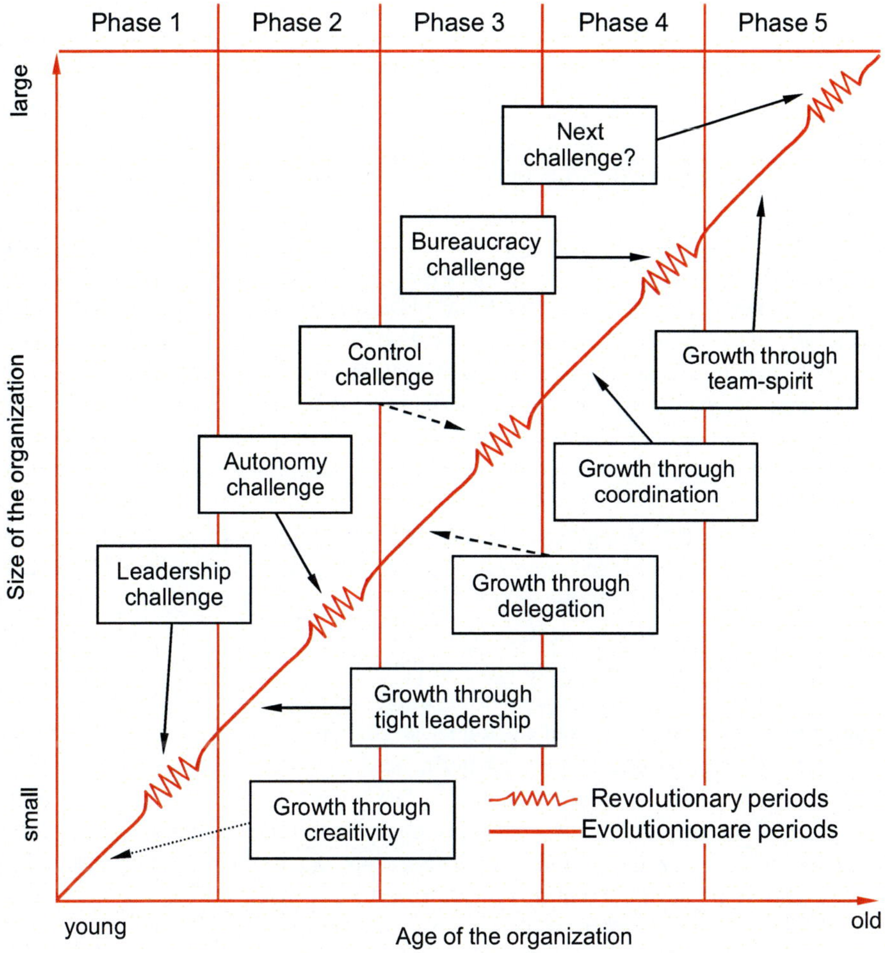

Fig. 3.3 Challenges resulting from an organization's growth (adapted from Greiner, 1972, p. 41)

They can only solve this challenge by giving up central decision-making and control through delegating tasks and responsibilities. Too much delegation may, however, successively lead to problems of coordination among people and organizational units and lead to uncoordinated actions. For example, such behavior is typical in strategic business units that act independently in the market. Thus, the same customers may get several uncoordinated offers from different business units of the same organization.

These uncoordinated actions will trigger a control challenge, which they can solve by introducing coordination mechanisms such as *one face to the customer*: One representative of the organization serves specific customers and coordinates the interface between the customers and the organization's different business units. Internally, many coordination efforts such as meetings, calls, and emails characterize this growth stage. After some time, increasing coordination efforts will call for more formal rules, standards and regulations. These efforts may eventually lead to increasing bureaucracy. They can solve the bureaucracy challenge by building on the team spirit in the organization and investing in training. These efforts will help organizational members internalize the right way of accomplishing work in the organization. Such an approach will make some of the rules and regulations obsolete. The subsequent growth stage may, however, lead to another leadership challenge.

This discussion of the stages of evolutionary growth illustrates that natural challenges eventually follow every growth stage. These emerge as a response to actions taken when solving the problems of one growth stage. However, the initially helpful interventions and changes will gradually develop increasingly negative aspects that may result in another challenge or even crisis if not addressed early and adequately enough. The evolutionary growth cycle illustrates that organizations are dynamic systems whose *way of being,* their routinized behavior patterns need to be consciously and deliberately addressed and checked regularly to prevent major problems or even crises.

Along with increasing revenue and organizational members, the developing organizational culture, the organization's designs with its structures and processes need to be critically examined and adapted in the respective periods of growth. After the founding stage, an organization will most likely establish different functions that require specifically trained people and experts. On the operational level, the generalists of the early stage handled everything themselves: research, development, finance, sales, marketing, and personnel issues. Once an organization grows, one or a few generalists can no longer handle these tasks. The respective functions and tasks require specially trained people to bring their professional perspective and expertise to the separate functional areas. Such a differentiation of an organization's design into organizational units—be it functions, departments, or business units—may lead to the development of subcultures.

3.2.4 The Development of Subcultures

As organizations grow, they differentiate into different organizational units such as functions, departments, projects, programs, or strategic business units. This internal differentiation is likely to be accompanied by developing subcultures if these organizational units exist for some time. The more often and intensely the members of a group interact and work with each other while, at the same time, being separated from other groups, the more likely it is for a subculture to emerge. Subcultures have developed an identity of their own and distinguish themselves from other groups regarding their directory and dictionary knowledge (Sackmann, 1992).

Different factors can lead to the development of subcultures in organizations (Trice & Beyer, 1993; Sackmann, 1997). Subcultures may form due to:

- function (e.g., marketing, sales, development, accounting, finances),
- length of tenure with an organization (long-term organizational members vs. newcomers),
- affiliation with a professional group (e.g., marketing specialists, engineers, doctors, nurses, psychotherapists, physiotherapists),
- gender (male-female-diverse),
- age (generations, young—older organizational members),
- experience (little experience—much experience),
- ethnicity,
- religion.

Organizational subcultures tend to develop along with structural interfaces since structural differentiation leads to separate groupings. As a result, the members working within the same organizational unit, communicate, interact and meet people from their organizational unit more often than colleagues who work in different organizational units.

The subcultures that may develop and their size depends on the respective organizational design and the developing organizational culture. Organizational members may also be simultaneous members of different subgroupings or subcultures. The existence of subcultures is by itself neither positive nor negative for an organization. The critical question is how they relate to each other and whether the organization has intended this specific relationship between subcultures. The three potential ways of subcultural relations and their impact on the organization are discussed in Sect. 3.3.1 of this chapter.

3.3 The Maturity Stage

Noticeable subcultures and various explicit and implicit norms in terms of rules, standards, and regulations characterize an organization's maturity stage and culture. Depending on the number of rules and standards, they may increasingly lead to bureaucracy. In addition, ceremonies, rites, and rituals exist and enforce the existing culture. Since organizational members have repeatedly handled the same tasks, issues, and problems, many solutions exist concerning problem-solving routines. As a result, the behavior in organizations is overdetermined in this maturity stage. Overdetermined behavior may lead to an organizational crisis. The specific interplay of subcultures, the development of the culture network with its rites, rituals, ceremonies, and overdetermined behavior are now discussed in more detail.

3.3.1 The Interplay of Subcultures

Essentially, existing subcultures may relate to each other in three different ways (Martin & Siehl, 1983). They may

- act independently from each other,
- complement each other, or
- be conflicting with each other.

Subcultures act independently from each other if they operate side by side, pursuing their own goals without any contact points. Such an independent relationship between subcultures may be intended and deliberately designed. For example, if the organization design is that of a holding company, the organization consists of different organizational entities that may operate in various industries and business areas. As such, each organization or subsidiary may have its own independent culture that may differ from others due to the different industries or lines of business. The same holds for strategic business units that may operate in different markets and industries. Since viable organizations need to be ambidextrous in that they have to be both efficient in what they do and innovate simultaneously (O'Reilly & Tushman, 2013). Some organizations separate these two essential tasks deliberately from each other, not to obstruct each other. Innovation requires exploration and experimentation, while efficiency requires established systems for smooth standard operations. Therefore, people working in these two areas need to think and act differently. Due to their other orientation, both groups will have different subcultures useful for their respective work. Examples are the cooperation between firms developing and producing a Covid-19 vaccine, such as between Biotech and Pfizer, Curevac and Bayer, or Moderna and Lonza.

An independent relationship between subcultures may be dysfunctional if the subcultures represent, for example, different functions or departments like marketing, sales, research and development (R&D), finance, or human resources (HR) that should interact and work with each other in coordinated ways. Dysfunctional subcultures are likely to develop in larger firms when the division between the various areas of operation or departments is too strict. Hence, if a lack of exchange and cooperation exists between these units, if nobody manages their interface, and if no incentives exist for collaboration between different departments, their subcultures are likely dysfunctional.

The automotive industry of the 1990s is one vivid example. Research results of a study on U.S., European and Japanese car manufacturers (Womack et al. (1990) challenged the U.S. and European manufacturers. They realized that their companies had developed so-called chimney careers with relatively independent subcultures. Organizational members who had once started in production stayed in production for the rest of their tenure with the organization. Those who had started in R&D stayed in R&D, and those who had started in sales stayed in sales. The resulting subcultures along these functional borders led to inefficiencies with adverse effects on the organizations' effectiveness and thus for their performance. If salespeople did not forward relevant customer data and customer desires to the R&D department, or if people in R&D would not listen to their sales colleagues, their information did not make its way into developing or adjusting products or services. It took, for example, several years until German car manufacturers eventually integrated a coffee cup holder in their cars since their engineers could not imagine that car drivers wanted to drink coffee when driving at high speed on the autobahn.

To counteract the problem of functions acting separately, a German car manufacturer introduced a "2 × 2 × 2"-rule for developing and recruiting their managers and future leaders. To be promoted to a higher management or leadership position, the candidate had to have worked at least two different functions, two different locations, and two different regions. With this rule, the firm wanted to ensure that future leaders had acquired a broader perspective. If various units or functional areas work together well and in coordinated ways despite their differing subcultures, they have *complimentary* subcultures. Such collaboration requires regular interactions between their members and an understanding of each other's tasks.

Subcultures may also *conflict with each other.* Even though a conflict of different subcultures is usually unintended, it leads to dysfunctional micro-political behavior and mostly culminates in the fight for scarce organization resources. Two examples illustrate the harmful effects of conflicting subcultures:

1. A former CEO and chairman of a large organization had two potential successors. Unfortunately, he did not choose for quite some time who was most likely to follow him. During this time of uncertainty, both potential successors developed their respective groups of followers that fought against each other. These fights ranged from not forwarding information, hiding papers, and files to behavior characterized today as mobbing.

2. Two related divisions of an international firm had been at odds with each other for more than a year. They worked against rather than with each other. The central issue of contention was the direct access to personnel files. Having direct access to these files was associated with having more power in the firm than those units that did not have access.

3.3.2 *The Development of Rites, Rituals, and Ceremonies*

As organizations age and mature, they develop cultural knowledge around their commonly-held basic beliefs—the culture core—by repeatedly dealing with the same or similar issues. Many tasks come up regularly both from the internal and external business environment. Once organizational members recognize a pattern of repetition, they tend to develop systems and routines in dealing with these tasks in the same way. In addition, stories, legends, myths, rites, rituals, and ceremonies emerge, which are part of the cultural network (see Fig. 3.1). This cultural network contains the organization's collective experience, including all its ups and downs.

Stories, legends, rites, rituals, celebrations, and ceremonies fulfill specific functions. Their primary function is to confirm, maintain, and enhance the existing culture with its commonly-held basic beliefs (Trice, 1985; Kieser, 1988). Several human resource management practices, for instance, have a ritualistic nature by reinforcing the existing groups or subcultures and, thus, the current social and power structures (Trice & Beyer, 1993). Selection and promotion mechanisms such as assessment centers or tests confirm those who passed them that they are now part of the *in-group*. At the same time, the successful passing of these tests reinforces the high value and identification of the in-group and their members. Successfully passing an assessment center as an entrance ticket to a particular leadership group or management circle has both a selection function and serves, at the same time, as initiating rite or rite of passage. As mentioned above, Trice et al. (1969) have explored and demonstrated this ritualistic nature of human resource practices still valid today.

Figure 3.4 shows the cross-section of a mature organizational culture, including its network, which has developed over time and with an increasing number of

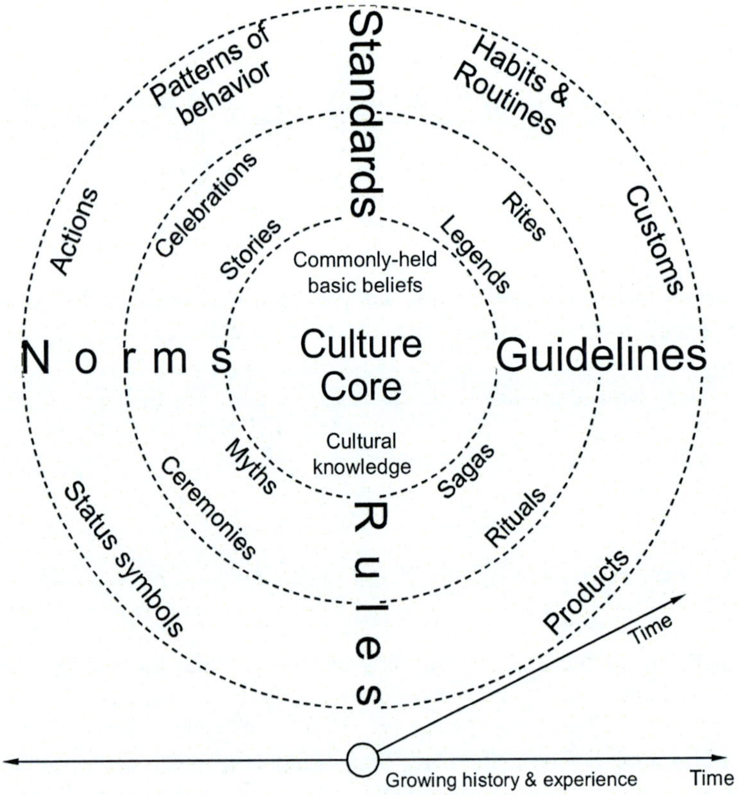

Fig. 3.4 A cross-section of an organization's culture

artifacts, similar to a tree trunk. The growing experience also enhances the number of norms, standards, rules, regulations, and stories that can transform into legends and myths. Rites, rituals, celebrations, and ceremonies are also part of the growing cultural network. All of those cultural elements have the positive effects of providing structure, orientation, and reducing complexity. However, they can also lead to problems and crises due to their routinized nature and automatic use.

3.3.3 The Problem of Overdetermined Behavior

With the increasing age of an organization and its respective culture, the existing cultural network becomes more elaborate regarding the number of existing implicit and explicit rules, standards, guidelines, systems, stories, rites, rituals, and ceremonies. These components of the culture network reinforce and confirm the underlying culture core composed of the commonly-held basic beliefs and cultural knowledge. As mentioned before, organizational members may not be aware of the specific meanings of the culture core in their daily actions. All the components of the culture network offer *orientation* to the culture carriers (see also, Sect. 2.3.2). This repertoire of orientation devices contains all the *right, good,* and *appropriate* answers to emerging problems that have turned into routines of thinking and action, as well as systems and procedures. These experientially developed solutions have worked well in the past in dealing with specific issues and problems. They have been used regularly and frequently and thus have started to act as autopilots. They come up automatically when confronted with these reoccurring issues and concerns.

Thus, organizational behavior has become overdetermined. Overdetermined behavior makes individuals use the stock of experientially based problem solutions habitually. They apply problem-solutions routinely without conscious reflection or thought since they have proven effective in their repeated use. This habitual use aligns with culture's function of reducing complexity (see, Sect. 2.3.5). Culture has become an aggregate of undecidable decision premises (Luhmann, 2000) that guide thinking and behavior pre-consciously. The overdetermined behavior in mature organizations becomes apparent in the number of existing routines and the extent of written rules, procedures, forms, and regulations.

The ample supply of well-proven solutions and their internalized routines in thinking and behavior may prevent organizational members from not recognizing the novelty of situations. However, the available cultural knowledge and behavior repertoire may not provide appropriate solutions for the new problem. Due to a culture's influence on the selective perception of organizational members (e.g., Jussim, 2012), new situations tend to be adjusted to and aligned with familiar situations. Hence, people use an available, well-known behavior pattern that has proven effective in handling a supposedly similar situation in the past automatically to deal with the new issue. When the existing culture and associated over-determined behavior prevents organizational members from recognizing the novelty of a task or problem, their automatic response may lead unnoticed to an unintended crisis.

Hence, it is essential to regularly question cultural beliefs and their routinized thinking patterns and acting to prevent an unintended crisis.

3.3.4 The Problem of Long-Term Success

Recipes of success and repeated success of an organization may cause another related problem. Learning theory predicts that individuals likely repeat behavior patterns that have resulted in desired outcomes, and they discard those that have not brought about the desired results. Successful consequences of decisions and their implementation reinforce these decisions and actions taken as a successful way of handling this issue. The respective thinking and behavior pattern may develop into a recipe of success explained above. Success recipes are used automatically and passed on to other organizational members. People may also use them for apparently similar situations. Thus, these success recipes become generalized, and individuals use them for a broader range of issues. They tend not to repeat those decisions and actions that have not led to the desired outcome and eliminate those from their behavioral repertoire.

Over time, the repeated use of success recipes can lead to an organization's inward-looking focus and a kind of organizational autism: the organization repeatedly applies strategies that have been successful in the past. In case of long periods of success, its members associate these strategies with a feeling of invincibility. However, those strategies may no longer be effective in dealing with emerging external issues and challenges. Due to the organization's inward focus, reliance on formerly developed recipes of success, and feeling of invincibility, organizational members apply their proven routines and recipes of success to all sorts of situations without noticing that critical issues in their environment may have changed. Accordingly, recipes for success developed in the past can lead to an organization's failure.

Many examples exist demonstrating the problem of long-term success. Several companies included in the research on the book *In Search of Excellence* (Peters & Waterman, 1982) experienced the pain of long-term success. Even though they were considered excellent at the time of the study, some of them ran into serious problems shortly after. Others even had to file for protection under Chap. 11 or were bought by another company. When companies such as Wang Global, DEC, Kodak, IBM, Hewlett Packard, Texas Instruments, and McDonald's got into trouble some years after the book's publication, some organizational scholars attributed these cases to bad research. However, these business cases demonstrate that organizations are living systems operating in a dynamic environment. More extended periods of success are no guarantee for future success if the same routines related to systems, strategies, and courses of action are repeatedly and unreflected applied. Hence, an organization needs to regularly check the existing recipes of success and failure and evaluate if they are still adequate for dealing with a changing environment to avoid potential problems and crises (Sackmann, 2013).

Furthermore, historically developed success recipes can lead to arrogance and blindness concerning developments in an organization's relevant environment with its emerging challenges and threats. This arrogance can cause managers and leaders to make strategically necessary decisions very late—and sometimes even too late. The automotive industry may serve as an example of such an arrogant attitude. In the 1980s, the U.S. automobile industry had belittled the competitors from Japan and Europe. A few years ago, none of the established car manufacturers would have thought newcomers to the automotive industry, such as Elon Musk with Tesla, or Alphabet could become a threat to the entire industry with their very different approach to conceptualizing and designing cars.

The over-generalization of recipes of success, an increasing inward focus, and selective perception of an organization's relevant external environment and growing bureaucracy may negatively influence an organization's agility. These negative influences can lead to an organization's calcification and eventually to significant problems and a crisis.

3.4 Crisis or Rejuvenation?

In our Western World, the term *crisis* has a negative connotation, even though a crisis may not necessarily be damaging. A crisis may be a time of decision or a turning point.[1] The Chinese symbol for crisis contains both an aspect of crisis as well as one of opportunity. As expressed in the Chinese character, each crisis may offer the opportunity for a new beginning or a new development.

It is hard to imagine that anybody would want to create a problem or even set off a crisis deliberately. In addition, nobody believes they will ever cause a crisis. If an organization and its culture are in the mature stage and its behavior is overdetermined, the risk of navigating into a crisis is high. As mentioned above, several studies in strategic management have shown that companies often do not react in time to critical changes in their external environment (e.g., Dutton, 1993), thus triggering severe problems or even a crisis.

Both internal and external factors can trigger a crisis. The following examples of external events triggered a crisis for many firms: the dot.com bubble at the beginning of this Millennium, the financial crisis in 2007/2008, and the outbreak of the Covid-19 pandemic. Examples of internal events leading to a crisis may be the sudden loss of a large order due to quality problems or bad customer relationships, the sudden loss of a top-level leader, or a lack of urgently needed experts. In addition, growing too fast and changing too slowly when faced with changes in the business environment also may lead to crises (Probst and Raisch 2005). Even evolutionary growth and maturing may cause problems resulting in a crisis, as discussed in Sect. 3.2.3 and Sect. 3.3. Knowing the developing process of an organization and the associated

[1] https://en.oxforddictionaries.com/definition/crisis. Received: February 19, 2021.

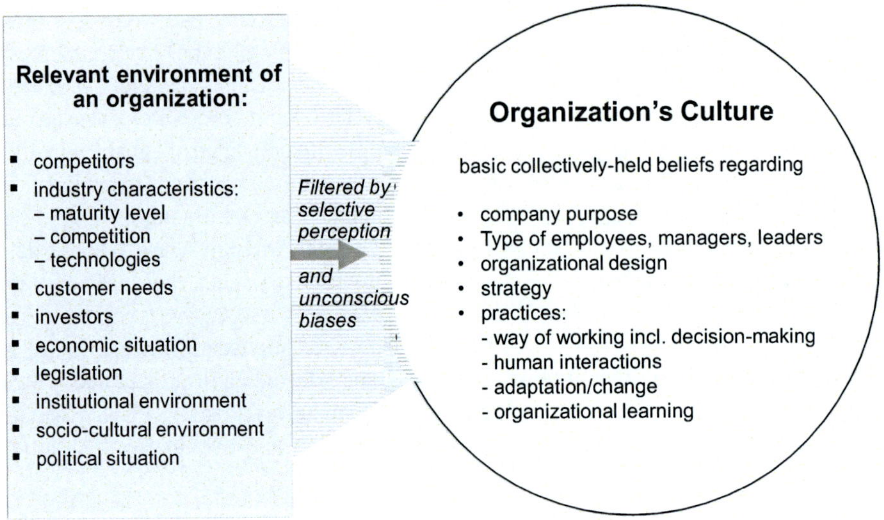

Fig. 3.5 Organizational culture's filter for perceiving its environment

growing pains can help prevent a crisis by implementing offsetting actions before the associated problems emerge.

Organizational members can never objectively perceive information about an organization's relevant environment. Instead, they perceive data about their competitors, partners, customers' needs, investors, economic, legal, political, and socio-cultural issues selectively. An organization's collective experiences influence its members' perceptions. Hence, its culture may lead to unconscious biases while taking in data and information and processing it. Figure 3.5 illustrates this process of culturally influenced selective perception and interpretation.

Furthermore, the unconscious confirmation bias (Pohl, 2004) distorts the information intake. According to the confirmation bias, people prefer, and hence notice, information congruent with their own beliefs, attitudes, and expectations. At the same time, available information that is incongruent with their beliefs or contradicts them tends to be either unnoticed, trivialized, or even negated. As a result, organizations notice necessary changes often too late. The later an organization responds to changes in its relevant external environment, the more restricted the range of potential actions or interventions and the more radical they need to be.[2]

If an organization's culture remains unreflected for too long, long-term organizational members are no longer aware of its cultural imprint and its potential implications. Due to a culture's function of complexity reduction, they notice only information and consider it essential if it confirms their respective culturally influenced beliefs. Information that questions the culture's basic beliefs is most likely not even noticed, classified as irrelevant, or even false (see, Jussim, 2012).

[2]Culture change is addressed in detail in Chap. 8.

People in our Western World usually perceive contradictions as uncomfortable or even painful, so that they want to dissolve contradictions as quickly as possible. Such complexity reducing cognitive processes shield organizations and their members unintentionally and systematically from information critical to their survival.

The following four examples illustrate crises caused by the collectively-held beliefs in the respective organization:

- U.S. Railroads proudly considered and defined themselves as being in the railroad business. Management recognized rather late that they were in the transportation and not in the railroad business. When new technologies allowed for significantly faster transportation by commercial air traveling, the U.S. Railroads revenues collapsed.
- Nixdorf Computers did not realize in time that their strength in sales was turning into a weakness: After a substantial period of growth, they adapted structures and systems too slowly. Excellent salespeople had conquered the markets. However, the products they had sold could neither be produced nor shipped in the time promised to customers. Hence, many customers turned to other firms.
- The Swiss watch industry did not recognize the implications of digitization for their products, business, and industry. When the inventor offered the patent to a Swiss watch manufacturer, the management declined, and a Japanese company bought the patent. Only by redefining themselves strategically, the Swiss watch manufacturers could regain competitiveness—both in the luxury segment (Ebel, Rolex, Patek Philippe) and the segment of inexpensive fashion items (Swatch).
- Nokia was the worldwide leading manufacturer of mobile phones from 1998 until 2011. When the small competitor Apple introduced the iPhone in 2007, the market started to change. Beginning in 2008, Nokia continuously lost market share. Samsung surpassed it in 2012, which had an estimated market share of 25.4 percent that year. Nokia's market share was down to 22.5 percent, and Apple had grown to 9.5 percent market share. While in 2010, Nokia's earnings were still 1.85 billion EUR, in 2012 Nokia made a loss of 2.3 billion EUR. In 2012 Nokia sold their entire mobile phone division to Microsoft for 5.4 billion EUR.

At the beginning of the Millenium, one could observe how established companies reacted to the changing market conditions triggered by the commercial use of the internet. These changes resulted in new business models, increasing internationalization and globalization, virtual cooperations, and born global firms. Established companies invested much money in e-commerce to be part of the new economy. The late reactions of many established firms enabled small start-up companies to benefit from the new economy at first. Several of these start-up companies experienced, however, the typical growing pains discussed in Sect. 3.2.3. With the entry of large established companies, the market redefined itself. Combining new ideas and mature market entry based on well-functioning logistics turned about to be a successful match.

Digital transformation still poses a big challenge for many organizations. These challenges became apparent when the Covid-19 pandemic struck in 2020. Artifical intelligene with its intelligent robots,[3] cyber-physical systems, the internet of things where machines interact with each other, and cloud computing will open up new avenues in all spheres of life that not all organizations will recognize or embrace. In addition, they will also come with some yet unknown challenges. Even though *Big Data* is considered the new oil, this new oil needs refinement before turning it into a sound business model (Singh, 2013). Hence, organizational members need to first translate the data into information to become knowledge that organizations can use. The associated challenges may lead to a crisis or a rejuvenation if organizational members recognize their inherent potential and the organization's culture allows them to tap into it.

3.5 Crisis or Demise?

Not every organization accomplishes a successful turnaround and rejuvenation when faced with a crisis. If the problems become overwhelming, if organizations misjudged the seriousness of the situation and underestimated the challenges, insolvency and finally bankruptcy are likely results. The following business cases illustrate such a culture initiated demise.

- In the 1960s, the production of typewriters was the core business of a U.S.-based organization. The top management collectively decided that the emerging developments in the IT sector were irrelevant to their business. When the company was facing some difficulties, it hired a so-called 'turnaround manager'. After getting to know the organization and trying to understand its specifics in more detail, it became clear to the turnaround manager how severe the business situation was for the company. When he explained the seriousness of the problem to his top-management colleagues and the board of directors, he also proposed a fast and radical change. In his opinion, this was the only way out of the situation. His colleagues and board members were so shocked that they conspired to make him leave the organization. Consequently, the company had to file for bankruptcy one year later (Pelton et al., 1990).
- A company founded in 1883 in Berlin and renamed a few years later into AEG[4] was once one of the World's largest electrical companies. In 1982, AEG had to file for bankruptcy. In 1985, the Daimler Benz corporation took over AEG, merged it with one of its subsidiaries, and later sold it. In the meantime, the trademark rights belong to Electrolux Global Brand Licensing.
- Founded in 1951, the US-American company Wang Laboratories had revenues of more than $ 3 billion per year and more than 30,000 employees in the 1980s. In 1992, it had to file for bankruptcy.

[3]The YouTube video by Boston Dynamics illustrates impressively the capability of these intelligent robots. www.youtube.com/watch?v=2SpNjBI1lu0. Retrieved: Sep 27, 2021.

[4]AEG is a German acronym standing for *Aus Erfahrung gut* (good due to experience).

- In 1998 Kodak had 170,000 employees and sold 85 percent of all photographic paper worldwide. As a result of digitization, Kodak's business model vanished. Although the digital camera was invented in 1975, Kodak did not take it seriously because of its low quality. In 2005, Kodak stopped the production of black-and-white photographic paper. Until 2008, they had to lay-off 15,000 of the remaining 60,000 employees. In 2009, they stopped production of the Kodachrome color film after 74 years. They made further efforts to restructure the company until its bankruptcy filing in January 2012. In 2013 Kodak, sold its filmstrip production and hence gave up its former core business.
- Even the long-term worldwide leading automobile manufacturer founded in 1908—General Motors (GM)—had to file for insolvency in June 2009 due to the financial crisis. Years before, the Head of Engineering was once asked at a social function why there were so many small foreign manufacturers' cars on the streets in Southern California. He had replied that GM was not interested in this "breakfast" since GM made its money with big cars.

The formerly worldwide largest power company Enron, the telecommunications corporation Worldcom, and the Fintech Wirecard are examples of a culture drift. In all three cases, the continued falsification of their balance sheets remained unnoticed for some time and finally led to their demise. A group of managers gradually undermined existing controls at Barings Bank to grant more freedom to its very successful broker Nick Leeson. However, they did not question or even check his business practices. His risky and unauthorized speculative trading led to the bankruptcy of the 150-year-old bank on February 26 in 1995.

Factors stemming from the internal and external environment of an organization can trigger existential crises. Rejuvenation is not possible because the problems are recognized too late, and the time does not suffice to accomplish a turnaround. All examples given above demonstrate that an organization's culture needs to be regularly addressed and examined regarding its potential impact. A regular check may help to avoid an unintended culture drift and thus prevent a crisis and an organization's demise.

The following Chap. 4 addresses the impact of organizational culture on its internal life and its way of functioning.

References

Adizes, I. (1979). Organizational passages: Diagnosing and treating life cycle problems on organizations. *Organizational Dynamics, 7*(1), 3–24.

Dutton, J. (1993). The making of organizational opportunities: An interpretive pathway to organizational change. In B. Staw & L. L. Cummings (Eds.), *Research in organization behavior* (pp. 195–226). JAI Press.

Flamholtz, E., & Randle, Y. (1990). *Growing pains: How to make the transition from an entrepreneurship to a professionally managed firm.* Jossey-Bass.

Greiner, L. (1972). Evolution and revolution as organizations grow: A company's past has clues for management that are critical to future success. *Harvard Business Review, 50*(4), 37–46.

Hilton, C. N. (1987). *Be my guest*. Prentice-Hall.

Illeris, K. (2018). *Contemporary theories of learning*. Routledge.

Jussim, L. (2012). *Social perception and social reality*. Oxford University Press.

Kay Ash, M. (1981). *Mary Kay*. Harper & Row.

Kieser, A. (1988). *Von der Morgensprache zum »gemeinsamen HP-Frühstück«. Zur Funktion von Werten, Mythen, Ritualen und Symbolen–»Organisationskulturen«–in der Zunft im modernen Unternehmen*. In E. Dülfer (Ed.), Organisationskultur (pp. 207–225). Poeschel.

Kilday, B. (2018). *Never lost again: The Google mapping revolution that sparked new industries and augmented our reality*. HarperCollins.

Knight, P. (2016). *Shoe Dog: Die offizielle Biografie des Nike Gründers*. FinanzBuch.

Küppers, A. (2000). If you're often late for the office, why not just scoot? *The Wall Street Journal Europe, XVIII*(6), 1–9.

Liker, J. (2004). *The Toyota way: 14 management principles from the World's greatest manufacturer*. McGraw-Hill.

Luhmann, N. (2000). *Organisation und Entscheidung*. Westdeutscher.

Martin, J., & Siehl, C. (1983). Organizational culture and counter-culture: An uneasy symbiosis. *Organizational Dynamics, 12*(2), 52–64.

Mezrich, B. (2009). *The accidental billionaires: The founding of Facebook*. Arrow Books.

O'Reilly, C. A., & Tushman, M. L. (2013). Ambidexterity: Past, present, and future. *Academy of Management Perspective, 27*(4). https://doi.org/10.5465/amp.2013.0025

Packard, D. (1995). *The HP way. How Bill Hewlett and I built our company*. HarperCollins.

Parsons, T. (1951). *The social system*. Free Press.

Pelton, W., Sackmann, S. A., & Boguslaw, R. (1990). *Tough choices. The decision-making styles of America's top 50 CEO's*. Dow Jones-Irwin.

Peters, T. J., & Waterman, R. H. (1982). *In search of excellence*. Harper & Row.

Pohl, R. (2004). *Cognitive illusions: A handbook on fallacies and biases in thinking, judgement and memory*. Psychology Press.

Probst, G., & Raisch, S. (2005). Organizational crisis: The logic of failure. *Academy of Management Perspectives, 19*(1), 90–105.

Rogers, E. M., & Larsen, J. K. (1984). *Silicon valley fever: The Apple store*. Basic Books.

Sackmann, S. A. (1983). Organisationskultur: Die unsichtbare Einflußgröße. *Gruppendynamik, 14* (4), 393–406.

Sackmann, S. A. (1992). Cultures and subcultures: An analysis of organizational knowledge. *Administrative Science Quarterly, 37*(1), 140–161. https://doi.org/10.2307/2393536

Sackmann, S. A. (Ed.). (1997). *Cultural complexity in organizations: Inherent contrasts and contradictions*. Sage.

Sackmann, S. A. (2013). Die Unternehmenskultur als kritischer Erfolgsfaktor zur Vermeidung und Beseitigung von Unternehmenskrisen. In F. Richter & C. Timmreck (Eds.), *Effizientes Sanierungsmanagement. Krisenunternehmen zielgerecht und konsequent restrukturieren* (pp. 43–62). Schäffer-Poeschel.

Schein, E. H. (2010). *Organizational culture and leadership* (4th ed.). Wiley.

Singh, A. (2013). Is big data the new black gold? *Wired Online*, February 13, 2013. Accessed Feb 4, 2021, from www.wired.com/insights/2013/02/is-big-data-the-new-black-gold

Trice, H. M. (1985). Rites and ceremonials in organizational cultures. *Research in the Sociology of Organizations, 4*(22), 221–270.

Trice, H. M., & Beyer, J. M. (1993). *The cultures of work organizations*. Prentice-Hall.

Trice, H. M., Belasco, J. E., & Allutto, J. A. (1969). The role of ceremonials in organization behavior. *Industrial & Labor Relations Review, 23*(1), 40–51.

WirtschaftsWoche. (2000). Plötzlich wahnsinnig heiß. Das Wirtschaftswoche-Tagebuch einer Unternehmensgründung. *Wirtschaftswoche, 39*, 106–112.

Womack, J. P., Jones, D. T., & Roos, D. (1990). *The machine that changed the world*. Macmillan.

Herdt, H. K. (1986). Bosch 1886–1986. In *Porträt eines Unternehmens*. DVA. ISBN 3-421-06324-9.

Chapter 4
The Influences of Culture on Organizations' Daily-Life

How does an organization's culture exert its influence on its members and its internal life? Chapter 4 first explains *how* culture exerts its influence and then how organizational members become full members of an organization. This is followed by exploring an organization's culture impact on strategy, its development and implementation, an organization's choice of design including structures and processes, management systems, and management instruments. Furthermore, the chapter discusses an organization's culture influence on leaders, their behavior and on leadership processes. The last section addresses an organization's culturally influenced expectations toward its members' behavior and explores its culture's impact on organizational members' motivation and identification with the organization, on their health and their work performance. Once in existence, these culturally influenced internal factors will, in turn, influence and maintain the existing culture.

4.1 How Does an Organization's Culture Influence Organizational Life?

In general, every organizational member is a culture carrier and thus transports the influences and effects of the organization's culture. New members may bring fresh ideas from the organization's external environment based on their experiences from other organizations (see, Sect. 3.1 *Founding stage*). Organizations may deliberately choose new members based on their fit with the existing organization's culture. Over time, newcomers' ideas of how to go about their work will increasingly overlap with the respective expectations of the group or division in which they work. These expectations always exist implicitly, and they may be voiced explicitly. Socialization processes enable the slowly developing overlap of ideas and expectations between new organizational members and the organization (see Bauer & Erdogan, 2011), as illustrated in Fig. 4.1.

S. A. Sackmann, *Culture in Organizations*, Contributions to Management Science,
https://doi.org/10.1007/978-3-030-86080-6_4

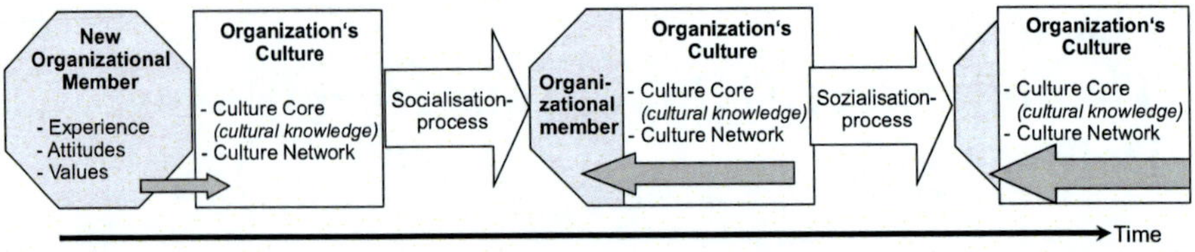

Fig. 4.1 Socialization process: From *newcomer* to *culture carrier*

The octagon in Fig. 4.1 represents newcomers who are gradually socialized into the organization and its culture. The disappearing octagon indicates that newcomers slowly become fully functioning organizational members. In this process, they add to their existing experience, attitudes, and values those of the organization and their work unit. In this process of becoming a fully accepted organizational member, the imported influences from prior workplace experiences start to shrink or become covered by those of the current organization. At the same time, the degree of conformity between newcomers and organizations increases due to the socialization process and its onboarding practices. The arrows pointing to the left illustrate this effect of an organization's culture on new organizational members. Studies have revealed that new employees learn the specific terminology and jargon used in their team within approximately one week. This knowledge is essential for effective communication and cooperation in their daily work processes. Learning and internalizing the organization's specific work practices and their routines, however, takes longer.

The longer people have worked in a specific group or organization, the more they are likely to identify with their work, team, and organization. In addition, the ideas that they have brought with them from the outside about work and organizing work processes are likely to have faded away, or they have been integrated into the existing organizational cultural knowledge base. Consequently, if newcomers decide to stay with an organization beyond the first three to six months, their critical externally influenced perspective and influence on the organization's culture will gradually vanish. At the same, time the impact of the organization's culture on the newcomers will increase. In this stage, organizational members will express that influence by automatically starting to use the term *we*—meaning their division or their organization. This verbal reference indicates that they no longer distinguish between themselves and *the organization*. Once organizational members identify with the organization and have internalized its basic beliefs and priorities, they can be considered culture carriers. Culture carriers will live and maintain the existing culture of their unit and/or of their organization by routinely displaying the cultural characteristics in their behavior. These cultural characteristics are passed on to other organizational members and thus influence organizational life. At the same time, culture carriers may influence an organization's culture and all aspects of the cultural network with their personal experience, skills, and perceptions that they have made inside and outside of the organization.

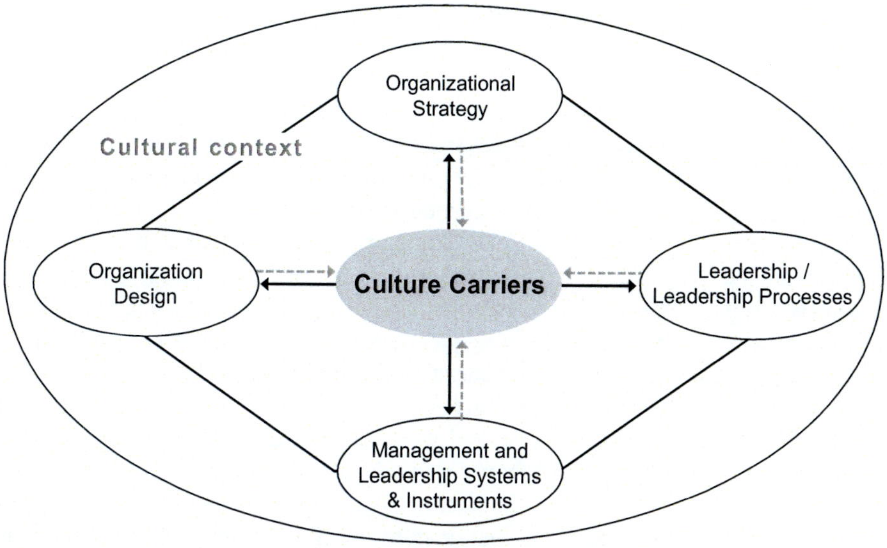

Fig. 4.2 Potential influences of culture carriers on organizational life

Whenever I discuss influences in the following sections, these are exerted by existing culture carriers. They use and negotiate culture in their daily interactions, thus creating cultural manifestations outlined by the arrows in Fig. 4.2. Once culture manifestations have become established, they will, in turn, influence and impact the culture carriers, as indicated by the dotted arrows in Fig. 4.2. All of the cultural manifestations shown in Fig. 4.2—the organization's strategy, its design, its management and leadership systems, and related instruments and its type of leaders and leadership processes—impact organizational members. Together, they define the cultural context of an organization or its units. The following sections discuss these influences and their effects in more detail.

4.2 The Influence of Organizational Culture on Strategy and its Development

Literature on strategic management suggests that strategy provides orientation for everything in an organization since strategy points to the organization's future direction (e.g., Chandler, 1962; Porter, 1980) according to the motto *structure follows strategy*. But where does the strategy come from? How is it developed? Depending on the size and culture of an organization, its strategy may develop in various ways and with different actors involved: These may be members of a strategy department, a person in charge of strategy development, the top management, the organization's founder/owner, or it may be the result of a mutual bottom-up/top-down-process (Hamel & Breen, 2007). Depending on the degree of professionalism in developing a strategy, top management may formulate the organization's strategy retrospectively as reconstructed logic (Mintzberg et al., 1998). Hence, it may evolve from organizational processes (Schreyögg, 1988), or a selective group of organizational members may plan it actively and proactively, considering essential stakeholder groups (Hamel & Breen, 2007). A more or less systematic scanning process of the organization's environment may result in the environmental analysis, including general observations of relevant markets with their customers, competitors, and technological, environmental, and socio-cultural developments. The group may use market studies, benchmark studies, competitors' analyses, observations, and research of socio-demographic trends and customers to acquire more systematic data. Subsequently, they need to condense and interpret these data regarding their possible meaning for the organization, its strategic positioning vis à vis its competitors, and its future development. Depending on the identified organization's strengths and weaknesses regarding these environmental opportunities and challenges, the group involved will decide on attractive markets and decide on strategic fields for action. These discussions will conclude in a business plan with goals, activities and responsiblites, required resources, and controls. Figure 4.3 illustrates an ideal strategy development process.

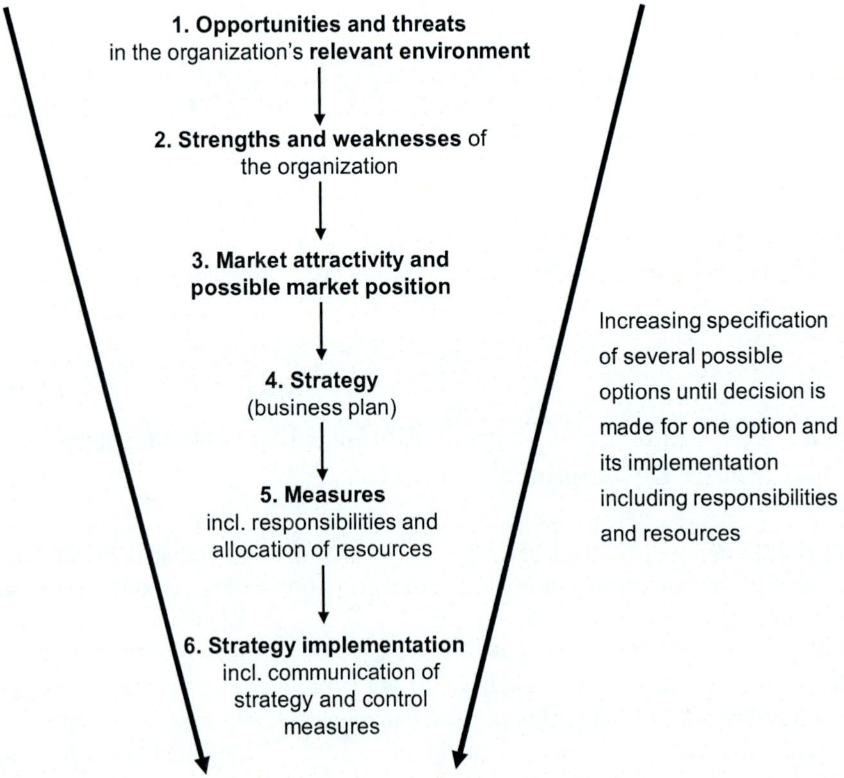

Fig. 4.3 Ideal strategy development process

During the strategy development process, the people and culture carriers involved influence every data, information, discussion, and decision. A so-called *objective* decision is therefore not possible. Accordingly, the quality of decisions is as good or as limited as the people involved in the process and the decision-makers' collective experiences, information bases, analyses, and interpretations that they bring to the discussion. All these factors ultimately influence their decisions. The organization's culture influences the information intake due to complexity reducing function leading to individuals' selective perception (see the discussion Chap. 3, Jussim, 2012). The cognitive structures and cognitive complexity of those involved influence the group's information processing (e.g., Bieri, 1955; McDaniel & Lawrence, 1990), and thus the outcome and quality of their discussions.[1]

Given these human factors, an organization's culture influences the strategy development process, its results, and the strategy implementation process. Hence, since the decision-makers involved in strategy development are simultaneously members of the organization's culture, they influence the strategy development process with their basic cultural beliefs and cognitive biases, blind spots, and related limitations. Figure 4.4 visualizes this mutual influencing process of collective beliefs and organizational strategy.

Fig. 4.4 Mutual influence of collective beliefs and organizational strategy

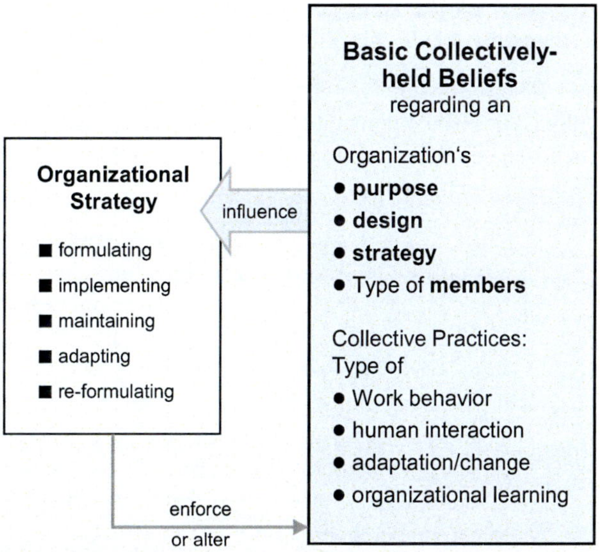

[1]Nobel Prize winner Herbert Simon already explained in the 1950s that individuals are limited in their perception and information processing; and Nobel Prize winner psychologist Kahneman has described the various cognitive biases and heuristics that influence decisions and opinions (Kahneman, 2011; Kahneman et al., 1982; Kahneman & Tversky, 2000).

A study of the strategic decision-making of two different top management groups illustrates this process of mutual influence (Sapienza, 1985). She investigated two hospitals that were comparable in size and services offered. Both hospitals faced the same environmental challenge: the entire hospital industry in the U.S. became deregulated by law. The top management of each hospital discussed the possible implications of this environmental challenge in several meetings. Sapienza observed these discussions of both groups in the role of a participant observer. Her observations and subsequent data analysis revealed that the evolving discussions significantly differed in the two groups. Each top management team drew almost opposite conclusions from their interpretations of the potential opportunities and threats due to the legal change. Hence, the resulting strategies, including corresponding action plans and implementation measures, were contrary. Based on their discussions over several weeks,

- the top management group of one of the hospitals concluded that the legal change provided an opportunity to expand. They saw the opportunity for offering new services, ultimately linked to an increase in staff and new building projects.
- The top management group of the other hospital derived more restrictions from the legal change. The metaphor that came up in their discussion was that of being confined by a "straitjacket". This metaphor and related discussions ultimately led to a retreat strategy leading to discontinuing services, reducing beds, and cutting jobs!

The following examples from the automotive industry, IBM, Nokia, and former Swissair also demonstrate the influence of decision makers' collective beliefs on the chosen strategies and implementation measures.

- The U.S., as well as the European automotive industry, are two of many examples. The Americans belittled the small cars from Europe, particularly from Japan, which offered much smaller profit margins than big cars. European car manufacturers hardly believed the feedback they received from scientists in the course of the MIT study. It clearly showed that productivity was significantly higher in Japan. In addition, certain process steps such as repair at the end of the production process did not exist in Japanese companies (Womack et al., 1990). Similarly, European car manufacturers' late decision to invest in electric mobility is another example of selective perception and misinterpretation due to specific beliefs and their cultural imprint.
- IBM had a similar experience concerning the development of their PC Junior. As the leading manufacturer of mainframes, the whole world consisted of mainframes to IBM. As a consequence, IBM's top executives realized the possible implications of PCs very late. Accordingly, adjusting to this entirely different world took longer than assumed because of their

(continued)

industry recipes (Grinyer & Spender, 1979). These are cultural beliefs at the industry level, including collective rules and routines that differed widely between the PC world and the mainframe world.

- Nokia once was the world's leading mobile phone manufacturer. However, their top executives and several product developers believed that consumers did not want a folding mobile phone. Consequently, Ericson gained a significant market share with its folding mobile phone that sold like hotcakes—especially in the U.S. market. A few years later, Nokia's top executives and product developers belittled Apple with its touchscreen. Once again, Nokia's decision-makers believed that touchscreens would not catch on with their consumers—and they were wrong with their guiding collective beliefs.
- For former airline Swissair, the basic commonly-held beliefs of its top executive group and their strategic decisions ultimately led to the company's grounding. Since the top executives wanted to play a leading role in an airline alliance, they finally decided not to join the Lufthansa-dominated Star Alliance. Instead, they established a separate partnership, the Qualiflyer Group. Over time, however, the Qualiflyer Group was less attractive than Star Alliance for bigger and more profitable airlines. Hence, one of its major partners, Austrian Airlines, switched to Star Alliance. Within the Qualiflyer Group, Swissair developed strategic alliances with Sabena, LTU, Air Europe, Air Littoral, Air Portugal, AOM, LOT, and Portugalia—partly including shareholdings. In hindsight, those shareholdings turned out to be bad strategic decisions and finally led to Swissair's grounding.

Numerous examples exist like the above. They illustrate the power and impact of an organization's culture with its basic commonly-held beliefs on strategic decisions, strategy development, and subsequent actions. This historical imprint of organizations and its effects are also discussed as *path dependency* (see contributions in Schreyögg & Sydow, 2009). To prevent possible adverse outcomes of such an imprint or historically developed path dependency, it is necessary to question the existing organizational culture with its basic beliefs critically (see Chap. 7 and 10).

Depending on priorities set in the organization's strategy and the respective goals, cultural manifestations and underlying beliefs may change over time. For example, entering a new market may lead to changes in an organization's design, including its structure and processes. As a consequence, work processes may become more customer-oriented. Hence, customer focus will receive a higher priority due to these changes.

4.3 The Influence of Culture on an Organization's Design

The specific design of an organization consists of its structures, processes, and job design including roles, and responsibilities. An organization's culture, its carriers, and significantly its key decision-makers influence the choice and specifications of an organization's design. An organization's design can be considered an instrument for leaders and managers. It is usually guided in its selection by the principle *structures follow processes follow strategy*. Since key decision-makers are culture carriers, their acquired cultural beliefs influence them in assessing what they consider the most appropriate organizational design for the organization or business unit. In addition, their positive and negative experiences with different kinds of designs influence their opinion about what is a good or a bad one. Once they have chosen and implemented a specific design, it will then, in turn, influence future decisions and actions of organizational members.

Various possible design options exist for differently sized organizations pursuing different strategies (e.g., Felin & Powell, 2016; Galbraith, 1995, 2012). The guiding principles for choosing a specific organization design may differ depending on the degree of environmental dynamics and the resulting necessity for flexibility and agility. However, every kind of organizational design has its strengths and weaknesses. None of them is ideal, and the search for the perfect design turns out to be Sisyphean labor (Kühl, 2015). Hence, an organization's culture with its basic beliefs offers an orientation for finding and choosing the most appropriate organizational design, including its principles, processes, jobs, roles, and responsibilities. Cultural beliefs influence how to work and accomplish results best. They prescribe how to execute existing tasks and processes such as product development, production, logistics, marketing, and sales most properly and best, and which guidelines and responsibilities organizational members need to observe in task accomplishment. Therefore, one major factor determining the choice and implementation of an organization's design is the type of person considered most appropriate for the organization.

Several examples demonstrate the positive and negative effects of cultural beliefs on an organization's design with its structures and processes.

> The CEO of Bell Industries, a company that had acquired 25 small and medium-sized businesses from diverse industries during three and a half years, wanted to establish a centrally managed conglomerate. Centralized corporate structures were the dominant trend in the 1960s. Most of the entrepreneurs, who had founded the acquired firms and made them successful, were dissatisfied working in such a centralized structure. They left Bell Industries once their contracts permitted them to do so. At the same time, the stock price of Bell Industries plummeted. The three majority shareholders of Bell—founders of acquired firms—then decided to have critical and

(continued)

fundamental discussions around Bell Industries' identity, strategy, organization design, and people. One of the majority shareholders became the new CEO and initiated what he called "philosophical discussions". In their one-year-long discussions, the new top executive group questioned the existing axiomatic knowledge and changed it to become the new basis of the company.

In their analysis of the situation, the new top executives concluded that they did not know enough about the many markets and industries to manage the wide range of acquired companies. These considerations led to three important conclusions:

1. They wanted to retain the acquired firms' leaders because they knew the market and customers of their former company. These entrepreneurs were, however, used to think and act within non-bureaucratic structures. Moreover, as entrepreneurs, they did not like the long decision-making processes nor the substantially smaller scope of responsibility and accountability of the centrally organized conglomerate.
2. They concluded that to retain these entrepreneurs, they needed to create an organization design that allowed these former entrepreneurs to act again like entrepreneurs within a larger structure. Consequently, the new top executive group decentralized and shifted responsibilities down into the organizations where operational decisions had to be made.
3. The conclusion was to recruit self-organized organizational members who acted like entrepreneurs. (Sackmann, 1991).

IBM recognized the potential of the PC market relatively late. When the top executives of the mainframe producer IBM finally decided to enter the PC market, they launched the PC Junior's development project. As usual, they located the project in their product development department. Despite high management attention, the PC Junior's development took much more time than planned and expected. Finally, the top executive group decided that the project reported directly to them without passing the usual hierarchical reporting lines within their hierarchy. This new structural arrangement helped the project progress much faster. In the meantime, however, they had lost precious time and had to postpone the announced market launch several times (Pelton et al., 1990).

Companies such as 3 M and ABB had similar experiences with developing new products or businesses and drew similar conclusions from their experience. They had learned that it was challenging to create an ambidextrous organization design by integrating units responsible for innovation into the existing organization, focusing on efficient operations. Innovation and efficiency require people who think and act differently. Placing organizational members responsible for entirely new products and services in the existing organization with its respective culture and routines created a culture clash. The culturally influenced decision-makers tended to adjust

Fig. 4.5 Optical illusion

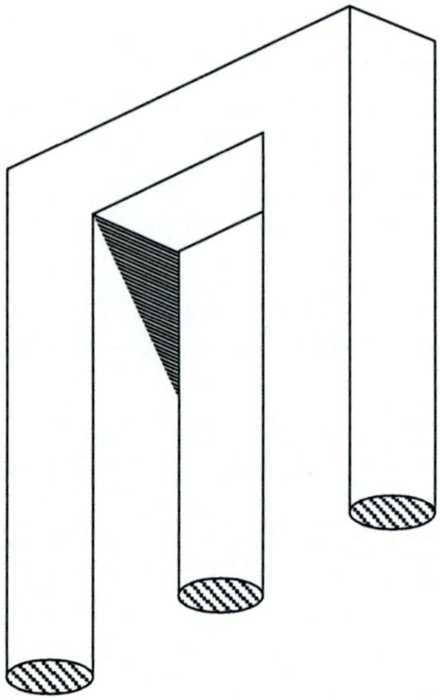

the new ideas to what they knew best and applied their proven success recipes. Figure 4.5 demonstrates this phenomenon of creative adjustment.

When looking at the figure, it seems to be wrong and tends to trigger an uncomfortable feeling in the observer. The eyes will inevitably concentrate either on the top half or the bottom half of the figure. Both halves by themselves look familiar and fit with prior experience. While the top half of the picture resembles an entrance, the bottom half shows three pillars. Combining both halves in the way as suggested in the picture results in an unknown figure. Immediately, we tend to consider the entire figure as strange and somehow wrong based on prior experience. This example illustrates that it is essential to examine existing organizational designs for their cultural imprint.

Besides the well-known options of organizational designs, less conventional ones exist. When Bill Gore founded W.L. Gore & Associates in 1958, he wanted an organization design allowing for agility and flexibility with large scopes of action and self-organization for organizational members. The result was a lattice or ameba structure in which people move in and out of management and leadership roles, and associates also elect their leaders. For example, an expert may receive a project leader's role and move back to the expert role once the project is finished. The classical hierarchy and titles do not exist: "no ranks, no title" is one of Gore's basic beliefs manifested in their use of the term associates. If associates meet with external constituencies used to titles on business cards, they may decide on the most appropriate title in such a case (Flik, 1990). In addition, associates choose their mentors, and this choice reflects positively on the leader's evaluation.

When organizations operate in a volatile, uncertain, complex, and ambiguous environment, hierarchical designs may no longer be the best choice. More flexible options are the viable systems model-based on principles of the human nervous

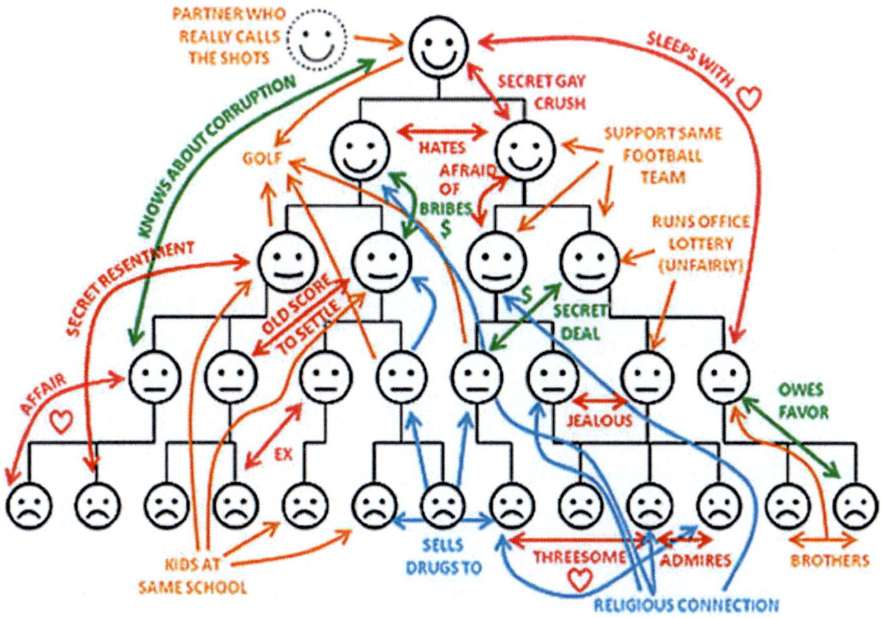

Fig. 4.6 The holacratic organization design at Zappos. (Source: Bartz (2018))

system (Beer, 1995a, b), and heterarchical or holacratic design principles. Heterarchic designs include shared power and decision-making based on self-organizing and equal rights (e.g., Winter, 2009). The human brain structure serves as the basis for holacratic designs (Mackenzie, 1991). For example, Zappos's former CEO introduced such a holacratic design because he believed that Zappos needed to become more flexible, productive, and self-organizing (see Fig. 4.6.).

Tony Hsieh, co-founder and CEO of Zappos until August 2020, justified his choice of the holacratic design that he introduced in 2013 as follows:

> Research shows that every time a town's number of citizens doubles, the rate of innovation and productivity per citizen increases by 15 percent. However, when companies grow, innovation and productivity usually decrease. That is why we try to organize Zappos more like a town and less like a bureaucratic organization. In a town, people and businesses are self-organized. We try to do the same thing by changing from a normal hierarchical structure to a system called holacracy that enables the employees to act more like entrepreneurs and to organize their work themselves instead of reporting to a manager that tells them what to do. (www.zapposinsights.com)

Dieter Zetsche, former CEO of Daimler, also tried to create a more flexible and agile organization by introducing swarm-organizing principles. In an interview, he mentioned that they could imagine relocating 20 percent of their employees to a swarm organization within half a year or one year. Other variations of heterarchical designs are cooperatives and network-based organizations. To become more flexible, the shoe retailer Deichmann reduced its 50 decision-making groups to three and provided its organizational members with more responsibilities and freedom to act based on trust.

Other flexible design options are team-based organizations as practiced, for example, in the Haier Group China-based multinational producing appliances and consumer electronics. The company deliberately moved away from a traditional hierarchical structure and created many microentrepreneurial teams. They formed based on mutual selection, and team members collaborate over networks of people and platforms. Another flexible option is a helix design consisting of two separate accountability lines, one focusing on speed and the other on stability.

All these examples demonstrate the strong influence of basic beliefs on the choice of an organization's design.

4.4 The Influence of an Organization's Culture on Management Systems and Management Instruments

An organization's culture also influences decision-makers choice of management systems and instruments, including their meaning, development, and implementation in a particular organization. Once established and running, the existing systems and tools influence the collective behavior of all organizational members. Hence, they sustain and even reinforce the current organizational culture. General management systems and instruments are, for instance:

- IT and management information systems (MIS),
- controlling systems and instruments,
- human resource management (HRM) systems and their respective instruments or tools,
- information and communication systems and instruments.

Why do these management systems and related instruments or tools exist, and what is their purpose within an organization? Many management systems and their tools typically develop over time to deal with recurring issues and problems. Systems and instruments help organizational members deal with these regularly occurring tasks or problems routinely by employing the defined quality standards and defined process steps (see, Sect. 3.3 *The maturity stage* and Sect. 3.3.3 *The problem of over-determined behavior*). They enable an organization to grow because they provide the standards and routines necessary for efficient operations. The following example of HRM systems and their respective instruments explains this process.

Every organization is faced with the recurring tasks of searching for, selecting, hiring, onboarding, paying, developing, and separating from organizational members. Start-ups typically deal with HR issues or tasks ad hoc whenever they occur. However, once an organization grows, it becomes increasingly important to address these recurring issues routinely. Consequently, organizational members have more time and energy to focus on non-routine novel challenges. Systems and instruments are routinized and formalized procedures ensuring that employees meet defined quality standards in efficient ways.

Several procedures exist for recruiting organizational members at different levels. These include interviews with varying corporate representatives, an assessment center, a taster day, a probation period, a prior internship, or project work. Such measures ensure that those people finally hired bring the required qualifications and fit with the organization's culture. Compensation systems provide appropriate compensation for specific functions, tasks, or met goals. The type of compensation system influences the attention of organizational members. Are they paid for their work efforts or successful teamwork? Are they paid to spend the agreed-upon working hours in the company or for their contribution and deliver the agreed-upon results on time? Is the achievement of short-term goals or long-term goals rewarded, or both? HR development systems help improve or develop skills considered necessary for current or future tasks and functions in the organization. But what kind of development measures exist, and how do they look like? What content do they convey? Do they occur on the organization's premises and involve leaders of the organization, or are they conducted in an external venue such as a hotel or a well-known university? An organization's culture influences all of these choices regarding HR development measures—their content, process, types of trainers, venue, and other issues relevant for their implementation. Besides developing the organization's members and future leaders, these HR systems and instruments also convey the organization's culture to participants.

Once in existence, these management systems and instruments are products of the organization's culture and serve two functions: On the one hand, they handle specific recurring tasks in an explicitly defined way to ensure efficiency, quality, and reliability. On the other hand, they maintain the existing culture and reinforce it with every single use. As long they are considered appropriate measures, management systems and instruments are helpful and enable efficient and reliable work processes. However, if the organization is launching a change process, existing management systems and instruments need to be critically examined and questioned whether they still will be appropriate for the future.

4.5 The Influence of Organizational Culture on Leaders and Leadership Processes

An organization's existing culture also influences leaders and leadership processes. This influence includes the type of leaders, an organization's expectations toward its leadership based on the promises to external and internal stakeholders, and finally, the enacted leadership behavior and leadership processes that translate these promises into practice.

4.5.1 The Influence of Organizational Culture on its Type of Leaders

An organization's culture defines the expectations towards its leaders concerning their professional and personal qualifications and behaviors. Which qualities characterize a *good* leader who fits well with the organization's culture? In some organizations and industries, *typical* leaders can be recognized because of their physical appearance. For example, the leaders of a traditional bank dress and behave differently from leaders of a start-up organization. Due to their culturally adequate clothing, leaders of an insurance company look different from leaders of a fashion company or an IT organization. Substantial differences may even exist across units and their subcultures within the same organization. These differences may be due to the different types of work. For example, divisions and individuals with direct customer contact are usually dressed more formally than leaders in administration or the IT department. In addition to an organization's and industry's culture, the spirit of the times may also influence the observed dress code. Nowadays, even top executives in rather traditional industries such as insurance or traditional banking dress less formally. Like people in start-ups, they may wear sneakers and no tie to appear young, dynamic, and future-oriented.

Therefore, more important than the physical appearance are leaders' mindsets and behavior influenced by specific cultural knowledge. What is the meaning of *good* leadership in a given organization, and what does it imply regarding leadership behavior? Which qualities does an organization consider essential for a *good* leader to have? At what time in the morning should a *good* leader be in the office and stay until when? Which qualities and actions are essential for being promoted: The number of working hours, loyalty, the developing organizational members, or the (over-)achieved results? How much is diplomatic or micro-political behavior necessary to survive? Which *do's* and *don'ts* exist in the organization for leaders? What characterizes a *bad* leader as defined by the organization's culture?

In addition, an organization's culture also defines the proper processes how to become a leader in the organization. What kind of qualifications, degrees, or diplomas are needed? Is a degree from a specific university helpful? Does the organization prefer candidates with no prior job experience? For example, Toyota hires people preferably right after they have finished their formal education. The firm wants to socialize, groom, and develop new employees themselves and not have them influenced beforehand by a different company. Other organizations may appreciate prior job experience and even require it. Is it only possible to be promoted to a leadership position if one has worked in a specific department or internal division? Are career changers welcome? At what age should one become a manager or leader? At what age is a leader considered too old for a particular job or function? Research has shown, for instance, that firms tend to have a so-called *age-grading*, which defines their meaning of *young* and *old* regarding specific career steps (e.g., Kunze et al., 2013; Lawrence, 1996). If existing leadership selection- and development processes remain unchallenged, they may unintendedly lead to a homogeneous group of leaders. If the leaders of an organization have too similar qualifications, the phenomenon of group-think (Sandhu, 2014) may occur with potentially adverse effects, especially in a fast-changing, dynamic environment.

4.5.2 Influences of Organizational Culture on Leadership and Leaders' Behavior

Leadership of and in an organization consists of two critical aspects. On the one hand, organizations declare and promise to external stakeholders what they can expect from the organization and its leadership. On the other hand, an organization has normative expectations towards its organizational members including leaders regarding their behavior in fulfilling these promises. Ultimately, these promises and expectations need to become manifest in leaders' and employees' daily behavior.

Organizations' Promises

An organization expresses its promises to its external stakeholders that comprise customers, future employees, suppliers, investors, and society, usually in its code of business conduct. This code serves as a benchmark for an organization's collective behavior and orientation for organizational members at all levels and functions. The formalized statement characterizes an organization's intended way of conduct and addresses its relationship with its employees, shareholders, customers, suppliers, and the immediate environment. Thus, it contains the basic principles and rules of conduct for all organizational members and their behavior when relating to internal and external partners and the general public. These guidelines intend to ensure ethically, legally, and also ecologically responsible behavior.

Today, all publicly listed companies and most larger organizations have such documented guidelines, even though these may be labeled differently. These guidelines are usually publicly accessible and thus available to people both inside and outside the organization. Even though they cover similar topics, they differ in scope, content, and detail. The following examples provide the central components of business conduct principles or guidelines for Apple, Siemens, Infineon, and the grocery discounter Lidl. The complete guidelines, principles, or code of business conduct can be accessed using the provided web links. The four examples illustrate the organization's different foci in their promises and expectations.

Example Apple: **Apple's Principles of Business Conduct**[2]
The way we do business worldwide (July 2010)

Apple's success is based on creating innovative, high-quality products and services and on demonstrating integrity in every business interaction. Apple's principles of business conduct define the way we do business worldwide. These principles are:

Honesty. Demonstrate honesty and high ethical standards in all business dealings.

Respect. Treat customers, suppliers, employees, and others with respect and courtesy.

Confidentiality. Protect the confidentiality of Apple's information and the information of our customers, suppliers, and employees.

Compliance. Ensure that business decisions comply with all applicable laws and regulations.

Your Responsibilities

Apple's Business Conduct Policy and principles apply to employees, independent contractors, consultants, and others who do business with Apple. All such individuals are expected to comply with Apple's Business Conduct Policy and principles and with all applicable legal requirements. Apple retains the right to discipline (up to and including termination of employment) or end working relationships with those who do not comply.

If you have knowledge of a possible violation of Apple's Business Conduct Policy or principles, other Apple policies, or legal or regulatory requirements, you are required to notify either your manager (provided your manager is not involved in the violation), Human Resources, Legal, Internal Audit, Finance, or the Business Conduct Helpline. If you have knowledge of a potential violation and fail to report it, you may be subject to disciplinary action.

Example Siemens: **Siemens Business Conduct Guidelines**[3]
We make real what matters.

The Business Conduct Guidelines help us apply our values:
innovative, excellent, and responsible.

- We are innovative to create sustainable value.
- We are excellent and achieve outstanding results.
- We act responsibly. This is how we jointly make real what matters.

(continued)

[2] https://corporate.findlaw.com/contracts/operations/business-conduct-policy-apple-inc.html. Retrieved: Sep 20, 2021.

[3] https://assets.new.siemens.com/siemens/assets/public.1580482594.5c242542-e991-4b97-af63-090ad509be74.2019-sag-bcg-en.pdf. Retrieved: September 20, 2021.

Our basic principles
Our basic principles guide our decisions and overall conduct as employees of Siemens.
A: We behave correctly.
B: We respect each other.
C: We create trust.
D: We protect our Company.
E: As managers, we have a special responsibility.
Our responsibility: We make real what matters.
F: We look after each other and ourselves.
G: Our markets: we act fairly and reliably.
H: Our Company: we create trust and protect what makes Siemens valuable.
I: Our portfolio: world-class products, services and industry solutions.
J: Our partners: we work with responsible partners.
K: Our responsibility to society and the environment.

Example Infineon: **The Business Conduct Guidelines**[4]
Infineon's code of ethics
We comply with the law and keep our promises
We are fair market players

- We abide by competition and anti-trust law
- We reject corruption
- We accept valuable gifts and invitations only in exceptional cases
- We deal with conflicts of interest openly
- We choose our business partners carefully
- We prevent money laundering
- We comply with export control laws

We treat each other with respect

- We observe and protect human rights and basic social rights
- We promote an employee culture of openness and respect
- We lead by example
- We value employee representative bodies
- We promote health and safety at work

We handle organization equipment and information carefully

- We treat property of Infineon with care
- We protect Infineon's intellectual property

(continued)

[4] www.infineon.com/dgdl/INFIN+Broschu%CC%88re+BCG_EN_VF.pdf?fileId=5546d46154530942015470cebd78006d. Sep 20, 2021.

- We safeguard organization secrets
- We comply with the regulations on data protection and information security
- We promote transparency, openness and reliability in documentation
- We do not exploit our insider knowledge

We are sincere in our social responsibility

- We are committed to sustainability, quality and product safety
- We protect our environment
- We show social commitment

We ensure that the Business Conduct Guidelines are observed and enforced

- We regularly take part in training on the BCG
- We report misconduct proactively
- We prosecute culpable violations in a balanced and comprehensible manner

Example Lidl: of Lidl[5]

As an international company, we are aware of our size and public visibility. We respect the variety of cultures and recognize the diversity of their values and traditions. Our work is characterized by the following company principles:

- Customer satisfaction is our highest priority.
- Superior quality for the lowest price possible determines our position in the market.
- Our continued growth is determined by expansion and constant improvement in our stores.
- As an efficient company, we work according to defined processes and procedures.
- Our success is ensured by short decision paths and simple work processes.
- We grow through development and continuous improvement in our stores—we believe success is never final.
- In our daily activities, we make sure to abide by the law and internal policies.
- We are an economically, socially and environmentally responsible company.
- Fairness to all in the Company is imperative.
- We respect and encourage each other.
- Agreements are upheld in an atmosphere of trust.

(continued)

[5] https://careers.lidl.com/lidl-as-an-employer/company-principles. Retrieved: September 20, 2021.

- Recognition, acknowledgment and constructive feedback determine the operating environment in our daily work.
- We foster an environment for leadership growth to ensure continuous success.

Twenty years ago, organizations may have provided some information on their values. With increasing internationalization and globalization, organizations have expanded their codes of conduct to help their multinational and multicultural members behave ethically and responsibly in critical situations around the globe.

Leadership Behavior
An organization's culture defines those behavior patterns that are expected from a *good* leader and characterizes what *good* leadership entails. At the same time, this entails what is considered *bad* leadership behavior. These culture-based normative expectations towards leaders and their appropriate behavior always exist implicitly, and an increasing number of organizations address them nowadays explicitly. Especially large companies provide these expectations regarding *good* leadership in documented leadership guidelines or leadership principles. These may become the basis for competence profiles or guidelines for recruiting and developing leaders in the organization. Contrary to the organization's promises or code of business guidelines, these expectations towards appropriate leadership and leadership behavior are available internally to organizational members but rarely to outsiders. Regarding the four examples given above, only Lidl makes its guidelines of conduct and leadership available on the internet. Siemens publicly provides their management manual[6] but not their leadership guidelines.

Figure 4.7 depicts the ideal process of deriving guidelines for the selection and development of leaders. Hence, practiced leadership behavior should express the essence of these guidelines.

Organizations differ regarding the existence of formalized normative expectations towards their leaders and their acceptable behavior. Leaders can use them as orientation for their behavior if they exist, and organizational members can claim these behaviors from their leaders. If these normative expectations do not exist as formal documents, one can derive them from a few indicators. Most meaningful is the observable leadership behavior, followed by leaders' behavior who move up the organizational ladder and those entrusted with more responsibility.

As mentioned above, it is rare to find leadership guidelines communicated in the public domain. If they are available to outsiders, they intend to attract potential

[6]https://assets.new.siemens.com/siemens/assets/api/uuid:89b72b08b7cf2ca467bb549924a438359cd271ec/management-manual-mobility.pdf. Retrieved: Sep 20, 2021.

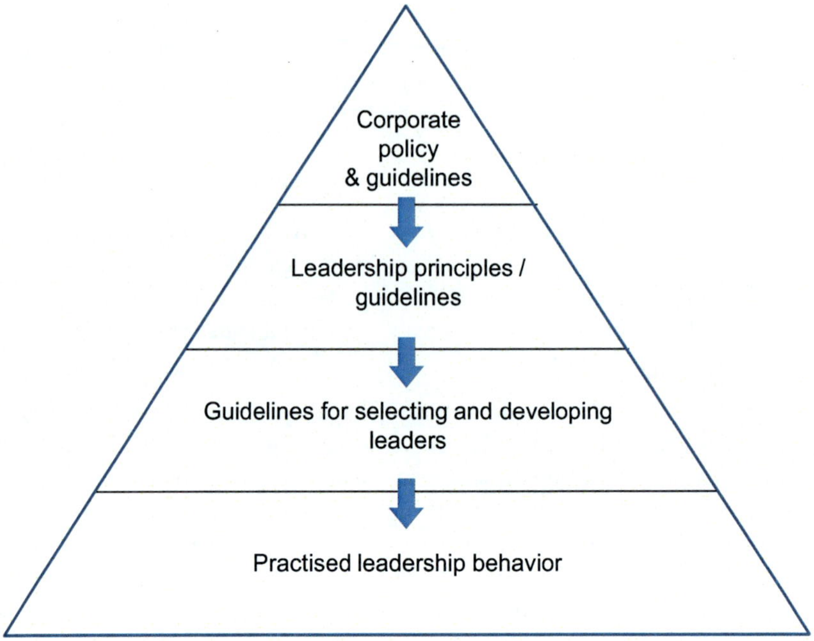

Fig. 4.7 From corporate policy to practiced leadership behavior

employees, as shown in the example of the grocery discounter Lidl. They may also be inferred from talking to insiders or from publications about the organization. Examples are books about Apple, Amazon, Siemens, or W.L. Gore.

Example of Leadership Principles or Guidelines

Example Lidl: Our Leadership Principles: What we stand for as an employer[7]

Leading through Communication

Communication at Lidl is simple and direct—just as our business model. We speak honestly and openly. If a conflict arises, we address issues directly and immediately and resolve them fairly. As managers, we create meaning by always explaining the overall context and appreciating the value and contribution of everyone's work. We create an inclusive environment by incorporating our employees in decisions. We thoroughly explain the reasons why when executive decisions are made. We ensure that our employees are the first to be informed. We take care of them by providing needed information. We

(continued)

[7] https://careers.lidl.com/lidl-as-an-employer/leadership-principles. Retrieved: Sep 20, 2021.

respect those employees who have the courage to ask questions, even if those questions are critical ones. We take time to respond to these questions.

Establishing Trust And Acting Fair

We trust our employees and have confidence that they meet their responsibilities. We strongly believe that every single team member does their best to bring Lidl forward. We create a culture in which employees dare to break fresh ground. Mistakes are opportunities to learn and grow. Supervision is practiced support. It is a contribution to the stability of our business model and helps us become better. We are predictable and reliable. We keep our word and promises. We stick to our agreements. We appreciate our employees and treat everyone fairly. We respect their individual personalities and skills. We treat our employees with the greatest respect and expect the same in return. We understand the responsibilities of being a manager and ensure to prevent any misuse of our roles. We treat our employees as partners.

Being a Role Model

Every single one of us assumes our own entrepreneurial responsibility and independently pushes our tasks—which are clearly defined. Details are important to us. We lead through questions and are interested in the business—we are involved. As managers, everything we do has a significant impact. Therefore, we set a good example in all of our actions. We give our employees free reign and at the same time set clear boundaries for independent decisions. When delegating tasks, we keep an eye on the skills and the experience of each employee. We consciously handle our resources. We are proud of our teams and acknowledge achievements within them.

Example from a Family-Owned International Company

Leadership combines our strengths into mutual success. Leaders focus on the task and not on themselves. We achieve our corporate goals together. The basis for our management is the corporate strategy along with our corporate values.

- We manage comprehensibly and consistently.
- We create a positive and results-oriented working atmosphere.
- We obtain results by providing our employees measurable goals for their orientation.
- We facilitate and demand independent and autonomous action on a clearly defined "playing field".
- We specify tasks, competencies, and responsibilities.
- We give and expect open and constructive feedback.
- We support our employees and use their potential.

(continued)

Example from a Global Firm
The following five leadership guidelines are based on explicitly described values. A leader of our organization

1. thinks and acts strategically and provides orientation,
2. initiates and promotes changes,
3. supports and enables top-performance,
4. handles knowledge and information professionally,
5. creates value and acts in the spirit of the organization.

Example from a Governmental Organization
1. We set goals and measure the results.
2. We concentrate on the essentials and set priorities.
3. We delegate as much as possible and assign clear responsibilities.
4. We use our resources economically, effectively, and sustainably.
5. We support learning processes, take responsibility, and let involved parties take part in decision-making processes.
6. We communicate openly, directly, and factually and promote respect and trust.
7. We live these leadership principles and demand them from each other.

As with an organization's promises and values, these normative expectations about leadership behavior are only one side of leadership. Whether, how, and to what extent these expectations are observable in everyday leadership practice is another question discussed further below. Written expectations towards leadership behavior can serve as a yardstick for the organization and the employees to evaluate the practiced leadership behavior. They may further serve as orientation for leadership development.

An organization's culture also determines the extent to which leaders should have specific skills and competencies. What degree and combination of organizational skills, management skills, and people skills do certain functions and levels require? How much is technical knowledge expected for specific management or leadership positions? What is the ratio between management and leadership skills that an organization considers *good and effective* compared to a leader evaluated as *ineffective*? How is *good* leadership practiced? When does it take place, and where? An organization's culture influences all of these questions concerning leadership.

In addition to an organization's culture, culture at the national and industry level may also influence the expectations toward *good* leadership. For example, in Germanic countries and Japan, employees expect substantially more technical knowledge and expertise from their leaders than in Anglo-Saxon countries. Furthermore, the acceptance of different leadership behavior differs across functions, regions, and nations. For instance, in production, employees may accept a more directive leadership style, while a directive leadership style is ineffective in R&D or marketing functions. In France, Mexico, and several Asian countries, employees expect a *good* leader to be decisive in the sense of patriarchic and benevolent-directive leadership. Such leadership behavior is less accepted in Germanic, Scandinavian or Anglo-Saxon countries (Brodbeck et al., 2016; Chhokar et al., 2008). In addition, young employees especially expect a participatory leadership style.

Practiced Leadership

An organization's culture influences leadership as practiced, hence the observable leadership behavior and leadership processes. A broad definition of leadership is influencing people (Northouse, 2018). How does this influencing process happen in a given organization and its culture? The existing leadership literature and everyday experience suggest that it can occur in all sorts of ways. It may range from directive to participatory and shared leadership, including self-management. Leaders may act transactional or transformational. In addition to professional leadership qualifications, what kind of personal characteristics are essential? They become visible in leaders' daily conduct and interactions with external and internal partners. To what extent do leaders practice the organization's normative expectations regarding leadership behavior, and to what extent does the organization hold leaders responsible for living up to these expectations?

If leaders do not behave within the organization's culture, the culture may be at risk. The following example describes a case in which an organization parted with a highly qualified leader of the top management group because he did not abide by the behavior expected by the organization.

A company was looking for a finance expert to fill the top finance position and found a highly qualified person. Informal interactions within and between hierarchical levels characterized the company's culture. They addressed each other by first names; they did not use their respective titles; they treated each other in a friendly manner across hierarchical levels. Doors were usually open, and employees could easily approach leaders at the top. The new Vice President (VP) of Finance, however, behaved differently. He wanted people to address him with his title and surname, his door was always closed, and employees from lower hierarchical levels were non-existent to him.

The firm's CEO had a long talk with him, explaining the particularities of the organization's essential culture. Since the VP of Finance did not change his behavior, the CEO had another conversation with him. He gave him feedback on his behavior and explained the importance of living the organization's culture again. When the third conversation did not result in observable behavioral changes of the VP Finance, the CEO decided together with his colleagues to dismiss him despite his outstanding qualifications. Sustaining the organizational culture was more important to the CEO and the existing top management group than employing one of the best financial experts (Sackmann, 1991).

Organizations that consider their culture important have similar examples of having parted with highly qualified people at different levels because they would not behave in line with their culture. For example, Grundfos, one of the world's leading water technology companies, and the pharmaceutical firm Novo Nordisk have a culture that allows organizational members to make mistakes concerning business matters. However, violating their organization's basic beliefs and values is not permitted and may lead to dismissal (Sackmann, 2006). After a culture development process, the hotel chain Upstalsboom part with leaders "when they consciously work against our values. Then we have to draw a red line. Otherwise we would become untrustworthy and dilute our culture". (Bodo Janssen, CEO at Upstalsboom cited in Martens, 2016).

Many organizations claim that their culture is vital to them, but they do not act as consistently as Grundfos, Novo Nordisk, or Upstalsboom to enforce their culture. When organizational members perform well and achieve good business results, organizations often tolerate behavior that deviates from the organization's culture. Business results are more important than culture according to the motto: *if the numbers are good, we allow exceptions*. From an organization's culture perspective, such an attitude is not conducive since it weakens its credibility. Baring Bank and its former broker Nick Leeson are a prominent example of this phenomenon. Given his successful track record, Baring Bank's management did not question how he had achieved his results. They even granted him special conditions before uncovering his fraudulent behavior, and Barings Bank had to file for insolvency.

Practiced leadership also entails communicating, setting priorities, exercising control, giving feedback, and developing people. Ideally, all these leadership practices align with the organization's normative expectations. Discrepancies between proclaimed organizational promises and organizational practices or between verbal accounts of leaders and their observable leadership behavior harm the organization's culture and its members. Unfortunately, many examples exist in the everyday work life of such discrepancies between written or oral statements and observable leadership behavior:

- The leaders of an organization announce that they had to cut expenses. Nevertheless, they extensively renovated upper management's offices, and a management meeting took place in an expensive venue.
- Despite the announcement that everybody had to fly economy class for short flights, the members of the top management group kept flying business or even first class.
- The CEO announces that the firm had to cut jobs. While affirming how sorry he was for taking these cuts, he had a smile on his face.
- Top managers and leaders communicated the importance of innovation. But, unfortunately, as soon as organizational members made a mistake, they imposed sanctions on them.

(continued)

- Top leaders emphasized that their door was always open to employees from all hierarchical levels if they could not resolve an issue with their direct supervisor. The next possible meeting, however, was only in a few months.
- Due to a new contract, managers assigned organizational members additional work packages with the highest priority without changing the priorities of the existing workload.

These are only a few of many examples. Often, those leaders who cause the discrepancies are unaware of their negative impact and are surprised by the organizational members' reactions and the deteriorating working climate. The extent of an existing difference is an informal measure for the quality of an organization's culture: the higher the discrepancy between the proclaimed and the practiced leadership behavior, the more problematic the state of the organization's culture and the more urgent the need for taking measure to reduce the discrepancy. A high congruence between proclaimed and observable behavior implies that the organization and its members walk the talk and live what they preach.

4.6 The Impact of an Organization's Culture on Employees

The specific content of an organization's culture influences the behavior of employees. This influence concerns their attitude and motivation, which influence their engagement and identification with their work, team, and the organization. Furthermore, an organization's culture affects employees' health, the level of cohesion in a group, and ultimately the performance of individuals, teams, and the entire organization. Once again, organizations have normative expectations towards their members' behavior. If employees meet these expectations in their daily work practices also depends on the organization's culture. These factors are linked and interrelated, as shown in Fig. 4.8., and addressed in this section, starting with the organization's normative expectations towards its members.

4.6.1 Organizational Expectations Towards its Employees' Behavior

An organization's principles and guidelines of behavior (see Sect. 4.5.2) usually specifies the organization's culturally-influenced expectations regarding its employees' behavior. Organizations expect that their members use these guidelines to choose the most appropriate behavior, abide by these normative expectations and show the proper behavior. Until the beginning of this millennium, codes of conduct or behavioral guidelines contained only a few principles or the basic beliefs and

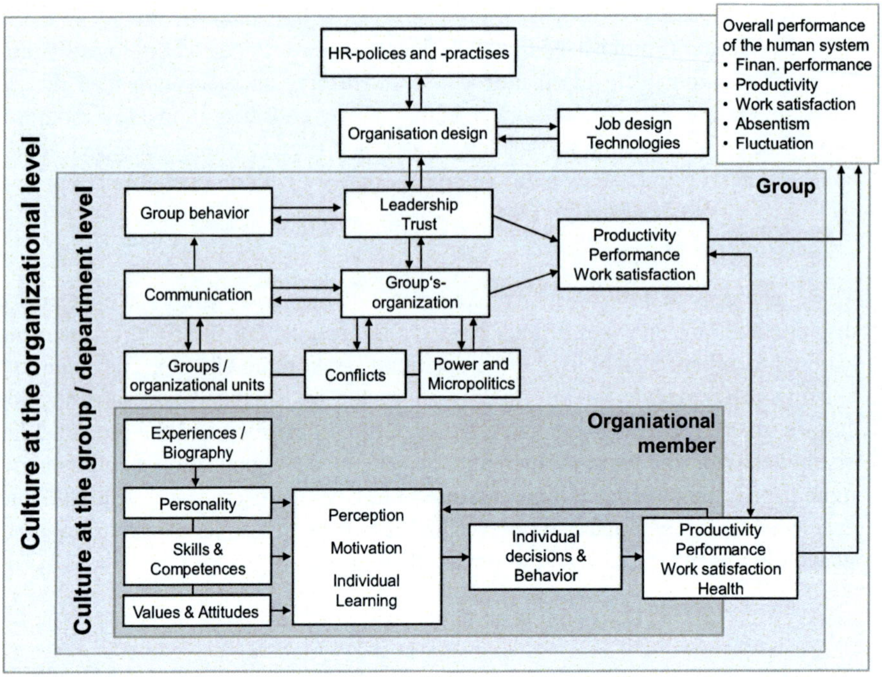

Fig. 4.8 Factors and their mutual influences contributing to performance at different levels of an organization

values of an organization, if they existed at all. Over the years, ethical guidelines complemented these codes of conduct. Meanwhile, these normative expectations regarding the organizational members' behavior have been expanded in form and content. The reasons for this development were twofold: increasing international or even global business operations, on the one hand, and the increasing importance of compliance on the other hand. While the behavior of an *honorable merchant* or a *good* employee may be known and observed in an organization because its members have internalized its culture and abide by it, this may not be the case when interacting with people in and from different countries and cultures (Sackmann & Horstmann, 2009; Stachowicz-Stanusch, 2009).

Furthermore, societal standards have also changed over the years. While the exchange of presents in some countries used to be accepted as *appropriate* business demeanor and partly still is, Western countries and jurisdictions consider such business behavior unfair and unethical. While at the turn of the millennium, expenses for initiating business contacts were tax-deductible in some countries, they are considered today corruptive behavior.

Because of these changes in prevailing standards and the growing importance of compliance issues, it is crucial for internationally and globally operating organizations to explain their expectations regarding appropriate and inappropriate behavior to their organizational members. Some organizations have integrated this information in their code of business conduct, such as Coca-Cola,[8] or in their code of conduct such as BASF,[9] while other organizations have developed a separate legal compliance code, such as the BMW Group.[10]

The reasons for having such a code of conduct is provided, for example, by Coca-Cola:

> What makes Coca-Cola one of the most admired brands in the world? It is not just our products. It is also how we do our work and the integrity of our actions. Ingrained in our culture, integrity inspires our work and strengthens our reputation as a Company that does extraordinary things and always does what is right. Integrity is the essential ingredient to our success. Sometimes, you might face a situation where the right thing to do is not obvious. That is where our Code of Business Conduct can help. It is always here as your guide to preserving our reputation and living our values. While the Code cannot answer every question, it can show you where to go for guidance when the answer is not clear.
>
> How Can the Code Help You? The Code enables you to . . .
>
> » Conduct yourself honestly and ethically.
>
> » Uphold our values and protect our reputation.
>
> » Understand what Coca-Cola expects from you.
>
> » Make good decisions every day.
>
> » Comply with the laws, regulations and standards that apply to our Company.
>
> » Understand where to go for assistance or guidance if you have questions.
>
> (Coca-Cola Company—Code of Business Conduct, p. 4)

The space provided to legal issues, both in Coca-Cola's Code of Business Conduct and BASF's Code of Conduct, demonstrates the increasing importance of legal compliance. At BASF, about six pages deal with why the code of conduct, the importance of adhering to it, and what the corporate values imply. In addition, about 29 pages deal with legal issues including anti-corruption, anti-trust laws, anti-money laundry, dealing with gifts and entertainment, human rights, labor laws, and social standards, environmental protection, dealing with sensitive company information, personal data, digital responsibility, company property, and accurate books and records. Coca-Cola's Code of Conduct mirrors this proportion and content.

---

[8] www.coca-colacompany.com/content/dam/journey/us/en/policies/pdf/corporate-governance/code-of-business-conduct/coca-cola-coc-external.pdf. Retrieved: Sep 20, 2021.

[9] www.basf.com/global/documents/en/about-us/management/BASF_Code-of-Conduct.pdf. Retrieved: Sep 20, 2021.

[10] www.bmwgroup.com/content/dam/grpw/websites/bmwgroup_com/company/downloads/en/2016/BMW_Group_LEGALCOMPLIANCECODE_EN.pdf. Retrieved: Sep 20, 2021.

The BMW Group's dedicated legal compliance code reminds organizational members of the Company's five values on the last page. About 25 pages deal with a wide range of legal issues such as the BMW Group products, services, customers, and markets; its competitors; corruption prevention; data protection; mutual esteem and principle of non-discrimination; safety at the workplace; environmental protection; protection of company assets; transparency for investors; fair treatment of contracting partners, and dealing with authorities.

While these codes of conduct emphasize primarily legal aspects, some firms also provide information about their organization's culture, focusing on their core values. The primary target group is potential organizational members. One example is the BMW Group[11]:

BMW: Fostering a Great Culture

We believe in supporting a progressive culture that allows all our associates to feel at home, enjoy equal opportunities, and grow with us. That's why our culture is founded on 5 core values, which set the tone for how we work together and treat each other in order to empower us all—and foster a unique team spirit.

Discover what it's really like to work with us, from the people who know the best.

Our Values

Responsibility

We take consistent decisions and commit to them personally. This allows us to work freely and more effectively.

Appreciation

We reflect on our actions, respect each other, offer clear feedback and celebrate success.

Transparency

We acknowledge concern and identify inconsistencies in a constructive way. We act with integrity.

Trust

We trust and rely on each other. This is essential if we are to act swiftly and achieve our goals.

Openness

We are excited by changes and open to new opportunities. We learn from our mistakes.

Tesla's culture builds on different values, which are explained in the context of its culture by Pauline Meyer (2019):

[11] www.bmwgroup.jobs/us/en/culture.html. Retrieved: Sep 20, 2021

1. Move Fast
2. Do the Impossible
3. Constantly Innovate
4. Reason from "First Principles"
5. Think Like Owners
6. We are ALL IN

Regarding the impact of an organization's culture, it is essential to know to what extent the verbalized normative expectations exist on paper and to what extent they are practiced in everyday work life and thus observable.

4.6.2 *The Influence of Organizational Culture on Employees' Motivation and Identification*

Depending on the specific content of an organization's culture, it may positively or negatively affect employees' motivation and level of identification with their team, division, and the entire organization. The culture of an organization with its subcultures provides the context in which organizational members work. Depending on its characteristics, this context may be inspiring, neutral, or even demotivating. The specific impact of an organization's culture on members' motivation and identification depends on its symbolic content and the meanings that employees assign to their work- and organizational context, including actions, decisions, and tasks (see Sect. 2.3.3).

If one asks three masons about their work, they may give three different answers shown in the picture.

Even though all three of them perform the same tasks, they assign different meanings to their work. The mason building a cathedral is likely to experience the highest and longest-lasting motivation even if she/he never sees the cathedral completed during his or her lifetime. Being part of a significant cause greater than oneself and that may outlive oneself can produce high motivation. To give another example: the security guard of an organization's computer center proudly explained that he was controlling the access to the heart of the organization. His professional self-image made him proud of his work. It had a positive influence on how he executed his guarding function and his identification with his work and employer. Given the importance that he felt in this role, he accomplished his work with care and a high level of attention. Furthermore, the symbolic meaning that he saw in his work positively influenced his job satisfaction and positively influenced his private life and general wellbeing. Off work, he probably talked proudly about his work and work organization when being with his family, friends, and neighbors.

Perceiving one's work as part of a bigger picture provides meaning with an uplifting and long-lasting motivational effect. Considering one's existence and contribution necessary can mobilize enormous energy and power as documented in studies on or accounts given by Holocaust survivors (Frankl, 1988). An organization's specific culture conveys the symbolic content of one's work. Depending on its content, it may offer more or less meaning for organizational members and thus influence their identification and motivation to a larger or lesser extent, positively or negatively. An internal study of the Bertelsmann Group provides evidence for this argument. The results show that the direct superiors' orientation toward their employees, supervisors' behavior, and the cooperation within and between the teams influenced development and training. All four factors influenced the level of autonomy and self-actualization of organizational members, which both had a strong influence on employees' identification with their task and company (Netta, 2009).

If it is difficult to identify with one's work and organization, the low identification is most likely associated with low motivation or even demotivation. Low motivation and identification may also impact employees' work ethics, evidenced by high absenteeism, sabotage, and data theft. The Bertelsmann Group study provides evidence for the effects of high and low motivation. Employees, who only loosely identified with their organization and were not satisfied with the leadership, had a 104 percent higher sickness rate and twice the number of sick-leave days than those who strongly identified with their organization and were highly satisfied with their leaders. A further data analysis suggests that the company could save 41 million EUR in labor costs if it could reduce the number of sick-leave days to those companies having high levels of identification (Netta, 2009).

Since 2001, the Gallup yearly surveys the degree of people's emotional attachment to their work and work organization and its effects on productivity. Results show that employees with a strong emotional attachment feel committed to their workplace. In contrast, employees with a medium-low attachment tend to do their work according to the book. And those without any emotional attachment are likely to sometimes even work against the organization's best interests. In addition, employees with a strong emotional attachment to their organization consider themselves more productive than those from the other two groups. Furthermore, they tend to have a lower absenteeism rate, tend to be more innovative in their behavior, experience less stress, report more fun at work and are more satisfied with their work and lives. The results also suggest that emotional attachment to the organization fosters loyalty if the essential needs of organizational members are considered (Gallup, 2019).

A longitudinal study reveals the dynamic nature of a culture's influence on organizational members' motivation and behavior. *West Coast Camelot* was a start-up software engineering company in Silicon Valley, California, characterized by a unique culture. All employees and managers were highly committed to the organization. The offices were brightly lit until late at night because people kept working. The organization was very successful and grew very fast from "9 people in a garage" to 3.000 and an annual turnover of 400 Million US dollars. When the organization entered a critical phase with a large project, the new management explicitly demanded that the project members worked overtime even though working overtime was part of Camelot's culture. Until then, organizational members had been highly committed and considerably contributed to the firm's success by voluntarily working overtime due to their high level of identification with the organization and their intrinsic motivation. When the new management explicitly demanded to work long hours, they started to resist even though it used to be their usual way of working (Schumacher, 1997). Their intrinsic motivation had been undermined (Ryan & Deci, 2000). Consequently, their commitment that had resulted in voluntary extra-role behavior (Organ, 1997) vanished. The explicitly voiced expectations regarding the formerly voluntary behavior evoked resistance (Crawford et al., 2002) with the respective adverse effects on their performance.

The examples mentioned above show that leaders play an essential role in conveying the symbolic content of a specific task or function. On the one hand, organizational members themselves attribute meaning to their work. On the other hand, colleagues and especially leaders may communicate the purpose of a specific task. They may place it in the larger context, pointing out its contribution to the organization's overall functioning. For instance, employees responsible for cleaning the offices may do so. Or their leader has communicated to them how vital clean offices are for the proper functioning of the organization. Furthermore, the level of appreciation that leaders show toward their employees will also influence their level of motivation.

4.6.3 The Influence of an Organization's Culture on its Members' Health

The culture of an organization also influences the health of organizational members. In dealing with health issues, reducing physical stress factors traditionally was the primary goal of work organizations. Today's illness statistics increasingly draw attention to mental illnesses. In the mid-1990s, mental illnesses were absent from work organizations' statistics. Taking Germany as an example, mental illnesses have become the second most frequent cause of sick leaves (Knies & Pfaff, 2015, p. 247). In 2015, the number of sick days caused by mental illnesses rose by 171,9 percent in Germany compared to 2004 (Meyer & Meschede, 2016, p. 279). At the same time,

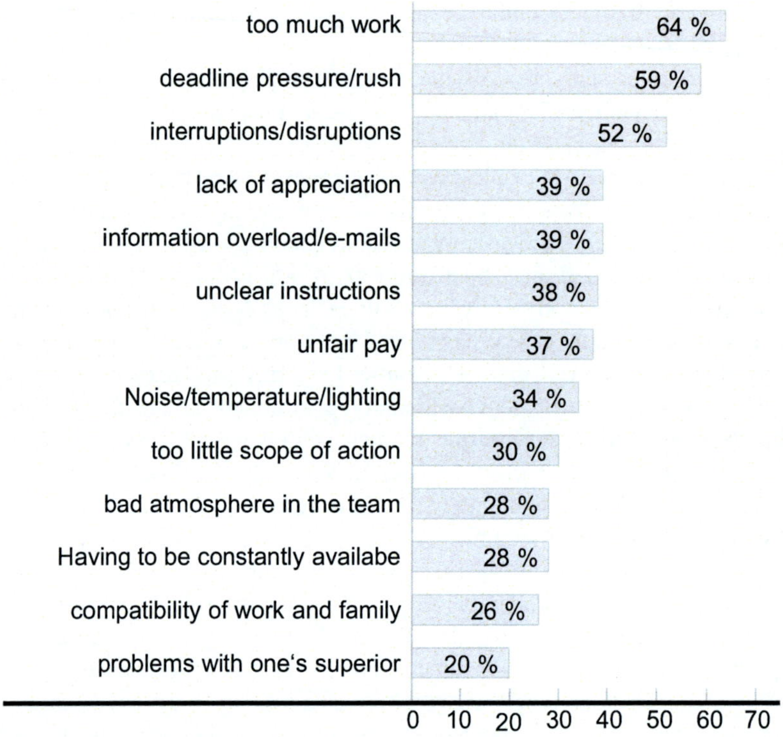

Fig. 4.9 Survey results: This is stressful about work (Source: Wohlers & Hombrecher, 2016, p. 24)

mental illnesses last on average for 39.1 days, which is three times the length of other diseases whose duration amounts to 13.3 days (Knies & Pfaff, 2015, p. 39). Furthermore, mental illnesses have become the most frequent cause for employees filing for early retirement. Between 1993 and 2020, the share of early retirement due to mental illness has risen from 15.3 to 41.7 percent.[12]

Psychological problems frequently result from experienced stress that a variety of factors can elicit. Those factors can reside within the individual and be part of the specific job and the work environment. The job is characterized by the type of work, the location, duration of working hours, the ability to manage the assigned task, the available time for completing a task, its complexity, the work equipment, and available resources. The work environment comprises the physical workplace, rules and regulations, and the social environment, including colleagues, managers, and the relationship with the direct superior, including their leadership behavior.

According to the results of a study conducted by a German health insurance firm, two-thirds of interviewed employees named work as their major stress factor (Wohlers & Hombrecher, 2016). In addition, factors concerning the organizational culture significantly influenced the reported stress level (Beckmann et al., 2016). As indicated in Fig. 4.9, the most significant stress-producing factors named were too

[12]Deutsche Rentenversicherung Bund: Rentenversicherung in Zeitreihen, 2020, p. 105.

much work, deadline pressure, and disturbances at work. Less severe but still stress-producing was a lack of appreciation, information overload, unclear instructions, unfair pay, being permanently available, too little freedom of action, and conflicts with the boss or colleagues.

Except for noise and temperature, an organization's culture influences all of these factors. These factors influence organizational members' perception of their job satisfaction, mental wellbeing, and stress in their combination and interaction. Other stress-inducing factors often not reported are micro-politics, mobbing, and bore-out. A worldwide survey including 11.238 respondents revealed that in Europe, 32 percent reported felt overqualified for their job (StepStone, 2012).

Depending on the specific content of an organization's culture, these psychological stress factors can be high and health-threatening or low and supporting the employee's self-esteem and subjective wellbeing. All studies reported above emphasize the importance of culturally influenced leadership behavior for organizational members` health and wellbeing. As superiors, leaders assign tasks, set deadlines, define the requirement, and ensure fair (or unfair) pay. They show or withhold appreciation, they may expect constant availability or not, they grant or discourage home office work, and they define the scope of action of their employees. A further data analysis of the Bertelsmann study revealed the critical influence on organizational members' perception of health protection. As depicted in Fig. 4.10, superiors allow the degree of self-determined actions and responsibility, which influences the satisfaction with work-time regulations with a direct and indirect effect on employees' perception of health protection. In addition, superiors communicate the organization's goals more or less clear and transparent, thus providing a certain degree of workplace security, which directly affects health protection.

The extent to which leaders themselves suffer from too much work, deadline pressure, disturbances, unclear specifications, or a lack of appreciation and pass it on

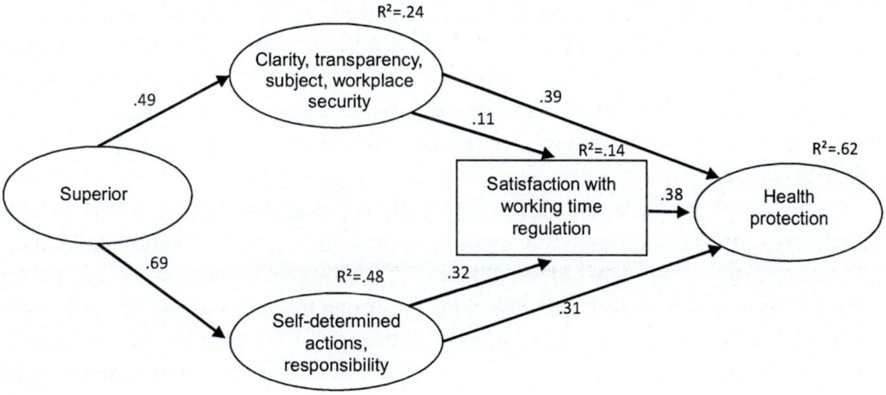

Fig. 4.10 Factors contributing to perceived health protection (Netta, 2009)

to their subordinates is also an expression of an organization's existing culture (see Sect. 4.5). Hence leaders and their practiced leadership behavior convey culturally influenced health-related issues to their employees. This leadership behavior does not only affect employees' wellbeing and health condition but also their job performance.

4.6.4 The Influence of an Organization's Culture on its Members' Work Performance

Work performance refers to the quality and quantity of achieved results with the invested resources. Inputs or resources such as information, knowledge, time, energy, financial and material resources are transformed into outputs.[13] As Fig. 4.8 shows, performance refers to results achieved by individuals, groups, and organizational units. Taken together, they determine the performance of the entire organization. Since an organization's culture provides the context in which these transformation processes occur, it considerably influences the results at all three levels.

This section focuses on the influence of an organization's culture on its members' performance, while Chap. 5 focuses on performance at the organizational level.

First of all, an organization's culture influences the extent to which qualified people can be recruited, hired, and further developed to do their work. A good fit between job requirements and qualifications is the best prerequisite for high performance. If people feel over- or underqualified for a specific job and the respective tasks, this will negatively affect their job performance. Both being overwhelmed and unchallenged can result in negative stress, as illustrated in Csikszentmihalyi's (2008) Flow model depicted in Fig. 4.11. Feeling either bored or anxious will also lead to suboptimal results. The best condition for experiencing flow at work is an optimal fit between an individual's abilities and skills and the perceived challenges at work.

On the individual and the group level, an organization's culture influences its members' perception, information processing, and assessment of the accumulated information and events. Depending on the outcome of the evaluation process, they take different kinds of actions, also influenced by the organization's culture. As *good* organizational members, they know culturally acceptable behavior. If they perceive their work context as stimulating and feel appreciated, their motivation and engagement are likely to be high. On the other hand, if they feel bored and not appreciated, their motivation is likely to be low with the respective effects on their job performance. Hence organizational members' abilities and skills are essential prerequisites for their level of performance, while the specifications of the organization's culture

[13] A differentiated discussion on performance from an organizational psychological perspective can be found amongst others in Roe (1999) and Arvinen-Muondo and Perkins (2013).

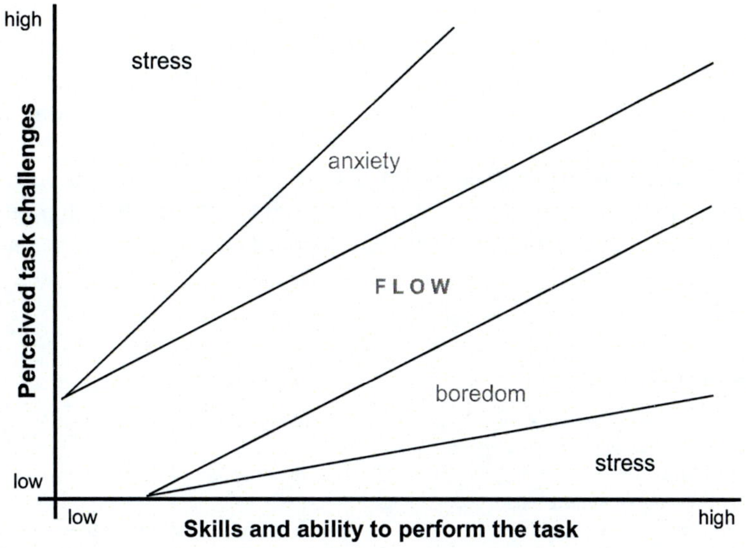

Fig. 4.11 Csikszentmihalyi's (2008) Flow model: Effects of different combinations of skill level and task challenge

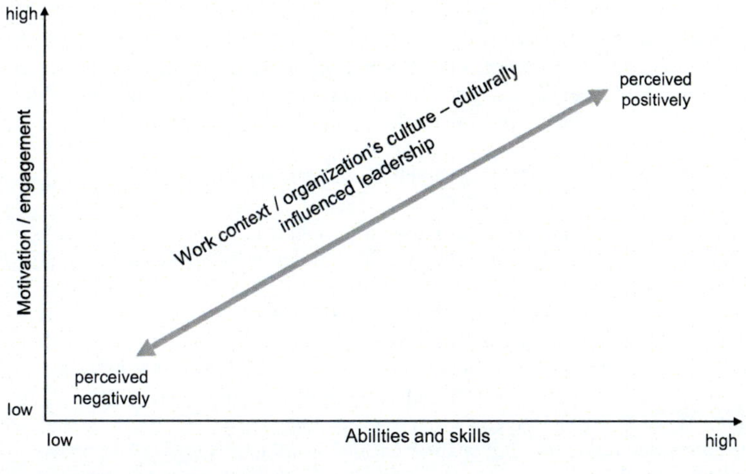

Fig. 4.12 Determinants of organizational members' performance

influence the extent to which they can use their skills and abilities, as visualized in Fig. 4.12.

The case of *West Coast Camelot* (Schumacher, 1997) in Sect. 4.6.2 illustrates that a cultural change influenced the motivation, commitment, and identification of organizational members with their employer negatively. In addition, the change also led to declining performance, problems, and even layoffs. The results of the analyses of the *Best Place to Work*-interviews revealed that those respondents, who rated their organization's culture the best, like to go to work, act in a coordinated way and toward common goals, feel recognized and appreciated as individuals, and think that their contributions are welcomed and respected. The results regarding these factors were 20–30 percent lower in companies whose culture was perceived mediocre. Hence, it is worth paying attention to one's culture.

The last section explored an organization's cultural influence on organizational members` performance. Chap. 5 sheds more light on the relationship between an organization's culture and various performance factors at the organization level.

References

Apple. *Code of conduct.* www.apple.com.

Arvinen-Muondo, R., & Perkins, S. (2013). *Organizational behaviour. People, process, work and human resource management.* Kogan Page.

Bartz, M. (2018, February 26). *Holacracy at Zappos.* New World of Work. Retrieved Sep 20, 2021, from https://newworldofwork.wordpress.com/2018/02/26/holacracy-at-zappos/

BASF. *Code of conduct.* www.basf.com.

Bauer, T. N., & Erdogan, B. (2011). Organizational socialization: The effective onboarding of new employees. In S. Zedeck (Ed.), *APA handbooks in psychology®. APA handbook of industrial and organizational psychology, Vol. 3. Maintaining, expanding, and contracting the organization* (pp. 51–64). American Psychological Association. https://doi.org/10.1037/12171-002

Beckmann, O., Meschede, J., & Zok, K. (2016). Unternehmenskultur und Gesundheit: Ergebnisse einer repräsentativen Umfrage unter Erwerbstätigen. In B. Badura, A. Ducki, H. Schröder, J. Klose, & M. Meyer (Eds.), *Fehlzeiten-Report 2016* (pp. 43–70). Springer.

Beer, S. (1995a). *The brain of the firm* (2nd ed.). Wiley. (1st ed. 1980.).

Beer, S. (1995b). *The heart of the enterprise.* Wiley.

Bieri, J. (1955). Cognitive complexity-simplicity and predictive behavior. *Journal of Abnormal and Social Psychology, 51*(2), 263–268.

BMW Group. *Legal compliance code.* www.bmwgroup.com.

Brodbeck, F. C., Kirchler, E., & Woschée, R. (2016). *Internationale Führung: Das GLOBE Brevier in der Praxis.* Springer.

Chandler, A. D. (1962). *Strategy and structure.* MIT Press.

Chhokar, J. S., Brodbeck, F. C., & House, R. J. (Eds.). (2008). *Culture and leadership across the world: The GLOBE book of in-depth studies of 25 societies.* Taylor & Francis.

Coca-Cola Company. *Code of business conduct.* www.coca-colacompany.com.

Crawford, M. T., McConnel, A. R., Lewis, A. C., & Sherman, S. J. (2002). Reactance, compliance, and anticipated regret. *Journal of Experimental Social Psychology, 38*(1), 56–63.

Csikszentmihalyi, M. (2008). *Flow: The psychology of optimal experience.* Harper.

Deutsche Rentenversicherung Bund. (Ed.). (2014). Positionspapier zur Bedeutung psychischer Erkrankungen in der Rehabilitation und bei Erwerbsminderung. Deutsche Rentenversicherung Bund, Geschäftsbereich Sozialmedizin und Rehabilitation. Accessed Sep 27, 2021, from www.deutsche-rentenversicherung.de/SharedDocs/Downloads/DE/Experten/infos_reha_einrichtungen/konzepte_systemfragen/positionspapiere/pospap_psych_Erkrankung.html

Deutsche Rentenversicherung Bund (Ed.). (2020) DRV-Schriften: Bd. 22. Rentenversicherung in Zeitreihen 2020. : Deutsche Rentenversicherung Bund. Retrieved: September 20, 2021, from www.deutsche-rentenversicherung.de/DRV/DE/Experten/Zahlen-und-Fakten/Statistiken-und-Berichte/statistiken_und_berichte.html

Felin, T., & Powell, T. C. (2016). Designing organizations for dynamic capabilities. *California Management Review, 58*(4). https://doi.org/10.1525/cmr.2016.58.4.78

Flik, H. (1990). The ameba concept . . . organizing around opportunity within the GORE culture. In H. Simon (Ed.), *Herausforderung Unternehmenskultur* (pp. 91–129). Schäffer.

Frankl, V. E. (1988). *The will to meaning*. Penguin Books.

Galbraith, J. R. (1995). *Designing organizations: An executive briefing on strategy, structure, and process*. Jossey-Bass.

Galbraith, J. R. (2012). The future of organization design. *Journal of Organization Design, 1*(1), 3–6. https://doi.org/10.7146/jod.6332

Gallup. (2019). Engagement Index Deutschland 2019. Accessed Feb 12, 2021, from www.gallup.com/de/engagement-index-deutschland.aspx

Grinyer, P. H., & Spender, J. (1979). Recipes, crisis and adaptation in mature business. *International Studies of Management and Organization, 9*(3), 113–133.

Hamel, G., & Breen, B. (2007). *The future of management*. Harvard Business School Press.

Infineon Technologies AG (Ed.). (2019). *Business conduct guidelines: Infineon's code of ethics*. Infineon Technologies AG. www.infineon.com

Jussim, L. J. (2012). *Social perception and social reality: Why accuracy dominates bias and self-fulfilling prophecy*. Oxford University Press.

Kahneman, D. (2011). *Thinking fast and slow*. Farrar, Straus and Giroux.

Kahneman, D., & Tversky, A. (Eds.). (2000). *Choices, values, and frames*. Cambridge University Press.

Kahneman, D., Slovic, P., & Tversky, A. (Eds.). (1982). *Judgment under uncertainty: Heuristics and biases*. Cambridge University Press. https://doi.org/10.1017/CBO9780511809477

Knies, F., & Pfaff, H. (Eds.). (2015). *BKK Gesundheitsreport 2015 (BKK health report 2015)*. MWV.

Kühl, S. (2015). *Sisyphos im Management: Die vergebliche Suche nach der optionalen Organisationsstruktur* (2nd ed.). Frankfurt a. M.: Campus.

Kunze, F., Boehm, S., & Bruch, H. (2013). Organizational performance consequences of age diversity: Inspecting the role of diversity-friendly HR policies and top managers' negative age stereotypes. *Journal of Management Studies, 50*(3), 413–442.

Lawrence, B. S. (1996). Organizational age norms: Why is it so hard to know one when you see one? *The Gerontologist, 36*(2), 209–220.

Lidl. *Leadership principles*. www.lidl-com.

Mackenzie, K. D. (1991). *The organizational hologram: The effective management of organizational change*. Kluwer Academic Publishers.

Martens, A. (2016). PE-Offensive bei Upstalsboom. Der andere Aufstieg. *ManagerSeminare, 223*, 18–27. Accessed Sep 20, 2021, from www.managerseminare.de/ms_Artikel/PE-Offensive-bei-Upstalsboom-Der-andere-Aufstieg,249440

McDaniel, E., & Lawrence, C. (1990). *Levels of cognitive complexity*. Springer.

Meyer, M., & Meschede, M. (2016). Krankheitsbedingte Fehlzeiten in der Wirtschaft im Jahr 2015. In B. Badura, A. Ducki, H. Schröder, J. Klose, & M. Meyer (Eds.), *Fehlzeiten-Report 2016* (pp. 251–306). Springer.

Meyer, P. (2019). *Tesla Inc.'s organizational culture & its characteristics (analysis)*. Panmure Institute (An online publishing platform and online network). Accessed Sept 20, 2021, from http://panmore.com/tesla-motors-inc-organizational-culture-characteristics-analysis

Mintzberg, H., Ahlstrand, B., & Lampel, J. (1998). *The strategy safari: A guided tour through the jungles of strategic management*. Free Press.

Netta, F. (2009). Gezielte Schwachstellenanalyse bis auf die untersten Führungsebenen. *HR Today, 5*, 25–28. Accessed Sep 20, 2021, from www.hrtoday.ch/de/article/gezielte-schwachstellenanalyse-bis-aufdie-untersten-fuehrungsebenen

Northouse, P. G. (2018). *Leadership: Theory and practice* (8th ed.). Sage.

Organ, D. W. (1997). Organizational citizenship behavior: It's construct clean-up time. *Human Performance, 10*(2), 85–97.

Pelton, W., Sackmann, S. A., & Boguslaw, R. (1990). *Tough choices. The decision-making styles of America's top 50 CEO's*. Dow Jones-Irwin.

Porter, M. E. (1980). *Competitive strategy: Techniques for analyzing industries and competitors*. Free Press. (Republished with a new introduction, 1998.).

Roe, R. A. (1999). Work performance: A multiple regulation perspective. In C. C. Cooper & I. T. Robertson (Eds.), *International review of industrial and organizational psychology 1999* (Vol. 14, pp. 231–335). Wiley.

Ryan, R. M., & Deci, E. L. (2000). Self-determination theory and the facilitation of intrinsic motivation, social development, and wellbeing. *American Psychologist, 55*(1), 68–78.

Sackmann, S. A. (1991). *Cultural knowledge in organizations. Exploring the collective mind*. Sage.

Sackmann, S. A. (2006). *Success factor: Corporate culture*. Developing a corporate culture for high performance and long-term competitiveness. Six best practices (1st ed.). BertelsmannStiftung (Ed.). Gütersloh: Verlag BertelsmannStiftung. (2nd ed. 2008. E-book 2011.)

Sackmann, S., & Horstmann, B. (2009). The role of corporate culture in developing and preventing corruption. In A. Stachowicz-Stanusch (Ed.), *Organizational immunity to corruption: Building theoretical and research foundations* (pp. 261–277). Katowice Branch of the Polish Academy of Sciences.

Sandhu, P. E. (2014). *Selektionspfade im Topmanagement: Homogenisierungsprozesse in Organisationen*. Springer.

Sapienza, A. M. (1985). Believing is seeing: How organizational culture influences the decisions top managers make. In R. H. Kilmann, M. J. Saxton, & R. Serpa (Eds.), *Gaining control of the corporate culture* (pp. 66–83). Jossey-Bass.

Schreyögg, G. (1988). Darf und kann man Unternehmenskulturen ändern? In E. Dülfer (Ed.), *Organisationskultur* (pp. 155–168). Poeschel.

Schreyögg, G., & Sydow, J. (Eds.). (2009). *The hidden dynamics of path dependence: Institutions and organizations*. Springer.

Schumacher, T. (1997). West coast Camelot: The rise and fall of an organizational culture. In S. A. Sackmann (Ed.), *Cultural complexity in organizations: Inherent contrasts and contradictions* (pp. 105–132). Sage.

Siemens. *Siemens business conduct guidelines*. www.siemens.com.

Stachowicz-Stanusch, A. (2009). Culture due diligence based on HP/Compaq merger case study. *Journal of Intercultural Management, 1*(1), 64–81.

StepStone Deutschland AG. (2012). "Do you feel underemployed in your job sometimes?" StepStone Online-Stellenmarkt. www.stepstone.de.

Winter, J. (2009). *Zwischen Hierarchie und Heterarchie: Kompetenzveränderungen in Tochterbetrieben internationaler Automobilunternehmen am Standort Polen*. LIT.

Wohlers, K., & Hombrecher, M. (2016). *Entspann dich, Deutschland—TK-Stressstudie 2016*. Techniker Krankenkasse.

Womack, J. P., Jones, D. T., & Roos, D. (1990). *The machine that changed the world*. Macmillan.

Zappos. *Real organization chart*. www.zapposinsights.com.

Chapter 5
Culture and Organizational Performance

Practitioners' primary interest in organizational culture is rooted in the belief about culture's influence on organizational performance. Several corporate leaders such as Reinhold Würth, former CEO and Chairman of the Board of the Würth-Group,[1] Michael and Martin Hilti, founder, CEOs, and Chairmen of the Hilti Group,[2] or Bill Gore, founder of W.L. Gore & Associates,[3] are convinced that corporate culture is a critical competitive factor that needs leaders' and managers' attention. Since the book's publication *In search of excellence* (Peters & Waterman, 1982/2004), managers and leaders try to tap into the identified success factor corporate culture. The results of Kotter and Heskett's study (1992) further nurtured this interest. Which executive would not like to see the firm's value increase by 682 percent, the net income by 756 percent, and the shareholder value by 901 percent within eleven years?

Accordingly, the number of empirical studies investigating the relationship between organizational culture and various performance indicators has steadily increased since the 1990s.

This chapter addresses the different ways used to measure both culture and performance. This information provides an understanding of the multifaceted nature of the relationship between culture and performance. The following five sections focus on: (1) research that investigated the direct link between culture and performance indicators; (2) research that investigated cultures perceived to be different and their impact on performance indicators; (3) studies that found an indirect link

---

[1]The Würth-Group is a family-owned business and world market leader in its core business, assembling and fastening materials. www.wuerth.com/web/en/wuerthcom/unternehmen/unternehmen_1.php. Retrieved: Sep 21, 2021.

[2]The Hilti Group is also a family-owned multinational company that develops, manufactures, and markets products for the construction, building maintenance, energy, and manufacturing industries, mainly to the professional end-user. www.hilti.com

[3]W.L. Gore & Associates is a material science company focused on discovery, product innovation, and rewarding careers for their Associates. www.gore.com

S. A. Sackmann, *Culture in Organizations*, Contributions to Management Science,
https://doi.org/10.1007/978-3-030-86080-6_5

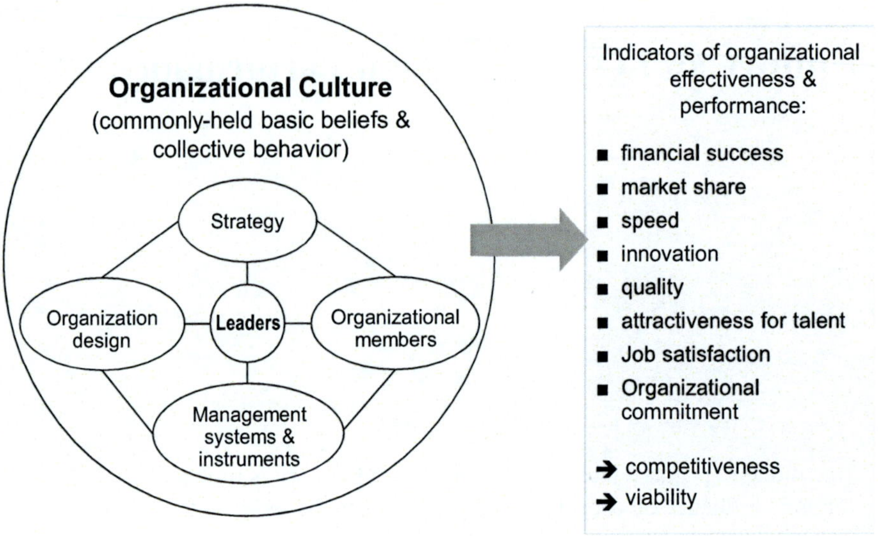

Fig. 5.1 Potential impact of an organization's culture on a range of effectiveness and performance indicators

between culture and performance; (4) research that suggests an interaction effect; (5) non-linear and reciprocal relationships between culture and performance. The chapter closes with a discussion if strong cultures tend to be better for organizational performance, as some authors and practitioners claim.

Most studies focused on a direct relationship between the two concepts using correlational statistics. Figure 5.1 illustrates the direct influence of organizational culture on several possible financial and non-financial performance.

Using more sophisticated research designs and research methods, more recent studies also reveal indirect, non-linear, and reciprocal relationships between organizational culture and performance indicators, including interaction- and moderator effects.

Given that organizational culture and performance are multidimensional concepts, researchers used several ways to measure organizational culture and a wide range of financial and non-financial performance indicators. Due to the wide range of indicators used, one can only compare a small number of studies directly. Nevertheless, the existing research gives insights into the various effects of different cultural dimensions on potential performance indicators. To better understand the diversity of studying the relationship between an organization's culture and its performance, the following section gives a short overview on the way researchers have measured culture and performance before discussing the current state of research on the topic.

5.1 Measuring Organizational Performance and Culture

The indicators used to operationalize organizational performance includes financial and non-financial measures. Among the financial measures are the following: revenue, profit and profitability, return on capital, expenses, the ratio of profit to revenue and investments, ROI (return on investment), ROS (return on sales), ROE (return on equity), ROA (return on assets), return on capital employed (ROCE), earnings before interest and taxes (EBIT), earnings before interest, taxes, depreciation and amortization (EBITDA), capital growth, sales and sales volume growth, growth of premiums in real terms, share price development, or dept to equity ratio. Most studies assessed the chosen indicators for one year; some studies collected them for two, three, six, or—in the case of Kotter and Heskett's research (1992)—over a period of eleven years.

The range of non-financial indicators to assess organizational effectiveness or performance in investigating its relation to culture is equally diverse. These non-financial measures include perceived market share, brand performance, market position, organizational performance, an organization's speed in recognizing new trends and adapting to them; the time needed to bring new products to the market; gaining and keeping market share; the type and extent of innovation, quality of products and services, product development, fluctuation, job-, employee-, and customer satisfaction, organizational commitment, engagement, and an organization's attractiveness to needed talent.

Some studies used only one indicator, while others combined several indicators. Many researchers employed objective measures for performance, while others chose perceptual assessments from organizational members. Both the type of organization and industry and the availability of data influence the specific choice of measure(s).

The operationalization of culture shows a similar variety in methods and instruments employed. Different perspectives of culture tend to underly their choice. Hence studies focused on various cultural components or dimensions as well as on different levels. Sackmann (2011) discusses 25 possibilities to assess culture in the context of organizations, and this list of measures is not exhaustive. In general, research that investigates organizational culture either uses a qualitative or a quantitative approach. An increasing number is employing multiple methods by combining both qualitative and quantitative data. When addressing the relationship between culture and organizational performance and the impact of culture on an organization's performance, researchers tend to choose large sample sizes. In such large-scale investigations, questionnaires have been the data collection method of choice mainly because of cost and comparability. Accordingly, most studies on the topic of culture and performance are quantitative in nature. Only a few case studies exist on the subject assessing culture with a combination of interviews, observations, and desk research.

In research investigating the relationship between culture and performance, the most commonly-used questionnaires are the Denison Organizational Culture Survey (DOCS) (Denison, 1990, 1996), the Organizational Culture Inventory (OCI) (Cooke

& Lafferty, 1983), and the Competing Values Framework (Cameron & Quinn, 1999). The DOCS assesses four primary dimensions of culture: involvement, consistency, adaptability, and mission. Involvement and consistency have an internal focus, while adaptability and mission have an external focus. The OCI assesses three culture types: constructive, passive-defensive, and aggressive-defensive cultures. The Competing Values Framework measures four different culture types: clan, adhocracy, hierarchy-, and market-oriented cultures.

In addition, researchers used a variety of different dimensions to examine organizational culture. These include orientations focusing on people, employees, teamwork, processes, tasks, improvements, external orientation, performance, work-related values and practices, trust and credibility, tight vs. loose control, normative vs. pragmatic orientation, or corporate citizenship. Furthermore, some studies assessed the *strength* of culture using the intensity that its members adhere to values and norms or the homogeneity/consistency between respondents' answers. A few studies measured the fit between an organization's culture and its strategy; the consistency between norms and values, as well as the discrepancy between perceived and preferred orientations (e.g., Wilderom & van den Berg, 1998) or the discrepancy between practiced and written values (Flamholtz & Kannan-Narasimhan, 2005). Similar to measuring performance, researchers used only a few dimensions of culture per study when assessing an organization's culture.

The following section addresses the direct relationship between an organization's culture and organizational performance.

5.2 Direct Relationship Between Culture and Performance Indicators

Several contributions provide an overview over the state of research regarding the relationship between dimensions of culture and organizational effectiveness or performance indicators (c.f., Baetge et al., 2007; Hartnell et al., 2011; Sackmann, 2011; Hartnell et al., 2019; Wilderom & van den Berg, 2000). Wilderom et al. (2000) included ten empirical studies, nine of which showed a direct relationship between different dimensions of culture and various performance indicators. The analysis of 55 empirical studies investigating the relationship between culture and performance published between 2000 and 2010 found that these studies primarily discovered a direct positive correlation between different dimensions of organizational culture and performance indicators (Sackmann, 2011). The listing in Fig. 5.2 illustrates the diversity of investigated culture aspects and their direct and positive correlation with several different performance indicators.

Reviewing 65 empirical studies conducted between 1990 and 2010 revealed that the investigated culture dimensions showed a predominantly positive correlation with the selected performance indicators. According to these studies, organizations tend to be more successful if their culture focuses on corporate citizenship,

- Shared goal orientation and humanistic values – financial success *(Ouchi & Jaeger, 1978)*
- *Strong* OC – (short-term) company success *(Peters & Waterman, 1982/2004)*
- *Strong* OC – strong growth *(Calori & Sarnin, 1991)*
- *Strong* OC – long-term economic performance *(Kotter & Heskett, 1992)*
- *Strong* OC and adaptability – short-term success *(Gordon & DiTomaso, 1992)*
- Competitive, entrepreneurial OC – (subjectively estimated) company success *(Deshpandé et al., 1993)*
- Involvement – short- and mid-term performance *(Denison, 1990)*
- Mission/consistency at large companies – profitability *(Denison & Mishra, 1995)*
- Mission – overall performance, revenue growth, increase of market share, return on assets *(Yilmaz & Ergun, 2008)*
- Involvement/adaptability – revenue growth *(Dension & Mishra, 1995)*
- Innovative, competitive corporate culture – company performance *(Obgonna & Harris, 2000)*
- Innovation-, team-, people- and task-orientation – return on assets, net income, revenue *(Lee & Yu, 2004)*
- Innovation- and market-orientation – brand performance *(O'Cass & Ngo, 2007)*
- market-oriented OC – company performance *(Lee et al., 2006)*
- Clan and market culture – market performance (*Dadzie et al., 2012*)
- Clan culture – product strategy change *(Wei et al., 2014)*
- OC – performance regarding balanced scorecard indicators *(Hilman & Siam, 2014)*
- OC – work motivation and human resource performance (*Al-Musadieq et al., 2018)*
- OC – customer loyalty and organizational performance *(Garcia-Fernández et al., 2018)*
- Market culture – knowledge sharing *(Rohim & Budhiasa, 2019)*
- Outcome- and team-orientation culture – financial and non-financial performance *(Bhuiyan et al., 2020)*
- Six cultural variables incl. dominant type – government performance (measured in terms of quality, quantity, timeliness, effectiveness, independence) *(Wazirman et al., 2020)*

Fig. 5.2 Positive correlations between organizational culture (OC) dimensions and performance indicators

innovation, goal- and performance orientation, and external than internal orientation. The stronger external compared to internal orientation keeps organizations flexible and ensures their focus on the market and their customers.

Four studies published between 2000 and 2010, Sackmann (2011) summarize the multifaceted research results regarding the relationship between organizational culture and different performance indicators. Table 12.1 included in Sackmann (2011, pp. 197-209), gives an overview of the specific assessment of culture, the performance measures used in the respective studies, organizations and respondents involved, and the major results regarding culture and performance. Two meta-analytical studies (Hartnell et al., 2011, 2019) focused on research using the competing values framework (Cameron & Quinn, 1999) for measuring culture. They found significant positive correlations between the different culture types and organizational effectiveness measures and several financial and non-financial performance measures. The four culture types were interrelated. They showed moderate to strong relationships with employees' job satisfaction and organizational commitment, quality of products and services, corporate innovation, and profit and growth assessed with subjective measures (Hartnell et al., 2011). The results of the latter study (Hartnell et al., 2019) indicate that the culture types explained 75% of the variance in the outcome variables. These effects were the highest for the following organizational-level effectiveness criteria: employee outcomes, followed by operational, customer- and innovation-related as well as financial results.

Besides the aforementioned positive correlations between culture and performance, some research results revealed no relationship between the measured culture dimensions and the included performance indicators. A few studies even found a negative correlation. For example, hierarchical cultures significantly negatively influenced knowledge sharing (Rohim & Budhiasa, 2019). In organizations with a defensive culture, the correlations between culture and performance at the individual and organizational level were also negative. Researchers measured the latter with the following indicators: quality of products and services, customer orientation, adaptability, intention to leave, and job quality (Balthazard et al., 2006). In addition, hierarchical-bureaucratic and consensus-oriented clan cultures correlated negatively with the performance measures used (Deshpandé & Farley, 2004). Furthermore, cultures with a hierarchical-bureaucratic orientation significantly negatively influenced organizations' innovation success (Deshpandé & Farley, 2004).

The findings of a qualitative study using documentary analysis to investigate the demise of a Swiss reading society support these results. Because the decision-makers rigidly held on to their historically developed, elitist beliefs and values, they did not recognize or acknowledge significant societal changes in reading preferences. Their selective perception eventually caused the reading society's decline (Eberle, 1997). Another study found ambivalent results when investigating the relationship between organizational culture and organizational performance during the transformation of an Australian college to a university (Lewis, 1994). Although the change achieved all management goals, the teachers' work-related values decayed in the transformation process.

Probst and Raisch (2005) chose a different research design with their focus on corporate failures. The researchers investigated companies in the U.S. and Europe that had experienced a crash defined as losing at least 40 percent of their value or having to file for bankruptcy between 1998 and 2003. Of the 100 companies included in their study, 57 firms were successful before their crash or bankruptcy. The researchers defined success as either being the market leader in their respective industry or continuously showing a net profit up to their failure. Within this group of formerly successful firms, the researchers identified two syndromes causing the failure due to different logics. Both logics were related to their organization's culture. The failures were homemade, and the firms could have avoided them with different logics.

40 (70 percent) of these companies showed a so-called burn-out syndrome characterized by a collective focus on excessive growth, uncontrolled change, autocratic leadership, and an extreme quest for success. They motivated their employees by paying high salaries and bonuses and providing opportunities for fast promotions. These characteristics came with a directive leadership style, rigid recruitment processes, a strong competitive orientation, and a mercenary mentality. They emphasized making money and did not care for loyalty.

Companies suffering from the so-called premature aging syndrome showed the following characteristics: stagnating growth, hesitant change, weak organizational leadership, and lacking a success orientation. Innovation hardly happened, and change was only introduced reluctantly and too late. The top executives were considered weak and clinging to the organization's past achievements. Organizational members felt comfortable within the culture characterized by loyalty and trust. However, necessary strategic and operational decisions happened too late or not at all due to their reluctant approach towards change.

5.3 Different Kinds of Organizational Cultures and their Relation to Performance Indicators

Several studies have investigated the cultural characteristics that differentiate financially successful firms from less successful ones or classified organizational cultures according to their members' perceptions. The two Harvard professors John Kotter and Jim Heskett, compared 207 companies from 22 industries over eleven years. When analyzing their data, they found two types of companies with widely different cultural characteristics and performance. The high-performing type A companies had managers at all hierarchical levels acting like leaders, and they firmly focused on three stakeholder groups: their customers, employees, and shareholders. The less successful type B companies initially had a strong position in their market and comparatively less competition, but they neglected their customers, employees, and shareholders. In addition, they only recognized needed changes and internal problems late or not enough. Within the 11 years, type A companies increased:

- their revenue by on average 682 percent as compared to the 166 percent increase of type B companies,
- the number of employees by 282 percent as compared to 36 pecent,
- their shareholder value by 901 percent as compared to 74 percent of type B companies, and
- their net income by 756 percent compared to 1 percent of the type B companies (Kotter & Heskett, 1992, p. 11).

The cross-sectional comparisons between successful and less successful companies (Denison & Mishra, 1995; Flamholtz & Kannan-Narasimhan, 2005; Hunsdiek, 2005) also reveal differences in the characteristics of the respective organizational cultures. For example, a research project conducted in South Africa showed that financially successful companies—compared with unsuccessful firms—had a strategic vision and regularly aligned their strategy with their organizations' culture measured as core values. They recruited new employees carefully to fit their culture. Once hired, they introduced newcomers into the specifics of the firms' culture. Newcomers received an orientation regarding appropriate and inappropriate behavior as defined by the organizations' culture. Furthermore, existing communication systems also conveyed the company's core values to organizational members (Van der Post & de Coning, 1998).

Some studies have classified an organization's culture from the perspective of organizational members and compared the effects of different kinds of cultures.

Taking emotional commitment towards an organization as an indicator for the quality of a given culture, the meta-analysis of the worldwide Gallup survey 2012 shows an interesting relationship between emotional commitment and performance indicators. Teams whose emotional commitment was in the upper quartile demonstrated the following characteristics compared to teams whose emotional commitment was in the lower quartile (Gallup, 2014).[4] Teams with high emotional commitment showed

- 22% higher profitability,
- 21% higher productivity,
- 10% better key customer performance indicators,
- up to 65% fewer fluctuation (depending on the respective industry),
- 48% fewer work accidents,
- 41% fewer quality problems,
- 37% less absence, and
- 28% less waste.

Because the Gallup-results for companies in Germany were only mediocre over several years, the German Federal Ministry of Labour and Social Affairs (BMAS) initiated a research project in 2008 to shed more light on the situation in Germany. The initiated study obtained data from 314 companies of different sizes from twelve industries. The results revealed a significant, positive relationship between employee commitment and organizational performance. To assess organizational culture, the researchers utilized indicators from the *Great Place to Work* survey. They measured organizational performance using a combination of three different quantitative and qualitative indicators. These included economic earning power (in terms of development of sales and EBIT over three years), sickness rate, and fluctuation rate.

The regression analysis results revealed that the culture dimensions explained 31 percent of the variance in organizational performance. Identification with the company had the most significant influence, followed by a sense of community, feeling accepted as a full-fledged member, perceived appreciation and interest in the individual (compared to being a mere production factor), and different dimensions of leadership. Interestingly, the direct effect of the culture dimensions on organizational performance turned out to be less strong than the indirect effect mediated by commitment. This finding implies that the measured dimensions of an organization's culture influenced employees' commitment which, in return, influenced the organization's performance.

Further data analyses show that specific aspects of an organization's culture determined two-thirds of employees' commitment. These were (c.f., Hauser et al., 2008, p. 122):

- Enjoy working in the respective organization.
- Being treated as a full-fledged member.

[4]These findings resulted from 192 organizations in 49 different industries involving almost 1.4 million respondents from 34 countries (Gallup, 2014).

- Being able to rely on cooperation with colleagues.
- The possibility of further developing one's skills and abilities.
- Maintaining and improving quality as part of daily work.

When researchers divided the sample into financially successful and financially less successful organizations, the study found that the financially successful companies had significantly more actively engaged employees (34%) and less acutely dissatisfied employees (14%) than the less successful companies. The latter only had 24% actively engaged employees and, at the same time, almost the same amount of acutely dissatisfied employees (21%). An analysis of the reasons for organizational members leaving the company uncovered that the organization's specific culture caused 32% of resignations. Respondents mentioned a lack of flexible working hours, a missed feeling of being welcomed when joining the organization, a lack of opportunities for professional development, low tolerance for mistakes, little fun at work, and only a few social benefits.

The two meta-analytic studies mentioned above also revealed that the four different types of culture showed somewhat different strategy, organization design, and leadership patterns. Furthermore, they differed in the strength of their relationships to organizational effectiveness criteria (Hartnell et al., 2011, 2019). Clan-type cultures had a stronger correlation with an exploration-type strategy than a market- or hierarchy-type culture. Together with the market- and adhocracy-type cultures, clan-type cultures correlated stronger with an organic structure and had a strong positive relationship with relational leadership. Regarding effectiveness criteria, clan-type cultures strongly correlated with job satisfaction and organizational commitment and had a small but significant association with profit. Market-type cultures showed moderate correlations with exploration strategy, organic design, relational leadership, satisfaction, and organizational commitment. Their correlation with innovation, quality of products, and services were strong yet small with profit. Adhocracy-type cultures had a stronger association with an exploration-type strategy, organic structure, and change leadership. They showed a moderate relationship with job satisfaction, innovation, quality of products and services, and a small association with profit. Hierarchy-type cultures had a stronger correlation with an exploitation-type strategy, a small negative relationship with organic structure, and a moderate correlation with relational leadership. Overall, market-type cultures showed the strongest positive correlations with all five outcome measures.

As mentioned above, the relationship between an organization's culture and organizational success is not only a direct one. It may also be indirect. The following Sect. 5.4. explores this indirect relationship further.

5.4 Indirect Relationships Between Organizational Culture and Organizational Performance

In an indirect relationship, additional factors or variables mediate the relationship between an organization's culture and organizational performance. Hence, culture as measured exerts its influence not directly on performance but through those mediating factors, while a moderator influences the strengths of the relationship between culture and performance indicators. Figure 5.3 shows both kinds of relationships.

Existing research has identified several mediators and moderators that influence the relationship between different dimensions of an organization's culture and organizational performance indicators. Depending on the focus of the research, these are employee engagement, individual and organizational communication, identification with the task and the company, leadership behavior, organizational trust, psychological capital, innovation, organizational learning activities, and customer satisfaction.

In the BMAS initiated study mentioned above, employee engagement was a crucial factor that mediated and even intensified the positive correlation between organizational culture and organizational performance indicators (Hauser et al., 2008). Hence, the cultural dimensions influenced the level of employee engagement that then affected organizational performance accordingly. This indirect relationship between organizational culture and organizational performance mediated by engagement was stronger than the direct influence of culture on performance indicators. Figure 5.4 depicts the correlations of the included culture dimensions with the employee engagement index. All correlations are high for correlational studies.

Communication is another mediator, and moderator that influences the relationship between organizational culture dimensions and performance indicators. In the study by Garnett, Marlowe and Pandey (2008), rule-based organizational cultures influenced communication which influenced perceived organizational performance.

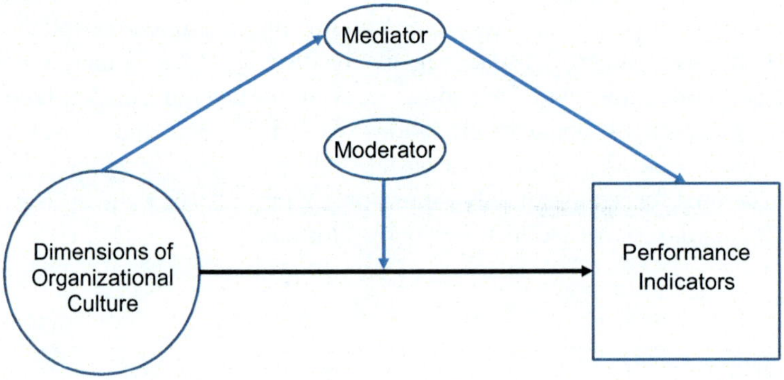

Fig. 5.3 The effects of moderators and mediators on the relationship between culture and performance indicators

Culture dimension (main drivers for engagement)	correlation
Identification	0,77
Team-orientation	0,70
Fairness (fully recognized member)	0,65
Encouragement (appreciation)	0,63
Care (interest in person)	0,62
Leadership: Competence (competent performance)	0,60
Leadership: Integrity (trust)	0,60
Change competence & innovation (developing skills)	0,60
Leadership: Communication (open answers)	0,54
Participation (proposals & ideas by employees)	0,51
Performance-orientation (quality as guiding principle)	0,48
Customer-orientation (meeting customer needs)	0,44

ENGAGEMENT

N = 37.151

Fig. 5.4 Correlation between culture dimensions and engagement (Source: Hauser et al., 2008, p. 126; translated by the author)

However, in goal-oriented cultures, communication directly affected the relationship between culture and organizational performance as perceived by respondents.

In an internal study including the different firms of the Bertelsmann group, the factor *identification with the task and the company* showed a similar effect as employee engagement mentioned above. The analysis of the global survey showed that aspects of the organization's culture influenced employees' identification with the task and their firm, and the extent of respondents' identification was reflected in the performance indicators. This kind of leadership turned out to be an important influencing factor for performance. Firms whose leaders were rated high on participative leadership had employees with the highest level of identification. If organizational members rated the level of participative leadership moderately, the level of identification was equally moderate. In firms with low levels of participative leadership, organizational members' identification with the task and the company was also low. In addition, the results showed that those companies with a high profit margin had leaders high in participative leadership and employees with high levels of identification. In firms with moderate participative leadership and moderated employee identification, the profit margin was moderate. In firms with low levels of participative leadership and employee identification, the profit margin was also low. (Hunsdiek, 2005). Another study found a similar indirect relationship between organizational culture and performance indicators mediated by transformational leadership (Wilderom & van den Berg, 2000).

5.5 Interaction Effects

An increasing number of studies reveal interaction effects between different dimensions of culture and performance indicators. An interaction effect implies that a different kind of culture may have a different impact on a chosen performance indicator. Using the typology of Cameron and Freeman (1991), Ernst (2003) investigated the relationship between the external environment, innovation, and culture type. The results showed that hierarchical-bureaucratic type cultures correlated significantly and negatively with a technologically dynamic environment. In contrast, adhocracy-type cultures characterized by flexibility and entrepreneurial spirit correlated significantly and positively with a technologically dynamic environment. The results also revealed that companies acting in a technologically dynamic environment had significantly more adhocracy-entrepreneurial type cultures than hierarchical-bureaucratic cultures. Furthermore, irrespective of the environment, hierarchical type cultures significantly negatively influenced innovation success, which in return influenced 30 percent of the profitability of new products.

A multiple case study also uncovered an interaction effect between four different organizational cultures and their different effects on knowledge sharing in their respective organization (Wiewiora et al., 2014). The identified cultures differed in their trustworthiness, use of controls, type of structure, the importance of achievement, and competition, focusing on winning.

5.6 Non-Linear and Reciprocal Relationships Between an Organization's Culture and Performance

A few studies and theoretical considerations also suggest non-linear and reciprocal relationships between aspects of organizational culture and performance indicators. The study mentioned above by Ernst (2003) revealed, for example, a non-linear relationship for adhocracy-entrepreneurial types of culture. While adhocracy-type cultures influenced innovation success positively in an early stage, this positive effect reversed at a later stage of an organization's growth. This result suggests that as organizations grow, innovation may require less adhoc behavior and a more stable internal work environment with defined roles and responsibilities. Another study complements these findings: Companies with a strong corporate culture—in terms of shared values—showed a reliable performance as long as they acted in a stable external business environment. However, this positive effect disappeared when they performed in a volatile business environment (Sørensen, 2002).

A reciprocal relationship between organizational culture and organizational effectiveness or performance may explain why companies with long-term success may run into serious problems. While Probst and Raisch (2005) explicitly focused on this question, some of the firms with long-term success included in Peters and Waterman's (1982/2004) research got into trouble or even failed after the study.

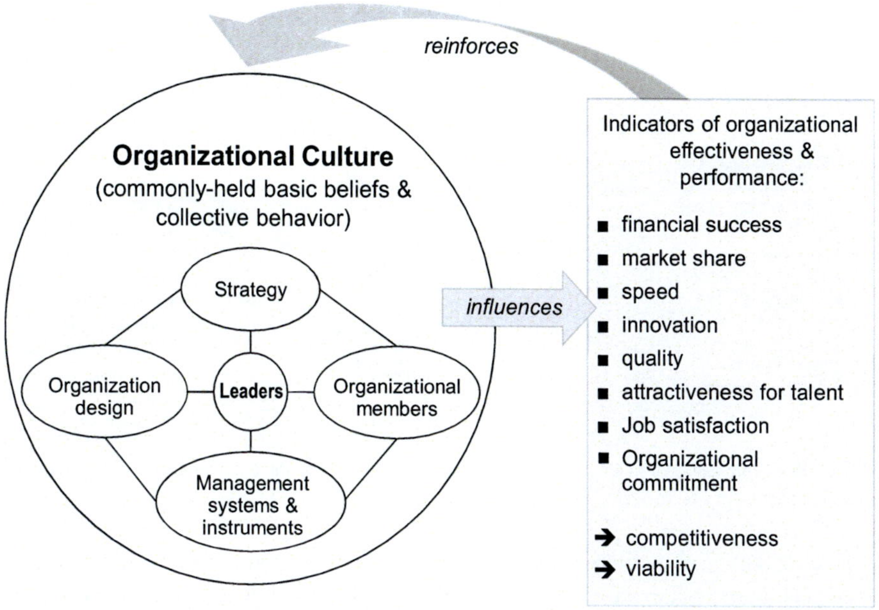

Fig. 5.5 Mutually reinforcing influences between an organization's culture and performance indicators

Rather than changing in time when faced with new environmental challenges, those firms kept applying their proven success recipes. According to learning theory, individuals tend to repeat behavior that has resulted in desired outcomes and thus reinforces the chosen behavior. When applying this principle to organizational behavior, those behavior patterns that have led to the desired outcomes will enforce and reinforce the selected behavior pattern. Accordingly, people use the same behavior pattern repeatedly in the hope and expectation to obtain similar positive results. This process eventually results in recipes of success. On the other hand, if a chosen behavior pattern did not lead to the desired outcome, this kind of behavior will most likely not be repeated and results in failure recipes (see Chap. 3). Figure 5.5 illustrates the basic principle of positive reinforcement.

The development of recipes of success and failure, respectively, is based on this reinforcement principle. If organizations do not regularly question their recipes of success and failure, they may unintendedly isolate themselves from their environment. Influenced by these patterns, organizational members perceive the relevant business environment rather selectively influenced by the organization's culture that may act as confirmation bias. Hence, they notice and search for information that supports their beliefs. Even if the proven practices fail to lead to the desired results, organizational members may find arguments and reasons to explain why, for example, the once successful products and services do not meet the expected sales volume, thus defending their proven practices and beliefs. Figure 5.6 depicts the mutually reinforcing processes, thus complementing Fig. 5.5 with the relevant

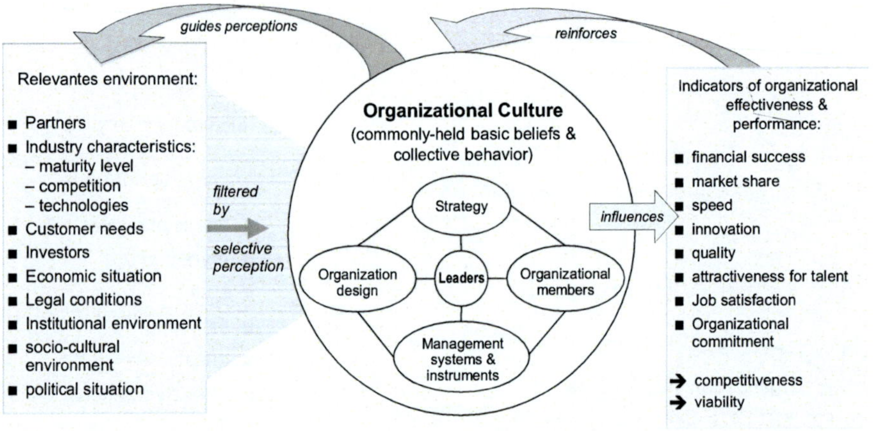

Fig. 5.6 Interdependencies between organizational culture, its environment, and performance indicators

environment and the selective perception of organizational members. In addition, the results of an organization's transformation processes, such as products and services, need to be absorbed by their environment. If practices are reinforced over a longer period, an organization may become increasingly inward-looking and thus acquires autistic features.

5.7 Are *Strong* Organizational Cultures Better?

Several publications and statements suggest that a *strong* organizational culture is essential for an organization's good performance. The notion that culture is the glue of an organization and, hence, important for internal integration and coordination may have promoted this idea. Interestingly, this notion only has been addressed in a few studies that defined and measured cultural *strength* differently. The obtained results are ambiguous. Calori and Sarnin (1991) examined cultural strength in terms of homogeneity as well as intensity. They defined homogeneity as the extent to which organizational members shared the company values and intensity regarding the importance of the organizations' values. Both dimensions correlated significantly with the short-term oriented criteria firm growth, but they did not correlate with the organizations' profitability. In their investigation of insurance companies, Gordon and DiTomaso (1992) measured the strength of organizational culture as the extent to which the employees shared the same perception. Culture strength as measured correlated with growth in insurance premiums and assets, while, at the same time, stability orientation correlated negatively with the two performance indicators.

In their study of ten companies in three different industries, Lee and Yu (2004) measured culture strength with shared perceptions. The results showed that their culture strength measure correlated positively and significantly with return on assets in manufacturing companies and with insurance sum in insurance companies. In hospitals, however, they found no relationship between culture strength and performance indicators. Sørensen (2002) investigated the effect of strong organizational cultures on the variability of firm performance. The results of his study, including a broad range of industries, revealed that in relatively stable environments, strong-culture firms had more reliable/less variable performance. In volatile environments, however, the reliability benefits of strong cultures disappeared. Ernst's (2003) research supports these findings. He found that firms acting in a dynamic business environment had a more flexible adhocracy culture.

Given these few and somewhat ambiguous findings, we suggest to part with the general term of culture strength and substituting it with more precise measures. In line with Chatman and O'Reilly (2016), measures could include consensus and intensity. The *degree of consensus* reflects how widely organizational members share cultural aspects such as beliefs, values, or norms across members. The *degree of intensity* gives insights into how important organizational members consider the cultural beliefs, values, or norms in a given organization.

The various findings and their discussion in this chapter demonstrate the multifaceted nature of the relationship between an organization's culture and organizational performance indicators. Once in existence, an organization's culture influences the entire behavior of its members and thus the collective behavior of an organization. Culture influences the discussions during a strategy development process, and it affects the implementation process. Culture influences the choice of a specific organization design and the respective management systems and management instruments. An organization's culture determines who fits into a given organization and who is considered a good or a not-so-good member or leader. Furthermore, an organization's culture may have a substantial direct, indirect, and non-linear relationship with several performance indicators, reinforcing the collective behavior typical for the organization and its culture.

For all these reasons, it is essential to be or become aware of an organization's culture, its specific characteristics, and its effects on individuals, teams, and the organization. Based on such awareness, one can examine its features if appropriate in a given business environment and for the organization's future. Chap. 6 discusses situations requiring explicit attention to an organization's culture for avoiding an unintended culture drift.

References

Al-Musadieq, M., Nurjannah, N., Raharjo, K., Solimun, S., & Achmad Rinaldo Fernandes, A. (2018). The mediating effect of work motivation on the influence of job design and organizational culture against HR performance. *Journal of Management Development, 37*(6), 452–469. https://doi.org/10.1108/JMD-07-2017-0239

Baetge, J., Schewe, G., Schulz, R., & Solmecke, H. (2007). Unternehmenskultur und Unternehmenserfolg: Stand der empirischen Forschung und Konsequenzen für die Entwicklung eines Messkonzeptes. *Journal für Betriebswirtschaft, 57*(3–4), 183–219.

Balthazard, P. A., Cooke, R. A., & Potter, R. E. (2006). Dysfunctional culture, dysfunctional organization: Capturing the behavioral norms that form organizational culture and drive performance. *Journal of Managerial Psychology, 21*(8), 709–732.

Bhuiyan, F., Baird, K., & Munir, R. (2020). The association between organisational culture, CSR practices and organisational performance in an emerging economy. *Meditari Accountancy Research, 28*(6), 977–1011. https://doi.org/10.1108/MEDAR-09-2019-0574

Calori, R., & Sarnin, P. (1991). Corporate culture and economic performance: A French study. *Organization Studies, 12*(1), 49–74.

Cameron, K. S., & Freeman, S. J. (1991). Cultural congruence, strength, and type: Relationships to effectiveness. In R. W. Woodman & W. A. Pasmore (Eds.), *Research in organizational change and development* (5th ed., pp. 23–58). JAI Press.

Cameron, K. S., & Quinn, R. E. (1999). *Diagnosing and changing organizational culture: Based on the competing values framework.* Jossey-Bass.

Chatman, J. A., & O'Reilly, C. A. (2016). Paradigm lost: Reinvigorating the study of organizational culture. *Research in Organizational Behavior, 36*, 199–224. https://doi.org/10.1016/j.riob.2016.11.004

Cooke, R., & Lafferty, J. (1983). *Level V: Organizational culture inventory (form I).* Human Synergistics.

Dadzie, C. A., Winston, E. M., & Dadzie, K. Q. (2012). Organizational culture, competitive strategy, and performance in Ghana. *Journal of African Business, 13*(3), 172–182. https://doi.org/10.1080/15228916.2012.727737

Denison, D. R. (1990). *Corporate culture and organizational effectiveness*. Wiley.

Denison, D. R. (1996). What is the difference between organizational culture and organizational climate? A native's point of view on a decade of paradigm wars. *Academy of Management Review, 21*(3), 619–654.

Denison, D. R., & Mishra, A. K. (1995). Toward a theory of organizational culture and effectiveness. *Organization Science, 6*(2), 204–233.

Deshpandé, R., & Farley, J. U. (2004). Organizational culture, market orientation, innovativeness, and firm performance: An international research odyssey. *International Journal of Research in Marketing, 21*(1), 3–22.

Deshpandé, R., Farley, J. U., & Webster, F. E., Jr. (1993). Corporate culture, customer orientation, and innovativeness in Japanese firms: A quadrant analysis. *Journal of Marketing, 57*(1), 23–37.

Eberle, T. S. (1997). Cultural contrasts in a democratic nonprofit organization: The case of a Swiss reading society. In S. A. Sackmann (Ed.), *Cultural complexity in organizations: Inherent contrasts and contradictions* (pp. 133–159). Sage.

Ernst, H. (2003). Unternehmenskultur und Innovationserfolg–Eine empirische Analyse. *Zeitschrift für Betriebswirtschaftliche Forschung, 55*(2), 23–44.

Flamholtz, E., & Kannan-Narasimhan, R. (2005). Differential impact of cultural elements on financial performance. *European Management Journal, 23*(1), 50–64.

Gallup. (2014). *Engagement Index Deutschland 2013*. (Chart Meta-Analyse: Weiche Faktoren zahlen sich in barer Münze aus). Gallup Engagement Index Deutschland 2019. Accessed Feb 19, 2021, from www.gallup.de/183104/engagement-indexdeutschland.aspx

Garnett, J. L., Marlowe, J., & Pandey, S. K. (2008). Penetrating the performance predicament: Communication as a mediator or moderator of organizational culture's impact on public organizational performance. *Public Administration Review, 68*(2), 266–281.

García-Fernández, J., Martelo-Landroguez, S., Vélez-Colon, L., & Cepeda-Carrión, G. (2018). An explanatory and predictive PLS-SEM approach to the relationship between organizational culture, organizational performance and customer loyalty. *Journal of Hospitality and Tourism Technology, 9*(3), 438–454. https://doi.org/10.1108/JHTT-09-2017-0100

Gordon, G. G., & DiTomaso, N. (1992). Predicting corporate performance from organizational culture. *Journal of Management Studies, 29*(6), 783–798.

Hartnell, C. A., Ou, A. Y., & Kinicki, A. J. (2011). Organizational culture and effectiveness: A meta-analytic investigation of the competing values framework's theoretical supposition. *Journal of Applied Psychology, 96*(4), 677–694. https://doi.org/10.1037/a0021987

Hartnell, C. A., Ou, A. Y., Kinicki, A. J., Choi, D., & Karam, E. P. (2019). A meta-analytic test of organizational culture's association with elements of an organization's system and its relative predictive validity on organizational outcomes. *The Journal of Applied Psychology, 104*(6), 832–850. https://doi.org/10.1037/apl0000380

Hauser, F., Schubert, A., Aicher, M., Fischer, L., Wegera, K., Erne, C., & Böth, I. (2008). *Unternehmenskultur, Arbeitsqualität und Mitarbeiterengagement in den Unternehmen in Deutschland. Abschlussbericht Forschungsprojekt Nr. 18/05.* Bundesministerium für Arbeit und Soziales (BMAS). Köln: Psychonomics. Accessed Feb 19, 2021, from www.bmas.de/SharedDocs/Downloads/DE/Publikationen/forschungsbericht-f371.pdf?__blob=publicationFile&v=1

Hilman, H., & Siam, M. (2014). The influence of organizational structure and organization culture on the organizational performance of higher educational institutions: The moderating role of strategy communication. *Asian Social Sciences, 10*(13), 142–154. https://doi.org/10.5539/ass.v10n13p142

Homburg, C., & Pflesser, C. (2000). A multiple-layer model of market-oriented organizational culture: Measurement issues and performance outcomes. *Journal of Marketing Research, 37*(4), 449–462.

Hunsdiek, D. (2005). *Messbarkeit von Unternehmenskultur anhand der internationalen Mitarbeiterbefragung*. Presentation given on the 1st Meeting of the International Network Corporate Culture. Gütersloh, Germany, March 2, 2005.

Kabanoff, B. (1991). Equity, equality, power and conflict. *Academy of Management Review, 16*(2), 416–441.

Kotter, J. P., & Heskett, J. L. (1992). *Corporate culture and performance*. Free Press.

Lee, S. K. J., & Yu, K. (2004). Corporate culture and organizational performance. *Journal of Managerial Psychology, 19*(4), 340–359. https://doi.org/10.1108/02683940410537927

Lee, S., Yoon, S.-J., Kim, S., & Kang, J.-W. (2006). The integrated effects of market-oriented culture and marketing strategy on firm performance. *Journal of Strategic Marketing, 14*(3), 245–261. https://doi.org/10.1080/09652540600825548

Lewis, D. S. (1994). Organizational change: Relationship between reactions, behavior and organizational performance. *Journal of Organizational Change Management, 7*(5), 41–55.

O'Cass, A., & Ngo, L. V. (2007). Market orientation versus innovative culture: Two routes to superior brand performance. *European Journal of Marketing, 41*(7/8), 868–887. https://doi.org/10.1108/03090560710752438

Obgonna, E., & Harris, L. C. (2000). Leadership style, organizational culture and performance: Empirical evidence form U.K. companies. *The International Journal of Human Resource Management, 11*(4), 766–788. https://doi.org/10.1080/09585190050075114

Ouchi, W. G., & Jaeger, A. M. (1978). Type Z organization: Stability in the midst of mobility. *Academy of Management Review, 3*(2), 305–314.

Peters, T. J., & Waterman, R. H. (1982/2004). *In search of excellence*. Harper & Row/HarperBusiness Essentials.

Probst, G., & Raisch, S. (2005). Organizational crisis: The logic of failure. *The Academy of Management Executive, 19*(1), 90–105.

Quinn, R. E., & Spreitzer, G. M. (1991). *The psychometrics of the competing values culture instrument and an analysis of the impact of organizational culture on quality of life*. Emerald.

Rohim, A., & Budhiasa, I. G. S. (2019). Organizational culture as moderator in the relationship between organizational reward on knowledge sharing and employee performance. *Journal of Management Development, 38*(7), 538–560. https://doi.org/10.1108/JMD-07-2018-0190

Sackmann, S. A. (2011). Culture and performance. In N. M. Ashkanasy, C. P. M. Wilderom, & M. F. Peterson (Eds.), *Handbook of organizational culture and climate* (2nd ed., pp. 188–224). Sage.

Sørensen, J. (2002). The strength of corporate culture and the reliability of firm performance. *Administrative Science Quarterly, 47*(1), 70–91.

Van der Post, W. Z., Coning, T. J. de, & Smit, E. vdM. (1998). The relationship between organizational culture and financial performance: Some south African evidence. South African Journal of Business Management, 29(1), 30–41.

Wazirman, W., Johannes, J., Edward, E., & Lubis, T. A. (2020). The influence of organizational culture, leadership behavior, civil servants characters, and planning quality of government performance. *Journal of Advanced Research in Dynamical and Control Systems, 12*(3), 628–634. https://doi.org/10.5373/JARDCS/V12I3/20201410

Wei, Y., Samiee, S., & Lee, R. P. (2014). The influence of organic organizational cultures, market responsiveness, and product strategy on firm performance in an emerging market. *Journal of the Academy of Marketing Science, 42*(1), 49–70. https://doi.org/10.1007/s11747-013-0337-6

Wiewiora, A., Murphy, G., Trigunarsyah, B., & Brown, K. (2014). Interactions between organizational culture, trustworthiness and mechanism for inter-project knowledge sharing. *Project Management Journal, 45*(2), 48–65. https://doi.org/10.1002/pmj.21407

Wilderom, C. P. M., & van den Berg, P. T. (1998). A test of the leadership-culture-performance model within a large Dutch financial organization. *Academy of Management Proceedings, 1998* (1), B1–B5. https://doi.org/10.5465/apbpp.1998.27658493

Wilderom, C. P. M., & van den Berg, P. T. (2000). Firm culture and leadership as firm performance predictors: A resource-based perspective. In *Discussion paper 2000–03*. Tilburg University.

Wilderom, C. P. M., Glunk, U., & Maslowski, R. (2000). Organizational culture as predictor of organizational performance. In N. M. Ashkanasy, C. P. M. Wilderom, & M. F. Peterson (Eds.), *Handbook of organizational culture and climate* (pp. 193–209). Sage.

Yilmaz, C., & Ergun, E. (2008). Organizational culture and firm effectiveness: An examination of relative effects of culture traits and the balanced culture hypothesis in an emerging economy. *Journal of World Business, 43*(3), 290–306.

Chapter 6
Situations when an Organization's Culture Needs Special Attention

The culture of organizations is omnipresent and influences organizational members' way of thinking and their actions in their daily work. The extent to which the culture of an organization supports its activities depends on its culture's characteristics. Since culture has developed over time in organizational members' interactions, who passed it on to new members, culture is based on their collective learning experiences. Thus, every organizational culture has a specific history that has shaped its particular characteristics and influences organizational members' current thinking and practices. Therefore, being confronted with a new situation or a change, it is critical to examine whether the specific characteristics of a given culture are appropriate, helpful, neutral, or even obstructive in handling the new situation. This chapter discusses several situations requiring knowledge about an organization's culture to deal with them effectively and avoid an unintended culture drift. These situations may originate from an organization's internal or external environment. Typical triggers for change in an organization's internal environment may include:

- the fast growth of an organization,
- stagnation,
- a change in leadership,
- strategic alliances,
- mergers and acquisitions, and
- internationalization efforts.

Given their importance, the discussion focuses on joint ventures and mergers and acquisitions. The chapter explores the cultural challenges involved when different cultures meet as well as various kinds of mergers and acquisitions and their impact on culture.

Typical triggers for change stemming from the external environment may be:

- Societal changes such as changes in demography and values,
- technological change such as digitization,
- politics and related insecurities including regulatory and legal changes.

S. A. Sackmann, *Culture in Organizations*, Contributions to Management Science,
https://doi.org/10.1007/978-3-030-86080-6_6

The exploration concentrates on societal changes in terms of values, their change over time, the value patterns of different generations, and those represented in today's increasingly diverse workforce. This chapter focuses on the challenges that these internally and externally triggered situations may pose for an organization and its culture. Every one of these situations requires an active engagement with the existing culture as well as management and leadership attention to avoid organizational problems and an untended culture drift.

6.1 Fast Growth

> It is difficult to transport the 10-people-company's spirit into an organization of 20, 30, and 100 people.[1]

Like human beings, organizations also go through a life cycle consisting of several phases (Greiner, 1972). Each phase places different demands and requirements on organizations and their culture. If these specific demands are not anticipated or noticed and tackled in time, growth-related crises may emerge (see Chap. 3). The particular challenge of fast-growing companies is sustaining their specific culture that has helped foster fast growth and passing the cultural specifics on to new organizational members. An organization's rapid growth requires integrating newly hired organizational members into the existing organization and its culture. The story of Boo.com's failure (Spiegel, 2000; Asch, 2000) illustrates problems of fast growth. Boo.com sold fashion on the internet and wanted to develop a global market presence quickly. The start-up, however, could not cope with its rapid growth and finally had to file for bankruptcy. These growing pains (Flamholtz & Randle, 2000; see also Sect. 3.2.3) impact not only finance and logistics, as in the case of Boo.com, they also affect the processes of onboarding, socialization, and integration of new organizational members into the organization and its culture.

Every successful start-up company and more seasoned organization experiences these growing pains in finding, hiring, and integrating new people when they grow fast. The former Nixdorf Computer AG once was one of Europe's most significant and innovative computer manufacturers. In 1972, Nixdorf Computer was present in 22 countries around the globe. Due to its fast growth, it had generated five billion German Marks (about 2.6 billion EUR) in revenues with 30,000 organizational members in 1986. At that time, top executives complained that Nixdorf had lost part of its entrepreneurial spirit due to the immense growth in terms of organizational members. A few years later, Nixdorf Computer lost its independence. Not losing the entrepreneurial spirit is a challenge for all fast-growing companies such as Amazon, Apple, Facebook, or Google.

[1] Bonhage et al. (2002), p. 10). Interview with Peter Pfluger, former CEO and Chairman of the Board of the Phonak-Group).

The more an organization's products and services depend on its organizational members, the more it needs to pay attention to fast growth and the implications for its culture. The growth rate of service-based organizations mainly depends on finding the right people that can deliver the desired quality and understand the essence of the unique services offered by the organization. To act in the spirit of the organization requires knowing the culture and working within its framework. It includes knowledge and appropriate practices in terms of an organization's specific way of dealing with customers. How are services delivered in the spirit of the organization and its culture? What are the main priorities? Which quality standards have to be met? The related collective practices typical for an organization are part of its cultural knowledge, which has yet to be passed on to new organizational members. Without having this cultural knowledge internalized, new organizational members act based on the past experiences they have acquired in other companies and during their formal education and training. Although this kind of general knowledge is precious, it lacks the organization's specific cultural imprint. How are services provided, and how does one deal with customers in the spirit of the organization? Without the organizational culture's unique imprint, the potential competitive advantage of an organization may get lost (Barney, 1986, 1991).

How do newcomers to an organization acquire its specific cultural knowledge? A study by Martin and Siehl (1983) revealed that new organizational members first learn the particular jargon of an organization (see Sect. 2.5.2) since its knowledge is essential for communicating and interacting with colleagues and superiors. The researchers' analysis of companies in Silicon Valley revealed that it took new organizational members about one week to learn the basic jargon typical for the industry and the respective organization. However, knowing the organization-specific label of things, their denotation does not necessarily imply that a new organizational member also understands their respective connotations, their underlying meanings in the organization's context. Becoming a full member of an organization and its culture implies thinking and acting within its specific cultural framework. Such an understanding is gained in a subtle yet thorough enculturation and socialization process during which newcomers turn into fully accepted insiders. Eventually, they let go of prior acquired orientations and practices and start thinking and acting in terms of the specific organizational culture. Once new organizational members have turned into insiders, they no longer need help navigating appropriately through the organization. The chief executive of the hotel chain Upstalsboom, Bodo Janssen, illustrates the difficulties of such a socialization process:

> A while ago, we hired a manager who had worked as associate director in a big hotel chain before. She wanted to continue working with the instruments that helped her succeed in the big hotel chain. She gave, for example, checklists with the daily tasks to the organizational members working at the reception desk. Those shook their heads and said: That's not the way we work here. It was very frustrating for the new manager. Although she got used to our leadership style and adopted it eventually, not everybody succeeds in doing that. Those who fail will leave (Martens, 2016; translated by the author).

Once newly-hired organizational members have internalized the most important characteristics of an organization's culture regarding its core beliefs and related practices, they will guide their perception, thinking, and actions as described in detail in Sect. 2.3.4. Chap. 8 addresses human resource management instruments that may assist in integrating new members into the organization. Selection and socialization processes and selecting people for key positions play an essential role in this process.

6.2 Stagnation

Stagnation is another symptom that requires a detailed examination of an organization's culture. Several cultural factors may lead to stagnation: organizational members may not recognize necessary changes. They may realize a need for change but do not implement it. An organization may lack entrepreneurial spirit and innovation, or its processes are too complicated. In a study of 100 bankruptcies and crashes in which organization's lost at least 40 percent of their value within five years, 20 percent of the sample suffered from the premature aging syndrome. This premature aging syndrome was characterized by stagnating growth and a reluctance to change. Companies belonging to this group, such as Kmart, Xerox, and Eastman Kodak, had stagnating earnings for years. Eastman Kodak ignored, for example, the trend of digital photography and lost 80 percent of its revenue (Probst & Raisch, 2005). Similarly, Nokia, the former global market leader of mobile phones, missed several consumer trends and consequently lost its leading position.

Essential factors that caused such a premature aging syndrome were, amongst others, weak leadership and management. Together with the rest of the organization, they held on to their organization's past successes and did not recognize the necessary changes required for viability. Furthermore, loyalty and trust were culturally more critical in these organizations than setting and achieving ambitious goals. As a consequence, they cut expenditures and staff reluctantly and often too late. Organizational members, including leaders, felt comfortable in this corporate culture (Probst & Raisch, 2005). However, they did not realize that a continuous loss of competitiveness can eventually threaten the organization's viability and its survival. Once signs of stagnation emerge, it is crucial to examine the existing organizational culture critically. Such an examination may reveal areas in need of change. If these are recognized early and followed by appropriate actions, an organization will maintain or regain its competitiveness and viability.

6.3 A Change in Leadership

Another situation requiring attention to culture is a change in leadership. The more visible the position of a leadership change, the more critical is deliberate attention to the organization's culture. If a change occurs at the top level, the new leaders will likely shape the position and organization according to their specific ideas. What is important to the new CEO, director, president, or chairman of the Board? How should the organization be positioned? Which future direction should it take? Which foci and competencies are necessary for achieving these intentions? Which ones are already part of the current organization's culture? Which orientations and competencies are missing and need to be developed or brought in from the outside?

If a change in leadership occurs, all of these questions need to be addressed concerning their impact on the organization's culture and its future development. For example, the following case of Nixdorf Computer AG shows the detrimental effects of a sudden change in leadership. In addition, the business case of Daimler illustrates the different kinds of imprints that leaders may make on organizations.

Nixdorf Computer AG

As mentioned in Sect. 6.1, Nixdorf Computer AG was a significant and highly successful computer manufacturer in the 1980s. At the peak of its success, its founder and CEO Heinz Nixdorf died unexpectedly from a heart attack in 1986. Heinz Nixdorf was a visionary and paternalistic leader with the idea of selling solutions to customers rather than hard-and software. He had developed the organization into a company with four billion DEM (about two billion EUR) in revenues, 172 million DEM (about 95 million EUR) profit, and 23′300 organizational members working in 44 countries in 1985 before his sudden death. His successor Klaus Luft reported record results for 1986 with more than 2.56 billion EUR in revenues and more than 30′000 organizational members worldwide. However, Heinz Nixdorf's death left a leadership void. The new top executive group did not recognize fundamental changes in the computer industry, such as the rapid success of the P.C. and the fast deteriorating margins in a market that became increasingly competitive and turned into a mass market. As a result, they made significant investments without much income. The Board parted with Klaus Luft in 1989, and the company was eventually sold due to considerable losses in the operational business.

Daimler-Benz AG / DaimlerChrysler AG / Daimler AG

For Daimler-Benz, the change in CEO from Edzard Reuter to Jürgen Schrempp entailed fundamental changes both in terms of strategic direction and internal cooperation (see e.g., Grässlin, 1995). Edzard Reuter's idea was to develop an integrated technology company acquiring several technology firms of different industries. However, due to heavy losses, the new CEO Schrempp changed the strategic focus to the core competencies of Daimler-Benz. As a result, non-core businesses eventually were sold, such as AEG, a consumer electronic company, and Fokker, an aircraft manufacturer. In addition, they transferred the larger part of DASA into the European joint venture EADS that became a publicly held company in 2000 and later became Airbus. At the same time, the top executive group with CEO Schrempp extended Daimler's core business: In 1998, Daimler merged with Chrysler; in 2000, Daimler held a stake in Mitsubishi and the Hyundai Motor Company.

(continued)

Schrempp's successor Dieter Zetsche continued this concentration on core competencies selling Chrysler and renaming Daimler AG.

Within the company, the change in top leadership from Reuter to Schrempp led to a restructuring and reorganization of the business units as well as to a shift in the organizational culture towards more innovation, openness, teamwork, agility, performance, and customer orientation ("one company—one vision"). When Zetsche became CEO, he intensified this new focus on teamwork. In addition, he wanted to increase flexibility by introducing principles of collective intelligence and new leadership guidelines, "leadership 2020" (WirtschaftsWoche, 2016).

Given the trend toward e-mobility, Zetsche's successor Ola Källenius announced that Daimler will offer all car models as electronic versions focusing on bigger-sized cars. Furthermore, with the *Project Focus,* he split Daimler AG into two independent companies in 2021, Mercedes-Benz for cars and vans and Daimler Truck for trucks and busses. Daimler Mobility AG will disappear, and the finance- and mobility services will be integrated into the two separate companies (Welt, 2021).

A change in leadership has two potential implications for an organization's culture. On the one hand, it can be used to change the organization's focus and strategy by deliberately introducing a new cultural orientation with a new leader. On the other hand, since newly elected leaders shape their respective position and role in the organization, it is essential that they also take a critical look at the existing culture. For example, is it still appropriate for what the organization wants to accomplish, or does it show signs of a premature aging syndrome? Does it support the necessary developments, or do specific orientations need a rejuvenation? The analysis and evaluation of the organization's culture help to learn about and understand its strength and weaknesses (see Chap. 7). This information will allow initiating appropriate actions to either maintain or further develop certain aspects of the culture (see Chap. 8).

6.4 Joint Ventures (JV)

Joint ventures have become increasingly popular during the past decades for a variety of reasons. Joint ventures are a strategic alliance of two or more organizations that collaborate by founding a new, combined organization. In this new organizational entity, members of two or more organizations meet, who carry their respective cultures. Hence the cultures involved require attention for the effective functioning of a joint venture. The following two sections list the goals of JV and discuss prerequisites for success as well as challenges of JV.s from an organizational culture perspective.

6.4.1 Goals and Prerequisites for Successful Joint Ventures

In general, several reasons may lead to deciding on a joint venture. Organizations involved may

- want to get to know each other better because of a potential future merger or acquisition.
- want to create a platform for knowledge and know-how transfer.
- pool resources because of cost-intensive activities such as research.
- want to create synergies by combining different core competencies.
- want to enter a new market that would otherwise be difficult or not possible. Or
- an acquisition or merger is impossible for political reasons.

No matter the underlying reasons, the parent companies with their different historically-grown cultures transfer several organizational members to work in the JV to succeed. The contractual framework of seconding employees to the JV is crucial for the JV's success since it influences their identification. Do seconded members have a work contract with the parent organization, or do they have it with the JV? The stronger the contractual and the emotional link is to the parent organization, the less likely will they identify with the JV. On the other hand, if the work contract is with the JV for at least some time, it is more likely that organizational members develop an identity with the JV.

In addition to the employment contract, the type of JV is an additional prerequisite for the JV's future success. The latter usually specifies shareholders' power, positions, rights, responsibilities, and accountabilities. Two types of JVs exist regarding shareholdings: JVs with equal or unequal shareholdings. Examples of JVs with equal shareholdings between the partners are the JV between MAN and PON,[2] and the 50%–50% JV between UBER and Volvo to produce driverless cars. In JVs with unequal shareholdings between partners involved, one or more partners dominate a minority shareholder, such as the JV between Google (45 percent) and Glaxo and Smith (55 percent). The two companies agreed on a seven-year JV to produce bioelectric medicines.

The contractual framework influences and shapes all activities and work processes—positively or negatively. When the different parent companies are involved with equal shareholdings, management and leadership positions tend to be equally divided, which may create problems. The percentage of ownership of the organization usually determines the amount of investment, the distribution of critical positions, the market presence, the use of assets and profits, and the bearing of financial losses.

From an organizational culture's perspective, it is important to leverage a JV's potentials. Since a new organizational entity is established with employees seconded from two or more different organizations and their respective cultures, the JV ideally uses their combined strengths and successful practices while avoiding the

[2] www.man.eu DJG/kla/jhe

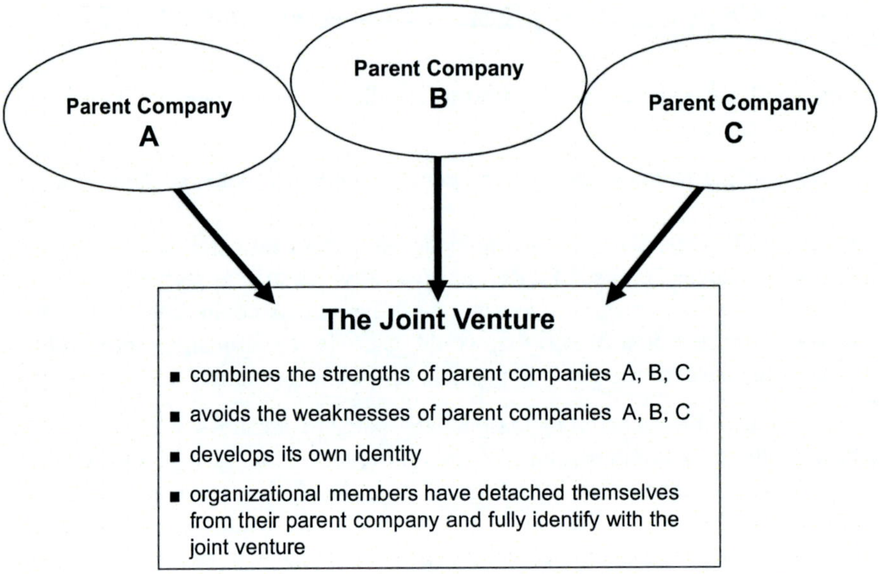

Fig. 6.1 The ideal joint venture and its synergy effects

weaknesses of the parent organizations. Such an ideal situation generates the highest synergies, as illustrated in Fig. 6.1.

Unfortunately, the organizational reality is not always ideal. Several business cases and empirical studies highlight several problems that get in the way of reaching the best of all possible worlds. These cultural challenges need to be overcome for working towards the above-mentioned ideal situation.

6.4.2 Cultural Challenges of Joint Ventures and Ways to Overcome Them

Research in different fields suggests that organizational members' identification with their organization and the JV, their openness toward other ideas and practices, and how cultural dynamics unfold in the newly created JV influence performance. Results from JV research (e.g., Killing, 1983; Cartwright & Cooper, 1996) suggests three critical phases. They pose different challenges that need to be addressed. A study of three international JV labeled these phases as *encounters*, *frame making or frame breaking*, and *consolidation* (Brannen & Salk, 2000; Salk, 1997).

Phase 1, *Encounter*, is characterized by structural and cultural influences. Three critical decisions come up in this phase:

- Where should the headquarters of the joint venture be located?
- In the case of cross-border joint ventures: which language is the official organizational language?
- What kind of career and reward systems will be chosen?

The cultural differences between organizational members of the different parent companies are visible in their behaviors, artifacts, and expectations. The fundamental problems in this phase are associated with organizational members' identities still tied to their parent organization. Their potential mutual stereotyping may lead to in- and outgroup typifications. In such a case, a dominant group within the joint venture is likely to emerge.

During phase 2, *Frame Making or Frame Breaking*, the question arises if the framework conditions for management, work, and interactions developed in phase 1 are maintained or if new identities, behaviors, and guidelines for orientation have to be developed. The critical problem is whether the group dynamics between organizational members of the different parent companies during phase 1 will intensify or if JV members can tackle them constructively and overcome them. The outcome of these negotiations will significantly impact the quality of work, collaboration, and eventually the JV results.

In phase 3, *Consolidation*, two different patterns emerged. The subgroups that had developed during phase 1 either solidified, including the respective identifications of organizational members, or a new jointly negotiated and integrating identity emerged as described in the ideal case above (see Fig. 6.1).

Research in the fields of project management and cross-cultural teams supports these dynamics and their related outcomes. Projects and teams are comparable to JVs since their members come from different functions, organizational units, and nations and need to work together in a newly formed entity. Over time, teams staffed with members from other countries and functions developed into three types of teams that researchers labeled destroyer, equalizer, and creator teams (DiStefano & Maznevski, 2000). Members of *destroyer* teams mistrusted each other, guarded information jealously, and used every opportunity to attack different team members. The performance of destroyer teams was poor, given their mutual stereotyping. The following statement illustrates the quality of their interactions: "Those Brits in our team are too serious. The Germans occupied with their engineering they don't think anyone else has a brain. And the French couldn't care less about production quotas."

Members of the *equalizer* teams felt that they worked well without letting their differences affect their performance. As a result, the team's outcome was satisfying. However, considering all team members' qualifications and know-how, the results were suboptimal and somewhat disappointing.

Members of *creator* teams first addressed their differences and invested time to get to know their differences. They learned to use their differences as a resource for developing better ideas and solutions. Understanding their differences enabled them to utilize these differences in the various project phases. Their specific form of collaboration—being attentive and responsive to each other and further developing other project members' ideas—resulted in synergy effects. Their team results were good, and no single member could have achieved it.

The insights gained from these different streams of research suggest that members of a newly founded JV need to invest time to get to know each other's differences and potential contributions. They need to be sensitive to their differences and learn how to constructively address and deal with their different thinking, working, interacting, and need to accept differing ideas as a vital part of their work. Their interactions require tolerance, trust, and some patience. In the process, a new JV culture will emerge that reflects part of the parent companies' cultures and includes unique features.

6.5 Mergers & Acquisitions (M&A)

Mergers usually take place between organizations considered equal, as illustrated in DaimlerChrylser's announcement of their deal as a *merger of equals*. In acquisitions, the dominant, financially more vital partner usually acquires a financially weaker or smaller organization. M&As were popular strategic choices in the 1960s, the 1990s and have become increasingly popular in the past decade. One recent example is the merger between Fiat Chrysler Automobiles and the PSA Group forming Stellantis N.V. for 52 billion USD in 2021. Furthermore, the major acquisitions of foreign companies by German corporations from 1998 to 2016 (Fig. 6.2) show that companies still consider acquisitions as attractive strategic options.

2016: Bayer increases its takeover bid for Monsanto to 64,8 billion USD and is awarded the contract

2016: the medical corporation Fresenius bought the Spanish hospital Quirónsalud for 5.75 billion USD

2016: the German stock exchange bids on London stock exchange – the planned stock exchange estimates LSE at 13.9 billion USD

2016: the VW subsidiary Truck & Bus buys 16.6% of the shares of the American Truck manufacturer Navistar for 256 billion USD

2014: Bayer buys the US company Merck for 14.2 billion USD in order to extend their product portfolio by over-the-counter medicine and health products

2014: Merck buys the American laboratory supplier Sigma-Aldrich for 16.4 billion USD.

2008: EON buys power plants from ENEL and Endesa in Italy, Spain, and France for 14.3 billion USD

2007: HeidelbergCement buys Hansom for 18.4 billions USD

2006: Linde buys BOC for 15.5 billion USD and becomes global market leader for industrial gas

2001: EON buys the British company Powergen for 15.11 billion USD and enters the US-American market

2000: German Telekom acquires Voicestream for 34 billion USD

1999: Mannesmann buys British mobile telecommunications company Orange for 35.5 billion USD

1999: Vodafone buys Mannesmann for 203 billion USD

1998: Daimler merges with Chrysler by exchanging stock worth 40.5 billion USD (when they separated, the worth had diminished to merely 6 billion USD)

Fig. 6.2 Examples of acquisitions by German corporations

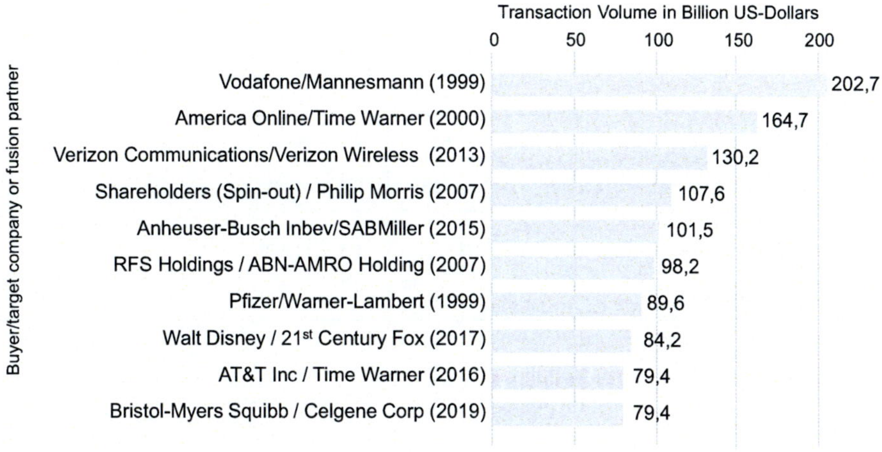

Fig. 6.3 The ten largest mergers & acquisitions worldwide according to their transaction volume (Source: Institute for Mergers, Acquisitions and Alliances: IMAA, 2021)

The transaction volume of the ten largest M&As worldwide (Fig. 6.3) shows the economic factor of M&As.

According to the Institute of Mergers, Acquisitions and Alliances, more than 790′000 M&A transactions have been announced worldwide since the year 2000, with a known value of over 57 trillion USD (IMAA, 2021). And the pace of acquisitions is expected to increase in 2021.

6.5.1 The Role of Organizational Culture in M&As

Several M&A examples show how difficult such a merger or acquisition can become after the companies involved have signed the contracts and the cartel authorities have given their permission. In many business cases, the M&A could not realize the proclaimed synergies. Vivid examples are the cases of BMW-Rover, Glaxo-Wellcome, DaimlerChrysler, or Bayer-Monsanto. Figure 6.4 shows two examples of the loss in market shares and profit compared to the companies' separate existence.

Organizational culture plays a significant role in M&As′ lack of success. According to a study by Ernst & Young (Böhlke & Walleyo, 2007), half of all mergers failed, primarily because of incompatibilities in the human system, including emotional factors. Differing cultures contributed to the failure of M&As due to diverging ideas about goals, priorities, and integration management. The problems tended to be rooted in the pre-merger phase because of limited attention to culture, and they became apparent in the post-merger phase. The respective companies' potentials were not assess professionally, synergies were not identified properly, and company values and financing were not calculated realistically. In addition, the

	Market share after merger (worldwide)		Market share before merger (worldwide)	Profitability (ROI)		
Glaxo + Wellcome	4,87 % (1994)	↓	4,6 % (1998)	12 % (pre-merger)	↓	4 % (3 years after merger)
Smith Kline Beckman + Beecham	3,44 % (1988)	↓	2,9 % (1998)			
Merck (Stand alone)	3,6 % (1990)	↑	4,5 % (1997)			
Pfizer (Stand alone)	2,1 % (1990)	↑	3,3 % (1998)			

Fig. 6.4 Market share and profitability after the merger. (Source: Economist, 1998)

cultural fit and related problems were frequently not assessed. Given the high volume of M&A transactions, the authors consider these mistakes an economic risk factor.

A study conducted by Business Week and Mercer Management Consulting (Zweig, 1995) support these conclusions. The results show that 50 percent of 150 mergers destroyed shareholder value, and a further 33 percent resulted in only marginal improvements. Due to the lack of attention to culture in the pre-M&A phase, several critical issues arose during the post-merger integration phase. An insufficiently managed integration of two different organizational cultures with their respective subcultures led to a strong internal focus neglecting customer demands and losing market share. Productivity and the ability to innovate decreased by 30 percent, fluctuation of organizational members at all levels resulted in the loss of valuable know-how and delays in innovation processes because of insecurities and inconsistencies (Zweig, 1995). In a more recent report, 92 percent of participants mentioned that their merger would have benefitted from a greater understanding of the organizational cultures involved before the merger. And 70 percent reported that not enough focus was placed on the topic of organizational culture during the post-M&A process (Deutsch & West, 2010).

These research results demonstrate that the cultural context of the organizations involved requires special attention before, during, and after signing an M&A contract. Knowledge about the cultural context provides the basis for realizing the expected potentials instead of destroying capital and the goodwill of employees, leaders, customers, and other stakeholders. Even if the strategic fit and financial synergies exist, organizations may decide against a planned merger or acquisition in case of a lack of cultural fit.

6.5.2 *What Happens when Different Organizations and their Cultures Merge?*

M&As can be either friendly or hostile. In both cases, at least two organizations come together with their historically grown cultures and subcultures under the heading of one organization. The future success of M&As depends on several factors influenced by their culture. These are the kind of developed strategy, the chosen organizational design including structures and processes, and the management systems and instruments used or introduced. In general, four potential outcomes may result regarding the cultural reality after an M&A:

- everything stays the same,
- organization A and its culture dominate organization B,
- organization B and its culture dominate organization A, or
- a new culture evolves.

From a strategic perspective, three related integration approaches can be distinguished (Haspeslagh & Jemison, 1991). These integration approaches result from combinations of the two dimensions *of strategic interdependence* between the two organizations involved and the required *organizational autonomy* after a merger or acquisition. Figure 6.5 illustrates these integration approaches including their implications for the organization's culture.

The following sections discuss these potential outcomes focusing on the cultural implications. Since the second and third outcomes are the same situation merely reversed and identical regarding their cultural implications, they are adressed together.

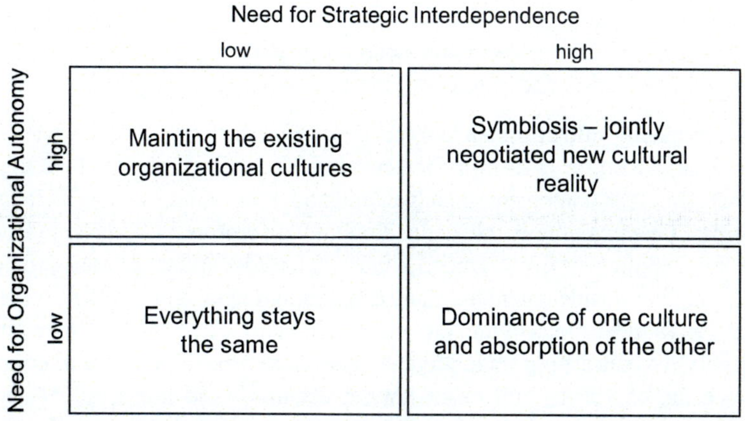

Fig. 6.5 Three types of integration in acquisitions and their implications for culture (expanded and adapted from Haspeslagh & Jemison, 1991, p. 145)

Everything Stays the Same

After an acquisition, retaining the existing organizational cultures is possible and even reasonable if both organizations continue operating in different strategic business areas. Lateral diversification is such a case: a European paper manufacturer buys, for example, a cattle farm in South America. Both companies continue to operate in their respective markets and different industries. The organization's cultures are likely to differ due to their different industry cultures reflected in their operational business. The resulting organization can maintain both cultures without harming the entire organization. On the contrary, trying to align two different organizational cultures in such a case may be counterproductive. It may be helpful if the top executive group decides on key performance indicators for each company to compare their relative performance and contribution to the overall company performance. The resulting organization design is most likely a holding.

Acquisitions based on horizontal diversification are somewhat different. Let's say an automotive manufacturer buys a brand from another car manufacturer. An example is Ford Motor Corporation's acquisition of Jaguar Cars Ltd. Since Ford entered the luxury market segment with this acquisition within the same industry, Ford's top executive group was very keen on communicating that the two companies continued to operate separately. They did not want to damage Jaguar's image (Mocraw, 2000). The media even reported that no Ford employee was allowed to enter the premises of Jaguar except for the CEO. However, a closer look revealed that some Ford managers moved to Jaguar to introduce some of the processes and instruments that had worked well for Ford in the past to raise Jaguar's efficiency. To the outside world, however, they wanted to keep the image of two separately operating companies with separate organizational cultures.

One Organization and its Culture Dominate the Other

Most frequently in M&As, one of the organizations is dominant due to its size, market capitalization, financial power, or know-how. Concerning organizational culture, it is crucial in such a case to know whether the takeover is friendly or hostile. Furthermore, it is essential to assess whether it makes sense that one organization will take a dominant position in deciding about their joint strategy, organizational design and processes, and their management systems.

A dominating role of organization A over organization B can, for example, make sense if organization B is in a financial or leadership crisis and thus depends on organization A's competent management and their financial, as well as human resources. One example is the acquisition and absorption of Zanussi by Electrolux, both home appliances firms. Due to Zanussi's founder and CEO's sudden death, and the succeeding mismanagement, Zanussi got into financial difficulties. Years before, Zanussi's founder voiced the intention to acquire Electrolux after assessing its compatibility concerning their products and market positioning. The compatibility between the two firms still existed when Zanussi's top management approached Electrolux in this critical situation. But now, Zanussi needed financial and managerial support from Electrolux. After Electrolux had agreed to acquire Zanussi, they quickly took all the necessary steps for a turnaround. In this process, Electrolux's management and leaders demonstrated a high level of determinism combined with some cultural sensitivity that contributed to the turnaround's success. Electrolux's leaders quickly replaced the incapable Zanussi management. They introduced needed management systems and their cultural specifics with related practices. They made clear to Zanussi's remaining people what was important to them in their way of operating. In addition, they developed organizational members so that former Zanussi people were later also promoted into management and leadership positions.

In such a case, dominance and absorption are logical decisions, even if they may be initially painful for the acquired organization. If the acquired organization will benefit from acquiring the organization's know-how and culture, it is reasonable to transfer the cultural strengths to the acquired organization. In a friendly acquisition, organizational members are likely to accept new cultural orientations and practices. In former years, General Electric (G.E.) received about 250 requests per year from companies interested in being taken over by G.E., equivalent to more than one request per workday. Based on the acquisition competencies that G.E. had developed over the years, a group of G.E. experts examined the requests applying strict rules to their decision-making. First of all, G.E. only looked at those companies in more detail that would match with its strategic focus and strengthen its market position. Furthermore, the acquired organization should benefit from G.E.'s knowledge and know-how by strengthening its market position and contributing to its bottom line. If companies did not meet these criteria, G.E. denied the request, which happened quite often.[3]

Former CEO and chairman of the Phonak[4] group's Executive Board would "not acquire a company whose organizational culture is opposed to our own" (Bonhage et al., 2002, p. 9). Hence, the degree of fit between the two organizations' cultures should already be examined and evaluated in detail in the pre-merger phase. The result will determine whether it makes sense to acquire a company from a cultural perspective, whether the two cultures require integration, and how risky such an integration would be. Quite a few M&As do not happen because the top leaders decide that an acquisition would be too risky. Toyota, for example, chose to grow internally rather than through acquisitions. They considered it too cumbersome to integrate an organization with a different culture. If Toyota is interested in an organization, they may take a financial stake in the company, get to know the company better, and vice versa. If it turns out to be a good fit over the years, they will increase their investment or fully acquire it (Sackmann, 2005).

In an unfriendly acquisition, organizational members are likely to act defensively toward the acquiring organization and try to hold on to their culture. Hence, the additional subculture may lead to frictions, a lack of information exchange,

[3]Personal conversation between the author and Bernhard Fink, at the time CEO GE Germany.

[4]www.phonak.com

communication, and collaboration combined with feelings of not being welcomed and accepted as full organization members.

Jointly Negotiating a New Culture

Even if a complete cultural integration of both organizations involved may be generally desirable, a symbiosis makes only sense in the case of a high degree of strategic interdependence. Symbiosis implies that the two different cultures form a mutually beneficial relationship. The expectations are that the new organization with its symbiotic culture will be much stronger due to its combined skills, business areas, or markets. Ideally, all these aspects complement each other. One example of a successful merger is the pharmaceutical company Novartis that resulted from Ciba-Geigy merging with Sandoz. The two top executives knew each other for several years before the merger. In secret meetings, they developed the new organizational design and thought about staffing important positions before announcing the merger. They had decided whom they wanted to keep and whom to offer which key positions. They chose a new name for the merged organization to symbolize a new, joint beginning and communicated it to both the inside and the outside world.

The cultural challenges of integrating two equally strong organizations and their cultures are similar to those of joint ventures. The critical difference is the entire organizations are involved instead of separated organizational units. How can two or more organizations with their distinct history and culture grow together and benefit from each other's strengths? How can they develop synergies while avoiding or reducing frictions due to their differences? The three potential cases and their respective outcomes may be:

1. The merger of the two different organizations is unsuccessful due to mutual distrust and lack of effort to understand and learn from each other. Organizational members hold on to *their* organization's culture and emphasize the existing differences, making these differences seem bigger than they are. Organizational members still—sometimes ostentatiously—identify with their original organization while distancing themselves from the others, and they apply stereotypes to their colleagues from the formerly other organization. The result is a rather hostile and challenging situation with negative impacts on performance at the individual, group, and organizational levels.
2. The merger of the two organizations is suboptimal since existing organizational members ignore differences due to their need for harmony. "We are all the same", "we have overcome our differences" are typical statements. Everybody holds back during daily work processes, trying to respect the others with their different ideas and ways of working rather than initiating necessary but difficult discussions. Hence, problems are covered rather than openly addressed. Synergy cannot emerge because organizational members don't know each other culture's strengths or weaknesses or address them openly. They still identify more with their original organization than with the new organization. The resulting performance is suboptimal given the potentially available cultural strengths, knowledge, and know-how of both organizations.

3. The merger of the two different organizations and their culture leads to synergies. Organizational members take time to know each other's cultural strengths and weaknesses and the existing differences. They make efforts to leverage both their these strengths. They avoid their weaknesses in a constructive and complementary way while focusing on their common goal to succeed together. They may still identify with the former organization to some extent but gradually develop an increasingly stronger identification with the new, joint organization and its jointly negotiated culture. The resulting performance tends to be high at all levels.

For achieving a cultural symbiosis and reaping the benefits of the organizations' cultures, activities in the pre-and, especially in the post-M&A phase, are essential.

6.5.3 Creating Conditions for a Successful Culture Integration

Several studies suggest that the performance of a strategic alliance tends to be better if the intentions for the joint venture, merger, or acquisition are clear and carefully thought through (Koller et al., 2015) in the pre-M&A phase. When Kraft Heinz withdrew its takeover bid for Unilever in 2017, the underlying reason was probably their respective cultures. Even external experts viewed them as being too different. Furthermore, knowing the strategic and cultural fit of the organizations involved and considering this information when deciding about the acquisition and the integration approach helps create conditions for a successful M&A (Weber, 2012; Weber & Tarba, 2012). Compiled findings from 600 companies and 6000 strategic alliances over 15 years revealed that the integration process contributed mainly to the more than 50 percent failure rate of those strategic alliances (Harbison & Pekar, 2000). About half of them had lost half of their market value since June 1998. Hence, after having signed the contract, the big challenge remains the actual integration of the organizations involved with their cultures. Based on their findings, the authors suggest the following actions as prerequisites for successful integration:

- developing a clear vision,
- deciding the leadership responsibilities,
- utilizing synergies,
- striving for profit early in the process,
- limiting risks,
- overcoming cultural differences, and
- communicating effectively.

Several studies of M&A integration processes point to similar actions needed in a post-M&A integration phase. For example, in an investigation of 103 mergers, respondents considered two actions most vital: quick decisions regarding key leadership and management positions and creating and implementing an internal and external communication strategy (Jansen & Körner, 2000). Other factors such as

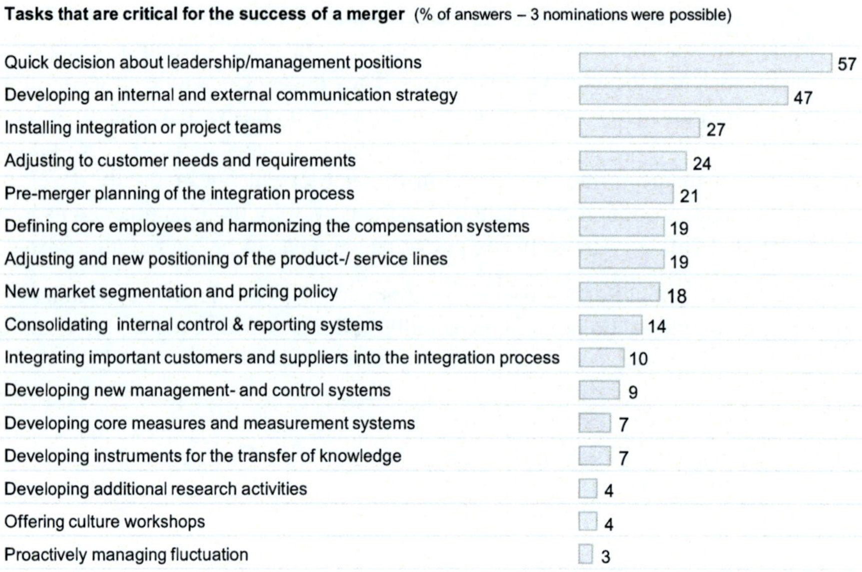

Fig. 6.6 Success factors of mergers (Source: Jansen & Körner, 2000; own translation)

installing integration- or project team, and the pre-merger planning of the integration process, were considered less important, as shown in the responses listed in Fig. 6.6.

If the decision-makers decide to integrate an acquired organization and its culture, they ideally start thinking about the future organization's design and staffing of key leadership positions before announcing the merger or acquisition, as was the case with Novartis. Merging with or integrating an organization that has operated independently before usually has all functions and positions assigned. Once the intention of a merger or acquisition becomes public, highly qualified organizational members may test their market value. They are likely to leave if they don't know their responsibilities in the future organization. Hence, the decision-makers need to inform those organizational members they want to keep after the merger or acquisition and discuss their potential roles. It is also important to realize that the acquirer must not discard everything of an acquired organization and its culture. The acquired organization may have valuable knowledge, practices, and processes from which the acquiring organization may benefit. Recognizing the cultural strengths of the acquired organization and existing complementarities and leveraging them will contribute to the success of an acquisition.

In cross-border M&As, the integration process follows the same path even though different cultures at the national level are involved. A few studies suggest that differing cultures at the organizational level have a stronger influence on the resulting success or failure in an integration process than cultural differences at the national level (e.g., Gerhart, 2009; Nelson & Gopalan, 2003). Hence, it is important to know the culture of the organizations involved.

A study of M&A practices and skills uncovered interesting cultural differences between successful and unsuccessful organizations (Doherty et al., 2015). Those 464 organizations that exceeded their cost and profit targets within five years evaluated their strategic options several times per year. The other 302 companies neither met their cost nor their profit targets within five years. According to respondents, the successful companies demonstrated significantly higher competencies in searching and initiating an acquisition, closing the deal, and integrating the two different organizations and their culture. Furthermore, the successful companies needed less time from the initial contact to the binding bid, indicating a more goal-oriented search and knowledge regarding the requirements of a good acquisition.

These results support the recommendation that successful M&As start with gaining detailed knowledge of the organizations' cultures involved. Chap. 7 addresses this issue.

6.6 International Expansion

Globalization affects large corporations as well as small and medium-sized organizations that face the question of how to leverage the opportunities of global markets and how to expand in different markets around the globe. They can choose from several internationalization strategies to enter new markets. These range from international distribution managed headquarters, opening production facilities abroad, to establishing independent subsidiaries in different countries. These strategies are well-documented and discussed in the respective literature with their advantages and disadvantages for vrious industries (e.g., contributions in Schmid, 2018).

From an organizational culture perspective, two critical and related questions arise: To what extent does the parent company need to transfer its culture to foreign business units? To what extent does the organization need to be open to the specifics of culture at the regional and national levels? The answer to these two questions may significantly impact the organization's effectiveness and performance in the different regions and countries. On the one hand, an organization wants to transport and keep its identity, image, and brand worldwide and be recognized for its products and services. On the other hand, it needs to be sensitive and responsive to local cultural specifics. Hence, the big challenge is finding a culturally appropriate balance between the organization's needs and global and local requirements. Furthermore, an organization must distinguish between its products and services as manifestations of its culture and its members' interactions within the organization and with external stakeholders (Sackmann, 2010).

Regarding products and services, the following principle may serve as orientation: the more products or services influence local customers' everyday lives, the more they are part of their daily practices, the more critical is cultural sensitivity to local practices and traditions. To give some examples: In extreme temperature differences and streets in bad shape with many potholes, local customers will need robust cars that can withstand the temperature differences and bad roads. In narrow streets and small parking spaces, customers are likely to want small cars and mopeds. If a company sells blenders, those countries and regions are most interesting for market expansion where typical dishes require mixing. The preparation of sushi or sashimi, for instance, does not need a blender.

However, customers also buy certain products because of their country of origin or their brand. The labels "Made in Germany" or "Made in Switzerland" still stand for high quality and technical precision (e.g., Breiding, 2013). Related products are cars, special instruments, and watches and tend to be in the high price segment. These visible manifestations deliberately demonstrate their country of origin because customers associate them with high quality and a certain status. They buy global brands such as Coca-Cola for their associated lifestyle. Hence, organizations should not adjust these products to local specifics.

When interacting with the local organizational members, different worlds may collide in an initial stage. If members are strongly influenced by and attached to their local culture, they will expect their employer to adapt to local customs. These refer to compensation practices, management systems, working time, work processes, behavior at work, interpersonal interactions, and leadership behavior. Hence, transferring management systems, working standards, and rules for behavior such as codes of conduct from the headquarters to subsidiaries in different countries may become culturally challenging, as several studies document. For example, Yousfi (2011) describes the difficulty in introducing American management techniques such as goal setting in a Tunisian organization. Its employees only accepted the tool once it was adjusted and reinterpreted to fit local cultural standards of good management. Likewise, the study of a US-based multinational firm reveals the many and rather complex intercultural challenges in implementing its code of conduct in its European subsidiaries (Barmeyer & Davoine, 2011). The authors conclude from their case study that it may be impossible to standardize the culture of a multinational organization with an instrument that is rooted in the cultural history of the parent company and profoundly impacts local culture with its different institutional environment.

Hence parent organizations need to carefully examine how they can adjust their culture's rules, systems, and practices to fit the different cultural frameworks and deal with expectations resulting from the local culture. If, for example, expectations regarding punctuality, quality, and work behavior differ due to different regional or national cultures, parent organizations need to communicate these expectations carefully and in a way that local organizational members can relate to and comprehend.

In the above mentioned cross-border acquisition of Zanussi by Electrolux (Sect. 6.6.2), the Swedish acquiring firm Electrolux had different understandings of, for example, punctuality and working time than organizational members from the acquired Italian firm Zanussi. Electrolux explained the meaning and importance of punctuality and practiced their culture daily by showing up exactly on time for work and meetings. Due to this role-modeling behavior, Zanussi's people quickly adjusted and changed their related behavior. Furthermore, organizational members' adherence to the expected standards of conduct needs to be monitored regularly with feedback to the local workforce. The parent company's expectations regarding organizational members' degree of emersion in an organization and its culture may also differ from the local culture. For example, in Germany, people appreciate separation between work and private life (Trompenaars, 1994). In contrast, organizational members in other countries and cultures, such as China or Russia, may expect their employer to also deal with family issues.

If it is essential to an organization that its central cultural beliefs are practiced worldwide, it needs to provide support. Such support includes discussing and explaining these beliefs and related practices in the local context and exploring their implications for different functions and roles. Consequently, the local organizational members will not only know the relevant labels of proclaimed values, such as teamwork, innovation, or participatory leadership. They will also learn the underlying meaning of these labels and their implications for their daily work practices. Such process requires dialogue in which members of the parent organization explain the meaning of the central beliefs and enrich them with examples that fit with the local culture. This dialogue will help local organizational members to understand their meaning and implications for their local work practices. The Chairman of Grundfos, the largest pump manufacturer worldwide based in Denmark, perceived one of his roles as a cultural ambassador. He visited all Grundfos organization sites around the globe at least once a year. During these visits, he discussed the values important to the parent organization and filled them with life. This discussion made them more understandable to the local organizational members (Sackmann & Bertelsmann Foundation, 2006).

6.7 Societal Changes

Societal developments also require a critical look at an organization's culture. Of particular interest are age demographics and social values since they have implications for the composition and expectations of the workforce. In the following section, age demographics are briefly discussed with their implications for an organization's culture. Given the increasing diversity in our workforce, a more detailed exploration focuses on changes in social values. This discussion includes differences among generations and different value patterns in the workforce. The resulting expectations have several implications for organizations and their culture.

6.7.1 Demographic Change

The demographic developments related to age are well-known. People now entering the job market were born at least two decades ago, and various statistics report their numbers. The retiring generation of organizational members is offset by a much

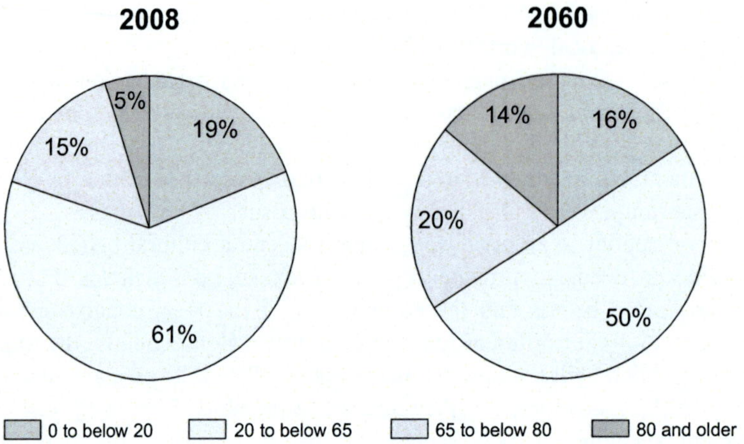

Fig. 6.7 Population according to age groups (Germany 2008/2060) (Source: Statistisches Bundesamt, 2009, p. 16)

smaller number of young people in Western countries, who are needed despite increasing automation. Figure 6.7 illustrates the changing distribution of age groups comparing 2008 to 2060 for Germany. This distribution between age groups is likely to be similar for many Western countries.

Apprenticeship positions in Germany remain vacant, and the lack of qualified workers is already slowing the growth of many companies. According to a recent study by the German Chamber of Industry and Commerce (DIHK), almost every second company cannot fill vacancies in the longer term. There was a shortage of around 440,000 qualified workers in 2018. This shortage of skilled workers is estimated to reduce economic output by 0.9 percent, corresponding to approximately 30 billion EUR (DIHK, 2018). Further consequences are an additional burden on the existing workforce as well as a loss of innovation capacity. Therefore, organizations may have to tap into the potential of qualified retired professionals. Some companies such as Bosch report good experiences in including retired experts and managers in their work processes (Schrödl & Hanen, 2019).

Consequently, the "war for talent" proclaimed at the beginning of the millennium (Michaels et al., 2001) is still ongoing. Many companies search for employees with similar qualifications, such as a STEM.[5] Engineers and computer scientists are in short supply, and even large corporations have problems filling vacant positions. It is yet unknown to what extend the inflow of educated immigrants and refugees from different parts of the world will influence the demographic development in Western societies and the availability of qualified people.

The future workforce will span wide age ranges with people having different skills and value-influenced expectations regarding their employer, work, and

[5] STEM stands for science, technology, engineering, and mathematics.

leadership. If an organization wants to stay attractive to qualified people, its culture needs to be responsive to the expectations of such a diverse group.

6.7.2 Changing Values

Values and their changes play an essential role for both customers and organizational members. The customers' values influence their needs, desires, interests, and expectations concerning products and services. An example is a growing desire to purchase healthy food even at a higher price. The personal values of organizational members influence their expectations regarding their employers' culture. These include expectations about the work environment, leadership behavior, job design, working time, physical working place, and remuneration. Hence, people's value sets are likely to influence their choice of favorite employer.

People acquire personal values in socialization processes in the family and educational settings, thus reflecting societal values (see e.g., Inglehart, 2008; Nextpractice, 2016; Paine Schofield & Honoré, 2011; Spickenreither & Sackmann, 2019). Societal values are a mixture of the current zeitgeist and values typical for the region and the respective nation. Since the 1950s, Western societies have experienced a move from materialistic to post-materialistic values. Until the 1960s, our Western societies were characterized by rather traditional, conservative values like survival, safety and security, discipline, loyalty, obedience, and duty. In work organizations, these values became manifest in patriarchal structures and a directive or patriarchal leadership behavior. However, the student revolution in the late 1960s initiated a democratization process that comprised all areas of life—family and child-rearing, schooling, education, training, and work organizations—and that influenced the respective practices. In this democratization process, post-materialistic values became more important. These are autonomy, loyalty towards oneself, self-actualization, enjoying life, and life balance. Table 6.1 gives a rough overview of the different generations, their formative experiences, their orientation towards work and life, their preferred technologies, and their means of communication.

Due to this shift in societal values, individuals' expectations towards work, their potential work organization with its culture and leadership have changed considerably in the last decades. Formerly, most organizational members being part of the traditionalist generation, were interested in job security and life-long employment. Members of younger generations such as generations X, Y, and Z want their expectations and needs met. Since members of all five generations or age cohorts, listed in Table 6.1, may be present and active in organizations, the resulting workforce is diverse. They have different value patterns resulting in different expectations towards work and their workplace. They prefer to communicate somewhat differently with different kinds of technologies.

This move from materialistic to post-materialistic values includes increasing individualism (e.g., Flamholtz et al., 1986; EVS, 2016; Nextpractice, 2016).

Table 6.1 Different generations and their orientations

	Traditionalists (up to 1955)	**Baby Boomer (1956–1965)**	**Generation X (1966–1980)**	**Generation Y (1981–1995)**	**Generation Z (from 1996 on)**
Formative experiences and influences	2nd World War, hard work and depriviations	Economic boom, social upheavals, student revolution, women's movement	«Generation Golf», television age, fall of the Berlin wall and the iron curtain, end of the cold war	«Millenials» Digital revolution,world-wide terror	«Generation YouTube», Globalization, climate change, Wikileaks
Orientation towards work and career	Work to finance livelihood	Work is important—coined the term workaholics	Life-balance: Professional career as important as private life	Work has to be fun, career is not so important, work and private life are not strictly separated	Fixed boundaries, clear structures, separation between work and private life
Orientation toward life, values	Conformity, obedience, respecting rules and authorities	Assertiveness, team spirit, idealism, protest	Independence, individualism, love of freedom, search for meaning	Self-actualization, freedom, living in the here and now	Self-actualization both in private and social sphere, authenticity, honesty
Use of technology	No to little relation to technology	New technology is used in the work context	Technological change from analogue to digital, tech-savvy	Digital natives: «24 hours online»	«Technoholics»: Virtual reality, cloud, music stream
Communication	Face-to-face	Face-to-face, telephone	SMS, email, messenger	Social media, messenger	FaceTime, messenger
Preferred media	Preference for traditional media (newspaper, phone, etc.)	Email, dialy newspaper, radio, TV, Facebook	Email, Facebook, TV, online-news	Twitter, Instagram, Facebook	Snapchat, Spotify, Wisper, YouTube, Tumlr

Hence, people want to be recognized as unique individuals with their interests, strengths, and weaknesses, and they expect to be treated accordingly. This change in expectations has implications for an organization's culture, especially human resource management, leadership practice, and an organization's design. A uniform and standard treatment of organizational members of a diverse workforce are no longer most effective. Results of collective bargaining processes meet the needs of a diverse workforce less and less. Instead, differential treatment of organizational members becomes increasingly essential as suggested in the concept of *differential human resource management* (Morick, 2002). Examples for differential human resource management are:

- individualized work contracts that consider the different needs of each individual;
- remuneration systems that meet the needs of various organizational members' including their changing needs over different life stages. Examples are *cafeteria systems* (e.g., Nieżurawska et al., 2016);
- leadership behavior acknowledges and considers organizational members' strengths and weaknesses, unique talents, development needs and interests, and specific life situations.

Example of Cafeteria Systems

The software company SAP offers organizational members a cafeteria system with a range of fringe benefits from which employees can flexibly choose according to their individual needs and circumstances. The system consists of two parts: one financed by the company and the other by organizational members. They decide about using the firm's yearly contribution either for their retirement plan or specific insurance such as disability insurance. Regarding their financed part, employees choose how much of their performance-related variable income they receive now or later. In addition, employees with three or more years of tenure qualify for a company car. The model is well received: 70 percent of organizational members who are eligible make use of the cafeteria system (Dilk, 1999).

Depending on the national labor and tax laws, organizations may offer products, services, or vouchers in addition to financial compensations and paid time off. Examples are contributions to child care, fitness studios, health checks, meals, or housing loans. The U.S. company DreamWorks SKG once scored with new organizational members by offering a remuneration package that, amongst others, offered a service that regularly stocked their refrigerator with their favorite food items.

Hence, the time of the *organization man* (Whyte, 1956) is gone. It has been replaced by generations guided by an orientation labeled as *what's in it for me*

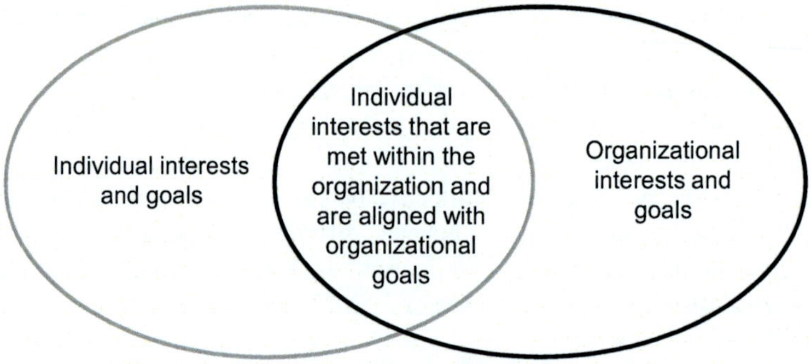

Fig. 6.8 Aligning personal interests and goals with organizational interests and goals

(Yankelovitch, 1981). As compared to Baby Boomers, members of the *GenMe,*[6] including generation Y and Z are more willing to change their jobs if employers do not meet their needs regarding personal development, advancement, or life balance. If organizations want to stay attractive for the talent of different generations, they need to be responsive to the interests of current and future organizational members.

Aligning these individual interests and goals with those of the organization thus becomes a crucial task for leaders. As indicated in Fig. 6.8, they have to actively work on achieving a reasonable overlap between their organizational members' interests and those of the organization.

Once established, the alignment of personal interests and goals with those of the organization cannot be taken for granted. Instead, developing and maintaining this overlap and alignment is an important, ongoing leadership task requiring appropriate communication and dialogue with organizational members. Leaders need to convey to their people how and to what extent they can fulfill their interests within the organization's context while meeting organizational goals during their daily work activities. However, achieving and maintaining such an overlap and alignment requires knowledge about employees' goals and interests and their strengths and weaknesses.

Several studies point to the increasing diversity in societal values even within one generation. These become manifest in different expectations, interests, and desires that people have regarding their work-life. A survey conducted among 20′000 graduates revealed three different types of professional goals (Wottawa et al., 2011):

- 38 percent were extrinsically motivated: They wanted to work to achieve goals; money and power played an essential role; ethics, fun, and the need for leisure were less important.
- 33 percent strove for self-actualization; friends and hobbies were important; money and power were secondary.

[6] *GenMe* stands for Generation Me.

- 29 percent were intrinsically motivated: they strove for fulfillment in their profession; important goals were power, image, ethics, and fun at work; hobbies, friends, and money were less important.

A government-funded values study using qualitative and quantitative data from 1200 respondents of Germany's working population reveals the diverse values in organizations. The results yielded seven different value patterns (Nextpractice, 2016):

1. Being able to live from work without worries (28 percent).
2. Working hard to achieve prosperity (15 percent).
3. Finding work-life balance (14 percent).
4. Searching for meaning outside of work (13 percent).
5. Achieving top performance with commitment (11 percent).
6. Finding self-actualization in work (10 percent).
7. Working in a strong community of solidarity (9 percent).

Similar value patterns are likely to exist in other countries with different priorities and distributions among value patterns. Furthermore, the results also revealed that the current organizational reality differs largely for the majority of respondents from their expectations towards work and work organizations. Table 6.2 summarizes some of the implications that the seven different value sets and their characteristics may have for an organization's culture and leadership. The column *characteristics* contains verbal statements that are typical for people adhering to the respective value pattern.

In addition to value differences between and within different generations, the study mentioned above, the 20′000 graduates supported the shift towards more post-materialistic values. Also, it revealed gender differences in value priorities (Wottawa et al., 2011). Female graduates mentioned the following priorities in their life-goals listed according to importance: Being able to realize their ethical claims was most important to them followed by a profession with a good image, being able to spend enough time with their family and hobbies, having fun at work and making money, and having influence. Male graduates showed almost the reversed sequence in priorities: Having time for their hobbies was most important to them, followed by making money, having an influential position, having sufficient time for family and friends, fun at work, a good professional image, and ethical standards.

The results of the studies mentioned above have three significant implications for organizations, their culture, and leaders:

1. organizations need to carefully select new people whose values fit with the current or intended culture.
2. An organization's culture and subcultures need to accommodate organizational members' differing needs and interests; and
3. Leaders need to be aware of these different value patterns and associated interests. They need to know the potentially different expectations that organizational members have depending on their life stage and situation. In addition, they

Table 6.2 Seven different value patterns, their characteristics and their implications for organizations, their culture, and leadership

Value pattern	Characteristics	Implications for organizations, their culture and leadership
Being able to live from work without worries (28%)	"It is important that my family can live without financial worries in a secure community. Work is part of life, but it tends to leave too little time for life outside of work. Life becomes more hectic with an increasing pressure to perform. Government should provide a secure income for those who contribute." • Material and traditional values such as security, diligence, sense of duty; recognition, accept set rules; prefer stability over change.	Provide a secure workplace with job security and a stable work environment; clear structures, rules and responsibilities; Focus on clear goals and performance, guaranteed compensation; Appreciate performance.
Working hard to achieve prosperity (15%)	"Naturally, work as become harder and it's not always fun. But I think that everyone who makes a real effort can achieve something. And when you've made it, you're allowed to indulge and treat yourself to some luxury. Top performers need to have a place in society." • Material and traditional values; acceptance of set rules; performance orientation; financial recognition; indulgences.	Provide a thriving and growth-oriented organization and work environment with a focus on performance; Provide opportunities to contribute; Delegate responsibilities and provide large latitudes of freedom at work based on mutual trust and respect; Tolerance for diversity; Variable pay component; pay for performance
Finding work-life-balance (14%)	"I want to align work, family and self-actualization. For me, personal responsibility and social participation go hand in hand. After all, it is a joint task to create good conditions for all. The system should adjust to people and not vice versa. I don't want to throw my principles overboard for some material security." • traditional values with a focus on balance between work, family and personal interests. Human orientation.	Provide people-oriented work and work place; Assign jobs according to strength and interest; Provide regular and flexible working time and hybrid work to accommodate changing needs and interests of organizational members (working 9 to 5, time off for family events; sabbaticals, etc.); Select new people carefully, provide transparent information upfront so that they know what to expect and to what extent they can realize their principles in the organization.
Searching for meaning outside of work (13%)	"I don't believe that the meaning of life should be sought only in gainful employment. All activities are equally valuable as long as they contribute to the Well-being of all.	Provide contractual arrangements; Agree mutually on goals, check work progress regularly and give regular feedback;

(continued)

Table 6.2 (continued)

Value pattern	Characteristics	Implications for organizations, their culture and leadership
	Humanity can become visible also in small and very personal things." • work is a job that serves to finance personal interests; human orientation; depending on the person: Social-, leisure-, health-, being challenged- orientation.	Negotiate working- and vacation time; provide hybrid work.
Achieving top performance with commitment (11%)	"Responsibility and a leading position don't mean pressure for me but pure adrenalin." I like to push myself to high performance. In view of digitization, life-long learning is a must." • performance, learning, and personal development orientation; seeks challenges; change oriented; does not accept the status quo.	Provide a challenging workplace with challenging tasks and stretched goals; Offer positions with high responsibility and leadership; Delegate responsibilities; involve people in strategic discussions and exploration of future opportunities; Provide latitudes of freedom for action; Providing appropriate resources; offer partnership or financial stake in the company.
Finding self-actualization in work (10%)	"We are moving towards a global working world in which you can invent yourself again and again with almost unlimited possibilities. It's a give and take: Society and employers support people on their way, for example, by providing flexible working conditions and childcare and organizational members show performance." • self-actualization; learning oriented; seeking challenges; family- or self- oriented	Provide an interesting, development-oriented workplace; Give transparent information in the hiring process so that people know if their interests can be met in the organization; Create opportunities for regular dialogue, feedback, and further development; Person-oriented leadership with regular alignment between personal and organizational goals; Offer flexible working time and hybrid work; cafeteria compensation system
Working in a strong community of solidarity (9%).	"Work for me is associated with loyalty, appreciation, participation, mutual trust and cohesion in a community of solidarity. Material values are important but not exclusively. In former years, companies still had the welfare of people in mind and there was work for everybody. Now, an increasing number of people no longer find work. This development worries me." • community oriented; combining material values with welfare for all.	Provide people-oriented work- and job design; Create opportunities for regular dialogue and feedback, time and space to mingle with colleagues; Arrange/allow social events; Provide flextime and hybrid work; Show personal and financial appreciation; Fixed salary with a bonus.

need to create and maintain an organizational context that meets those expectations both to attract and retain qualified people.

Given the diverse value patterns in the workforce, organizational cultures attractive to younger talent are responsive to individuals' desires for open, honest, and transparent information and communication. They allow possibilities for cooperation and participation, provide feedback and opportunities to develop. They act transparent with good governance and take ethical responsibility towards the society and its ecological environment.

Overall, the increasing diversity in values poses several critical questions for organizations and their culture that require answers and knowledge of the organization's culture. What kind of diversity does an organization want to have in its workforce? What kind of personal values fit with the organization's culture or subculture, and which ones should new organizational members hold and live by? How much diversity in personal values does an organization want, how much can it handle, and how can it handle the existing diversity?

6.8 Technological Changes: Digitization

With the commercial use of the internet, digitization has found its way into our lives. Technological developments will continue to emerge and find their way into organizations, thus influencing their culture. E-commerce and social exchange via mobile tools have become an integral part of our lives. The options offered by the internet have changed companies' sales channels as well as their entire business processes fundamentally. Digital tools such as smartphones and tablets have enabled the collaboration of people without considering physical locations. Our societies and organizations are in the midst of a digital transformation (Baller et al., 2016).

Digitization refers to applying digital tools and technologies for organizations' business models, service portfolios, and work practices. Digital technologies can be grouped into five areas: Interconnectedness and availability (mobile, IoT, Cloud computing); information and intelligence (big data analytics); automation and efficiency (robotics, artificial intelligence); communication and collaboration (social media); and privacy and security (Foerster-Metz et al., 2018). The extent to which organizations implement these digital technologies and tools in their work processes depends largely on their strategy, knowledge regarding utilizing these digital technologies and tools, and respective industries. While some organizations are still contemplating what digitization may mean to them, others have employed a Chief Digital Officer in charge of the organization's digital transformation process. What can be digitalized? Which work processes and functions benefit from digitization, and what is the impact on organizational members, their work and interactions, and hence the organization's culture?

An organization's digitization process depends first and foremost on its people. Its leaders have to recognize opportunities for digitization and include them in their strategic focus. Furthermore, organizational members have to use digital technologies and tools and hence implement the developed digitization strategy. Finally, customers need to be receptive and use the respective products and services offered. Some people may not like eating in a restaurant with drones flying around serving beverages and food. Some people may still want to read today's news in a traditional newspaper and not on their tablet or smartphone.

While studies on alternating telework revealed that managers had the biggest issues with mobile work, the COVID-19 pandemic gave them no choice. Due to sudden lock-downs and physical distancing, organizations had to allow mobile work from home, and managers were surprised how well it worked—provided the technology was available and functioning (e.g., Chung et al., 2021). However, virtual organizations and virtual collaboration pose several challenges for organizations, their culture, and their members. Since globally operating organizations can work 24 hours and seven days a week, synchronous technologically mediated interactions between organizational members become difficult when located in different time zones.

Mobile and virtual work also put employee commitment and organizational identification to the test (e.g., Wiesenfeld et al., 2001). Several studies revealed that mobile and virtual modes of working provide both benefits and challenges. Among the benefits is that people are no longer involved in daily conflicts at work. Maintaining organizational members' identification with their employing organization and maintaining its culture is more challenging (Klatte, 2015). Nevertheless, the lock-down accelerated the digitization process in almost every organization. Overnight, schools and universities had to provide tools and technology for online teaching. Companies subject to lock-downs had to invest in their online presence. Online shopping, including food, surged, and online services for fitness, educational programs, and entertainment. Technic-savvy digital natives, who grew up with digital technologies and tools, hardly knew it any different, while older people struggled with the overnight change.

If organizations want to use and exploit digitization opportunities, they will need to ensure that their organizational members have the respective qualifications for using the chosen technologies and tools. Former CEO and president of Hewlett-Packard, Meg Whitney, mentioned in a panel discussion during the World Economic Forum in Davos in 2016 that the critical issue in an organization's digital transformation is not the new technologies but its culture. To redesign and implement business processes and work procedures, organizational members impacted by the digitization process need to reorient themselves, even requiring a mental transformation. Bringing in new people with the relevant digital qualifications will also call for new organizational designs and new conceptions of work. Digital natives tend to have different expectations towards work, work organization, and leadership than older generations, as discussed in Sect. 6.4.

Several studies on digital natives who belong to the generations Y and Z suggest that digital media, social interactions generally, their work, and physical workplace are important. They want to contribute with their ideas, shape work designs, participate in decision-making. They want freedom for developing and implementing their initiatives. They expect appreciation from their superiors, who are expected to coach them rather than lead them in the traditional sense. Their job and their work environment should be fun. They want to use their digital tools and consider the boundaries between work and play floating because they constantly being online. Nevertheless, they expect sufficient time for their personal lives away from work. If organizations want to stay competitive and exploit the opportunities of digitization, they will have to become attractive employers for digital natives with their respective expectations. These developments have implications for their culture (see e.g., Dingli & Seychell, 2015).

On the other hand, not all organizational members and organizational units will be affected to the same extent by digitization. Hence, several subcultures may exist simultaneously within one organization. As discussed in Chap. 3, the existence of different subcultures does not necessarily create problems. The critical question is how these different subcultures relate to each other. If they function independently from each other and don't require any contact, no actions are needed. However, if members of different organizational units should but do not cooperate or even work against each other, there is an urgent need for action. Overall, increasing digitization may lead to a more colorful and more diverse workforce providing inherent potential for synergies and conflicts.

Digitization concerns all aspects of an organization's culture. Its specific characteristics influence the organization's internally developed strategy and business models. It affects the organization's design with its structure and processes, its leadership, and management instruments used in the various functional areas of the organization. The people and their qualifications recruited and integrated into the organization are central to the digitization process. Digitization requires organizations to employ people who can handle digital technologies and tools and recognize their potential for digital business models, products, services, and work processes. Current surveys show that young, highly qualified organizational members often criticize the slow digitization process in their organization, including management's reserved attitude toward the topic. Top management will need to include digital natives from different value chain areas in their strategy development process. In addition to users or customers, they will add their voices and perspectives in an open dialogue. The result points to an organization's needs for development and eventually shapes its future.

Furthermore, digital transformation requires fast actions, experiments, and evaluations, including organizational members with different backgrounds and experiences in the process. The results of such experiments are never perfect. They need to be adjusted and improved in further iterations eliminating flaws and mistakes. Such an experimentation mode requires an organizational culture that is open to new ideas, provides freedom to experiment, and tolerates errors that will occur in such a step-wise process (Thomke, 2020).

Since digital technologies and tools enable the decoupling of workplace and working hours, traditional hierarchical structures and the traditional ideas about a workplace will become obsolete. For instance, organizational members can accomplish administrative tasks, conceptual work, and handling customer issues from anywhere globally, given the required technical equipment and software tools. A physical work environment needs a flexible design as, for example, practiced by the firm IDEO. The San Francisco-based firm has an open office space with moveable furniture. Depending on the tasks, organizational members rearrange the work setting several times a day to foster interaction or provide privacy for conceptual work.

Leaders and their behavior play a crucial role in the digitization process. In addition to their leadership qualifications, they need relevant digital competencies and especially openness for digitization opportunities. Regarding their leadership qualifications, the digital natives and the more diverse workforce expects *modern* leadership behavior beyond wearing jeans and sneakers. As mentioned above, digital natives expect to use digital tools. They expect appreciation and regular exchange, as well as instant and frequent feedback. They want to try out things and learn from their mistakes. They want to take part in decision-making and design processes. They want to know where they stand and what kind of perspectives the organization has to offer. They expect their leaders to coach and support them in the course of their further development process. They want leaders who are responsive to their needs and concerns and available to discuss their questions. Hence, the old-style leadership behavior has become obsolete; *modern* leaders act as coaches, partners, coordinators, communicators, and mentors depending on the situation. In addition, leaders should allow mistakes and reflect them together with their people in an atmosphere of mutual trust. Leaders not only have to deal effectively with cultural diversity, but they also have to know how to leverage it. Leadership and management instruments need to be aligned with the digitization process to support leaders and maintain the desired organizational culture.

All these developments have significant implications for an organization's culture that needs to support and embrace a digitization process.

6.9 Politics

Political factors play a vital role for organizations and their cultures because they set the boundaries for legally acceptable business activities and behavior. For example, when the Fukushima nuclear catastrophe happened, no one had anticipated German Chancellor Angela Merkel's overnight decision to move the entire country out of atomic energy. As a result, energy providers' share values dropped. Companies owning nuclear power plants had to change their business model and their strategic orientation immediately. Germany's so-called "energy turnaround" has led to the highest worldwide energy costs (Breitkopf, 2020), influencing the competitiveness of German-based companies.

As a consequence of Enron's and WorldCom's accounting scandal at the beginning of this century, the U.S. American government passed the Sarbanes-Oxley Act to reestablish the investors' trust in companies listed on the stock exchange. This law had a considerable impact on the reporting duties of listed companies. From then on, organizations had to provide evidence for the effectiveness of their internal control systems both internally by management and externally by public accountants. The additional administrative costs were estimated to be 40 percent. Furthermore, the financial crisis of 2007 resulted in a myriad of new regulations that also affected and still affect organizations and their customers.

The election of populist leaders in several countries around the globe fostered increasing uncertainties, de-globalization, and bureaucracy. Under Donald Trump's presidency, the U.S.A. became an unreliable partner for some U.S. businesses, and especially its international allies. With a short Twitter message, he could send stock markets up or down. His slogan "America First" could be translated into "our country first". The canceling of multilateral treaties created new business conditions leading to new trade barriers such as re-installed tariffs and related bureaucracy. The tariffs imposed during Trump's presidency were estimated to have impacted over USD 460 billion of imports and exports by 2019. This increased annual consumer costs by roughly USD 57 billion (Lee & Vara, 2020) and resulted in job losses. Brexit, with its new regulations between the U.K. and the European Union, complicated cross-border business and increased bureaucracy. With Brexit in effect, the transport of fresh fish took five instead of one day to cross the border from England to the continent, often reaching its destination spoiled. In e-commerce, the tariffs on returns have become so high that customers and companies think of destroying ordered products rather than returning them.

Political decisions during the COVID-19 pandemic are another example of the challenges they may pose for organizations and their culture. From one day to the next, governments closed borders impacting supply chains and cross-border commuters. They shut down schools, universities, and businesses in many European countries despite their investments in hygiene concepts (Adler & Sackmann, 2021). While online business boomed, entire industries were closed repeatedly for an indefinite time, such as the travel, hospitality, and tourism industries. From one day to the next, children and their parents had to work from home, and managers and leaders had to get used to leading virtually and maintaining the organization's culture from a distance.

Even though some of the incidents mentioned above are examples of black swans—sudden and unexpected events—they may trigger rules, regulations, and laws that have a lasting effect on organizations. They impact organizations and their culture, including organizations' strategy, their design, products, service delivery, ways of working, and working standards. However, the need for rules and regulations may differ from one culture to another at the national level, including their implementation. Over the decades, Germany experienced, for example, an increase in the density of regulation—partly due to imposed E.U. law, partly due to its national culture. Several studies show that uncertainty avoidance or the need for security is higher in Germany than, for instance, in Switzerland, Scandinavian countries, the Netherlands, or the USA (Hofstede et al., 2010). This need for security fosters the introduction of new regulations as soon as a problem occurs to avoid similar issues in the future.

On the one hand, rules, standards, and norms provide security and stability and enable efficient processes once established. On the other hand, the number of rules and regulations may also impede experimentation behavior, agility, and new ideas and innovations. Research in the automotive industry has shown that the single focus on efficiency and adherence to existing rules may impede the organization's innovation capacity (Abernathy, 1978). While documenting individual process steps in detail can increase efficiency, innovation suffers Benner and Tushman's (2003, 2015). If organizations want to stay viable, they need both—efficient routines and explorative behavior enabling innovations.

Overall, political uncertainties imply that organizational cultures need to enable and support an organization's flexibility, resilience, and ambidexterity combining efficient processes with experimentation. Furthermore, depending on the characteristics of an organization's culture, fewer rules could suffice if organizational members have internalized the critical standards for appropriate and inappropriate behavior. Replacing rules with the cognitive guiding principles of culture requires specific characteristics of culture and careful socialization of their organizational members into the cultural specifics. Both require an understanding of a given organization's culture. How to gain such an understanding is the focus of Chap. 7.

References

Abernathy, W. J. (1978). *The productivity dilemma: Roadblock to innovation in the automobile industry*. Johns Hopkins University Press.

Adler, N. J., & Sackmann, S. A. (2021, in press). The grand challenge none of us chose: Succeeding (and failing) against the global pandemic. With S. Arieli, M. Akter, C. Barmeyer, C. Barzantny, D. Caprar, Y. Lee, L.A. Liu, G. Magnani, J. Marcus, C. Miska, F. Moore, S.H. Park, B.S. Reiche, and A.-M. Søderberg. In J. S. Osland, S. B. Reiche, B. Szkudlarek, & M. E. Mendenhall (Eds.), *Advances in global leadership* (Vol. 14, pp. xx–xx). Emerald.

Asch, F. (2000). Unsinnige Pleitenhysterie. *Spiegel Online*, 9. Juni. Accessed Sep 22, 2021, from www.spiegel.de/wirtschaft/der-markt-forscher-unsinnige-pleitenhysterie-a-80395.html

Baller, S., Dutta, S., & Lanvin, B. (Eds.). (2016). The global information technology report 2016: Innovating in the digital economy. World Economic Forum. Accessed Sep 22, 2021, from http://www3.weforum.org/docs/GITR2016/WEF_GITR_Full_Report.pdf

Barmeyer, C. I., & Davoine, E. (2011). The intercultural challenges in the transfer of codes of conduct from the US to Europe. In H. Primecz, L. Romani, & S. Sackmann (Eds.), *Cross-cultural management in practice* (pp. 53–63). Edward Elgar.

Barney, J. B. (1986). Organizational culture: Can it be a source of sustained competitive advantage? *Academy of Management Review, 11*(3), 656–665.

Barney, J. B. (1991). Firm resources and sustained competitive advantage. *Journal of Management, 17*(1), 99–120.

Benner, M. J., & Tushman, M. L. (2003). Exploitation, exploration and process management: The productivity dilemma revisited. *Academy of Management Review, 28*(2), 238–256.

Benner, M. J., & Tushman, M. L. (2015). Reflections on the 2013 decade award: "Exploitation, exploration, and process management: The productivity dilemma revisited" ten years later. *Academy of Management Review, 40*(4), 497–514.

Böhlke, R., & Walleyo, S. (2007). Handeln wider besseres Wissen–Warum viele Transaktionen scheitern, ohne es zu müssen. In K. Rausch (Ed.), *Organisation gestalten–Struktur mit Kultur versöhnen* (pp. 254–279). Pabst Science.

Bonhage, A., Gagnebin, P., & Aerberhard, U. (2002). Erfolgsfaktor Unternehmenskultur. Interview mit Peter Pfluger, CEO und Vorsitzender der Phonak-Gruppe. *Vision Das Schweizer Magazin für Wirtschaft und Innovation, 1*(2002), 6–10.

Brannen, M.-Y., & Salk, J. (2000). Partnering across borders: Negotiating organizational culture in a German-Japanese joint venture. *Human Relations, 53*(4), 451–487.

Breiding, R. J. (2013). *Swiss made: The untold story behind Switzerland's success*. Profile Books.

Breitkopf, A. (2020). Strompreise nach Länern weltweit. Accessed Sep 22, 2021, from https://de.statista.com/statistik/daten/studie/13020/umfrage/strompreise-inausgewaehlten-laendern/#statisticContainer, https://de.statista.com/statistik/daten/studie/13020/umfrage/strompreise-in-ausgewaehltenlaendern/#statisticContainer

Cartwright, S., & Cooper, C. (1996). *Managing mergers and acquisitions and strategic alliances*. Butterworth-Heinemann.

Chung, H, Seo, H., Forbes, S., & Birkett, H. (2021). *Working from home during COVID-19 lockdown: Changing preferences and the future of work*. University of Birmingham/University of Kent. Accessed Sep 22, 2021, from www.birmingham.ac.uk/Documents/college-social-sciences/business/research/wirc/epp-working-from-home-COVID-19-lockdown.pdf

Deutsch, C., & West, A. (2010, June). *A new generation of M&A: A McKinsey perspective on opportunities and challenges*. Perspectives on Mergers and Integration. McKinsey. Accessed Sep 22, 2021, from https://www.mckinsey.com/client_service/organization/latest_thinking/~/media/1002A11EEA4045899124B917EAC7404C.ashx

DIHK (2018). Arbeitsmarktreport 2018: Fachkräfte gesucht wie nie. *Gesellschaft für innovative Beschäftigungsförderung Online, March 13*. Accessed Sep 22, 2021, from www.gib.nrw.de/service/gib-newsletter/newsletter_archiv/g-i-b-newsletter-nr-365/arbeitsgestaltung-und-fachkraeftesicherung/dihk-arbeitsmarktreport-2018-fachkraefte-gesucht-wie-nie

Dilk, A. (1999). Cafeteria-Systeme. In E. Eyer (Ed.), *Report Vergütung: Entgeltgestaltung für Mitarbeiter und Manager* (pp. 135–139). Symposion Publishing.

Dingli, A., & Seychell, D. (2015). *The new digital natives*. Springer.

DiStefano, J. J., & Maznevski, M. L. (2000). Creating value with diverse teams in global management. *Organizational Dynamics, 29*(1), 45–63.

Doherty, R., Liu, S., & West, A. (2015). How M&A practitioners enable their success. Survey. *McKinsey & Company Online*, October 1. Accessed Sep 22, 2021, from www.mckinsey.com/business-functions/strategy-and-corporate-finance/our-insights/how-m-and-a-practitioners-enable-their-success

Economist (1998, February). *The mother of all mergers*. The Ecomomist 7, 65–66. www.economist.com.

EVS. (2016). *European values study 2008: Integrated dataset (EVS 2008)*. GESIS Data Archive, Cologne. ZA4800 Data file Version 4.0.0. https://doi.org/10.4232/1.12458.

Flamholtz, E., & Randle, Y. (2000). *Growing pains: Transitioning from an entrepreneurship to a professionally managed firm* (3rd ed.). Jossey-Bass.

Flamholtz, E., Randle, Y., & Sackmann, S. A. (1986). Future directions of human resource management from 1985 to the year 2000: An environmental scan overview. In E. Flamholtz, Y. Randle, & S. A. Sackmann (Eds.), *Future directions of human resource management. Monograph and research* (Vol. 46, pp. 6–75). University of California Los Angeles.

Foerster-Metz, U. S., Marquardt, K., Golowko, N., Kompalla, A., & Hell, C. (2018). Digital transformation and its implications on organizational behavior. *Journal of EU Research in Business*. https://doi.org/10.5171/2018.340873

Gerhart, B. (2009). How much does national culture constrain organizational culture? *Managemen and Organization Review, 5*(2), 241–259.

Grässlin, J. (1995). *Daimler-Benz: Der Konzern und seine Republik*. Droemer Knaur.

Greiner, L. (1972). Evolution and revolution as organizations grow: A company's past has clues for management that are critical to future success. *Harvard Business Review, 50*(4), 37–46.

Harbison, J., & Pekar, P. (2000). *Smart alliances: A practical guide to repeatable success. . Jossey-Bass Management Series*. Jossey-Bass.

Haspeslagh, P. C., & Jemison, D. B. (1991). *Managing acquisitions*. Free Press.

Hofstede, G., Hofstede, G. J., & Minkov, M. (2010). *Cultures and organizations: Software of the mind* (3rd ed.). McGraw-Hill.

Inglehart, R. (2008). Changing values among Western publics from 1970 to 2006. *West European Politics, 31*(1), 130–146.

IMAA (2021). *Number & value of M&A worldwide*. Accessed Sep 22, 2021, from https://imaa-institute.org/mergers-and-acquisitions-statistics

Jansen, S., & Körner, K. (2000). Szenen einiger Unternehmens-Ehen: Vier Hochzeiten und drei Todesfälle. *Frankfurter Allgemeine Zeitung, 260*, 49.

Killing, J. P. (1983). *Strategies for joint venture success*. Praeger Press.

Klatte, B. (2015). *Bildung von Wissensarbeitern in virtuellen Arbeitsstrukturen. Eine vergleichende Untersuchung organisationspsychologischer Determinanten der Bindung bei Mitarbeitern in virtuellen und klassischen rbeitsverhältnissen mit Implikationen für ein erfolgreiches Bindungsmanagement.* Dissertation. Neubiberg: Universität der Bundeswehr München.

Koller, T., Goedhart, M., & Wessels, D. (2015). *Valuation: Measuring and managing the values of companies* (6th ed.). Wiley.

Lee, T., & Vara, J. (2020). The total costs of Trump's tariffs. *American Action Forum Online*, September 16. Accessed Sep 22, 2021, from www.americanactionforum.org/research/the-total-cost-of-trumps-new-tariffs

Martens, A. (2016). PE-Offensive bei Ubstalsboom: Der andere Aufstieg. *ManagerSeminare, 223*, October, 18–27. Accessed Sep 22, 2021, from www.managerseminare.de/ms_Artikel/PE-Offensive-bei-Upstalsboom-Der-andere-Aufstieg-249440

Martin, J., & Siehl, C. (1983). Organizational culture and counter-culture: An uneasy symbiosis. *Organizational Dynamics, 12*(2), 52–64.

Michaels, E., Handfield-Jones, H., & Axelrod, B. (2001). *The war for talent*. Harvard Business School Press.

Mocraw, J. (2000). »*. . . and then there were seven*«. www.cuoresportivo.org: *Articles*, as well as European Car (magazine), July 2001.

Morick, H. (2002). *Differentielle Personalwirtschaft: Theoretisches Fundament und praktische Konsequenzen. Dissertation*. Universität der Bundeswehr München.

Nelson, R. E., & Gopalan, S. (2003). Do organizational cultures replicate national cutlures? Isomorphism, rejection and reciprocal opposition in the corporate value of three countries. *Organization Studies, 24*(7), 1115–1151. https://doi.org/10.1177/01708406030247006

Nextpractice. (2016). *Wertewelten. Arbeiten 4.0*. Bremen: Nextpraxis GmbH & BMAS Bundesministerium für Arbeit und Soziales. Accessed Sep 22, 2021, from www.bmas.de/SharedDocs/Downloads/DE/Publikationen/Forschungsberichte/wertewelten-arbeiten-vier-null.pdf?__blob=publicationFile&v=1

Nieżurawska, J., Karaszewska, H., & Dziadkiewicz, A. (2016). Attractiveness of cafeteria systems a viewed by generation Z. *International Journal of Social, Behavioral, Educational, Economic, Business and Industrial Engineering, 10*(2), 684–688.

Paine Schofield, C. & Honoré, S. (2011). *Great expectations: Managing generation Y. Ashridge Business School report.* Institute of Leadership and Management. Accessed Sep 22, 2021, from www.institutelm.com/resourceLibrary/great-expectations-managing-generation-y.html

Probst, G., & Raisch, S. (2005). Organizational crisis: The logic of failure. *Academy of Management Executive, 19*(1), 90–105.

Sackmann, S. A. (2005). *Toyota. Eine Fallstudie aus unternehmenskultureller Sicht. (Toyota. A case study from a corporate culture perspective)*. Bertelsmann Foundation.

Sackmann, S. A. (2010). Critical issues of corporate culture in a global perspective. In T. T. Goydke (Ed.), *Corporate culture in China and Japan* (pp. 11–26). Verlagshaus Monsenstein und Vannerdat.

Sackmann, S. A., & Bertelsmann Foundation. (2006). *Success factor corporate culture*. Bertelsmann.

Salk, J. E. (1997). Partners and other strangers: Cultural boundaries and cross-cultural encounters in international joint venture teams. *International Studies of Management and Organization, 26* (4), 48–72.

Schmid, S. (Ed.). (2018). *Internationalization of business. MIR series in international business*. Springer.

Schrödl, K.-H., & Hanen, D. G. (2019). Senior-Experten: Ihre Bedeutung für die Wirtschaft am Beispiel der Bosch Management Support GmbH. In S. A. Sackmann (Ed.), *Führung und ihre Herausforderungen* (pp. 371–382). Springer Gabler.

Spickenreither, N., & Sackmann, S. A. (2019). Herausforderung Millenials – ihre Charakteristika und Erwartungen mit Implikationen für wirksame Führung und Zusammenarbeit. In S. A. Sackmann (Ed.), *Führung und ihre Herausforderungen* (pp. 65–82). Springer Gabler.

Spiegel. (2000). Boo.com macht dicht. *Spiegel Online*, May 18. Accessed Sep 22, 2021, from www.spiegel.de/netzwelt/tech/konkurs-boo-com-macht-dicht-a-77027.html

Thomke, S. H. (2020). *Experimentation works: The surprising power of business experiments*. Harvard Business Press.

Trompenaars, F. (1994). *Riding the waves of culture*. Irwin.

Weber, Y. (Ed.). (2012). *Handbook on research of mergers and acquisitions*. Edward Elgar.

Weber, Y., & Tarba, A. (2012). Merger and acquisitions process: The use of corporate culture analysis. *Cross Cultural Management: An International Journal, 19*(3), 288–303.

Welt. (2021). Daimler spaltet sich auf–Lastwagensparte an die Börse. *Welt Online*, February 3. . Accessed Sep 22, 2021, from www.welt.de/newsticker/dpa_nt/infoline_nt/wirtschaft_nt/article225645207/Daimler-spaltet-sich-auf-Lastwagen-Sparte-an-die-Boerse.html

Whyte, W. F. (1956). *The organisation man*. Simon & Schuster.

Wiesenfeld, B. M., Raghuram, S., & Garud, R. (2001). Organizational identification among virtual workers: The role of need for affiliation and perceived work-based social support. *Journal of Management, 27*(2), 213–229.

Wirtschaftswoche. (2016). Daimler stößt Kulturwandel an. *WirtschaftsWoche Online, November 1*. Accessed Sep 22, 2021, from www.wiwo.de/unternehmen/auto/daimler-daimler-stoesst-kulturwandel-an/14766332.html

World Economic Forum (2016). *The future of jobs. Employment, skills and workforce strategy for the fourth industrial revolution*. Global challenge insight report. World Economic Forum. Accessed Sep 22, 2021, from http://reports.weforum.org/future-of-jobs-2016

Wottawa, H., Montel, C., Mette, C., Zimmer, B., & Hiltmann, M. (2011). ELIGO-Studie: Berufliche Lebensziele und Leistungspotenziale junger Hochschulabsolventinnen und Hochschulabsolventen. *Wirtschaftspsychologie, 13*(3), 85–111.

Yankelovitch, D. (1981). *The new rules*. Random House.

Yousfi, H. (2011). When American management system meets Tunisian culture: The Poulina case. In H. Primecz, L. Romani, & S. Sackmann (Eds.), *Cross-cultural management in practice* (pp. 64–76). Edward Elgar.

Zweig, P. L. (1995). The case against mergers. *Business Week,* 30. October, pp. 122–130.

way data is collected.[2] Based on the definition of organizational culture as *set of basic beliefs commonly-held by a group of people* (see Chap. 2), those characteristics that influence its analysis are further discussed with their implications for the analysis. These characteristics are:

- The essence of organizational culture consists of its basic commonly-held beliefs.
- Culture is the property of a group—the larger an organization, the more likely it is that subcultures may exist.
- Organizational culture, its commonly-held basic beliefs, and collective practices are routinized.

The Core of Culture Consists of Basic Beliefs

An organization's culture consists of several components located at different levels (see Chap. 2, Fig. 2.3). The top-level or outer layer of culture entails visible manifestations. These may be buildings, documents, products, and collective behavior such as practices, rites, rituals, or ceremonies. Rules, standards, and norms constitute the next level of culture, followed by postulated values. Basic beliefs and assumptions are at the deepest level of culture and form its core. These layers have immediate implications for gaining an understanding of a given culture. Even though the visible manifestations of the cultural network are directly observable, their meaning may neither be clear to new organizational members nor to outsiders. Understanding the specific connotations of these visible manifestations involves investigating the meanings that organizational members attribute to those manifestations. Such an understanding requires an investigation of the deepest level of culture or its inner core. The commonly-held basic beliefs and assumptions that constitute the deepest level cannot be directly observed due to their cognitive nature.

How can these underlying commonly-held beliefs be surfaced for gaining an understanding of an organization's culture core? And what kind of collective beliefs are relevant? Based on the social construction of reality (Berger & Luckmann, 1966), cognitive science, and empirical research, a framework of cultural knowledge proved helpful in understanding culture in the context of organizations (Sackmann, 1991a, b). The framework consists of four knowledge types: *Dictionary, directory, recipe, and axiomatic knowledge.*

- *Dictionary knowledge* comprises the descriptions or denotations typical for a group, such as specific labels, terms, and definitions.
- *Directory knowledge* contains collectively-held beliefs regarding practices: how is work accomplished? Which priorities exist in a given culture? What kind of standards exists for quality, punctuality, or cleanliness? How do organizational members learn and innovate? How do organizational members interact with each other, with insiders and outsiders, between and across hierarchical levels?

[2] In a study of four change agents' practices, Tichy (1975) found that they used different diagnostic categories that influenced their value orientation and the change techniques they employed.

- *Recipe knowledge* refers to normative beliefs: what should be done to obtain a specific result? What should be improved or changed?
- *Axiomatic knowledge* comprises four underlying axioms or basic beliefs about (1) an organization's purpose (who are we and why?), (2) its strategy (what do we want to accomplish and why?), (3) its most appropriate design (how do we organize ourselves and why? and (4). the most appropriate organizational members (had kind of people fit best and why?).

These four types of cultural knowledge can serve as a framework when collecting data in the context of a culture's analysis. Furthermore, a comparison between verbal and observed behavior may reveal whether organizational members practice the underlying beliefs in daily work.

Culture Is the Property of a Group
Culture is *commonly-held* and therefore a collective phenomenon. Even though individual group members are carriers of culture, culture is the property of a group. The group may refer to a team, a department, any other organizational unit, or the entire organization. Because of its collective nature, one cannot draw conclusions about a culture from individual statements. And personal accounts cannot be generalized to the group level since they do not necessarily represent the group's collective beliefs. Instead, personal accounts of organizational members need to be compared with those of other group members to understand whether they reflect a subjective opinion or whether they are typical for the group and its culture. When analyzing the culture of a single department or a small organizational unit, choosing the most appropriate interview partners is easy because it is possible to include all members of the department or unit in data collection. However, analyzing the culture of a larger organization requires a representative sample of that organization across all organizational units and all hierarchical levels.

The larger an organization, the more likely it is that subcultures may exist. Those members who hold the same basic beliefs belong to the same subculture. The process of data analysis may uncover different subcultures if data were collected across organizational units and hierarchical levels. Different subcultures may also hold some cultural knowledge, such as axiomatic knowledge, in common and differ in respect to the other types of cultural knowledge. As mentioned in Chap. 2, subcultures as such are neither good nor bad for an organization. Their specific characteristics and their way of interrelating determine if they supporte or hinder the organization's functioning. These issues need to be considered in planning and executing a culture analysis.

Culture Is Routinized
When new people join an organization, they are socialized into the organization's culture. They learn the ropes, the cultural knowledge, both from explicit information and predominantly from being exposed to daily work practices. If they want to fit in, the acquired cultural knowledge starts guiding their thinking and behavior. Once they have shifted from a newcomer to an organizational member, the cultural knowledge that guides their thinking and behavior drops out of their awareness.

Regular use has turned cultural knowledge into routines of thinking and behavior. As a consequence, cultural knowledge is applied automatically without paying any conscious thought.

This routinized nature of culture and cultural knowledge affects the data collection process, methods used, and the choice of individuals for data collection. Having dropped out of awareness, organizational members cannot reproduce routinized thought and action patterns when asked. Instead, they need first to surface them and bring them to their attention. Once accomplished, the commonly-held basic beliefs, the different types of cultural knowledge can be critically reflected and checked for their appropriateness.

7.1.2 *Designing a Culture Analysis Process*

Several questions guide the process of an organization's culture analysis:

- What kind of data needs to be collected?
- Where is the information gathered?
- Who is collecting the data?
- When is the data collected?
- How is the data collected?

The answer to these questions depends largely on investigators' theoretical model of culture and the approach they choose for the analysis. Due to its routinized nature, it is helpful if an outsider conducts the culture analysis in cooperation with insiders. While outsiders bring knowledge about the analysis methods and processes, insiders know the organization, its members, critical events, or available documents.

In general, two different types of approaches exist for analyzing an organization's culture: an inductive and a deductive approach. Both have advantages and disadvantages that need consideration. Combining the two in a multiple methods approach can minimize several weaknesses. The *deductive approach* is based on a positivist paradigm.[3] Existing concepts, models, and theories of culture serve as the basis in either choosing among existing data collection methods or developing new ones. The culture analyst makes assumptions about the culture before the data collection based on existing theoretical models and concepts. He or she takes the role of an emotionally uninvolved observer and acts as an *onlooker*. Examples are data collection with existing standardized questionnaires that consist of previously developed dimensions. Such a deductive approach has several advantages: large sample sizes can be investigated with a potential online tool using statistic packages for the data analysis. The results are quantifiable. The major disadvantage of a

[3] A paradigm is comparable with a worldview that influences the choice of questions that researchers investigate and the methodology and methods they consider most appropriate for investigating the research question.

deductive approach is that the previously chosen dimensions and questions may only partly reflect those issues typical for a given organizational culture. In many cases, the previously defined dimensions reveal more about the investigators' assumptions, preferences, and interests than about the specific cultural setting. Furthermore, investigators have to choose which culture elements they focus on: perceived practices, norms, values, or strategic orientation?

The goal of an *inductive approach* is to understand a particular cultural setting better. Investigators set their preconceived notions about culture aside. They interact with the members of the respective organization and are thus personally involved. Hypotheses and relevant dimensions of the organization's culture emerge in this process. An inductive approach is especially fruitful if the goal is to surface the essence or specific facets of an organization's culture for gaining its understanding. Participant observation and an ethnographic approach are typical ways of collecting data within the inductive research paradigm. The significant advantage of an inductive approach is the context-specific findings that reveal the essence of the given culture or those issues typical for the culture under investigation. The data analysis is more demanding and time-consuming when compared to the statistical analysis of questionnaires. Many rich, context-specific data need to be condensed and the specifics of a given culture extracted from the data. The dimensions and priorities that are relevant for a given cultural setting emerge from the data analysis. As a result, such an approach uncovers those cultural aspects that are genuinely relevant to the organization's culture.

Disadvantages associated with the inductive method are that the findings cannot be generalized beyond the investigated setting. Furthermore, a potential risk exists that investigators *go native* due to their getting increasingly closer to the research setting and the data. The investigators' biases and imperfections may also influence the data collection and data analysis. Selective perception[4] or halo-effects[5] are well-known examples of systematic biases. These unintended influences may be reduced if external people collect the culture-relevant data and present the results of their analysis to a predetermined group of decision-makers and selected organizational members. The findings can then be challenged and validated in the mutual discussion and dialogue.

Possible methods for data collection can be depicted on a continuum ranging from deductive or *outsider perspective* to inductive or *insider* perspective. Examples are structured interviews, desk research, secondary data evaluation, group discussions, assumption analysis, and unstructured interviews such as narrative or phenomenological interviews. Most of these data collection methods are *reactive* in that

[4]Selective perception means that the perceiving person never sees the whole surrounding reality but unconsciously selects excerpts of the reality. For example, personal experience, attitudes, interests, or social status steer this selection process. That explains why, e.g., after a car accident, three witnesses may tell three different stories to describe what happened.

[5]The halo-effect is a type of cognitive bias that describes how people perceive one seemingly central quality in a person and align other assumed characteristics with that quality. So, for example, someone who lies will also steal.

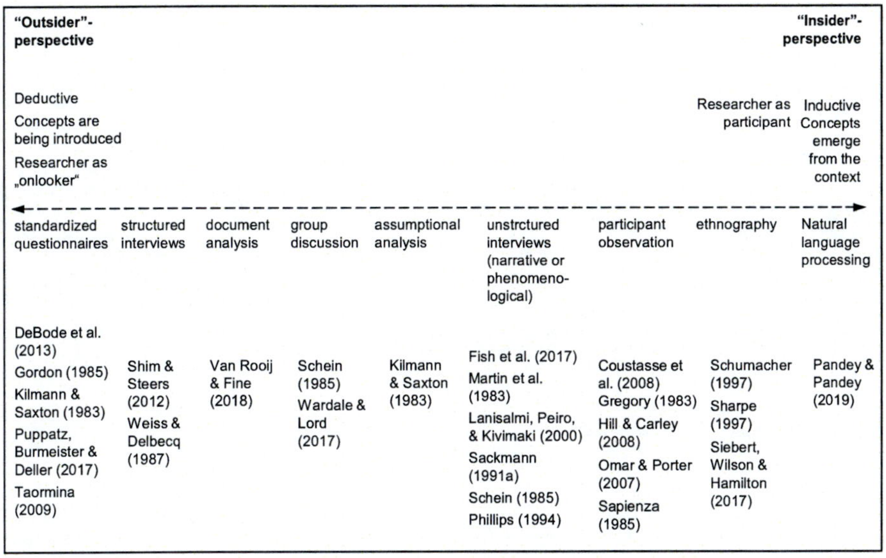

Fig. 7.2 Range of data collection methods for analyzing organizational culture, including research examples (Adapted and updated from Sackmann, 1996, p. 81)

organizational members show a reaction when filling out a questionnaire or being interviewed. In contrast, secondary data are non-reactive from the perspective of the culture analysis since they exist already. A recently developed method analyzes large amounts of secondary data using natural language processing (NLP) (Pandey & Pandey, 2019). Figure 7.2 illustrates these methods of data collection, including examples from empirical investigations. The following Sect. 7.1.3 describes them in more detail.

7.1.3 Data Collection Methods

Several different social sciences methods are available for gathering data to gain insights into an organization's culture. Given that no ideal data collection method exists, it is essential to know the strengths and shortcomings, and challenges associated with a particular data collection method. The following section discusses six different kinds of reactive and non-reactive data collection methods with their strengths, challenges, and shortcomings:

- Interviews
- Workshops
- Questionnaires
- Observations
- Secondary data and other non-reactive methods
- Projective measures (collages, paintings, and drawings)

Method	Strengths	Critical Issues
Interviews (individual and group interviews)	- Relationship can be established, empathy shown - Flexible, wide range of topics can be covered - Immediate reactions, clarification possible - Rich, contextual data	- time-consuming - Interivewer may distort answers - Possible distortions due to interviewee´s personal view and memory effects - Coding and interpration may be challenging
Workshops	- Same strengths and interiews - Interactions between participants can be used to further probe emerging issues	- Facilitator may distort responses - Distortions due to personal views - Data analysis and their interpretation may be challenging
Questionnaires	- Large sample sizes at same cost - Quantifiable results - Differferent kinds of statistical analysis	- No control over who answers qustionnaire - No clarifications possible - Reference points for answers may differ - Questions may miss important issues - Danger of overinterpreting of results
Observations	- Capture observable behavior in context - No distortion due to memory effects - flexible	- Time-consuming - Access and sampling may be difficult - Potential observation biasis - Recording, coding and interpretation of results bay be challenging
Secondary Data (non-reactive methods incl. Natural Language Processing)	- Data already exist - No systematic distortions in data collection - High face validity - quantifiable	- Access may be difficult - Coding and interpretation may be challenging - Validity may be an issue
Projective Methods (drawings, collages)	- non-verbal, rich, contextual data - Clarifications possible esp.regarding interpretation - Emotions may be captured - May reveal areas of conflict, discrepancies - Indications for needed changes, problem solutions	- time-consuming - Ideosyncratic – comparison across people may be difficult

Fig. 7.3 Data collection methods with their strengths and critical issues

Figure 7.3 provides an overview of the strengths and critical issues associated with these data collection methods:

Interviews can be conducted individually or in a group. While individual interviews render in-depth information from a single person's perspective, group interviews may surface additional issues during a discussion process and uncover taboos. Interviews can have various degrees of structure and may last roughly for one hour in the context of a culture analysis. A narrative interview uses, for example, general, open-ended questions and probes further into issues raised by the interviewee. Highly structured interviews may cover a set of predetermined questions. In general, interviews are very flexible if the interviewer is skilled. During the course of an interview, additional data collection instruments can be used, such as a Q-sort technique (Chatman et al., 2014), the critical incidents technique (e.g., Gundry & Rousseau, 1994), or the Kelly Repertory Grid (e.g., Langan-Fox & Tan, 1997; Krafft, 1998). Interviewees will be more open if the interviewer is an outsider who ensures anonymity. Furthermore, recording the interview may prevent distortions due to memory effects.

Example of an Interview Guideline in the Context of an Open Interview[6]

- What is typical for the organization?
- Who had/has a strong influence on the organization, and what kind of influence did/do they have?
- Who are the major competitors, and how do they differ from the organization?
- What are the organization's strengths?
- What kind of weaknesses does the organization have?
- How did these strengths and weaknesses develop over time?
- What characterizes a typical leader in the organization?
- What characterizes a typical employee in the organization?
- What characterizes *good* work?
- How does the organization deal with emerging problems?
- How are decisions made?
- In which ways do certain groups/organizational units differ from others?

Workshops include several organizational members ideally selected from different organizational units and hierarchical levels. Depending on the number of people and issues to be covered, a culture analysis workshop may range from two hours to one day. Typically, a group of seven to 15 people gathers for about three hours. In addition to individual interviews, workshops may uncover basic commonly-held beliefs and even taboos during participants' mutual discussions. These can be further probed by the workshop facilitator and validated by participants. Workshops also give insights into broader perspectives and issues than individual interviews in a relatively short amount of time. However, workshop participants need to be carefully selected, and the workshop itself needs to be well planned. It requires skilled facilitation; the obtained data and information need to be carefully documented and analyzed. Participants will be more open if the facilitator is an outsider, while insiders need to help select the workshop participants according to the facilitator's criteria. Furthermore, the workshop facilitator will be better able to concentrate on the process if an additional person assists in the documentation during the workshop.

Example of a Culture Analysis Workshop

(The focus can be on an organizational unit's culture, on the entire organization's culture, or both)

The workshop may cover the following issues:

(continued)

[6]The appendix of Sackmann and Bertelsmann Fondation (2006) provides another checklist for a detailed interview.

- What are we proud of? What works well?
- What is typical for us/our organization?
- What kind of challenges are we facing now, and what kind of challenges will we face in the next few years?
- How should our organizational unit/organization look like in three years from now to manage these challenges?
- What are our strengths regarding the upcoming challenges?
- What are our weaknesses regarding the upcoming challenges?
- What are our blind spots?
- How can we build on our strengths?
- How can we minimize or eliminate our weaknesses?
- What or whom do we need to developed (people, competencies, skills, methods, techniques, etc.)?
- What do we have to let go of?

Questionnaires

Several questionnaires exist and can be used in analyzing an organization's culture. Examples are the Dension Organizational Culture Survey (Denison, 2000), the Organizational Culture Assessment Instrument (Cameron & Quinn, 1999), the Organizational Culture Inventory (Cooke, 1997), the Organizational Culture Profile (Ashkanasy et al., 2000), or the Culture Analysis Questionnaire (Sackmann, 2011)[7] to name of a few. Each of these questionnaires is based on a specific culture model and focuses on particular culture components such as norms, values, or perceived practices. Using a questionnaire for a culture analysis has several advantages. Data from a large number of people can be collected with questionnaires at roughly the same cost, and their results can be analyzed using different kinds of statistics. In the case of using an electronic version, there are neither distribution nor data entry costs. Their use has, however, several drawbacks. Organizational members receiving the questionnaire may not answer it themselves. They may choose different references in answering the questions. They cannot ask for clarifications, and the pre-set questions reveal information, but they may not address culturally relevant issues. Adding some open-ended questions may resolve the last point. If a larger sample needs to be covered, another option is to develop a custom-made questionnaire based on previously conducted interviews.

Furthermore, organizational members tend to be more open if an external institution sends the questionnaire and analysis the data collected.

Observations

One can always conduct observations while being in an organization whose culture is under investigation. Observations can occur as part of an interview, during a first

[7] Sackmann (2011) describes 25 different methods for analyzing organizational culture, including several questionnaires.

visit, during a meeting, waiting in the elevator, or during lunch in the organization's cafeteria. The significant advantages of observations are that they capture behavior as it happens in context. Observations are very flexible, and observed people cannot distort the data due to their selective memory. At the same time, observations come with several challenges. Access may be an issue if one wants to observe, for example, an important top executive meeting or an organizational unit that requires special entry permission. An outside observer may collect a lot of data, but the sample of observation sites may be biased regarding a culture analysis. For example, if observations are conducted in a retail organization the week before Christmas, the results may not be typical for the organization when considering the entire year. Hence, insiders need to help in choosing the most appropriate sites, events, and time for observation. Furthermore, observers may be overwhelmed by the amount of data being available, and selective perception may bias observed data. Hence, it is crucial to record the observations during or shortly after they occur. When conducting observations, it is also essential to distinguish between observations and interpretations since individuals tend to jump quickly from an observation to its interpretation based on the observer's personal experience. Hence, it may be helpful to record observations in one column and potential interpretations in a separate column. These may then serve as hypotheses and be tested in subsequent steps of data gathering. In addition, observations of verbal accounts can be compared with the accompanying nonverbal behavior to check discrepancies. Investigators may address these hypotheses immediately or in subsequent data collection processes to understand their underlying reasons.

At the beginning of a culture analysis, it is helpful to conduct a tour through the organization for a first orientation. In doing so, outside analysts can consider themselves as the *instrument* of culture analysis. The following questions may guide observations while touring the organization:

- What is the geographic location of the organization?
- What kind of architecture does the organization have? Does the architecture express functionality or status? Does it support or impede interaction and cooperation?
- How carefully do organizational members treat their built environment and spaces? Are spaces well-kept, clean, dirty?
- What seems to symbolize status, and to what extent? What kind of furniture exists in which areas/offices? How big are the offices? What type of art, organizational products, etc., are displayed? Are specific spaces reserved for certain groups of organizational members?
- What kind of signs, papers, books, pictures, etc., are lying/hanging/standing around?
- How do the people interact with each other? How do they greet each other?
- How much openness-closeness do working spaces have?
- How do employees/leaders treat external people?

The checklist in Fig. 7.4 can help prepare, structure, and analyze the first impressions gained while touring an organization.

1. Geographic location / environment
- Where are the headquarters and organizational units located? How convenient are the geographic locations (logistics, public transportation)? How attractive are the locations for potential employees?
- How many and which competitors are close?
- Do sufficient parking facilities exist? Do they have reserved parking spaces, if yes, for whom?

2. Architecture
- To what extent does the architecture support/ impede interaction?
- How large are the buildings? How big are offices, work areas?
- What does the architecture symbolize (hierarchy, status, functionality)?
- What is the structural condition of the building?
- How easy/difficult is it to move around?
- How well are the buildings maintained?
- Does the architecture support or impede interaction?

3. Reception
- What is the first impression of the reception area?
- What is exhibited? What kind of information is available to are visitors?
- To what extent does the interior design and the furniture convey status?
- How friendly are the employees at the reception desk?
- How easy/ complicated / bureaucratic is the registration?
- How helpful/ service-oriented are the employees at the reception desk?
- How formal/ informal is their dress?
- How long is the wait when having an appointment?

4. Organization tour:

Escort
- How well is the escort informed (e.g., company history, products, services, information about different divisions, anecdotes, informal stories etc.)?
- How formal/ informal is the escort's dress?
- How proud is the escort of the organization (e.g., when explaining different areas, products, stories)?

Organizational members´ behavior
- How formal/ informal is the dress of employees and leaders?
- How does do people greet each other (degree of formality, friendliness)?
- How do people of different hierarchical levels greet each other? How do they interact with each other (degree of formality, friendliness)? How open are organizational members? How tense/relaxed do they appear at their work?
- How do employees and leaders treat you as an external person? (Are you being introduced? How curious are they about you? How much time do they take? Are you being ignored?)

Work space
- What is the layout the working spaces (degree of flexibility, openness)?
- What is the size of the work spaces?
- How friendly/ warm/ cold do they appear?
- How much noise is there?
- How many people are moving around the work space?
- How clean and orderly are they?
- What is lying and standing around (e.g., plants, material, pictures, etc.)?
- How modern is the technological equipment)?
- What is hanging on the walls – in the offices and the hallways? What kind of pictures and art work (classic, modern, expensive, made by organizational members, etc.)?
- What kind of furniture like (functional/ status-oriented, movable)?
- How does production look like (age, machines, layout, noise, cleanliness, rest, etc.)?
- How clean are the restrooms?

Meeting rooms
- What is the atmosphere of the cafeteria/ canteen (e.g., friendly, cozy, uncomfortable, loud, clean, untended, etc.)?
- What is the relation of the canteen size to number of employees at the site?
- What kind of drinks and foods are offered (nutritious, healthy)?
- How expensive are meals and beverages (e.g., does the organization subsidize parts of the costs)?
- To what extent do leaders and employees actually use the cafeteria/ canteen?
- How much do employees interact/ talk during meals and standing in line?
- Are leaders and employees sit together or separately?
- Do managers/leaders have a separate eating area?
- Are there (additional) break areas? If yes, where are they located and how many? Are they easily accessible?
- Who is using them to what extent?
- How do organizational members interact with each other in these break areas/ canteen?

Fig. 7.4 Checklist for touring an organization

Secondary Data

Secondary data is data about an organization that already exists and gathered for different purposes. Examples are all kinds of information about the organization from external and internal sources. External sources can be scientific journals, popular press, employer evaluation portals, video clips on YouTube, advertisements, postings on Facebook or Twitter, TV commercials, or information on an organization's website. Internal secondary data may include statistics, documents, internal survey results, memos, annual reports, speeches, emails, chats, etc. Usually, much more secondary data exists than one expects at the beginning of a culture analysis. The checklist in Fig. 7.5 lists possible documents that can be used for a culture analysis if they are accessible.

The significant advantage of secondary data is that they exist already and cannot be influenced or distorted by the culture analyst. A challenge may be selecting the

What kind of information does the organization provide to outsiders? How does the web page look like? What kind of image does the organization present to outsiders? How detailed is the information? In which languages is the information available?

1. Organization history
- How detailed is the? Are milestones, important events and people mentioned?
- Do anniversary brochures exist?
- In which languages is the information available?

2. Organizational policy & strategy; environmental, social & governance (ESG)
- Do clearly formulated policy, strategy, vision, values statements exist?
- Annual reports: How do they look like? In which languages are they available?
- Do written guidelines exist regarding organizational/ethical conduct; the organizations ESG contribution?
- Regulations & standards (e.g., working hours, timekeeping; employee participation system)?

3. Organization
- Is there one or several organization charts? How recent are they? How do they look like
- Are functional responsibilities documented?
- Do job descriptions exist? How recent and detailed are they?
- How are working hours across different divisions?
- Is home office possible? For whom and to what extent?

4. Leader/ Employees/ Human resources
- Do leadership guidelines exist?
- What kind of documents do new employees receive?
- Is there a code of ethics?
- What kind of human resource instruments exist (e.g., hiring, onboarding, goal agreement, personal development, giving feedback, performance review, training & education, employee surveys, regulation of working hours, etc.)?
- What kind of statistics exist (e.g., sick leaves/ absence, fluctuation)?
- Do results exist from participation in surveys, e.g., Best Place to Work? Employer ratings? What are the results?
- Do employee forums exist? What kind of information do they contain?
- What do employees write about the organization on external portals such as Kununu?

5. Internal and external communication
- Marketing material, internal videos; films on YouTube
- Job advertisements
- Public relations, marketing brochures
- Website
- Results of internal audits
- Speeches (written or online)
- External reviews

Fig. 7.5 Checklist of potential secondary data useful for culture analysis

Fig. 7.6 Example of a word cloud

most appropriate secondary data, their interpretation, and their validity to gain insights into an organization's culture.

Natural language processing (NLP) is a recently developed tool also used for analyzing an organization's culture. NLP is a computer-based method for analyzing both audible and verbal accounts of organizational members, such as speeches, emails, or chats (e.g., Pandey & Pandey, 2019). One may present results, for example, as word clouds highlighting those issues most frequently mentioned in an organizational unit or an entire organization. Figure 7.6 gives an example of a word cloud.

All the above-mentioned secondary data and NLP are non-reactive methods. Non-reactive methods[8] are based on data that already exists. Hence, neither the culture analyst nor organizational members have influenced them to use for the culture analysis. As such, observations made during an organization's tour represent non-reactive data to complement other data. Examples of non-reactive data are physical manifestations such as room sizes, type of furniture, wear of floors, and artwork displayed. Non-reactive data include the number, content and physical appearance of signs, rules, information boards, and organizational artifacts such as organization-specific clothing, certificates, cups, badges, buttons as signs for identification with the organization.

Projective Methods

Projective methods refer to techniques that use a stimulus to encourage open exploration of a topic or issue to uncover basic motives, values, and characteristics of an individual or organizational unit. They comprise, for example, free verbal

[8] Non-reactive methods use data that the researcher did not influence during their collection, and the data sources did not react to the researcher in the data collection process.

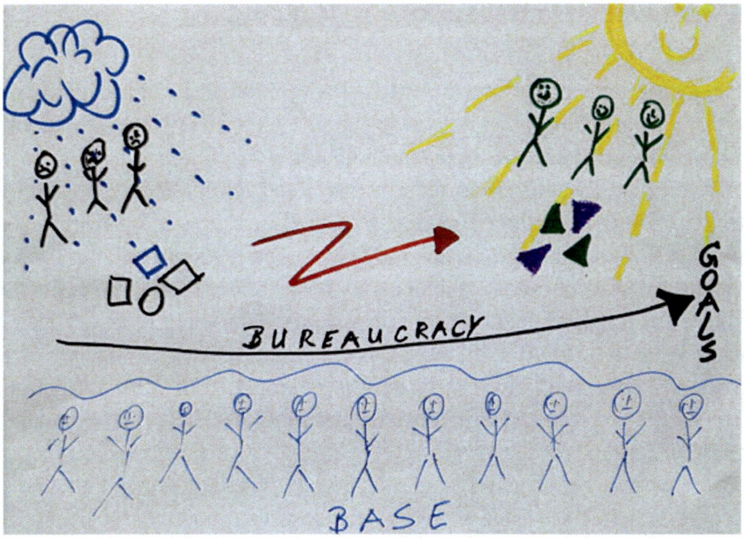

Fig. 7.7 Example for a drawing

associations, collages, or drawings. As such, the sentence completion technique, the critical incident technique (Kujala et al., 2014), the Q-sort technique (Peterson et al., 1999), and an open version of the Kelly Repertory Grid (Langan-Fox & Tan, 1997; Reger, 1990) have a projective nature. Participants of a culture analysis workshop may produce drawings and collages. Possible questions that can guide the production of collages or drawings during such a framework are, for example:

- What is characteristic for our current organizational unit (or organization) (including functions, core tasks, essential members, customers etc., and who plays what kind of roles?)
- How should it look like in one to three years (core functions and tasks, essential members, customers, etc.?)

Figure 7.7 shows an example of a drawing.

The process of interpreting, discussing, and further probing its various features with the artist and the entire group is critical. It will reveal valuable insights into the organization's culture and potential options for needed development. Groups of organizational members can also collectively draw or collage their organizational unit or organization and its typical way of being.

The significant advantage of using projective techniques in the process of a culture analysis is the surfacing of information that organizational members may not be able to verbalize. Projective techniques help surface data, information, and emotions that organizational members may no longer be aware of. Once these are uncovered, they can be jointly explored, discussed, and reflected in detail, including their implications for organizational members, the organization, and its functioning.

7.1.4 Securing Data Quality

Since every single method reveals only a fraction of the complex nature of culture, using a multiple-methods approach is recommended. Such an approach implies combining several data collection methods either simultaneously or sequentially. One method may be chosen as focal method and complemented by other data to ensure the validity of obtained results. Especially data resulting from interviews or questionnaires should be complemented by data obtained with other methods such as participant observation and/or the analysis of secondary data. As defined by triangulation,[9] the resulting data from the various data types and sources are then compared and contrasted with each other. Additional data must be collected if inconsistencies emerge between the results obtained from different data types and data sources to explore these inconsistencies further. These may not only refer to inconsistent content or characteristics regarding culture. Inconsistencies may also emerge between written and verbal statements, between documents and observed practices, and between verbal accounts and observed practices.

During designing a culture analysis process and collecting data, the general characteristics of organizational culture need to be considered that are outlined in Sect. 7.1.1. Given its collective nature, one cannot grasp an organization's culture by conducting a single interview with the CEO or interviewing the entire top management team. If one interviews only the CEO or the top management, the results will reflect the CEO's or top management's opinion about their organizational culture. However, their perspective may not necessarily reflect the culture as practiced in the various organizational units and hierarchical levels. These interviews may be a starting point, but the resulting data must be complemented by data collected from organizational members across functions, units, and hierarchical levels. In this way, the data analysis may identify potentially existing subcultures, and individual opinions can be separated from cultural knowledge.

Following the method of successive comparisons (Diesing, 1971), data can first be collected inductively in a step-wise approach using triangulation. After a set of interviews, observations, and document analysis, the investigator analysis collected data, resulting in initial insights into the culture and data inconsistencies. The next step of data collection may be narrower, validating the first insights and further explore the discrepancies. Depending on the size of the organization, this process may be repeated. The final analysis of all collected data and their preliminary analysis may result in hypotheses. These can be tested using a deductive approach. The final results are critically discussed with selected organizational members to ensure their validity and finally presented to the top executive group and the entire organization.

A step-wise investigation starts very broad and focuses increasingly on the organization's culture-relevant characteristics. Figure 7.8 gives an overview of a culture analysis project that used the design principle of successive comparisons (Sackmann, 1992).

[9]Triangulation refers to using different types of data and data collection methods to ensure the validity of the research findings. For further information, see also Denzin (2012).

Design of the culture analysis

- Method of successive comparisons

Data collection

- problem-oriented, focused interviews on a phenomenological basis complemented by
- participant observation and
- document analysis.

Data analysis

- theme-focused content analysis on the
    1. individual level and on
    2. group level.

Sample: n = 52 (chosen from three divisions of the same company)

- random sample (across divisions and hierarchies) complemented by
- a target sample.

Validation

- Triangulation
- Data feedback and check with selected organizational members
- Discussion of results with leaders / management

Securing objectivity and reliability

• Data collection:	Test questions during the interview.
• Data analysis and interpretation:	Critical discussion with informed researchers probing into the obtained results.
	Repeated data analysis and comparison with earlier analysis.

Fig. 7.8 Example of an organizational culture analysis combining inductive and deductive methods in a step-wise approach of successive comparisons

When analyzing an organizational culture, the investigator also needs to critically question to what extent obtained cultural beliefs are organization specific. As pointed out in Chap. 2, organizations are embedded in regional and national cultures, and some of their cultural beliefs may also be influenced by their industry's culture. In addition, professions may play a role in influencing potential subcultures identified in the organization. Fig. 2.8 shows the possible cultural influences that may exist within the boundaries of an organization.

7.1.5 Making Sense of the Data: Potential Dimensions and Visualization

If one chooses a deductive approach, the culture analysis starts with deciding about the culture model and its respective dimensions or typology. This decision influences the instrument used for the data collection process and guides the data analysis. The

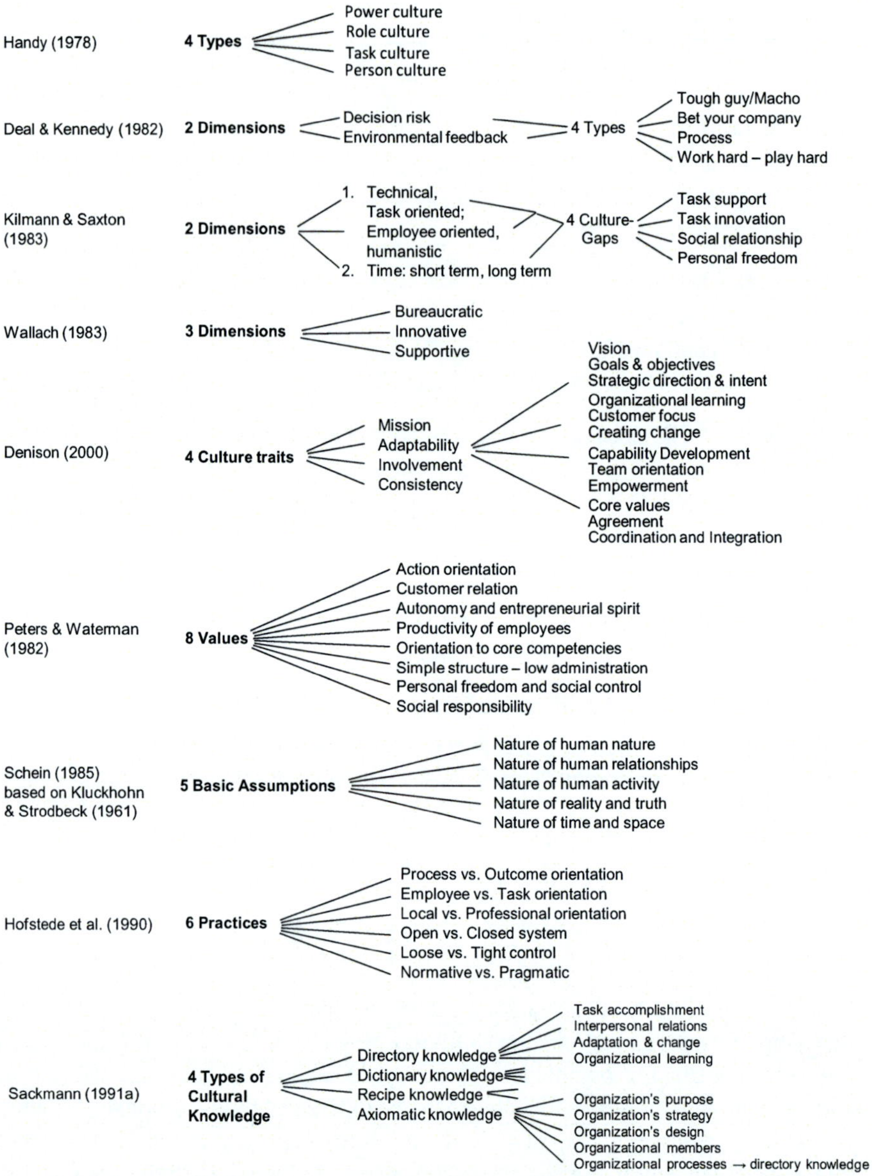

Fig. 7.9 Existing dimensions and types of organizational culture

statistically analyzed data are reported along these predefined dimensions. Figure 7.9 depicts a selection of existing organizational culture models and their respective dimensions or typology.

One may also use the dimensions or categories of an existing culture model as a guiding framework for collecting data. Research with the inductively developed framework of cultural knowledge (Sackmann, 1991a) revealed, for example, that the

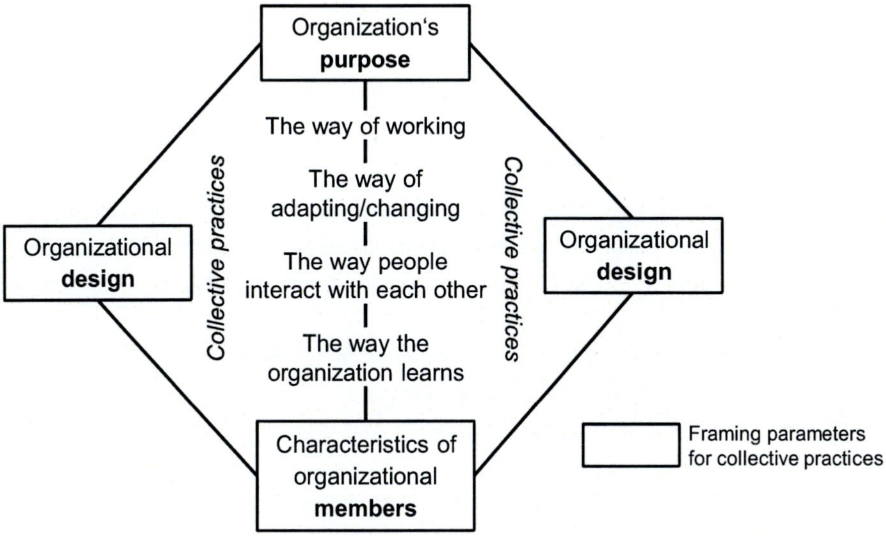

Fig. 7.10 Central areas of content concerning cultural knowledge

four areas organizational purpose, an organization's strategy, design, and organizational members frame and define the specific nature of an organization's collective practices. Four practices turned out to be relevant in characterizing an organization's culture: the way work is accomplished, the way people relate to each other, the way how an organization adapts and changes, and its mechanisms for learning. These four organizational practice areas and their four framing parameters shown in Fig. 7.10 may serve as categories specified and illustrated with specific examples from the data analysis.

When choosing an inductive approach, investigators typically use content analysis and its respective tools (Krippendorff, 2018) to reduce verbal accounts, written data, and observations and develop categories that capture the essence of the data. Figure 7.11 gives an example of the main categories resulting from an organization's culture analysis. These were then described and characterized in more detail.

Given the multifaceted nature of culture, it is impossible to capture all of its characteristics in one analysis. Usually, specific reasons exist why an organization wants to gain a better understanding of its culture. This particular interest may guide the selection of an analysis process and thus influence the areas in which data are collected. In addition, the results can be visualized in different ways. Examples are profiles, spider diagrams, or bar charts.

Once the results of a culture analysis exist, the question arises of what they mean within the organization's context and their implications. The following section addresses these questions.

Overview of GAMA´s Culture Characteristics

1. Strong employee orientation
2. Qualified, interested and mostly experienced employees
3. High level of employee identification and employer attractiveness
4. High level of intrinsic motivation
5. Appreciateive, polite and friendly interactions among organizational members
6. A lot of communication that is mostly indirect rather than addressing issues directly
7. Need for harmony → consensorientation → conflict avoidance → hardly any feedback
8. Hedging behavior – avoiding mistakes
9. Some entrepreneurial behavior – some have it pretty cushy
10. Cautious interacting with superiors who set the priorities
11. Large variety of leadership behavior
12. Weakness in decision making
13. Existing knowledge and systems are used suboptimale
14. Rigid, complicated and slow processes
15. Complicated systems and instruments
16. Reluctance to change

* the organization's name is changed

Fig. 7.11 Example of categories and characterizations resulting from an inductive organizational culture analysis

7.2 Assessing the Results of a Culture Analysis

The results of a culture analysis are descriptive and therefore mostly neutral regarding their implications for a particular organization. If one wants to know if the specific results are *good* or *bad*, *better* or *worse*, *helpful* or *hindering* for a particular organization, the results need to be evaluated against a standard. An evaluation may result from a benchmark comparison with another organization or a group of organizations. One may also compare the obtained results with an internally established standard based on the organization's future strategic direction.

In general, an organization's culture is dysfunctional if it makes its members sick, if micropolitics, power games, and distrust dominate, or if internal power struggles exist between different subcultures. These cultural characteristics absorb much attention, time, and energy from organizational members to use more productively. For example, if an organization's culture is characterized by distrust and fear, its members are likely to take protective measures and thus be distracted from their actual work and tasks. Suppose different functions or organizational units have subcultures that should complement each other act independently of or even against each other. In that case, they are dysfunctional because they hinder work, cooperation, and goal achievement. Furthermore, large discrepancies between written or verbal statements and collective practices do not contribute to an organization's success. Instead, they are indications of cultural problems that require attention.

The extent to which an organization's culture supports the organization's viability depends on its concrete characteristics and the extent to which they support organizational members in their work and implementation of an organization's strategy. Hence, assessing an organization's existing culture requires a definition of the desired or required culture.

7.2.1 Defining the Required Culture

If an organization wants to tap into its culture's potential of being the source for sustainable competitive advantage (Barney, 1986, 2002), the standard for evaluating its current culture is the organization's future direction. Hence, the required cultural characteristics can be derived from the organization's strategy. The comparison of the existing organizational culture with the required cultural characteristics needed to reach its anticipated future will reveal the strengths and shortcomings of a given culture.

An organization's strategy results from regularly monitoring an organization's relevant environment with its actors, factors, and developments that may provide both opportunities and threats. Important actors are competitors and consumers with their demands. Important factors are the economy, ecology, socio-cultural factors, relevant technologies, and potential developments or substitutions. A holistic discussion of these aspects and their possible development may lead to best- and worst-case scenarios. These provide both opportunities and threats for an organization with its' strengths and weaknesses regarding its anticipated future.

A strategy development process also requires critical discussions since the people involved influence the discussion and decisions with their cultural beliefs (see Chap. 4). On the other hand, the successful implementation of a developed strategy requires support from the organization's culture. If an organization does not assign high importance to the strategic direction, the strategic goals will mostly remain lip service documented on paper. It is therefore essential to include cultural considerations and their potential implications in the strategy development process. The best strategy is of no use if it is not implemented due to its culture. The automobile manufacturer Daimler, for example, involved around 1000 leaders and employees in developing its organizational culture 2020, incorporating a swarm organization to base the specification of the future required culture on a wide range of internal knowledge and experience.

7.2.2 Visualizing the Results of a Culture Assessment

A culture assessment is a result of comparing the existing analyzed culture with the required cultural characteristics. The result can be visualized in different ways

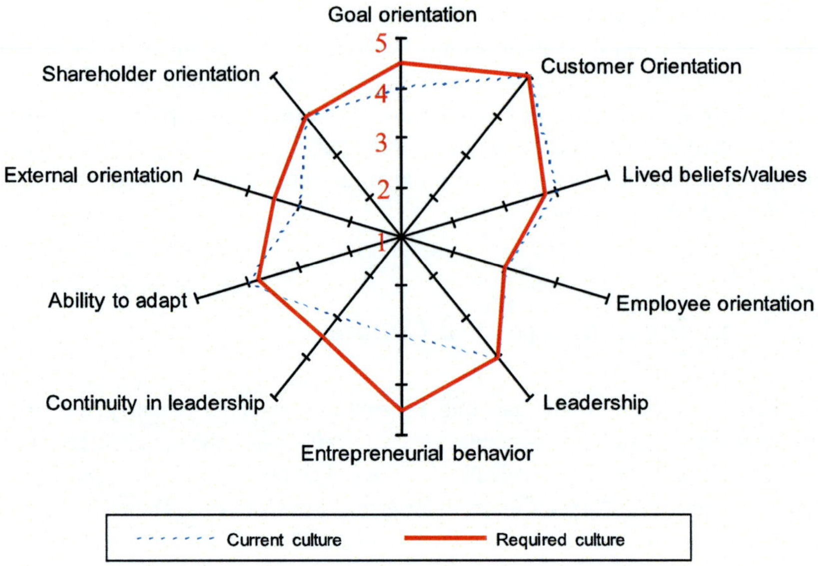

Fig. 7.12 Example of a culture assessment

depending on the way the current culture was analyzed. Figure 7.12 illustrated the results of a culture assessment in the form of a spider diagram. The analysis revealed ten dimensions critical for the required culture to support the organization's strategy implementation. The comparison shows that six out of the ten dimensions have a good fit between the current culture and its future cultural requirements. Hence, the existing culture supports the organization in the way it treats customers, employees, and shareholders. Furthermore, the organization's culture enables the organization to change the leadership behavior is considered appropriate and organizational members walk the talk. Areas in which the existing culture needs further development are its goal- and external orientations and entrepreneurial behavior.

7.3 Examples of a Culture Assessment

Different approaches exist to conduct a culture assessment and several options to collect and analyze a current culture. In trying to understand an organization's culture and evaluating it, the critical aspect is surfacing commonly-held beliefs and related routines that have dropped out of awareness and identifying their implications for the organization and its envisioned future. The following subsections describe two different cases of a culture assessment: assumption analysis and an issue-focused assessment.

7.3.1 Assumption Analysis

Assumption analysis was originally developed for addressing and solving strategic problems (Mitroff et al., 1979). Its adaptation to assess an organization's culture consists of four major phases:

1. identifying the most important culture carriers,
2. surfacing and identifying the commonly-held basic beliefs and assumptions,
3. addressing the implications of these basic beliefs and assumptions for the organization,
4. developing alternative beliefs and assumptions, including an action plan.

In the **first phase**, insiders help identify those organizational members that have the strongest influence on the organization's culture in terms of maintaining and shaping it. Important culture influencers may be decision-makers, formal and informal leaders, and members of the dominant coalitions (Cyert & March, 1963). Influential culture carriers can be organizational members that have had a strong influence on the organization's culture in the organization's historical development, such as founders. Examples of well-known company founders are Henry Ford, Walt Disney, Bill Gates (Microsoft), Steve Jobs (Apple), Bill Gore (W.L. Gore & Associates), Elon Musk (Tesla), Mary Kay Ash (Cosmetics). Robert Bosch, Carl Benz (Mercedes Benz, Germany), or Ingvar Kamprad, founder of the furniture company IKEA. These examples show that their influence may still be present today, but the older an organization is, the more its culture may have changed over time, and more recent culture influencers need to be identified.

CEOs and long-term board members may also influence an organization's culture. A well-known example is Jack Welch (Tichy & Sherman, 2001), who significantly influenced General Electric and its culture for many years. Former CEO *Robert Shapiro* impacted Monsanto's culture when he transformed the chemical company into a biotech firm. Edzard Reuter, a former CEO of Daimler Benz, is remembered for trying to change the car manufacturer into an integrated technology corporation; and *Jürgen Schrempp* for attempting to transform it into a global player within the automotive sector, for merging Daimler-Benz with Chrysler and for failing at successfully integrating the two car manufacturers. Both former CEOs have destroying immense company value. Today, the Daimler AG is back to its roots and former CEO Dieter Zetsche tried to change its hierarchically oriented culture into a more flexible, agile one that embraces change.

Important culture influencers can be identified by analyzing documents, interviewing organizational members, and using sociograms. Sociograms capture the frequency and preference of interpersonal interactions (Moreno, 1996). They can be developed through observations as well as interviews.

After having identified these cultural influencers within the context of an organizational unit or the entire organization, the analyst tries to identify those beliefs and assumptions that seem to have influenced the organization's current culture (**phase 2**). These serve as hypotheses that need further exploration and validation for their support using interview data, on-site observations, document analysis, and interviews.

The **third phase** consists of a workshop with a group of current decision-makers—usually the top management team. The workshop facilitator confronts them with the identified hypotheses about the influential cultural beliefs and assumptions and their implications for the organization. During the subsequent discussion, these hypotheses may be validated, changed, or discarded, and additional assumptions and taboos may emerge with their implications for the organization and its future. Finally, the decision-makers assess the appropriateness of the identified influential cultural beliefs and assumptions for the organization's anticipated future and decide which ones are still supporting the organization and which ones have become dysfunctional.

During the **fourth phase**, the group develops a best-case scenario based on its anticipated future strategic positioning. Then the group explores what kind of basic beliefs and assumptions are needed to move the organization toward this desired state. The following discussion identifies necessary steps for developing these new beliefs and assumptions and how to let go of the dysfunctional ones. Furthermore, they also need to discuss which factors could interfere with or even prevent the implementation of the new cultural reality and develop protective measures for the implementation process.

Surfacing guiding cultural beliefs and assumptions is essential in raising organizational members' awareness about their unreflective thinking and routines. However, given an organization's complexity and the interdependence between basic beliefs/assumptions, norms, practices, and attached emotions, awareness alone does not lead to reaching the desired future state as Pfeffer and Sutton's (2000) have pointed out in their research about the knowing and doing gap. Hence, the implementation of the developed action plan is critical for cultural changes to happen.

7.3.2 Issue-Focused Culture Assessment

An organization's culture consists of many facets that are difficult to capture altogether in one culture assessment. In most cases, organizations are confronted with challenges that can serve as the focus of a culture assessment, or a specific research question. In the following case, an organization faced increasing global competition, and it had difficulties keeping product development schedules and milestones. Overall, the top executive group felt that their organization needed to become more competitive and agile to stay viable, thus requiring a culture change.

After several initial discussions, they the top executive group chose an organization-specific approach for the culture assessment. Its goal was to uncover the basic cultural beliefs and supporting routines that needed to be changed. In a first step, the future required culture was defined based on an analysis of the organization's relevant business environment and its strategy. The second step consisted of the current culture's analysis using the following data collection methods:

- Individual interviews with the top management team as well as with people in key positions across all managerial levels and organizational units (38 persons).
- Workshop with the top executive team.
- Two workshops with high potentials and organizational members, who knew the organization well, wanted to further develop it, and were willing to be part of a change process.
- Two workshops with team leaders as well as employees who had several years of tenure.
- Participant observation during interviews and workshops, while being on-site, such as eating in the firm's cafeteria and during different kinds of company events.
- Analysis of a wide range of internal documents.

Based on the culture assessment goals, the firm's strategic orientation, and initial document analysis, the researchers developed an interview guideline with open questions for conducting semi-structured individual interviews. The guideline ensured the collecting of comparable information across individual interviewees. All interviews were recorded, documented, and content-analyzed. For the workshops, the facilitators chose several open questions. These were first answered by each participant individually and then discussed and critically reflected by all participants. The facilitators documented the findings from the workshops, content-analyzed them, and compared them with the interviews and document analysis findings. Researchers used participant observations to complement and test the continuously collected data and hypotheses that resulted from preliminary analyses. They further explored conflicting information and critical issues. Finally, they compared all data and information, condensed it, and organized it in a report, including resulting recommendations for developing the organization's culture.

The culture assessment results and developed recommendations were first presented to the top executive group and then to leaders and key decision-makers. They reflected, discussed, and thus validated the results and recommendations. The top executive group then decided on development measures based on the recommendations. Finally, all organizational members received the culture assessment results in a condensed form with an opportunity for clarifying potential questions in a personal dialogue.

Figure 7.13 visualizes the central results of the culture assessment and their interrelations. The headings in each box represent the categories that resulted from the issue-focused culture analysis. The text below the headings characterize issues in need of development given the anticipated future direction of the organization in mind.

The questions now arise about what to do to address the identified areas in need of culture development. How can one design such a process, and what needs consideration during a development or the change process? Chap. 8 addresses these questions.

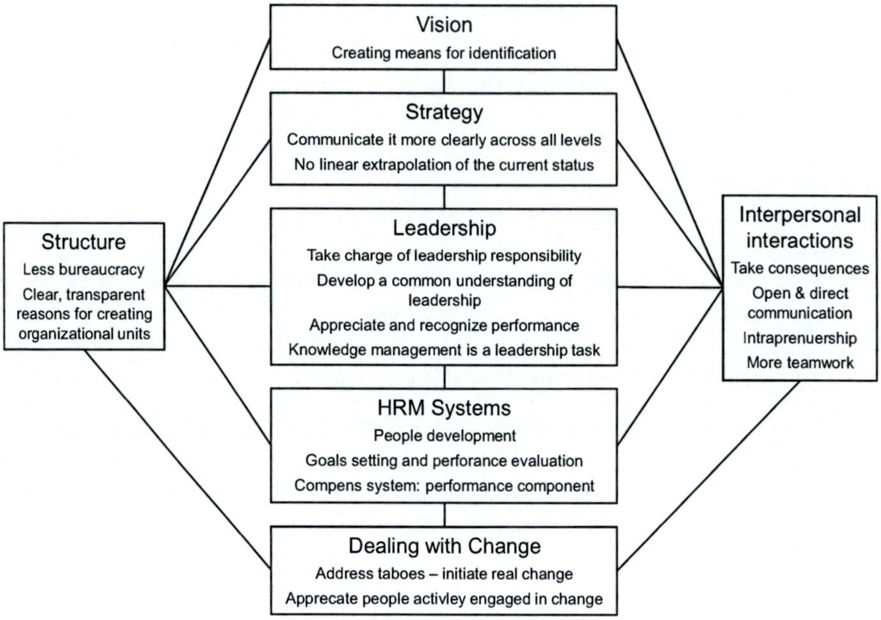

Fig. 7.13 Issue-focused culture assessment including areas for culture development

References

Ashkanasy, N. M., Broadfoot, L. E., & Falkus, S. (2000). Questionnaire measures of organizational culture. In N. M. Ashkanasi, C. P. M. Wilderom, & M. F. Peterson (Eds.), *Handbook of organizational culture and climate* (pp. 129–145). Sage.

Barney, J. B. (1986). Organizational culture: Can it be a source of sustained competitive advantage? *Academy of Management Review, 11*(3), 656–665.

Barney, J. B. (2002). *Gaining and sustaining competitive advantage* (2nd ed.). Prentice-Hall.

Berger, P. L., & Luckmann, T. (1966). *The social construction of reality*. Penguin.

Cameron, K. S., & Quinn, R. E. (1999). *Diagnosing and changing organizational culture*. Addison Wesley Longman.

Chatman, J. A., Caldwell, D. F., O'Reilly, C. A., & Doerr, B. (2014). Parsing organizational culture: How the norm for adaptability influences the relationship between culture consensus and financial performance in high-technology firms. *Journal of Organizational Behavior, 35*(6), 785–808. https://doi.org/10.1002/job.1928

Cooke, R. A. (1997). *Organizational culture inventory*. Human Synergistics.

Cyert, R. M., & March, J. G. (1963). *A behavioral theory of the firm*. Prentice-Hall.

Deal, T. E., & Kennedy, A. A. (1982). *Corporate cultures: The rites and rituals of corporate life*. Addison Wesley.

Denison, D. R. (2000). *Bringing organizational culture and leadership to the bottom-line: The Denison Organizational Culture Survey*. Denison Consulting. www.denisonculture.com; Accessed Sep 22, 2021, from https://denisonconsultingeurope.com/denison-organisational-culture-survey

Denzin, N. K. (2012). Triangulation 2.0. *Journal of Research Methods, 6*(2), 80–88. https://doi.org/10.1177/1558689812437186

Diesing, P. (1971). *Patterns of discovery in the social sciences*. Aldine Atherton.

Gordon, G. G. (1985). The relationship of corporate culture to industry sector and corporate performance. In R. Kilmann, M. Saxton, R. Serpa, & Associates (Eds.), *Gaining control of the corporate culture* (pp. 103–126). Jossey-Bass.

Gundry, L. K., & Rousseau, D. M. (1994). Critical incidents in communicating culture to newcomers: The meaning is the message. *Human Relations, 47*(9), 1063–1088. https://doi.org/10.1177/001872679404700903

Handy, C. B. (1978). Zur Entwicklung der Unternehmenskultur einer Unternehmung durch Management Development-Methoden. *Zeitschrift für Organisation, 47*(7), 404–410.

Hill, V., & Carley, K. M. (2008). Win friends and influence people: Relationships as conduits of organizational culture in temporary placement agencies. *Journal of Management Inquiry, 20*(4), 432–442. https://doi.org/10.1177/1056492611432807

Hofstede, G., Neuijen, B., Ohayv, D. D., & Sanders, G. (1990). Measuring organizational cultures: A qualitative and quantitative study across twenty cases. *Administrative Science Quarterly, 35* (2), 286–316. https://doi.org/10.2307/2393392

Kilmann, R. H., & Saxton, M. J. (1983). *The culture-gap survey*. Organizational Design Consultants. Accessed Sep 22, 2021, from https://kilmanndiagnostics.com/assessments/kilmann-saxton-culture-gap-survey

Kluckhohn, F. R., & Strodbeck, F. L. (1961). *Variations in value orientations*. Row, Peterson.

Krafft, A. M. (1998). *Organisationale Identität. Einheit von Vielfalt und Differenz (organizational identity: Unity of variety and difference). Dissertation Nr. 2115, Universität St. Gallen*. Difo-Druck.

Krippendorff, K. (2018). *Content analysis* (4th ed.). Sage.

Kujala, S., Walsh, T., Nurkka, P., & Crisan, M. (2014). Sentence completion for understanding users and evaluating user experience. *Interacting with Computers, 26*(3), 238–255. https://doi.org/10.1093/iwc/iwt036

Langan-Fox, J., & Tan, P. (1997). Images of a culture in transition: Personal constructs of organizational stability and change. *Journal of Occupational and Organizational Psychology, 70*(3), 273–293. https://doi.org/10.1111/j.2044-8325.1997.tb00648.x

Lansisalmi, H., Peiro, J. M., & Kivimaki, M., IV. (2000). Collective stress and coping in the context of organizational culture. *European Journal of Work and Organizational Psychology, 9*(4), 527–559. https://doi.org/10.1080/13594320050203120

Mitroff, I. I., Emshoff, J. R., & Kilmann, R. H. (1979). Assumption analysis: A methodology for strategic problem solving. *Management Science, 25*(6), 583–593. https://doi.org/10.1287/mnsc.25.6.583

Moreno, J. L. (1996). *Die Grundlagen der Soziometrie. Wege zur Neuordnung der Gesellschaft* (3rd ed.). Leske + Budrich.

Omar, M., & Porter, M. (2007). Organizational power and culture shift at Ducati motorcycles. *Global Business and Organizational Excellence, 27*(1), 20–27. https://doi.org/10.1002/joe.20181

Pandey, S., & Pandey, S. K. (2019). Applying natural language processing capabilities in computerized textual analysis to measure organizational culture. *Organizational Research Methods, 22* (3), 765–797. https://doi.org/10.1177/1094428117745648

Peters, T. J., & Waterman, R. H. (1982). *In search of excellence*. Harper & Row.

Peterson, R. S., Owens, P. D., & Martorana, P. V. (1999). The group dynamics q-sort in organizational research: A new method for studying familiar problems. *Organizational Research Methods, 2*(2), 107–139. https://doi.org/10.1177/109442819922001

Pfeffer, J., & Sutton, R. I. (2000). *The knowing-doing gap: How smart firms turn knowledge into action*. Harvard Business School Press.

Phillips, M. E. (1994). Industry mindsets: Exploring the cultures of two macro-organizational settings. *Organization Science, 5*(3), 384–402. https://doi.org/10.1287/orsc.5.3.384

Puppatz, M., Burmeister, A., & Deller, J. (2017). The assessment of organizational culture in cross-cultural settings: Investigating the psychometric quality and cultural equivalence of three quantitative instruments. *International Journal of Selection and Assessment, 25*(1), 43–60. https://doi.org/10.1111/ijsa.12159

Reger, R. J. (1990). The repertory grid for exliciting the content and structure of cognitive constructive systems. In A. S. Huff (Ed.), *Mapping strategic thought* (pp. 301–309). Wiley.

Sackmann, S. A. (1991a). *Cultural knowledge in organizations. Exploring the collective mind.* Sage.

Sackmann, S. A. (1991b). Uncovering culture in organizations. *Journal of Applied Behavioral Sciences, 27*(3), 295–317. https://doi.org/10.1177/0021886391273005

Sackmann, S. A. (1992). Cultures and subcultures: An analysis of organizational knowledge. *Administrative Science Quarterly, 37*(1), 140–161.

Sackmann, S. A. (1996). Erfassung und Analyse von National- und Organisationskultur: Eine kritische Betrachtung. In R. Lang (Ed.), *Wandel von Unternehmenskulturen in Ostdeutschland und Osteuropa* (pp. 55–64). Hampp.

Sackmann, S. A., & Bertelsmann Foundation. (2006). *Success factor: Corporate culture. Developing a corporate culture for high performance and long-term competitiveness. Six best practices*. Verlag Bertelsmann Stiftung.

Sackmann, S. A. (2011). Culture and performance. In N. M. Ashkanasy, C. P. M. Wilderom, & M. F. Peterson (Eds.), *Handbook of organizational culture and climate* (2nd ed., pp. 188–224). Sage.

Sapienza, A. M. (1985). Believing is seeing: How organizational culture influences the decisions top managers make. In R. H. Kilmann, M. J. Saxton, & R. Serpa (Eds.), *Gaining control of the corporate culture* (pp. 66–83). Jossey-Bass.

Schein, E. H. (1985). *Organizational culture and leadership*. Jossey-Bass.

Schumacher, T. (1997). West coast Camelot: The rise and fall of an organizational culture. In S. A. Sackmann (Ed.), *Cultural complexity in organizations: Inherent contrasts and contradictions* (pp. 105–132). Sage.

Sharpe, D. R. (1997). Managerial control strategies and subcultural processes: On the shop floor in a Japanese manufacturing organization in the United Kingdom. In S. A. Sackmann (Ed.), *Cultural complexity in organizations: Inherent contrasts and contradictions* (pp. 228–251). Sage.

Shim, W. S., & Steers, R. M. (2012). Symmetric and asymmetric leadership cultures: A comparative study of leadership and organizational culture at Hyundai and Toyota. *Journal of World Business, 47*(4), 581–591. https://doi.org/10.1016/j.jwb.2012.01.011

Siebert, S., Wilson, F., & Hamilton, J. R. A. (2017). "Devils may sit here:" the role of enchantment in institutional maintenance. *Academy of Management Journal, 60*(4), 1607–1632. https://doi.org/10.5465/amj.2014.0487

Taormina, R. J. (2009). Organizational socialization: The missing link between employee needs and organizational culture. *Journal of Managerial Psychology, 24*(7), 650–676. https://doi.org/10.1108/02683940910989039

Tichy, N. M. (1975). How different types of change agents diagnose organizations. *Human Relations, 28*(9), 771–799. https://doi.org/10.1177/001872677502800901

Tichy, N. M., & Sherman, S. (2001). *Control your destiny or someone else will.* Harper Business.

Van Rooij, B., & Fine, A. (2018). Toxic corporate culture: Assessing organizational processes of deviancy. *Administrative Sciences, 8*(3), 23. https://doi.org/10.3390/admsci8030023

Wallach, E. J. (1983). Individuals and organizations. The cultural match. *Training and Development Journal, 37*(2), 29–36.

Wardale, D., & Lord, L. (2017). Psychogeography–providing a lens on corporate culture and its potential impact on career success: A novel and efficient approach. *Electronic Journal of Business Research Methods, 15*(2), 99–108. URI: http://hdl.handle.net/20.500.11937/67228

Weiss, J., & Delbecq, A. (1987). High-technology cultures and management: Silicon Valley and route 128. *Group and Organization Studies, 12*(1), 39–54. https://doi.org/10.1177/105960118701200104

Chapter 8
Developing and Changing Organizational Culture

How can a given culture be further developed or even changed? These questions are addressed in this chapter with its focus on an organizational culture's planned development and change. First, the challenges and steps of a culture change process are outlined and shown how the associated risk can be assessed. Planned culture change can occur either in a revolutionary and an evolutionary way. Both strategies are examined with their characteristics and process steps. A model of change highlights the various phases in a culture change process and its implications before addressing the peculiarities of human systems that impact a culture change process. Several interventions, methods, and instruments are discussed grouped into methods focusing directly on people and the organization's context.

8.1 Challenges and Steps of Culture Development and Change

Research and practice document that planned change efforts are not easily implemented and not necessarily successful (e.g., Burnes, 2011). The results of our Change-Fitness surveys in German-speaking countries revealed that although almost every surveyed company faced change, its successful implementation is still an issue. Only about 50 percent rated their change processes of the past two to three years as successful (Sackmann et al., 2019).

The difficulties associated with culture change become apparent in the failures of change projects and as mergers and acquisitions over the past decades. The enthusiasm about corporate culture and its change quickly faded away in the late 1980s and early 1990s (see Chap. 1) when culture change projects did not bring about the desired results. The concepts and interventions of reengineering and lean management replaced attention to culture and culture change initiatives. While these new concepts appealed to people trained in engineering, the change and implementation

S. A. Sackmann, *Culture in Organizations*, Contributions to Management Science,
https://doi.org/10.1007/978-3-030-86080-6_8

of reengineering and lean management efforts were also not that successful with their 70–75 reported unmet goals (Scott-Morgan, 1994).

Strategic alliances and acquisitions, initiated to increase firms' competitiveness, frequently face culture change and development when two or even more organizational cultures encounter each other. Change efforts to align or develop differing cultures into one that is the best of both worlds were not always successful. Critical examples of the past are Volkswagen and Ford, GM and EDS, Rover and BMW, or Daimler and Chrysler (see also Calipha et al., 2010; Doherty et al., 2015; Harbison & Pekar, 2000; Rehm et al., 2012; Morosini, 1998). Organizational and cultural integration processes need time, as demonstrated by the examples of Ciba-Geigy and Novartis. However, it is not always clear what needs to be changed in such a culture integration process, how change will unfold, and who adapts to whom or to what.

Advice on culture change is abundant. Many publications exist on the topic, and management consultants offer more or less well-developed concepts and support. All these activities are usually based on a purposeful and systematic approach towards culture change. These systematic approaches convey to the help seekers that they will achieve the desired results once they implement the proposed measures and follow the prescribed course of action. Unfortunately, human systems operate neither as rational nor mechanistic as the underlying concepts frequently assume or managers and consultants would like companies to behave. Organizations abide by their own established laws and secret rules. If those are not addressed, organization charts, concepts on paper, and rhetorics may change, but the thinking of people and the way they work and act in their day-to-day activities will not change. Reengineering efforts and initiatives to make organizations leaner by taking out one layer of management in the organization chart, scratch the surface without real change (Sackmann, 1995). At the same time, the newly developed organization charts and new rhetorics often serve as an alibi for the intended change: They are visible and audible signs of change. They are used to demonstrate that change has happened and that things are different now while nothing has truly changed in the organization. Instead, successful change results from thorough knowledge, of an organization and its culture, planning and consistent and persistent implementation accompanied by regular evaluations.

Figure 8.1 illustrates the necessary steps in a culture development or change process following a culture assessment. After defining the required culture, one needs to assess the risk for developing identified characteristics of the current culture toward those of the desired future state. This assessment serves as the basis for defining and planning the change strategy, change process, and specific interventions. Regular checks and evaluations make sure that the change process stays on track. In case the situation has changed, these process evaluations help identify required adjustments in time. A planned culture change process is successful once leaders and managers practice culture-sensitive management and embark on a conscious and mindful culture journey (Sackmann, 2006) (see Chap. 10).

The following sections outline the risk analysis first before exploring potential change strategies and change interventions. Then, two possible change strategies are

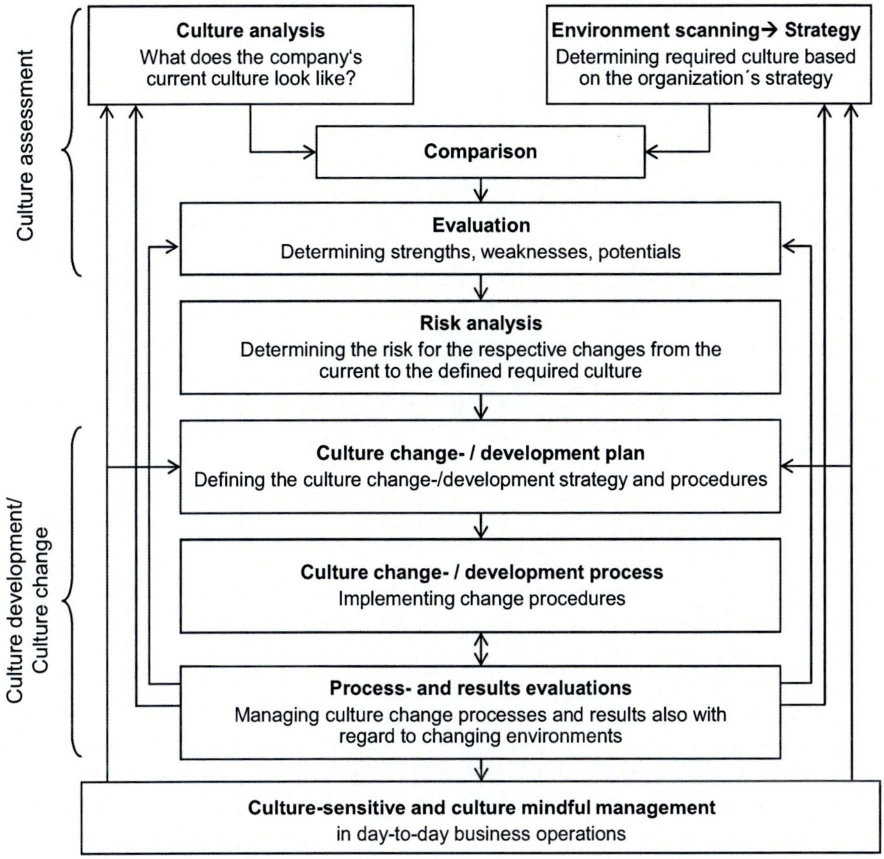

Fig. 8.1 Culture assessment and culture change process

discussed with their inherent challenges and requirements: evolutionary and revolutionary culture change. The choice of change strategy depends on the time available for a culture change.

8.2 Risk Analysis

The risk analysis determines the risk, or probability of success, associated with a particular change from the current to the required culture. It pursues two goals: to raise awareness for the dangers inherent in a culture change process and outline the change process's needed range and depth using two dimensions (Schwartz & Davis, 1981):

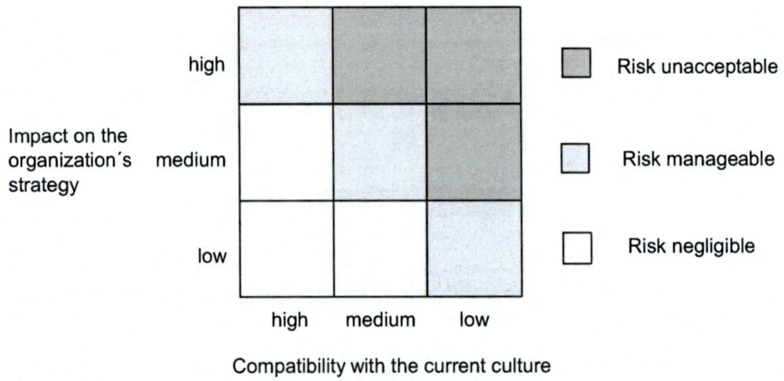

Fig. 8.2 Risk assessment of an organizational culture change initiative

- the importance of the culture change for the required corporate strategy, and
- the compatibility with the current culture.

When combined, these two dimensions differentiate three different forms of risks, as shown in Fig. 8.2:

- a negligible risk,
- a manageable risk, and
- an unacceptable risk.

According to Schwartz and Davis (1981), the risk of a culture change is unacceptable if the anticipated change has a high to medium impact on the strategy and is not very compatible (medium to low) with the current culture. In case of low compatibility of the required culture with the current culture, the change would entail a fundamental, company-wide change process questioning everything, including the culture's core. In case of such a high risk, one possible decision is to refrain from a culture change. For example, when Kraft Heinz withdrew its takeover bid for Unilever in 2017, the underlying reason was their rather different cultures. Alternatively, the organization could decide to stop investing in the business unit in question and instead start investing in a new area that already has the culture required for the future.

The risk of a culture change is manageable or acceptable if

(a) the impact of the culture change process on the strategy and the compatibility between current and required culture are both *high,*
(b) the impact of culture change on the organization's strategy and the compatibility between current and required culture are both *medium*, and if
(c) the effect of the culture change on the strategy and the compatibility between current and required organizational culture are both *low*.

In the latter case c), managers and leaders need to critically question the added value of the organization's change process and examined whether they should undertake such a culture change process at all.

The risk of a culture change is also negligible if it has only a low to medium impact on the organization's strategy and the culture compatibility is medium to high. Such a situation may only require a culture development—not a culture change—process within the context of culture-mindful management (see Chap. 10).

Once decision-makers have assessed the risk associated with a culture change and have become aware of the inherent dangers, they need to decide if they still want to conduct a culture change and what kind of change strategy they want or need to implement.

8.3 Strategies for Culture Change

Planned change of an existing culture requires first insight that a culture change is needed. Secondly, it requires knowledge of the current culture and which specific characteristics need change or development. Organizational culture provides its members with a cognitive framework that they apply routinely in their day-to-day business activities. Such a taken-for-granted and routinely used orientation does not require conscious effort, thoughts, or critical reflection. Hence, decision-makers and people involved in the change process first need to become aware of their culture and necessary change. This knowledge enables them to reflect on their current culture and decide what kind of change they need. Depending on the perceived urgency for change, the appropriate change strategy is either evolutionary or revolutionary. Low perceived urgency calls for an evolutionary change process, while high perceived urgency calls for a revolutionary change process.

Figure 8.3 illustrates the process of how organizational members may become aware of their taken-for-granted collective routines through a perceived need for

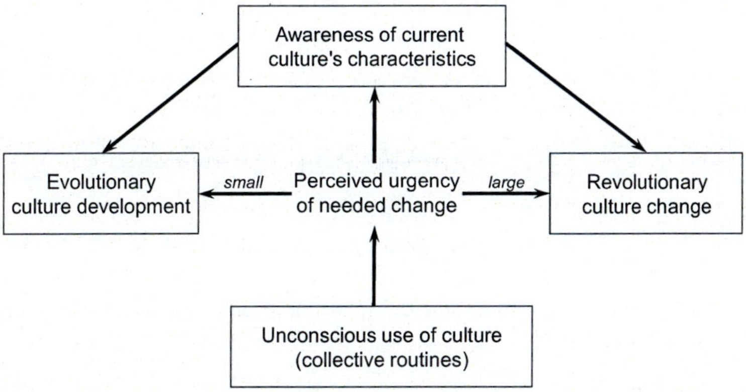

Fig. 8.3 Two strategies of culture change

change. Depending on the perceived urgency for change, they may choose an evolutionary or a revolutionary change strategy. The following section discusses both approaches.

8.3.1 Need for Revolutionary Change

Internal or external pressures may require immediate actions. In a high urgency situation, revolutionary change is the strategy of choice. Perceived pressure for change may emerge when well-established and proven practices fail to deliver desired results or if an organization is already in a crisis. Nystrom and Starbuck's (1984) research showed that most organizational crises emerged because their leaders failed to break their routine perception, thought, and behavior patterns. Thus they did not recognize in time that a change was necessary. Probst and Raisch's study (2005) on organizational failure support these results.

A typical reaction is to intensify existing efforts when faced with a difficult or unexpected situation—be it a new technology, an aggressive competitor, changing customer needs, or negative business results. By relying on routines that have worked well in the past, managers and leaders alike want to demonstrate that these proven practices and well-established paths still work. When intensified efforts fail to deliver expected results, people may realize that they need fundamental rethinking and different actions. To gain such awareness requires a confrontation with facts that they cannot negate. Such facts may be a loss in market share, revenues, quality, customer satisfaction, financial losses, or several employees' resignations.

Once top executives acknowledge a crisis, the pressure for change has usually become high, and time is pressing—a typical situation for revolutionary change. Revolutionary change requires taking radical actions. The business literature provides many examples of crises of, especially large organizations. Many years of continued success can make organizations stale (c.f., Probst & Raisch, 2005). Blinded by their long-term success, top executives and their management may no longer be able to recognize a need for change. Well-known business cases are Kodac, Blockbuster, Xerox, Pan-AM, Nike, or Nokia. Nokia had negated customers' desire for folding mobile phones. Nike had missed the upcoming aerobic trend in the 1990s (Herles, 1999). Pan-American Airlines was a company successfully fighting radical change for a long time. Rather than accepting and acting in response to the changing business environment, they sold off all their assets over the years, resulting in the firm's bankruptcy. Switzerland's flagship airline Swissair experienced the same fate even though the conditions for its grounding differed. Top executives' bad judgment and related decisions finally led to its bankruptcy (Swissinfo, 2016). A revolutionary culture change may have prevented the failures in some cases.

8.3.2 Need for Evolutionary Culture Development

An evolutionary change strategy becomes the choice if the perceived urgency for change is low and allows a development process. Nevertheless, initiating such an evolutionary change process requires a *catalyst* that explicitly addresses the taken-for-granted cultural beliefs, assumptions, and related routines. A new member in the top management team or people who are not (yet) members of the existing culture and bring experiences from different cultural contexts may act as catalysts. Newcomers may question existing routines and can explicitly address culture specifics. They may compare these specifics to other cultural settings and thus verbalize existing perception, thought, and behavior routines more easily, including their potential emotional impact and implications for the organization. Once culture carriers are confronted with the collective beliefs that guide their thinking and behavior, they may reflect on these cultural beliefs' and discuss their implications for the future. External to the cultural setting may also act as a *translator* and *mediator* between existing subcultures. A culture analysis conducted by a non-culture member can reveal blind spots and weaknesses in time and, thus, counterbalance the negative effects of groupthink or actively avoid its emergence (Janis, 1982). Such an awareness-raising process may help prevent a well-established culture from becoming stale and calcified or prevent an unintended culture drift. The procedures of culture assessment (see Chap. 7) helps uncover the predominant collectively-held basic beliefs.

A culture analysis may already act as a change intervention since the questions asked in the process may raise awareness about routines that organizational members use without conscious thought (Lewin, 1953). A critical reflection of those routines may help people realize that these routines are no longer functional for the organization and thus may need to be changed or abolished. Unfortunately, awareness alone is insufficient for initiating and implementing lasting changes, as Pfeffer and Sutton (2000) pointed out in their work on the knowing-doing-gap. Awareness and knowledge need to translate into a strategy for change and concrete actions. The latter includes specific goals for the change, activities for achieving those goals, and transparent responsibilities in the entire process. Furthermore, appropriate indicators need to be determined that signal early if the change process moves in the anticipated direction and brings about the desired results.

Before discussing concrete measures for evolutionary culture development and revolutionary culture change, the following section highlights some specifics of change processes that also apply to culture change and development.

8.4 Implications of a Culture Change Process

Changing culture with lasting effects requires knowledge about the characteristics of change processes in general and some specifics of change management and organizational development. The extant literature on organizational development and planned change provides detailed information on these topics, including recommendations and interventions. In the context of culture change, the following fours characteristics of change processes are relevant:

- incremental vs. quantum change,
- required steps of a culture change process,
- phases of a change process, and
- individual differences in dealing with change.

8.4.1 Incremental Vs. Quantum Change

Planned changes can typically be located on a continuum from *incremental change* to *quantum change* (e.g., Nadler, 1988). Incremental change addresses only a few aspects of an organization and its culture and solves a particular problem. Examples are problems in one organizational unit or a certain level, such as decision-making at the top level. Change interventions are conducted within the framework of existing strategies, structures, and the current culture. According to Argyris and Schön (1995), incremental change is associated with *single-loop learning*. The problem is solved in an incremental change process, but the organization does not gain more general problem-solving skills addressing future challenges. Thus, incremental changes are typically part of a culture development process.

On the other hand, quantum change is a fundamental change in an organization's orientation, its way of operating, and, hence, its culture. Quantum change entails several dimensions and hierarchical levels within an organization. Typically, it addresses the organization's culture and affects its strategy, design, and management systems and instruments. Burke (1994) claims that real and lasting change always implies a culture change. Quantum changes produce *double-loop learning* (Argyris & Schön, 1995). In the process of change and solving its associated problems, the organization and its members develop new competencies that they may apply when dealing with similar issues in the future.

8.4.2 Steps and Stages in a Culture Change Process

Sustainable culture change entails the following five steps:

- Surfacing existing patterns of thought and behavior and evaluating their fit with the organization's envisioned strategy;
- Letting go of some of the familiar routines and *unlearning* behavior patterns that were successful in the past and routinely used;
- Developing and negotiating a new cultural reality that is likely to enable the organization to move toward its desired future;
- Practicing the new thought and behavior patterns, developing necessary competencies and skills, and establishing them as new routines.
- Practicing and maintaining the new cultural reality.

Change is usually associated with new and unfamiliar things. Change at an adult age, however, does not only imply learning something new. It often requires to part with familiar routines first and unlearn them. This process of unlearning ingrained habits and patterns often makes change so difficult for people. The regular use of their routinized practices had created familiarity and emotional attachment over time. Organizational members know these routines and habits well and can retrieve and reproduce them without conscious effort. The longer routines have been used and therefore influenced perception, thinking, and behavior, the more difficult is their change for individuals and organizations (Akgün et al., 2007).

Several models describe the unfolding process of change in terms of three, five, seven, or nine stages. They build on the three phases introduced by social scientist Kurt Lewin (1963): unfreezing, changing, and freezing. The change model illustrated in Fig. 8.4 consists of seven phases.[1] This curve describes processes of change and transformation and can be applied to change at the individual, the group, and the organizational level. A long-term study on culture change tested the model (de Caluwé & Geurts, 2002).

At the beginning of a change process, people may be surprised about what they encounter in the new situation since the actual situation usually differs from what they had imagined before starting the change. Examples are the first weeks in a new (change) project, the first month in a new role, or moving to a different location. If the difference between expectations before entering the new situation and actual reality is small, people may experience it as a *surprise*. If the discrepancy between expectations and encountered reality is large, the person—or the organization—may experience a *shock*. When surprised or even shocked by the new situation, individuals feel insecure, and their perceived level of competence decreases. Not feeling sufficiently competent makes individuals uncomfortable, and they try to move back to a more comfortable zone. The first reaction is to ask themselves what qualities, behaviors, competencies, or skills have helped them become and be successful in the past. What are they good at? This reflection makes them (re-) use more of their familiar behaviors, skills, and routines. Hence, they feel good and competent again.

[1] Clarke (1994) provides a detailed description of this change model.

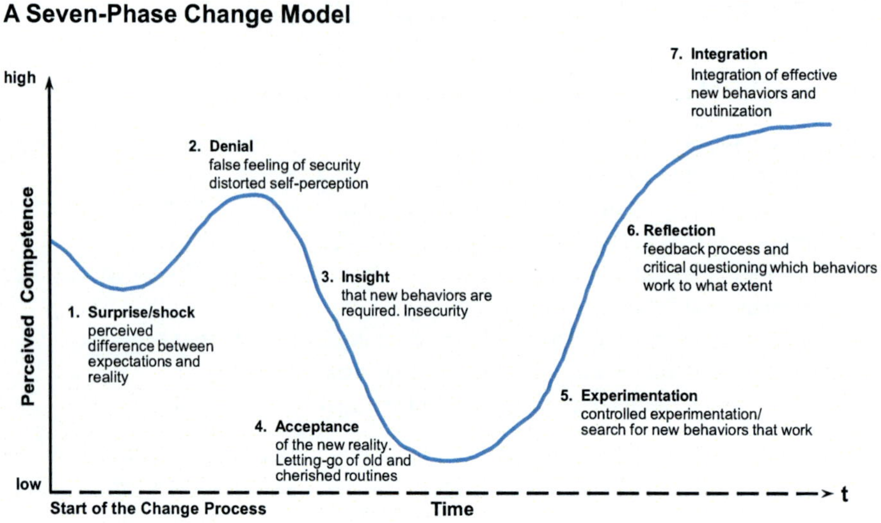

Fig. 8.4 The seven critical stages of a change process

The negative aspect is that they stick to the status quo. Looking back into the past and applying those behaviors that brought about desired results implies that they do not recognize the current situation's novelty or negate it. A false sense of security tends to evolve associated with a feeling of personal competence. This distorted self-perception and self-evaluation may, in an extreme case, lead to their isolation from the outside world. As a result, a change does and cannot take place. To move forward, individuals, groups, or entire organizations need the *insight* and *acceptance* that the situation is new and different from the past and calls for different kinds of behaviors. This process implies letting go of well-established and familiar routines. Unfortunately, the move from *negation* to *insight* and *acceptance* of the new situation is associated with growing insecurity and feelings of incompetence since one does not yet know what to do. This uncomfortable feeling may provoke a move back to the phase of *negation* and old routines.

Accepting that the situation is new and different from one's prior experiences and thus requires new behavior and skills will trigger an actual change process. The *acceptance stage* is difficult because people have not yet established new behaviors appropriate for the situation while letting go of old and familiar habits. Hence, they feel stuck between the old and the new cultural reality—without really knowing what to do. The level of uncertainty and the feeling of personal insecurity is highest at this stage, associated with the lowest level of perceived competence at the individual or collective level. Therefore, it is quite likely that people return to the established culture and its familiar patterns of thinking and behavior. The only way to move forward in the change process is accepting and living with these uncertainties and trying out or *experimenting* with new behaviors.

However, this phase of *experimentation* should not turn into a shot-gun approach by initiating several activities simultaneously. Instead, new behavior needs to be used and tested in a controlled way by critically evaluating how appropriate and effective it is in handling the new situation. In this phase, expectations regarding the outcome of the new behavior may be too ambitious. Hence, if the new behavior does not bring about desired results, it may be taken as a signal that the former practices and routines were better after all. The phase of experimentation requires patience with oneself and the work environment since the new behavior needs training. In addition, it is crucial in this phase to give and accept feedback so that the new behavior can be adjusted, improved, or discarded. In the *reflection* phase, it is helpful to have a *sparring partner* who supports, encourages, and gives differentiated feedback about what works well and needs adjustment. The new behavior can be adapted, refined, and finally integrated into the repertory of behaviors as a new routine in this process.

In a radical and quantum change, most organizational members have to go through these phases quickly. As described above, they have to deal with being personally destabilized during the stages of surprise or shock, unlearning, and experimentation. In addition, the entire organization is destabilized, and performance is most likely lower than expected following the same pattern as the change curve. The model explains and helps understand why some people prefer sticking to the old routines since nobody likes the sense of losing control while feeling less competent. In case the rhetorics have changed, but not the behavior, culture change has not occurred.

8.4.3 Individual Differences in Coping with Change

Even though there is nothing as permanent as change, doing something different is often difficult for individuals, as described above. Nevertheless, change processes are ubiquitous in everyday life, be it one's aging process or colleagues and family members. Nature, seasons, cities, and villages are permanently changing—change is one of the few constants in life.

Individuals differ in their skills and abilities in seeking or avoiding change and their ability to cope with change. Personality differences and past experiences with change processes contribute to these individual differences. The personality differences refer to either being drawn to new things, actively seeking out new situations, and initiating and embracing change or trying to stick with the familiar. In motivation, one theory differentiates individuals seeking success or avoiding failure (Atkinson, 1957). Seekers of success or *initiators* actively choose situations in which they can prove themselves and behave in a way that increases the probability of success. On the other hand, *pawns* do everything to avoid failure and preserve the current situation (De Charms, 1968). These specific orientations and behavior patterns develop during early childhood in interactions with their environment and their feedback from significant others (Rosen & d'Andrade, 1959). Due to their basic orientation, *initiators* tend to be much more open toward change, initiate change more easily, and implement change processes more readily while *pawns* try to avoid change.

Over time, the respective experiences with change become patterned and influence future actions. Individuals who experienced success over a more extended time may have difficulties facing and dealing with a setback or failure. Those who have learned early in life that change processes are associated with positive aspects and challenges, setbacks, and failures can better accept and deal with difficulties. Research also suggests that individuals who have a track record of dealing with new situations and change move faster through the entire change curve. Rather than getting stuck in the phases of negating, insight and acceptance, they move directly from the surprise phase to the experimentation phase. Even though change-experienced people may not have faced the same situation before, they have developed trust in their competencies in dealing with change. This confidence helps them deal with new and unknown situations. Thus, they feel less uncomfortable when faced with uncertainty. Individuals experienced in change neither stick to the old nor are they shocked by the new. Instead, they start right away experimenting with new behavior when faced with a new challenge.

Given these individual differences in dealing with change, a culture assessment should evaluate organizational members' readiness for change and their competencies in coping with change. In addition to individuals, organizations also have some peculiarities that need consideration in a culture change process.

8.5 Culture Change in Organizations: Peculiarities of Human Systems

Human systems differ from mechanical systems such as machines. Mechanical systems are deterministic and built to function with high precision, such as cars or airplanes. Human systems function in a probabilistic way: the outcome of human behavior such as a decision is never one hundred percent certain (e.g., Boulding, 1968; Buckley, 1968; Tannenbaum et al., 1985; Morgan, 1997). Due to the many facets of culture change and its dynamics, one cannot predict a culture development or change project outcome. To increase the probability of success, the following general principles of human systems need consideration in a culture change process:

1. In a culture change process, individuals may need to change
2. Isolated change initiatives and interventions will lead to failure
3. Resistance is part of a change process.

The following sections discuss these principles in more detail.

8.5.1 In a Culture Change Process, Individuals May Need to Change

The members of an organization have developed and negotiated its culture. Every organizational member is a carrier of and contributor to the culture. Therefore, a culture change or development process needs to include individuals and groups. In human systems, it is merely possible to create conditions under which the probability of desired behavior increases and less desirable behavior decreases. To increase success, all organizational members need to participate in the culture change—also managers and leaders. Depending on their current behavior and the envisioned future culture, some of them may need to embark on a personal development journey—regardless of position and hierarchy. Given the importance of managers and leaders in achieving lasting culture change, Chap. 10 addresses their role in more detail.

The collective nature of culture implies that it is not sufficient if one or a few organizational members change. All group members have to address the culture change that needs to occur at the group level. If an organization's culture consists of several subcultures, their intra- and inter-subcultural dynamics also need consideration in a culture development or change process (see, e.g., Sackmann, 1991, 1992, 1997; Trice & Beyer, 1993). How many subcultures exist? What are their basic beliefs and routines? How do they interact with each other? To what extent have they developed a life of their own and distanced themselves from other subcultures? To what extent are the existing subcultures functional for the envisioned future? Which aspects need change or development? Does the current culture entail sufficient variety in skills and competencies required for the future cultural reality? All these questions need to be addressed.

8.5.2 *Isolated Change Initiatives and Interventions Are Set up for Failure*

A large number of methods and interventions exist for a planned culture change. One critical issue is considering all relevant aspects of the human system and including them in the change or development process. On the one hand, this refers to all human elements such as organizational members' collectively-held basic beliefs, verbal and nonverbal behavior, and attached emotions. On the other hand, one also needs to address the *cultural context* in which these beliefs and routines occur. Hence, the system *organization* needs to be considered with its strategy, design, and leadership and management instruments. Depending on the result of the culture assessment, one needs to examine each component regarding its fit with the envisioned cultural reality. Given their mutual influence that sustains the organization as a system, necessary changes in one of these areas need to be aligned with changes in the other areas to move together toward the envisioned future. Hence, all aspects shown in Fig. 8.5 need to be addressed simultaneously in a planned culture development or change process, with the strategy providing the direction.

If an organizational culture needs to move from individual work to more team-based work, the organization's design needs to develop toward team-based systems. Individuals need to change their work behavior and become team players. For teamwork to happen, managers or leaders need to delegate work to teams and not

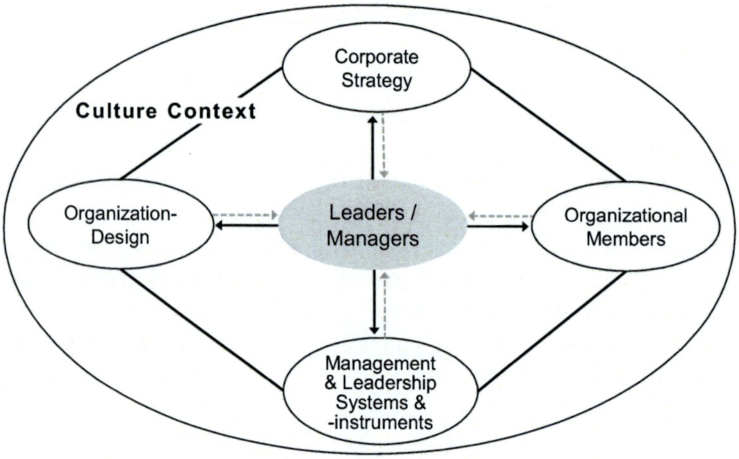

Fig. 8.5 Network of relevant components in a corporate culture development process

individuals and provide the necessary resources for the groups. In addition, the reward system needs to include a team-based component. Otherwise, people will move back to their individual work practices.

This example illustrates the mutual reinforcement process of these different components. Hence, planned change efforts focusing only on an organization's design or its members will not lead to sustainable culture change. Those system components not addressed in the change effort will pull the system back into its original state. One may visualize this pulling-back force if all the connections between the five components were rubber bands in Fig. 8.5. For moving the entire system sustainably, all five components need to move together in the same direction to avoid the pull-back into the system's original state.

8.5.3 Resistance Is Part of a Change Process

Change in human systems tends to produce resistance[2] in some people and groups. Depending on the nature of the culture development or change process, emerging resistance may be small or large, and it may manifest itself directly or indirectly.

Possible forms of open resistance are, for example, open protest, strike, accusing others, asking for a job transfer, or handing in resignations. Examples of covert forms of resistance are general demotivation, lack of participation, absenteeism, an increasing number of sick leaves, mental resignation, disregarding decisions or rules,

[2] Several researchers have addressed different resistance issues and how to handle them in a change process (Ford & Ford, 2010; Jones & Van de Ven, 2016).

or sabotage. In general, the degree of resistance associated with a culture change process depends on

- the degree to which the change affects existing power structures,
- the relative strength and impact of existing power structures,
- key people's loss of reputation and power in the company,
- the level of uncertainty and threats associated with the change,
- the duration and extensity of the change,
- the expected contribution of the culture change to the organization's viability,
- the degree of loyalty of people affected by the change and their level of identification with the organization, and
- the kind and timing of involving affected people in the change process.

Every change implies a change in existing power structures. Most likely, those who do not anticipate a loss of power are more willing to actively support the change process than those who feel that the change threatens their power. If the dominant coalition does not support the planned culture change and has a great deal of power in the organization, it can prevent the change process. This may happen directly and openly, but the dominant coalition members may also act in very subtle ways. The dismissal or transfer of key people who support the change process is an example of subtle resistance to culture change.

The case of Buehler, a former leader of an AT&T business unit, illustrates subtle resistance.

> When Mr. Buehler became head of the business unit, he initiated radical changes to cut bureaucracy and ineffective work procedures. Initially, he encountered quite a bit of reluctant behavior and resistance from his team. However, when they started to realize the benefits of the changes for their work, the team, and the business unit, he was able to win his team for the ongoing change process. Eventually, the highly motivated team contributed to a significant performance increase of the business unit outperforming all other business units. Instead of asking Buehler to continue with the change process at a larger scale, including other business units, he was transferred to a less important and less visible position. Most likely, colleagues and superiors in power perceived his actions as too threatening and wanted to elude his influence.

The more extensive and radical a change process, the higher is the probability that resistance develops. If organizational members express their resistance openly, leaders can address and handle it directly. However, if resistance occurs covertly, it first must be uncovered before the respective leaders can deal with it. A long-term study investigating the handling of the change in 40 hospitals over a period of three years found that resistance—if not uncovered and handled effectively—will become more rigid with the increasing duration of the change process (Jones & Van de Ven,

2016). Hence, it is essential to uncover, address, and actively handle existing resistance.

Frequently, organizational members resist change because they do not know or understand the reasons for the planned change. Or they may perceive the change initiative as unnecessary and cannot see its benefits for the organization. For example, why should money be spent on changing the color of the organization's logo? If the leaders can convincingly communicate the reasons behind the change and its necessity for the organization, resistance is less likely to occur. In addition, if organizational members highly identify with their organization and understand the reasons for the change, they are likely to support the change process without showing signs of resistance. The following example illustrates such a case.

The top executives had decided on a new corporate strategy associated with a more decentralized organization design. The decentralization process affected one of the seven organization units most severely since all of their unit members' workplaces had been in the company's headquarter and now moved to the various regional locations of the company. In addition, the managers of this unit had perceived their tasks as rather administrative in nature. The change process required them to relocate and adopt entrepreneurial and managerial thinking and managerial competencies. Hence, the new division leader initiated several measures to support his managers in this change. One year into the change process, the unit leader initiated an evaluation of the change. The results revealed that the managers perceived the supporting measures as very helpful in developing entrepreneurial and managerial competencies. Due to their high level of identification with the company, they also mentioned that they would support future change processes. Still, they wanted to be included earlier in the planning of change (c.f., Sackmann et al., 2009).

Several studies show that the early inclusion of those concerned by the change lowers their resistance. It seems that the level of resistance is inversely proportional to the timing of inclusion. Being involved in an early phase of a change process develops identification with the change as designed and planned. As a result, organizational members become engaged in implementation because they want to see their efforts succeed.

Another important principle in dealing with potential resistance is to understand people's concerns and take them seriously. Organizational members' questions, concerns, and fears can differ widely due to their differences in dealing with change and their different organizational roles. Therefore, superiors must address these individual differences, including early and sufficient information and clear and timely communication. Employees address their concerns more likely in personal discussions and dialogue. Once people understand why the change is necessary for the organization, they may have difficulties letting go of old routines and acquiring new ones. Still, they will not resist the change process.

These general principles of change in human systems provide the basis for discussing interventions suitable for a planned culture development or an evolutionary culture change process.

8.6 Culture Change Interventions in an Evolutionary Change Process

Once top management has decided to initiate and implement a culture development or change process and decided on the change strategy, the next step is to select specific change interventions for the various areas to start the journey.

Culture change and development interventions fall into two general categories depending on their focus. The focus can be on:

1. culture carriers,
2. organizational context.

The following sections discuss possible interventions in these two areas.

8.6.1 Change Interventions Concerning Culture Carriers

The entire human resources (HR) management function with its HR activities, systems, and instruments can be utilized in a planned culture change. These activities and their related tools addressing organizational members include

- HR planning,
- personnel selection,
- onboarding of newcomers,
- promotion and transfer,
- job rotation,
- education and training.

Compensation and reward systems are not included in this list since they provide a frame for the behavior of organizational members. As such, they are part of the contextual interventions and discussed in Sect. 8.6.2.

8.6.1.1 Culture-Sensitive HR Planning and Selection

Personnel planning and selection are essential tools for developing and maintaining an organization's culture. Existing collectively-held beliefs and behavior patterns can be enforced or changed with the kind of people hired. However, this requires conscious decisions about the type of basic orientations in thinking and behavior the organization expects from its people in the future. If organizational members, including managers and leaders, already live the required culture in their daily work, they still need to reinforce and maintain the existing culture. These activities are part of culture-sensitive and culture-mindful management and leadership (see Chap. 10).

An organization's culture constitutes a form of social control. At the age of twenty, people have developed their personality including certain attitudes, values, and behaviors. Even though these may change over their life span with different life stages, organizations should not assume they can change organizational members' values. Hence the most effective way to develop, change, or maintain an organization's culture is to hire people who fit the basic beliefs and values. Toyota, for instance, recruits its employees as soon as they have finished their education so that they are not yet influenced by other companies (c.f., Sackmann, 2005). Organizations that consider their culture important select individuals with a fitting—or required—general orientation, including attitude, values, and behavior.

In the following example, a CEO describes such a conscious and careful selection process of new organizational members.

The Role of Selection in Shaping Culture

"... you can talk about qualification for a certain job and then check whether or not someone qualifies for it. What is their background and attitude—these show whether they fit in the company. And for every company, there is a type of person that fits. Our specific type of person is—we need people who are self-motivated, you know, initiators. We need profit-oriented people. We need people who can communicate, who are people-oriented, people who are willing to take responsibility ... Many companies are oriented differently. They look for very specific qualifications, for people who are task-oriented and who become human robots and do the same thing over and over all day. There is no real interlock of different skills and talents ... We have a completely different notion in our company. There is no strict centralized control. In principle, we have a lot of people thinking and acting as entrepreneurs in the field who keep our divisions running. You know, it is much better having all these superstars in the field than confining them to the headquarter and having them tell all those out there what to do. That would never work here."

"... so that's something managers value, the attitude with which we deal with one another. Everybody has a bad day once in a while ... But if there is a real, lasting problem you will be transferred, or something else will have to happen. We work too closely together for too many hours to be keeping someone like that around. And that is something we look for in job interviews. We spend about 20 minutes with the applicant, just talking with them. You know, it is much easier to employ someone for administration and train them accordingly than change a person's attitude, i.e., his/her convictions. Everyone

(continued)

can learn how to write an order or whatsoever. Maybe not everyone at the same pace, but everyone can definitely learn. But you cannot teach someone an attitude or a certain work ethic they don't have to begin with ... When I hired a woman the other day, I wanted to make sure she was really willing ... I told her that she wasn't going to be hired only for the order inbox or whatsoever. She would be hired to do whatever was to be done. And that is the attitude I'm looking for. An attitude like that can, of course, be displayed during the job interview, and after three months, the novelty is gone, and the old attitude comes back out. That's why I believe that it has a lot to do with the right attitude."

(Personal conversation of the CEO with the author)

In this company, managers and leaders at all hierarchy levels were aware of the importance of consciously selecting people who fit their culture. Employees also noticed these deliberate actions (Sackmann, 1991). If one considers the cost associated with recruiting, hiring, and onboarding new employees, a careful selection process that includes attention to culture fit is definitely worth the effort (see also Major, 2000). Recruiting new employees also offers the possibility of introducing new ways of thinking and behavior patterns or support desired ones that are still a minority. Such a cultural shaping may avoid having to initiate a planned culture change process.

A careful selection process in terms of an organization's culture may also help prevent groupthink and thus becoming increasingly blind to the organization's weaknesses. New employees are not yet infused with and trapped by the existing cultural reality. This allows them to pose questions that insiders would not even be able to pose because they don't see the issue at hand or because the topic is considered taboo. New employees may critically question why specific processes are conducted the way they are and thus uncover inefficiencies. The culture, however, needs to be open to allow critical questions by newcomers and take their observations and opinion seriously. These cultural characteristics frequently do not exist. Often, long-term organizational members belittle or do not listen to the ideas and opinions of new employees because they don't know its culture and how things work. However, once new organizational members know and have become part of the culture, they will no longer pose critical questions. Hence, organizations need to make a consciuos effort if they want to deliberately use newcomers to uncover inefficiencies or dysfunctional aspects of their organization's culture. They can ask them to identify improvement potentials and suggest new, more efficient ways of operating.

If an organization consciously hires people with different basic beliefs and work practices to develop or change the current culture, these newcomers need protection from the current culture. For example, they could join a project team or business unit that works on new business ideas outside the regular or dominant organizational structure and culture. If these differently oriented newcomers are immediately integrated into the organization, two things may happen: They will either adjust to the existing culture or leave the organization because they cannot practice for what they were hired. As a result, the conscious selection effort intended to change or develop the culture was in vain. Many examples exist for well-intended yet unsuccessful culture change processes regarding hiring practices.

In the mid-1990s, several European-based international organizations hired MBA graduates from elite universities to professionalize their organizations. To successfully acquire these high potentials, the firms even paid part of the high tuition fees. When the high potentials started working in the companies, they were told that they had to first learn and adapt to the organization's culture and work their way up in the hierarchy. However, their MBA education had socialized them for a fast-moving career with high levels of responsibility. When the high potentials realized that this would not happen soon, they quit their jobs and sought challenges in different companies.

8.6.1.2 Onboarding of New Organizational Members

The appropriate introduction of new employees to an organization and its culture is an essential intervention for actively maintaining or developing a specific culture or subculture. The onboarding process provides the newcomers with an orientation for their new work environment and its way of working. In this process, they learn the priorities of the cultural setting and get informed about the unit's and superior's expectations regarding their work and work behavior. In addition, they learn what kind of role(s) they should enact and appropriate and inappropriate interpretation patterns. Hence, the entire onboarding process is a unique opportunity of infusing new organizational members with the appropriate cultural beliefs and related practices. If this process is not planned with cultural socialization in mind, a valuable opportunity is missed for maintaining or changing the culture. In addition, the danger exists of a potential culture drift. For example, the results of a study revealed that new employees learn the company's most essential jargon on the job during the first week of employment and that new employees deduce insights for their survival in an organization from stories told by long-term colleagues (Martin et al., 1983). Other studies show how important and formative new employees' experiences are, especially during the first weeks of employment (Van der Post et al., 1998).

Providing organizational guidelines and support systems for the initial orientation phase meets new organizational members' needs and active search for orientation (see Sect. 2.3.4) in the new work environment. Organizational guidelines may consist of a combination of written orientation materials, a guided visit, and walks around the organization, including their introduction to colleagues, co-workers, and managers. Providing a mentor for the first few months may also be helpful and effective in helping them learn their way around in the organization and getting familiar with the culture. In addition, a mentor may help newcomers answering several questions that come up during their first months. Decision-makers, however, need to make sure that the chosen mentors are good representatives of the desired culture to help new organizational members develop the *right* and preferred cultural interpretations.

To ensure that new employees learn the central characteristics of their culture right from the start, Toyota, for example, conducts an onboarding week at their locations. This onboarding week takes place in specifically designed rooms that visualize and explain the essential characteristics of Toyota's culture with plenty of information displayed on the walls in the room. These visualizations support the individual presentations and conversations during the introduction week (Sackmann, 2005). Other organizations use a rotation program for new organizational members introducing them to the different organizational functions and their respective work quickly.

8.6.1.3 Staffing, Promotion, and Transfer

The filling of a position, every promotion or transfer of organizational members conveys a message to all others regarding the organization's desired or unwanted behavior. The staffing of a key position and a promotion communicate to organizational members what kind of qualifications and attributes the organization is expecting from its people; what makes a *good* employee, manager, or leader. A transfer to a less desirable role or position signals what kind of behavior is not appreciated. Hence, decision-makers need to carefully examine their staffing, promotion, and transfer decisions regarding their cultural implications, including the symbolic message they communicate to organizational members. In addition to having achieved excellent business results, are those people up for promotion also good representatives of the organization's desired culture? If, for example, the organization wants to emphasize more teamwork in the future, it is crucial to fill visible positions with positive team player examples.

In a culture development or change process, decision-makers also need to ask themselves which organizational members do not represent the organization's culture and either part with them or remove them from visible positions. Most organizations that pay conscious attention to their culture have examples of having parted with people who had violated basic cultural beliefs and practices (c.f., Sackmann and Bertelsmann Stiftung, 2006). Thus, the following question is a kind of litmus test of whether an organization truly considers its culture important: Are we ready to part with an employee, manager, or leader who delivers good performance but does not adhere to our culture's basic principles and practices?

The following example illustrates the negative impact of a promotion that was incongruent with or even adverse to the goals of a culture change process.

A Culturally Counter-Productive Promotion Decision

A global company started a large initiative to change and develop its current culture with three objectives:

1. Moving away from a strong focus on individual contributions toward more teamwork;
2. Moving away from mistrust toward building trust;
3. moving away from reacting to change toward actively initiating change.

With the help of external consultants, they designed a three-month management and leadership development program, including an on-the-job project phase and follow-ups. Leaders and managers from different units and hierarchical levels attended the programs. The program's goal was to professionalize managers and leaders and accomplish the culture change mentioned above. A personal development program was part of the six-week professional skill development program. The participants could apply and deepen their learnings in the following three-month project phase while working in their jobs. Based on its content, intensity, duration, and coverage, the program triggered change at the personal, divisional and organizational levels.

The culture change process was well on its way in the company when headquarters staffed a key leadership position with a person who exemplified the old culture. The leader epitomized individual work, mistrusted people, and delegated work to individuals instead of teams. This promotion made many people question the intentions of the culture change process. The new culture orientation with its respective thought and behavior patterns could survive in those areas where it was well established and more distant from the new leader's areas of responsibility. The focus on teamwork was, however, no longer actively pushed or supported.

Promotions and transfers of people with respective qualifications and the appropriate culture orientation can signal a culture development or a culture change and thus act as visible signs for its start. For example, having to reapply for one's job is a strong signal. The desired effect is that managers and leaders need to critically reflect their skills and competencies, including their contribution to their role and organization—also in terms of its culture. This intervention is unsettling to most people and the entire organization, but it signals the beginning of a culture change process that cannot be negated or trivialized. Several organizations have used this intervention in the past. Top executives need to communicate the reasons for this intervention and provide support for organizational members.

8.6.1.4 Job Rotation

Job rotation is an intervention that can be effectively used in the context of a culture change or development effort. It is especially effective if an organization has several subcultures that work independently, even though they should cooperate. These subcultures may exist in different departments, divisions, business units, line management, and projects in a matrix organization. A well-designed job rotation in which people move between those organizational units and the subcultures in question will be helpful to improve the units' cooperation and alignment. Job rotating people need to work in each unit long enough to understand its way of functioning. Then, when moving back to their original unit, the rotating people have acquired the perspectives of the other units. This knowledge helps to design and practice more effective communication and coordination processes.

With this purpose in mind, job rotation has been successfully implemented in many organizations. For instance, a firm operating in the high-technology sector had severe cooperation problems between several divisions. Every division worked independently, and their lack of cooperation hindered some of the divisions in accomplishing their work in time. During a culture change process, job rotation was implemented between these divisions. As a consequence, the cooperation between the divisions improved considerably.

Some organizations argue that job rotation is not feasible since gaining the expected benefits requires staying several months in other divisions. However, shorter stays in different units are possible if these are well planned and the rotating people receive support in learning the particularities of another organizational unit. Only if they know the unit's particular way of working can they bring this knowledge back to their division and improve the cooperation and alignment between these organizational units.

8.6.1.5 Education and Training

Education and training can and should be purposefully used in changing and developing culture. Besides providing professional qualifications, both are essential instruments of socialization. Education and training programs inform employees about an organization's priorities and expectations about the appropriate orientation of organizational members, including important cultural beliefs and expected behavior.

The choice of content, context, and delivery of education and training programs indicate the organization's priorities and the *right* and *wrong* way of thinking and behaving. Even the absence of education and training programs orientate organizational members. It conveys to them that the organization does not consider such learning activities as necessary. Many organizations could design and implement their education and training programs more carefully with their cultural socialization function in mind. The following subsection discusses this issue for managers and leaders.

8.6.1.6 Management and Leadership Development

Developing managers and leaders play a crucial role in culture change, development, and maintaining a given culture because of their visible position that has leverage effects. Managers and leaders are the first anchors for their employees' orientation. Superiors' verbal and nonverbal communication informs their employees about the organization's priorities. What kind of behavior do managers and leaders consider relevant for their immediate work? Their daily work behavior demonstrates desirable as well as undesirable behavior to their direct reports. Thus they personify the organization's culture with its expectations toward organizational members (see also Chap. 9). For these reasons, it is essential to carefully design management and leadership development programs. Since these programs act as means of socialization into and reinforcement of the desired culture, the choices of venues and participants are also critical.

The choice of venue communicates the importance and status that an organization attributes to the respective program and its participants. For example, does a program take place on the organization's premises or in an expensive hotel in an attractive location? Does the organization have its own venue for management and executive development efforts, or does it conduct those in cooperation with external providers such as universities? Which providers does the organization use for which management level?

The choice of participants for specific programs signals position and status both to the participants and to all other organizational members. For example, who is considered a first, second, or third-line manager? Who belongs to the group of high potentials or a so-called goldfish pond? Who belongs to the group of prospective leaders? The current holders of key positions and those who move into a key position indicates direction, goals, and priorities to the other organizational members.

The choice of content for management and leadership development programs is essential since they provide specific mindsets for the participants. For example, what does the organization consider appropriate management and leadership? What kind of leadership model, concepts, and management instruments learn participants from those programs? Are all managers and leaders exposed to the same management and leadership models and concepts or different ones? Are internal speakers involved, and if so, how many and for what kind of content?

Many organizations plan education and training measures based on their hierarchical level. The lower management level attends a management development internally designed in cooperation with an external trainer at a local venue. The next management level is sent to a renowned institution in Europe, and the executive level attends a program of a famous university in the U.S. Such an approach acknowledges the status differences between these hierarchical groups but neglects the cognitive socialization aspect of these programs. If different providers expose them to other management and leadership models and teach them different management instruments, participants across programs do not share the same mental models and concepts that guide their behavior in their role as manager or leader. Thus communication across hierarchical levels becomes more difficult. From an organizational culture perspective, the concepts, models, and instruments taught in the various management and leadership development programs need to be aligned.

8.6.2 *Culture Change Interventions Focusing on the Organizational Context*

Organizational context refers to the entire work environment with its material, structural, and instrumental aspects. These are, among others

- the organization design including structures, processes, responsibilities and accountabilities,
- job design,
- reward practices,
- management and leadership systems and their respective instruments,
- technologies and techniques,
- architecture and interior design.

All these aspects constitute the organization's frame for its members' collective thinking and acting. They operate indirectly, define the field for appropriate behavior for organizational members and serve them as means for orientation, providing guidelines for their actions.

8.6.2.1 Organization Design

The organization design defines the basic principles of an organization's structuring. Hence, it determines the responsibilities in the organization and regulates the division of work, formal ways of information and communication, and the kind of cooperation between people and organizational units. An organization's design can follow different logics, such as a functional, divisional, project-, matrix, or network structure. Furthermore, it can be geared to value chains, strategic business units, systemic or holographical principles, or the principles of collective intelligence, and it can contain hybrid or virtual structures (c.f., Ríos, 2014). Every organization design has strengths as well as weaknesses and requires certain behaviors from organizational members. Hence, it influences their behavior since each type of design enables and impedes certain kinds of behavior (c.f., Tushman, 2014). For example, while hierarchical structures clearly define responsibilities and accountabilities, they inhibit innovative and self-initiated behavior. On the other hand, a design relying on the principles of self-organization requires qualified employees who are capable of leading themselves and leaders who are willing to delegate and release power.

An organization design can also combine different logics that coexist (c.f., Kotter, 2014). For example, routine work requires stability, while innovation requires creative search and experiments (c.f., Tushman & O'Reilly, 1996; O'Reilly III & Tushman, 2016). From a culture change and development perspective, top decision-makers must choose their organization's design carefully so that desired behaviors are enabled, and less desirable behavior is discouraged.

The specific organizational design also acts as a selection mechanism in attracting, acquiring, and retaining organizational members. *Bell Industries*' case illustrates that the organization design served as a framework for the firm's current cultural context and its specific type of people that fit. Thus, organization design and the type of people are interdependent and mutually influence each other.

Bell Industries

Over the course of three years, Bell Industries had grown quickly by acquiring 25 small entrepreneurial firms. Their founders and owners sold their companies to Bell Industries for shares. The then CEO and chairman of the board wanted to form an organization as centralized as possible. The former entrepreneurs were neither used nor could they cope with the bureaucracy, relinquishing power to the headquarter and slowing down decision-making associated with the new corporate design. These entrepreneurs left the company as soon as their contracts permitted.

As a consequence, the share price of the company plummeted. The major shareholders who had stayed with the company gathered and discussed the situation. They concluded that they would need the former owners' knowledge of the respective markets and customers, given its diverse portfolio. Since all of the acquired companies had been well managed and financially successful, the new top management decided to develop organizational structures that would allow entrepreneurs to stay within an appropriate corporate framework.

Consequently, they decentralized the company as much as possible, i.e., they shifted tasks, competencies, responsibilities, and accountability down as far as possible to keep the entrepreneurs in the company. The newly developed organizational design was flat and decentralized. It contained only three hierarchy levels. The business units were independent and manageable and based on the principle of self-organization. There was no organization chart because the new top executive group did not want the employees to feel responsible for an individual box on that chart but the entire company. In addition, the group adopted key performance indicators to apply to every business unit and served as orientation for them. Furthermore, they adapted the reward system so that entrepreneurial behavior that targeted the entire

(continued)

company's success was rewarded instead of rewarding self-optimizing behavior.

Once they introduced the new organizational design, the top executive team regularly observed and consciously cultivated it as part of their daily routine to keep those thinking and acting like entrepreneurs. In addition, newly-hired people had to be entrepreneurially oriented.

The case of *Bell Industries* illustrates that certain organization designs attract specific types of organizational members and are not attractive to others. The degree of attractiveness may depend on their need for structure and orientation instead of freedom at work and taking the initiative. Hence, self-selection processes operate to create a fit between the type of people and the type of organization design with its structures and processes. People who have a high need for structure and orientation will prefer a hierarchical design with clearly spelled out rules, roles, tasks, and responsibilities. On the other hand, those who are self-organized and like to take the initiative and shape their roles. They would feel stifled in a bureaucratic organization and instead apply and stay in an organization based on self-organization principles such as *Gore & Associates*.

Gore & Associates Ameba Concept

Gore & Associates, one of the 200 largest privately-held U.S. firms, was founded in 1958 and now has more than 11'000 organizational members (www.gore.com/about/the-gore-story#overview). Its design is built on the ameba concept with fluid structures (Flik, 1990). No job, function, or role descriptions exist. Next to their qualifications, *Gore & Associates* hires people based on their potential. Once hired, new employees can move around in the firm and join those projects where they believe they can contribute based on their knowledge and experience. All new employees are astonished about this high level of freedom, and some newly hired cannot handle it. Those who expect more structure and guidance tend to quit in the first few months.

Given the influences mentioned above of an organization's design, it needs to support an organization's strategy implementation and alignment with the basic principles of the required culture. For example, entrepreneurial, innovative behavior will be less likely in the context of a rigid, bureaucratic design since it requires freedom to act. Hence, one may deliberately use organization design to initiate culture change and development. The acquisition of Electronic Data Systems (EDS) by General Motors (GM) illustrates a well-intended but unsuccessful attempt of such a culture change effort.

GMs Attempt to Become more Flexible by Acquiring EDS
EDS was founded in 1962 by Ross Perot with an initial focus on facility management. It moved into providing computer expertise and services to the banking, insurance, and the travel industry with USD 230 million revenues and 8000 employees in 1979. In 1984, GM acquired EDS to automate everything from GM's medical insurance claims processing to its assembly lines, thus making GM faster and more flexible and infusing EDS'entrepreneurial spritit. However, GM people developed barriers to block the EDS influence. Especially GM managers perceived EDS'people's direct and agile way of working as threatening. EDS people did not seem to care for status or power. The GM manager were scared to lose their status and their power. The two companies'cultures were so different that GM bought out entrepreneurially oriented EDS founder Ross Perot, who supposedly said that trying to change GM's corporate culture was like trying to teach an elephant to tap dance (Holusha, 1986). EDS eventually became an independent company and relisted on the New York Stock Exchange.

Siemens' acquisition of former Nixdorf Computer AG is another example of a purposeful, intended culture change initiated by a structural change. The agile and market-oriented firm Nixdorf added an entrepreneurial orientation to much larger and older Siemens. Siemens, in turn, could offer Nixdorf standardized systems and processes needed for the company's next growth stage and further development.

Another option for making large organizations with hierarchical or even calcified structures more innovative is establishing a parallel structure. Rather than changing a *well-oiled machine* that runs very efficiently, innovation may happen in a parallel organization built on self-organizing principles, thus providing organizational members with the required freedom to act. This parallel organization reports directly to the top executive group or an innovation board of advisers To prevent internal barriers. Introducing the principles of collective intelligence can also result in more flexibility and agility.

Since no single organizational design is ideal and has certain advantages and disadvantages, top decision-makers need to check the various effects of their organization's design regularly. Such a regular check prevents the calcification of collective thought and behavior patterns and helps uncover potential misalignment with the organization's culture early. The Liechtenstein-based multinational Hilti AG, for example, regularly checks their structures and processes regarding their support of the firm's customer orientation. If they find friction losses due to suboptimal working processes, they will implement measures or change those processes (Sackmann & Bertelsmann Foundation, 2006).

8.6.2.2 Compensation and Reward Systems

Compensation policies and related compensation and reward systems play a central role in shaping and maintaining the specific orientation of an organization's culture. Strictly speaking, reward systems are part of an organization's management- and leadership systems, but because of their important role in maintaining and changing an organization's culture, they are discussed separately. Compensation policies, reward systems, and the respective practices[3] indicate to organizational members which behaviors are desirable: which behaviors are–literally–valued in an organization and which do not have a financial or career-advancing impact. Thus, existing policies, systems, and practices guide organizational members' attention and work behavior. They will show and repeat more likely those behaviors and work practices for which they are compensated and rewarded. In his classic article, "On the Folly of Rewarding A, While Hoping for B," Steve Kerr (1975/1995) pointed out that organizations invariably violate a fundamental law of human nature by rewarding the very behaviors which they are supposedly trying to discourage while failing to reward the behaviors they desire to reinforce. Hence, a culture change or development process needs to examine compensation and especially reward systems critically.

In this process, decision-makers have to ask two critical questions: for what kind of orientation and behavior are organizational members at all hierarchical levels currently rewarded? And what kind of orientation and behaviors does the desired culture require?

Traditionally, organizations compensate people in several functions primarily for time spent in the organization—both daily and regarding their tenure. However, the time spent in an organization does not necessarily reflect the contribution that organizational members make to the organization. In production and sales, performance-based pay and reward systems are more common. The question is, however, what kind of performance is compensated and rewarded? Is it the number of pieces produced and contracts closed or a combination of quantity and quality? Is efficiency or effectiveness rewarded or both? Are routine work or creativity, innovation, and entrepreneurial behavior rewarded? Is individual work or teamwork rewarded or both? Is a short-term- or a longer-term orientation valued or both? The financial crisis in 2008/2009 triggered critical discussions about the design of compensation and reward system. How could an organization compensate and reward not just for the immediate win but for a long-term orientation at all levels of an organization? Are all organizational members treated as employees, or can they take financial ownership in the company? An if so, what are the criteria for becoming a partial owner of one's employer?

The answer to these questions is not straightforward and suggests that combinations of different components are most likely required. In case an organization's

[3] For a detailed discussion of the design and effects of reward systems, see, for example, Agarwal (1998), Cissell (1987), Kerr (1975, 2009), Kerr and Slocum (2005).

culture needs to change from a focus on individual contribution toward more team- or project-based work, the compensation system should have a team- or project-based component. Otherwise, organizational members will neglect their team or project work if they are under time pressure and only rewarded for their individual contributions. If their contribution to the team or project counts and if the team or project performance is part of organizational members' evaluation, they will most likely try to satisfy work demands from the team or project and the line organization. The following examples give some insights into the various facets and effects of compensation and reward systems.

Examples of Compensation and Reward Systems and Related Practices

1. The top management of a large corporation complained that people were not collaborating across business units and instead seemed to treat their business units like separate organizations. This behavior was astonishing since compensation packages contained a pay component based on the company's overall performance that could exceed organizational members' variable pay component. Nevertheless, they seemed to do those things that optimized their personal performance and their business unit's performance. A closer examination of the entire compensation- and reward system and work practices revealed that personal advancement depended on the direct superior in the business units. Bosses decided both on the type of projects and their managers' next career steps. Some projects were more attractive to the engineers due to the cutting-edge technology and visibility in the external industry community. Furthermore, the next carrier step was associated with a more significant pay increase over time than the pay component based on the company's overall performance. This information helped redesign the compensation and reward system to provide a more enabling context for cooperation between the different business units.
2. In a production-based firm, the management wanted their production people to act like entrepreneurs and balanced four somewhat conflicting goals. These were output (units produced), quality, innovation, and continuous improvement. The company developed a compensation system that rewarded their production people based on the number of units produced. However, the company deduced units returned due to quality issues from the output number and, hence, from their pay. If employees made improvement suggestions for their work areas, they received a share of the cost savings or the gains calculated over a specific time. These reward system components focused organizational members' attention to simultaneously consider contradictory elements in their work such as efficiency and effectiveness, speed and quality, and improvement and innovation
3. The top executive group of a multinational organization realized that their leadership appraisal system allowed them to assess their managers' and

(continued)

leaders' competencies and skills but would not necessarily lead to better-qualified leaders. Furthermore, their leaders neglected the people management side in their work. The improved qualification system contained two new components: *employee development* and *leadership*. The various facets of both components were clearly defined and discussed regarding the organization's expectations and effects. Both components became part of the yearly goal agreement. The company rewarded the degree of attaining these new objects with a variable pay component. As a consequence, the quality of leadership improved, and the number of qualified leaders increased.

4. The intended culture change of an international bank started with a culture assessment workshop with high-level managers. All of them complained about their culture and especially the kind of leadership behavior of their direct superiors. However, when discussing concrete actions for change, they refused to commit to any of them. Further probing revealed that they were afraid of addressing critical issues with their superior because it might harm their relationship. They considered the relationship important for affecting their yearly bonus since their superior decided on their bonus at the end of each year partly independent of their personal goal attainment. Given that the bonus was a significant amount of money and a big part of their compensation package, they were unwilling to change their culture and used the workshop to let off steam instead. This was the end of the culture change effort.

These examples illustrate the various facets of compensation and reward systems and underline the importance of analyzing these systems in a culture change or development effort and aligning them with the future direction. The power of compensation and reward systems lies in their orientation function. They provide clear indicators for employees, managers, and leaders alike for what the organization expects from them; what they need to do to survive, get rewarded, and advance in an organization. Unless compensation and reward systems and their respective instruments are aligned with changes initiated for moving toward the desired culture, the culture change will eventually not be successful. However, similar to an organization's design, no compensation or reward system is perfect. Hence, they need a regular check regarding the kind of behaviors they encourage and discourage and if certain aspects need better alignment with the desired culture.

8.6.2.3 Management Systems and Instruments

In addition to an organization's strategy and design, management and leadership systems are also part of framing an organization's culture because they serve as orientation and guidelines for organizational members' behavior. A management or leadership system usually subsumes the general logic of an organization's aligned planning, control, information, and human resources (HR) systems. Management- as well as leadership systems, can refer to strategic or operational aspects of business management.

In culture change and development, those aspects are essential that determine whether and which systems are introduced in quality-, information-, energy-, environment-, or people management. In addition, every management and leadership system contains instruments for implementing specific measures. Generally, a culture change or development effort can use the orientation function of all management and leadership systems and their respective instruments. Of particular interest and importance are the systems and instruments in HR, communication, and controlling.

In addition to the compensation and reward systems discussed in a separate section, selected HR management and leadership systems and their respective instruments include, for example:

- Management by objectives,
- Leadership principles or leadership guidelines,
- Feedback systems and instruments such as upward-, 180°-, 270°- and 360°-feedback,
- Employee surveys,
- Appraisal interviews,
- career planning instruments,
- exit interviews.

Systems and instruments in the area of *information and communication* include

- management information systems,
- information and communication systems.

Selected management systems and instruments in the area of *managerial control* comprise, for instance:

- the Balanced Scorecard,
- planning instruments,
- budgeting,
- controlling and reporting.

HR Systems and Instrument

HR management and leadership systems and their respective instruments guide organizational members' attention and behavior. The introduction, implementation, and existence of a management system, such as management by objectives, signals organizational members the importance of setting goals, including respective priorities and achieving them. In the context of a culture change and development effort, the agreed-upon goals need to reflect the orientation of the desired culture. In addition, specific goals can be set for implementing the new cultural reality. Furthermore, it is necessary to check and assess the level of attainment of the agreed-upon goals for being effective. If organizational members know the measures of control and assessment, they can monitor their level of goal attainment themselves. Transparent measures and controls are essential antecedents of well-organized work. Without measuring and assessing goal attainment—either by employees themselves or by their boss—the system and instrument are worthless.

The same applies to all other leadership systems and instruments. Their existence is essential, but also the way they are used and especially their consistent use. For example, leadership principles and guidelines serve as an orientation device both for leaders in their daily leadership practice and for their employees regarding what behavior they can expect from their leaders. If a leader's deviation from these guidelines does not have any consequence for the leader, such a system or instrument is worthless. A leadership feedback instrument, for instance, could supplement the system of leadership principles or guidelines and monitor the degree of their implementation by the leaders in their daily work.

Employee surveys can also be used to monitor an organization's culture, change, or development. It requires a custom-designed instrument that reflects a culture's dominant orientations. Appraisal interviews can be structured in a way that they serve the goal of culture development. Their framing, content, and resulting consequences for organizational members need alignment with the culture and its change or development. The same is true for career planning instruments. Such leadership instruments are crucial, but also their use in the daily work routines. Does the career plan only exist on paper, or does it translate into concrete and visible staffing decisions?

Exit interviews provide an opportunity to uncover critical aspects of an organization's culture. People who have decided to leave the organization are more willing to address critical issues that others would not necessarily voice openly. These can translate into measures to develop the organization's culture further.

The specific design of all management and leadership systems and their respective instruments focus organizational members' attention on those cultural aspects routinely checked, discussed, and controlled. Large organizations tend to have a variety of these systems and tools. Even though they had once been implemented systematically and carefully, including support in using them appropriately, their use may become automatized. If it is more important to document that an instrument has been used rather than using the tool for initiating a development process, the instrument has lost its intended effect. Hence it is better to use a limited number of aligned systems and instruments and regularly check their impact on developing organizational members and their culture.

Information and Communication Systems and Instruments

Concerning management information and communication systems, it is vital to know what type of information they provide, how frequently, and how user-friendly. In our age of digitalization, the danger exists of information overload, making the distinction between important and unimportant information increasingly difficult. Therefore it is crucial to prepare important information to be easily noticed and processed in a culture change or development process. To give an example, a multinational firm annually prepares a culture balance sheet for its leaders. It contains information about those cultural parameters the top executives consider relevant. This information about a unit's and the organization's culture is provided on one page, indicating areas of strength and areas for improvement.

Given the multiplicity of potential digital tools available in information and communication systems, leaders have to make a conscious choice which ones to promote and use—both as a manifestation of their culture and in informing about a culture change or development effort. Which tools are helpful and reasonable for an organization's internal and external exchange of information, and which rules apply in handling them? The daily processing of incoming e-mails, for instance, requires much time and mailing lists need regular checks. Decision-makers have to discuss the pros and cons of using chatrooms, Wikis, YouTube, social media, and other digital tools. They need to specify who can use what, how, and when, including what kind of information.

Management information and communication systems and their tools are, on the one hand, an expression of an organization's culture, and, on the other hand, they influence the culture once in existence. Introducing digital systems and tools in organizations comes with a democratization process. The digital natives know how they can quickly access desired information and may be faster and better informed than their superiors. For example, a leader reported about an intern that he gave her a challenging research task. The leader assumed that it would take her at least two weeks to develop a good solution. The intern, however, returned to the leader's office two hours later and presented an excellent solution. In her worldwide web inquiry, an expert in the field contacted her and provided the answer.

This example illustrates how modern information and communication systems may change work processes, influence the organization's culture, and shift company borders. As mentioned, the internet allows worldwide access to knowledge, expertise, and open innovation processes. Harvard Professor Michael Tushman, for example, asks himself whether our developed management theories and knowledge will still apply in the future when innovation processes take place in the global community rather than within the boundaries of individual companies (Benner & Tushman, 2015; Sackmann, 2017).

Controlling Systems and Instruments

Regarding culture change and development, top executives' choice of key performance indicators is crucial because they signal their organizational members what they should focus on in their work. This focus influences their priorities and subsequent behavior. The Balanced Scorecard (Kaplan & Norton, 1992) demonstrates the effect of controlling systems and instruments. The hitherto existing controlling instruments were past-oriented and did not inform about a firm's viability. In addition, knowledge-based companies were difficult to manage based on existing controlling instruments. Motivated by this criticism, Kaplan and Norton (1992) developed the balanced scorecard. It combines quantitative with qualitative elements, including financial indicators, internal processes, customer relationships, and education and growth. As implied by its name, the intention is to balance different perspectives so that organizational members also pay attention to an organization's future development and not only to those aspects that are easily measurable such as revenues.

Budgeting is another management instrument that sets priorities for an organization's members and its culture. Because every organization has limited resources, the budgeting process determines the emphasis placed on different areas. Concerning culture, the question is if the budget's resource allocation and budgeting process reflect the cultural priorities. In case of a culture development or change effort, one also needs to reassess the resource allocation. Does it support the future culture direction? How much time does the budgeting process require? Finally, reporting is a related tool that needs to be examined regarding what is reported to whom, how frequently, and in which form.

Summing up, management and leadership systems and their related instruments play an essential role in a planned culture change and development process. On the one hand, they express the priorities of an organization's culture. On the other hand, they serve organizational members as orientation, guiding their attention and the choice of behavior. Therefore, existing systems and instruments need to be evaluated in terms of five different aspects: the priorities they set; their alignment with the strategy and the cultural development process; the coordination and alignment between existing systems and instruments; the kind of use by organizational members; and if violations in their intended use have consequences for organizational members.

8.6.2.4 Technologies and Techniques

Technology structures work processes and, at the same time, influences organizational members' collective thought and problem-solving processes. Technology includes all facets of digitization such as information and communication technologies with their hardware and software, production technologies, -procedures, -tools, and working techniques in general. The ongoing digitization process will change business models and interactions with organizational members, customers, suppliers, and the general public. It will impact innovation processes, definitions of performance, performance indicators (see also Sect. 6.8), and thus an organization's culture. Industrialization 4.0 and developments in artificial intelligence will provide intelligent machines and robots that will increasingly overtake routine tasks and jobs. On the one hand, they assist in areas such as nursing practice; on the other hand, they will change established working processes in yet unknown ways.

From a culture perspective, the questions arise if decision-makers recognize the potential inherent in available and future technologies and techniques, if they adopt them in time; and if they recognize the impact on their culture. If the latest technology is available, people will use it even if it may not be necessary. For example, clinical diagnostics use magnetic resonance tomographies in cases when the much cheaper X-ray technology would suffice. Thus, all technologies and tools have two sides: On the one hand, they enable and facilitate specific work processes.

On the other hand, they pre-structure collective thinking and behavior. Thus, while tools and technologies allow specific problem solutions, they may also limit problem-solving possibilities.

At the California Institute of Technology in Pasadena, a well-known research institute and alma mater of several Nobel prize winners, scientists had to apply for the technologies and equipment that they want to use in a specific research project. Then, only if an evaluation of their proposal indicated that they were the most appropriate technologies, the university bought the equipment. In other institutions, researchers request new technologies and equipment because it is the latest on the market, and they develop research projects around their use.

8.6.2.5 Architecture and Interior Design

A company's architecture and interior design are probably the most visible of all cultural artifacts (see Chap. 2) that reveal cultural priorities. At the same time, they structure the physical environment and thus influence organizational members' behavior, interactions and movements. The allocation of space and the type of furniture signal the priorities of an organization's culture. Who and what are important? Who has power and status? The architectural design, the particular layout of rooms, and their allocation to people within the building enable or disable communication and the flow of information between people. Large distances reduce the possibilities for informal face-to-face communication that is still important despite modern communication devices. A lack of personal contact is frequently the reason for the lack of communication between departments or different units.

Example of a Deliberately Designed Floor Plan
When a company moved its headquarters to a new location, the top executive group deliberately developed a specific floor plan that should facilitate interaction and communication as much as possible. The reception area, back-office, and administrative support were located in the center with an adjoining kitchen area where people could meet. The offices of the top executive team were arranged in a half-circle around this center with doors that were usually open to allow easy access and facilitate interaction among top executives. At the other side of the reception and back-office area were the offices of IT and corporate controlling (see Fig. 8.6).

In a culture change or development effort, the architecture and interior design also need to be examined regarding their behavioral and symbolic implications. The

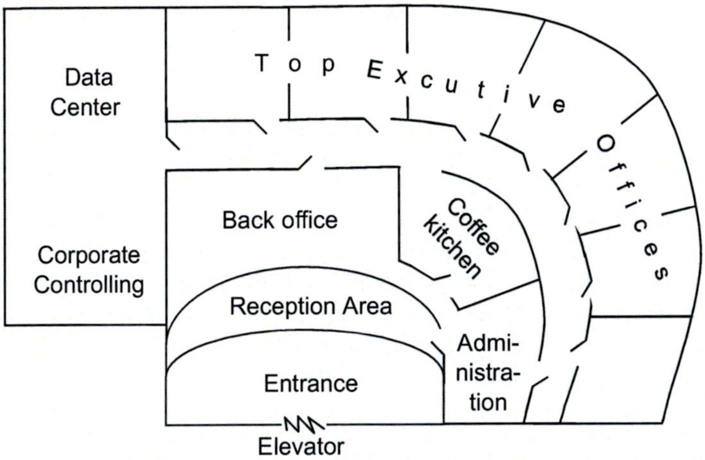

Fig. 8.6 Floor plan deliberately designed for facilitating interaction and communication

critical questions are to what extent the architecture and interior design facilitate or hinder desired behavior and the symbolic meanings they convey to organizational members and outsiders. At present, many organizations want to increase their agility and flexibility and build transparent office buildings with open floor plans and working spaces, hoping to encourage information flow and communication among organizational members. Some research results, however, indicate that this is not always the case. Depending on the materials and furniture, the noise level negatively affects focused working. It does not necessarily promote work-enhancing interactions between employees in open-space offices with more than twelve people. Furthermore, the need for personalization of the workspace varies substantially between employees.

Some organizations no longer offer designated workspaces for specific functions. Instead, employees choose their workplace once they come to work and enter the building. Other companies choose an entirely different approach: they take pictures of their employees' living rooms and rebuild them on the company premises to make employees feel at home. Google tries to meet its employees' needs in its interior design and workspace offers. In addition to regular workspaces and the availability of food around the clock, it offers possibilities for creative work, relaxation, sleep, play, and sports. The headquarters of U.S.-based Nike resembles a sports center. Next to regular offices and conference rooms, it offers a swimming pool, fitness rooms, and a running track. Organizational members report that a meeting may be interrupted to breathe and get new ideas while going out for a run. A one-on-one meeting may also take place while jogging. W. L. Gore & Associates chose yet another approach. According to their principle, *no ranks—no title*, office designs do not convey any status. Open spaces with coffee machines, food, bar stools, and respective tables invite informal conversations among organizational members. Reportedly, these discussions helped solve as many issues as prearranged meetings.

The concept of design thinking that the San Francisco-based firm Ideo has adopted uses another logic. The walls of their office in San Francisco display the principles of Design Thinking openly to everyone. After passing small reception areas, one reaches a grand, loft-style workspace with moveable furniture. Organizational members deliberately create the workspace that fits best depending on the kind of work—be it a team discussion or focused individual work. Larger meetings can take place in an open conference area. Organizational members cook and eat together in an open kitchen. A separate, well-equipped workshop contains all kinds of materials and tools that people use for translating their ideas into prototypes that are successively improved.

These examples illustrate that even the physical context of an organization impacts its members' thought processes and behavior and hence needs to be examined regarding its impact on the planned culture change or development process. The discussion of contextual factors in culture change and development does not cover the entire range of possibilities. Instead, the examples may inspire other ideas for use in a planned culture change or development process. Nevertheless, it is central that all components align both with the desired reorientation and with each other.

8.7 Culture Change Interventions in a Revolutionary Change Process

Revolutionary change requires fast actions. Hence, there is no time for culture development processes that take a longer-term perspective. Necessary changes need quick, immediate, and almost simultaneous execution. In general, all the components discussed above (see Fig. 8.5) also need to be considered in a revolutionary culture change—however, in a condensed time. Structures and processes require a redesign to support the implementation of the newly developed strategy. Existing management and leadership systems and their related instruments need to be evaluated, adjusted, or changed. The required culture needs a specification in line with the relevant aspects of the new corporate strategy.

Since organizational culture is maintained and shaped by people, the existing human system in terms of its members should be capable of implementing the new orientation. People, however, are no machines and have no buttons one can push so that organizational members will suddenly think and act according to the new culture and strategy. Hence, a critical assessment needs to reveal whether all existing organizational members can accomplish the change and able to learn and live the new cultural reality quickly. People usually need time to move through a change process associated with unlearning old routines and learning new skills, competencies, and behaviors, as discussed in Sect. 8.4.2. Hence, revolutionary change may imply letting go of some people who cannot adjust to the quick changes needed. The following example illustrates a situation requiring revolutionary change.

Revolutionary Change Process

Roy Ash, co-founder and president of Litton Industries, and former director of the U.S. Office of Management and Budget, describes this situation. He was appointed new CEO and Chairman of a company that required a turnaround. Only after a couple of weeks of intensive search and learning about the details did he become aware of the seriousness of the situation. According to him, the company's main strength was "to still be alive":

I told them (the board of directors) at a board meeting—I am sure I scared them, I possibly scared them too much—I told them, "To me, this company seems like we are all sitting in a rowboat on a peaceful, beautiful lake. We keep on rowing in different circles, and it is somehow comfortable and nice to go out there and paddle around in the sun and the fresh air on this beautiful lake. Unfortunately, though, the lake is gradually drying up, and we are left with only one possibility. That is getting new, better oars with which we can actually move because we have to row up the rapids and find new lakes. But it is not going to be easy. We will need all our strength the whole way. We will make mistakes due to our actions, but not mistakes of not doing things or doing things too late. Actually, we have no choice. This lake is drying up from under us, and we have to paddle very quickly. We will get wet a couple of times during this process, but we simply have to find a new lake for this one will soon be dried up."

Our time was running out, and I saw the lake drying up so swiftly ... Unfortunately, because I didn't have enough time, I really had to make all changes in two or three years' time. I had to change our technology, our products, our people, our corporate structure with its procedures ... everything had to be implemented and changed within two to three years.

(Personal talk with the author)

In a culture change process, people need orientation to navigate the new cultural reality. Since people in key positions act as role models, these key people need to live the new cultural reality. These considerations raise the questions:

1. Are the existing leaders and people in key positions able to live to the new cultural reality?
2. Does the organization have people with leadership potential who are role models of the new cultural reality?

If the organization cannot answer these two questions satisfactorily, two additional questions arise:

1. How can the organization attract and win leaders who live and fit with the new cultural reality?

2. What can the organization do with organizational members who cannot or do not want to develop into the required direction?

Similar to political revolutions, revolutionary culture changes often are associated with bloodshed—a replacement and exchange of people in key positions who do not act as role models for the required culture. The Wickes Corporation case illustrates the difficult decisions associated with a transformation process.

Wickes Corporation
(Excerpt from a conversation with Sanford C. Sigoloff, the then-CEO, newly appointed for the turnaround, chairman, and president of the Wickes Corporation.)

It isn't easy to introduce a turnaround to a company. But in the end, it is a matter of saving maybe ten thousand of twenty-two thousand jobs or losing all. And this means acting quickly. I had a look at the management and knew: some would make it, others might not. But how could I keep those fittest for the transformation at it? So I made clear the challenges we were facing, and the only thing I could guarantee was that those who accepted the challenge and helped to turn the boat around would have a future with us. But it wasn't easy.

(Personal talk with the author)

At Hilti, the conscious attention to its culture also started with a revolutionary culture change. At the end of the 1980s, co-founder and CEO Martin Hilti believed that the upper management was pursuing their own rather than the company's interests. He exchanged the whole top executive team, and his son and successor Michael Hilti took the entire company on a *culture journey*. Based on this revolutionary change process, Hilti developed a new corporate culture. Since the CEO and Chairman of the Board wanted to prevent an unintended culture drift, they monitor their culture regularly. If a need for adjustment arises, Hilti immediately implements appropriate measures.

Generally, it is preferable to embark on an evolutionary culture development process. The time pressure inherent in revolutionary change limits the scope of actions and usually calls for more drastic measures to achieve a successful culture change. The conscious and mindful attention to culture helps to prevent crises (c.f., Chap. 10).

8.8 Some Concluding Remarks Regarding Culture Change and Development

Culture change and development are possible, but it is not easy. Because of the nature of human systems, culture change efforts are challenging, complex, and their outcome is not predictable even if carefully planned. Since human systems do not follow deterministic principles, change efforts are less manageable and controllable than often assumed. Routines developed in the past and emotions limit rational planning efforts. While culture development builds on the existing culture, culture change affects its core. It involves a new orientation of an organization with its collective assumptions and belief system that affects its way of operating and thus every organizational member. A sustainable culture change addresses all components depicted in Fig. 8.5: an organization's strategy, its design, its management and leadership systems, and related instruments and members. Furthermore, all of these components need to be aligned and move together in the same direction. Otherwise, the organization and its culture will move back into its old position.

Culture change implies not only doing something new but also letting go of ingrained, familiar routines. The feeling of insecurity associated with letting go of familiar routines while not having established yet new routines is challenging to cope with. Hence, the danger exists of moving back into the comfort zone relying on familiar routines. However, a sustainable culture change is only possible if organizational members move forward and accept the associated insecurities, feelings of low competence, and letting go of familiar routines. The only way forward is moving into new territories and trying out new behaviors. In such a change process, it is not sufficient if *all others* change and develop except oneself. Most likely, more people in key positions are affected by a culture change process than initially expected at the outset of the process. Once organizational members accept their involvement in the change process, including their imperfections and the necessity of learning new ways of thinking and acting, they have taken a significant hurdle. Since early successes ignite motivation and help win those that still contemplate what to do, early successes help overcome hurdles, doubts, and lack of self-confidence. Hence, one needs to plan for early successes at the outset of the culture change process.

Culture change is challenging due to its fundamental reorientation that resembles a paradigm shift (Kuhn, 1996). Hence, an organization should avoid it whenever possible and replaced it with careful attention to its culture and ongoing development. Such attention requires cultural-sensitive and culture-mindful leaders and managers. They are aware of the importance of culture and its influences on daily operations and performance (see Chap. 10).

References

Agarwal, N. C. (1998). Reward systems: Emerging trends and issues. *Canadian Psychology/ Psychologie Canadienne, 39*(1–2), 60–70. https://doi.org/10.1037/h0086795

Akgün, A. E., Byrne, J. C., Lynn, G. S., & Keskin, H. (2007). Organizational unlearning as changes in beliefs and routines in organizations. *Journal of Organizational Change Management, 20*(6), 794–812. https://doi.org/10.1108/09534810710831028

Argyris, C., & Schön, D. (1995). *Organizational learning* (2nd ed.). Addison-Wesley.

Atkinson, J. W. (1957). Motivational determinants of risk-taking behavior. *Psychological Review, 64*(6, Pt.1), 359–372. https://doi.org/10.1037/h0043445

Benner, M. J., & Tushman, M. L. (2015). Reflections on the 2013 decade award: "exploitation, exploration, and process management: The productivity dilemma revisited" ten years later. *Academy of Management Review, 40*(4), 497–514.

Boulding, K. E. (1968). General systems theory: The skeleton of science. In W. Buckley (Ed.), *Modern systems research for the behavioral scientist* (pp. 3–10). Aldine.

Buckley, W. (Ed.). (1968). *Modern systems research for the behavioral scientist*. Aldine.

Burke, W. (1994). *Organization development: Principles and practices* (2nd ed.). Little, Brown.

Burnes, B. (2011). Introduction: Why does change fail, and what can we do about it? *Journal of Change Management, 11*(4), 445–450. https://doi.org/10.1080/14697017.2011.630507

Calipha, R., Tarba, S., & Brock, D. (2010). Mergers and acquisitions. A review of phases, motives, and success factors. In C. L. Cooper & S. Finkelstein (Eds.), *Advances in mergers and acquisitions* (Vol. 9, pp. 1–24). Emerald. https://doi.org/10.1108/S1479-361X(2010)0000009004

Caluwé, L. de, & Geurts, J. (2002). Measuring and explaining effects of culture change intervention. Unpublished working paper, Freie Universität Amsterdam & Tilburg University.

Cissell, M. J. (1987). Designing effective reward systems. Compensation & Benefits Review, 19(6), 49-55. DOI: https://doi.org/10.1177/088636878701900605.

Clarke, L. (1994). *The essence of change*. Prentice-Hall.

De Charms, R. (1968). *Personal causation*. Academic.

Doherty, R., Liu, S., & West, A. (2015). How M&A practitioners enable their success. Survey. *McKinsey & Company Online*, October 1st. Accessed Sep 23, 2021, from www.mckinsey.com/business-functions/strategy-and-corporate-finance/our-insights/how-m-and-a-practitioners-enable-their-success

Flik, H. (1990). *The ameba concept . . . organizing around opportunity within the GORE culture*. In H. Simon (Ed.), *Herausforderung Unternehmenskultur* (pp. 91–129). Schäffer. Accessed Sep 23, 2021, from https://michaelpacanowsky.files.wordpress.com/2013/04/ameba-concept.pdf

Ford, J. D., & Ford, L. W. (2010). Stop blaming resistance to change and start using it. *Organizational Dynamics, 39*(1), 24–36. https://doi.org/10.1016/j.orgdyn.2009.10.002

Harbison, J., & Pekar, P. (2000). *Smart alliances: A practical guide to repeatable success*. Jossey-Bass.

Herles, W. (1999). *Machtspiele. Hinter den Kulissen großer Konzerne*. Econ & List.

Holusha, J. (1986). *Perot is removed from G.M. board, but has big profit*. The New York Times Online, December 2nd. Accessed Sep 23, 2021, from www.nytimes.com/1986/12/02/business/perot-is-removed-from-gm-board-but-has-big-profit.html

Janis, I. L. (1982). *Groupthink: Psychological studies of policy decisions and fiascos*. Houghton-Mifflin.

Jones, S. L., & Van de Ven, A. H. (2016). The changing nature of change resistance: An examination of the moderating impact of time. *Journal of Applied Behavioral Science, 52*(4), 482–506. https://doi.org/10.1177/0021886316671409

Kaplan, R. S., & Norton, D. P. (1992). The balanced scorecard–measures that drive performance. *Harvard Business Review, 70*(1), 71–79. Accessed Sep 23, 2021, from https://hbr.org/1992/01/the-balanced-scorecard-measures-that-drive-performance-2

Kerr, S. (1975/1995). On the folly of rewarding a, while hoping for B. *Academy of Management Executive,* 9(1), 7-14. Accessed Sep 23, 2021, from www.csus.edu/indiv/s/sablynskic/documents/rewardinga.pdf; www.ou.edu/russell/UGcomp/Kerr.pdf

Kerr, S. (2009). *Reward systems: Does yours measure up?* Harvard Business Press.

Kerr, J., & Slocum, J. S. (2005). Managing corporate culture through reward systems. *Academy of Management Perspectives, 19*(4), 130–137. https://doi.org/10.5465/ame.2005.19417915

Kotter, J. P. (2014). *Accelerate: Building strategic agility for a faster-moving world*. Harvard Business Review Press.

Kuhn, T. S. (1996). *The structure of scientific revolutions* (3rd ed.). University of Chicago Press.

Lewin, K. (1953). Studies in group decision. In D. Cartwright & A. Zander (Eds.), *Group dynamics: Research and theory* (pp. 287–301). Row, Peterson &.

Lewin, K. (1963). *Feldtheorie in den Sozialwissenschaften*. Huber.

Major, D. A. (2000). Effective newcomer socialization into high-performance organizational cultures. In N. M. Ashkanasy, C. P. M. Wilderom, & M. F. Peterson (Eds.), *Handbook of organizational culture and climate* (pp. 355–368). Sage.

Martin, J., Feldman, M. S., Hatch, M. J., & Sitkin, S. B. (1983). The uniqueness paradox in organizational stories. *Administrative Science Quarterly, 28*(3), 438–453. https://doi.org/10.2307/2392251

Morgan, G. (1997). *Images of organizations* (2nd ed.). Sage.

Morosini, P. (1998). *Managing cultural differences. Effective strategy and execution across cultures in global corporate alliances*. Pergamon.

Nadler, D. (1988). Organizational frame-bending: Types of change in the complex organization. In R. Kilmann & T. Covin (Eds.), *Corporate transformation* (pp. 66–83). Jossey-Bass.

Nystrom, P. C., & Starbuck, W. H. (1984). To avoid organizational crises, unlearn. *Organizational Dynamics, 12*(4), 53–65. https://doi.org/10.1016/0090-2616(84)90011-1

O'Reilly, C. A., III, & Tushman, M. L. (2016). *Lead and disrupt: How to solve the innovator's dilemma*. Stanford University Books.

Pfeffer, J., & Sutton, R. I. (2000). *The knowing-doing gap: How smart firms turn knowledge into action*. Harvard Business School Press.

Probst, G., & Raisch, B. (2005). Organizational crisis: The logic of failure. *Academy of Management Perspectives,* 19(1), 90-105 Academy of Management Perspectives. DOI: https://doi.org/10.5465/ame.2005.15841958.

Rehm, W., Uhlander, R., & West, A. (2012). Taking a longer term look at M&A value creation. *McKinsey & Company Online*, January 1st. Accessed Sep 23, 2021, from www.mckinsey.com/business-functions/strategy-and-corporate-finance/our-insights/taking-a-longer-term-look-at-m-and-a-value-creation

Ríos, J. P. (2014). *Design and diagnosis for sustainable organizations*. Springer.

Rosen, B., & D'Andrade, R. (1959). The psychosocial origins of achievement motivation. *Sociometry, 22*(3), 185–218. https://doi.org/10.2307/2785664

Sackmann, S. A. (1991). *Cultural knowledge in organizations. Exploring the collective mind*. Sage.

Sackmann, S. A. (1992). Cultures and subcultures: An analysis of organizational knowledge. *Administrative Science Quarterly, 37*(1), 140–161. https://doi.org/10.2307/2393536

Sackmann, S. A. (1995). Introducing this year's buzz words is not enough if old beliefs reign managerial practice. Symposium »*European Critiques of Management*« (pp. 6–8). The 36th Annual Western Academy of Management Conference, San Diego, CA, April 1995.

Sackmann, S. A. (Ed.). (1997). *Cultural complexity in organizations: Inherent contrasts and contradictions*. Sage.

Sackmann, S. A. (2005). In Bertelsmann Stiftung (Ed.), *Toyota Motor Corporation. Eine Fallstudie aus unternehmenskultureller Perspektive*. Bertelsmann Stiftung.

Sackmann, S. A. (2017). Michael L. Tushman: A practice informed explorer and organizational scholar with a focus on viable organizations. In D. Szabla, B. Pasmore, M. Barnes, & A. N. Gibson (Eds.), *The Palgrave handbook of organizational change thinkers* (pp. 1373–1388). Palgrave Macmillan. https://doi.org/10.1007/978-3-319-52878-6_97

Sackmann, S. A., & Bertelsmann Foundation. (2006). *Success factor corporate culture*. Verlag Bertelsmann Stiftung.

Sackmann, S. A., Eggenhofer-Rehart, P. M., & Friesl, M. (2009). Sustainable change: Long-term efforts toward developing a learning organization. *Journal of Applied Behavioral Science, 45*(4), 521–549. https://doi.org/10.1177/0021886309346001

Sackmann, S. A., Eichel, V., & Schmidt, C. (2019). Wie ist es um die Change-Fitness von Unternehmen bestellt? In S. A. Sackmann (Ed.), *Herausforderung Führung–Führung für die Zukunft* (pp. 175–200). Springer Gabler.

Schwartz, H., & Davis, S. (1981). Matching corporate culture and business strategy. *Organizational Dynamics, 10*(1), 30–48. https://doi.org/10.1016/0090-2616(81)90010-3

Scott-Morgan, P. (1994). *The unwritten rules of the game*. MacGraw Hill.

Swissinfo (2016). *Swiss grounding: 15 years on. SWI schwissinfo.ch Online*, October 2nd. Accessed Sep 23, 2021, from www.swissinfo.ch/eng/national-legend_swissair-grounding-15-years-on/42481312

Tannenbaum, R., Margulies, N., & Massarik, F. (1985). *Human systems development*. Jossey-Bass.

Trice, H. M., & Beyer, J. M. (1993). *The cultures of work organizations*. Prentice-Hall.

Tushman, M. L., & O'Reilly, C. A. (1996). Ambidextrous organizations: Managing evolutionary and revolutionary change. *California Business Review, 38*(4), 8–29. https://doi.org/10.2307/41165852

Tushman, M. L. (2014). Leadership tips for today to stay in the game tomorrow: The ambidextrous leader. *IESE Insight,* 23(4), 31–38. Accessed Sep 23, 2021, from www.hbs.edu/faculty/Pages/item.aspx?num=50403

Van der Post, W. Z., de Coning, T. J., & Smit, E. V. D. M. (1998). The relationship between organizational culture and financial performance: Some south African evidence. *South African Journal of Business Management, 29*(1), 30–40. https://doi.org/10.4102/sajbm.v29i1.768

Chapter 9
Characteristics of Culture Sustaining Competitiveness and Viability

Consciously developing and maintaining an organization's culture raises questions regarding those content-related characteristics of a culture that enables an organization's sustained competitiveness and viability. Researchers have argued that depending on its specific characteristics, an organization's culture can be a source of competitive advantage (Barney, 1986, 1991). Studies have supported this assertion (Bogdanowicz, 2014). As discussed in Chap. 8, one condition for enabling a firm's competitiveness and viability is that its culture is aligned with the organization's strategy and supports the strategy implementation process. Furthermore, such a culture requires certain characteristics. Even though every organization has its unique culture, some generic characteristics do exist vital for organizations acting in a volatile, uncertain, complex, and ambiguous (VUCA) environment. This chapter discusses ten generic content-related characteristics and three quality criteria that support an organization's competitiveness and viability—especially in a volatile and dynamic environment.

As discussed in Chap. 2, an organization's culture serves several functions. These pertain to the two main primary functions of internal integration and external adaptation. Screening the relevant literature regarding these two general functions, ten content-related characteristics emerge that are central to an organization's viability in a VUCA environment and its performance. Furthermore, three criteria complement these ten content-related characteristics that offer insights into an organizational culture's quality.

The ten content-related characteristics supporting an organization's competitiveness and viability in a VUCA-environment are:

1. A clearly communicated identity and purpose.
2. A consistent strategic (goal-) orientation.
3. Customer orientation.
4. Learning orientation and ability to adapt.
5. Ability to innovative.
6. Utilizing the potential of all organizational members.

S. A. Sackmann, *Culture in Organizations*, Contributions to Management Science,
https://doi.org/10.1007/978-3-030-86080-6_9

7. Partnership based and culture-conscious leadership.
8. Open, trust-based communication and interactions.
9. Performance orientation.
10. A balanced stakeholder orientation.

Three quality criteria of organizational culture are:

1. Strategic fit.
2. Multidimensional orientation.
3. Consistency between normative expectations and daily practices.

9.1 Clearly Communicated Identity and Purpose

Several studies suggest that successful and viable organizations have a clear *identity*, a clear *purpose*, or *a mission* (e.g., Ellsworth, 2002; Collins, 2001). Organizations with a purpose know what they stand for, what is important to the organization, what kind of attitudes and behaviors the organization values, and the resulting priorities for the entire organization and its members. Successful companies communicate their identity, their purpose, their mission, and their values internally and externally. Their organizational members know what their employer stands for, and outsiders such as customers, suppliers, shareholders, the community, and the wider public understand what to expect from the organization.

However, the purpose and identity are not only documented on paper. The organization communicates them in a comprehensible way to its members and external stakeholders. Hence, organizational members know them, and they can act upon them by setting the appropriate priorities in their daily behavior. In addition, the communicated organizational identity and purpose offer members an opportunity for identifying with the organization (Gast et al., 2020; Simpson, 2020). This identification positively influences their organizational commitment, engagement, and performance, which eventually affects the organization's performance (Amran, 2012).

9.2 Consistent Strategic (Goal-) Orientation

Strategic (goal-) orientation is closely linked to a clearly communicated identity and purpose. Successful organizations have a clear identity and purpose that translate into their strategy and related goals for implementing the strategy. This process provides the organization and its members with a direction. It requires strategic leadership and leaders who regularly monitor the organization's environment and adapt its strategy if necessary (see Sect. 9.11.1 *Strategic fit*). As with the organization's identity and purpose, it is important that organizational members know and understand the strategy and related goals. This knowledge and understanding helps them direct their work efforts toward the overarching goal. Thus, their actions become aligned and coordinated despite different tasks, functions, and responsibilities. Research results show that effective organizations have aligned goals across different hierarchies, functions, and organizational units. Furthermore, this goal orientation and the respective goals are deep-seated in all organizational members guiding their daily work efforts (c.f., Sackmann & Bertelsmann Stiftung, 2006; Den Hartog & Verburg, 2004; Denison & Mishra, 1995; Ellsworth, 2002; Kotter & Heskett, 1992; Ouchi & Jaeger, 1978; Van der Post et al., 1998).

9.3 Customer Orientation

Customer orientation is another essential characteristic of an organization's competitiveness and viability. It represents an external orientation that needs to be anchored in the organization's strategy and culture. Several studies show that strategically anchored customer orientation is central to an organization's short-term and long-term success (e.g., Collins, 2001; Ellsworth, 2002; Flamholtz, 2005; Kotter & Heskett, 1992; Sackmann & Bertelsmann Foundation, 2006). In one study investigating the effects of different cultural dimensions on companies' financial success, customer orientation had the largest impact of all culture dimensions included in the study on financial success (Flamholtz & Kannan-Narasimhan, 2005).

The degree of customer orientation can be assessed by asking customers themselves as well as organizational members. A variety of objective indicators exist for its measurement. Examples are: the number of customer complaints; the number of returns; the number of new customers acquired through recommendations; the level of inclusion of customers into the product development process; the number of customer contacts per employee and leader; or the share of work time that sales and service people spend with the customer. The Liechtenstein-based multinational Hilti Group surveys their customers' satisfaction regularly using the feedback from their salespeople and information from social media channels. In addition, they periodically check their organizational design in terms of its customer orientation and adjust it if work processes in the various functional areas tend to become inefficient and lose sight of customer orientation (Sackmann & Bertelsmann Foundation, 2006).

9.4 Learning Orientation and Ability to Adapt

A VUCA-environment requires flexibility, change, and adaptability. Hence, if organizations want to survive in such a VUCA-environment, they need a culture that enables them to recognize, act in time and respond fast to changing environmental conditions and related challenges. Research in the field of organizational strategy revealed the reason for firms' lack of adapting to changing environmental conditions or for reacting too late: the organizations or rather their top executives did not perceive those changes at all, or they thought that these changes were not crucial for their organization (Dutton, 1993; Starbuck et al., 1978; Probst & Raisch, 2005).

Learning orientation includes both the ability and the willingness to learn and adapt and apply both to changes in the internal and external environment. Learning orientation implies that organizations are open to changes in their organization's relevant external and internal environment; they recognize these changes and examine the appropriateness of their existing practices and routines regular*ly. The ability to adapt* implies that an organization can identify necessary changes, take action and implement the required change. These changes may refer to work practices and routines, the organization's design, or management and leadership systems (c.f., Sackmann, 2006). Hence, these organizations do not fall into the trap of the knowing-doing gap (Pfeffer & Sutton, 2000). Several studies found that the dimension of adaptability is positively correlated with organization success (Denison & Mishra, 1995; Fey & Denison, 2003; Kotter & Heskett, 1992).

Research and practice also show that the competitiveness and success of an organization are not a steady-state that remains once it is achieved (Probst & Raisch, 2005). To stay successful requires regular checks and adapting practices. Despite many years of success, organizations are neither blinded by their success nor take their success for granted. Instead, their learning orientation enables them to question their practices regularly, and their ability to adapt enables them to initiate and implement necessary changes. This combination of critical questioning and taking actions helps organizations to act when there is still time. In addition, it prevents the organization and its culture from becoming either calcified or drifting toward an unintended direction (c.f., Collins, 2001; Kotter & Heskett, 1992; Sackmann & Bertelsmann Foundation, 2006).

9.5 Ability to Innovate

The ability to innovate is closely linked to the learning orientation, but it goes a step further toward reinvention. While learning orientation is evolutionary in nature, the ability to innovate is revolutionary. It implies questioning the status quo and venturing into new territories. It enables an organization to develop new products, or services that will ensure an organization's future survival. The ability to innovate also concerns new processes and systems that enhance both an organization's efficiency and effectiveness and thus help the organization staying competitive. In addition to questioning everything, the ability to innovate includes trying out new behaviors and work processes, experimenting with new practices, procedures, materials, or services. A meta-analysis involving 148 independent samples showed that a culture's innovation focus accounted for 53.7 percent of the relative weights in organizational effectiveness criteria (Hartnell et al., 2019). Furthermore, other studies suggest that organizations with more externally oriented cultures are associated with a higher competitive and innovative orientation. These, in turn, are positively correlated with factors of organization success (Ogbonna & Harris, 2000; Den Hartog & Verburg, 2004).

The simultaneously existing combination of learning orientation, ability to adapt and innovate are also prerequisites for ambidexterity. Ambidexterity implies that an organization focuses simultaneously on efficient processes and organizational adaptation and innovation (Benner & Tushman, 2003, 2015).

9.6 Utilizing the Potential of all Organizational Members

Research shows that genuinely utilizing the potential of all organizational members is a critical success factor. Employee outcome accounted for 92.1 percent of the relative weights in organizational effectiveness criteria in the meta-analysis of Hartnell et al. (2019) investigating the association of organizational culture and organizational outcomes. Several studies have revealed a positive correlation between humanistic values and financial success (e.g., Ouchi & Jaeger, 1978; Herrmann et al., 2004) as well as employee orientation, teamwork, and performance (Flamholtz, 2005; Koene, 1996; Petty et al., 1995). Others found that the inclusion of organizational members correlated with short- and mid-term performance (Denison, 1990). Furthermore, a constructive style characterized by self-actualization, a human orientation, motivation, extraversion (Cooke, 1997), and performance was linked to a low theft rate, increased growth in revenues, fewer warranty cases, and an increasing number of customers.

Organizational members, their knowledge, and talent are critical in service-based and knowledge-intensive industries to ensure an organization's viability. To recognize, appreciate and utilize the knowledge and skills of all organizational members requires a special kind of leadership, including open and trust-based communication.

9.7 Partnership-Based and Culture-Mindful Leadership

Partnership-based leadership is one of the prerequisites for utilizing the knowledge and skills of all organizational members and allowing their potentials to flourish. Partnership-based leadership implies that superiors and subordinates accept and deal with each other as equal partners at work. They interact with each other at eye level and know about each other's strengths and contributions. Several studies indicate that the specific kind of leadership significantly impacts employee engagement and identification with the organization. Hence, it indirectly enables or disables employee motivation and performance and their identification with the organization. A longitudinal study revealed a strong positive correlation between partnership-based leadership and organizational members' identification with the organization. Furthermore, a conglomerate's financially successful firms showed a substantially higher level of partnership-based leadership and organizational members' identification than less successful firms of the same corporation (Hunsdiek, 2005; Netta, 2009). Another study also indicated an indirect relationship between participative leadership and organization success (Ogbonna & Harris, 2000).

Culture-mindful leadership implies that the leaders are aware of the organization's culture, of the symbolic meaning of a leadership position, and their function as role models. In their role as leaders, they personify the organization's culture. Hence, they must live the required culture daily and comply with the organization's expectations regarding cultural norms. Several qualitative studies highlight the crucial role of culture-mindful and culture-compliant leadership (e.g., Sackmann, 2005; Sackmann & Bertelsmann Foundation, 2006). Successful companies that consciously handle their organization's culture-mindfully select leaders who fit with the desired organizational culture. If leaders do not comply with the desired culture, organizations that consider their culture important will rather part with otherwise well-qualified and high-performing leaders because it does not want to jeopardize culture (Sackmann, 1991; Sackmann & Bertelsmann Foundation, 2006).

9.8 Open and Trust-Based Communication

Open and trust-based communication is another prerequisite for utilizing the potential of all organizational members besides partnership-based leadership. Open and trust-based communication allows them to share information and their knowledge readily with colleagues, superiors, and subordinates. They communicate openly within and across organizational units and hierarchies. Hence, open and trust-based communication enables open and constructive feedback and efficient and effective work processes. It helps to solve problems fast and, at the same time, helps avoid micropolitical maneuvering. Open and trust-based communication focuses on the issues at hand without pursuing a hidden agenda. Critical issues can be addressed and openly discussed without having to fear potentially harmful consequences. In combination with partnership-based, culture-mindful leadership, communication processes also convey and support an organization's culture (c.f., Van der Post et al., 1998).

9.9 Performance Orientation

Performance orientation is another content-related characteristic of organizational culture that is vital for organizations' sustained success. Performance orientation includes both the willingness and the ability to perform and the focus on achieving results. Indicators of performance orientation are, for example, working efficiently and effectively, accomplishing tasks and goals on time, self-initiated ideas, and improvement suggestions—behavior typical for entrepreneurs. Several studies found that organizational cultures based on competitiveness and entrepreneurship correlated with the organization's success (Desphandé et al., 1993; Ogbonna & Harris, 2000). In the meta-analysis of Hartnell et al. (2019), high-performance work practices could explain variance in all five included outcome measures and accounted for 66.8 percent of the variance in financial performance. Several qualitative case studies took another approach by selecting high-performing organizations and then analyzed their culture. The results based on interviews and documentary analysis revealed a strong willingness and ability to perform among organizational members (Sackmann, 2005; Sackmann & Bertelsmann Foundtion, 2006).

A performance-oriented culture requires all organizational members to focus their minds and actions on the organization's mission and purpose, the related goals, and goal achievement. Concerning the cultural knowledge base of an organization, it implies that performance orientation is part of the axiomatic, dictionary, and directory knowledge. Accordingly, the organization's strategy, design, leadership, and management systems, including related instruments, are geared towards performance-oriented behavior. In addition, performance orientation is one selection criteria for new organizational members, who shape all collective practices with their behavior. Hence, little recipe knowledge exists because normative recommendations for improvement are immediately translated into effective measures and implemented.

9.10 Balanced Stakeholder-Orientation

In the field of organizational culture, few research efforts have considered an organization's shareholder- or stakeholder orientation. Several case studies indicate that an organization's stakeholder orientation contributes to its sustained success and viability (c.f., Sackmann, 2005), not the often-discussed shareholder orientation. Furthermore, research revealed that the balanced consideration of the three major stakeholders—customers, organizational members, and shareholders—was important for the organization's long-term success (Kotter & Heskett, 1992; Sackmann, 1991). In addition, research results suggest that an orientation toward social responsibility is another key success factor (Flamholtz & Kannan-Narasimhan, 2005; Sackmann & Bertelsmann Stiftung, 2006). Although customer orientation had the greatest impact on financial performance indicators, social responsibility also impacted their engagement in the organizations' community (Flamholtz & Kannan-Narasimhan, 2005). In addition to society, the environment is likely to become another critical stakeholder to consider in a culture's orientation.

Figure 9.1 summarizes these ten content-related characteristics of cultures that enable an organization's long-term success and viability in a VUCA environment.

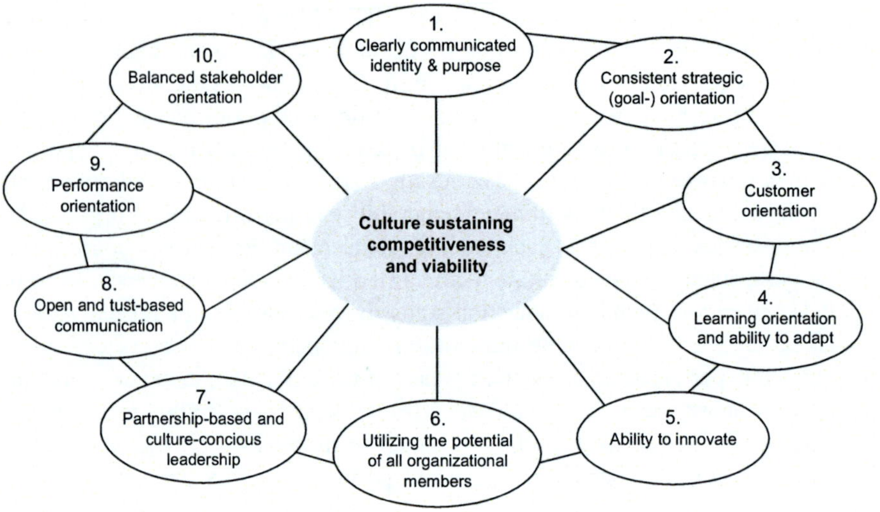

Fig. 9.1 Characteristics of culture sustaining competitiveness and viability

9.11 Three Quality Criteria

While the above-discussed ten characteristics refer to the content of an organization's culture relevant when operating in a VUCA environment, the quality of an organization's culture depends on the following three criteria strategic fit, multidimensional orientation, and congruence between normative expectations and practiced behavior. These three critera allow evaluating the degree of a culture's functionality for its organization.

9.11.1 Strategic Fit

The fit of an organization's culture with the organization's strategy emerged as a critical success factor in several studies (c.f., Flamholtz, 2005; Kotter & Heskett, 1992; Sackmann & Bertelsmann Stiftung, 2006; Van der Post et al., 1998; Wilderom & van den Berg, 1998). *Strategic fit* implies that the organization's culture is well aligned with its strategy and thus supports its implementation. However, this requires a carefully developed strategy based on a regular scanning of the organization's relevant environment and its positioning in its market. The executive group regularly checks the developed strategy, adjusts it if necessary, and further develops it with the involvement of organizational members. Hence, it also implies that responsible organizational members periodically monitor the needs and desires of the organization's current and potential customers, competitors, relevant stakeholders, and the existing and emerging technologies, including societal developments and bring this information into the organization. If perceived changes are considered relevant for the organization, the top executive group adapts both their strategy and culture to meet the environmental changes and maintain a high strategic fit between the strategy and its culture.

Given the multifaceted business environment, the content-related characteristics of organizational culture will most likely vary across organizations and industries. What is considered best in terms of enabling an organization's viability depends, among others, on the specific environmental conditions and requirements as well as an organization's purpose and life cycle. The criterion of strategic fit may help explain some of the seemingly contradictory assertions and research results regarding the quality of *strength* and *homogeneity* of an organization's culture. Several publications assert that *strong* and *homogenous* organizational cultures are better for an organization's success. However, other studies refuted this assertion. While organizations with strong and homogenous cultures may successfully operate in stable environments (c.f., Sørensen, 2002), dynamic VUCA environments require flexibility and various alternatives in thinking and action (c.f., Ernst, 2003).

Several studies provide evidence for the notion of strategic fit. One study found that the two stabilizing culture dimensions *mission* and *consistency* of their culture measure correlated stronger with profitability, while the two flexibility-oriented dimensions, *adaptability* and *participation/inclusion,* correlated stronger with organization growth (Denison & Mishra, 1995). Another study supported these results whose authors explained the differences in their results with the different national cultures (the USA vs. Hong Kong) (Chan et al., 2004). Further research also showed that the dimension *mission* was stronger associated with perceived corporate success in the USA. In contrast, the two dimensions *adaptability* and *participation* were more important for corporate success in Russia (Fey & Denison, 2003). Sørensen (2002) found that *strong* cultures—measured as consistent style—will only lead to extraordinary and reliable financial performance (measured as ROI[1] and operative cashflow), if they act in stable environments. Ernst (2003) found that organizational cultures characterized by flexibility affect innovative success in non-linear ways in environments with high technological dynamics. Regarding innovation, there seems to exist an optimum in a culture's flexibility while too little and too much flexibility reduces innovation. In contrast, bureaucratic organizational cultures significantly reduce innovative success even in environments with low technological dynamics.

These results substantiate several results from strategy research. On the one hand, studies indicate that depending on an organization's strategic positioning, life-cycle phase and size, different cultural characteristics may be more success-enhancing than others. On the other hand, extant research also suggests that culture characteristics correlating highly with success indicators will not necessarily guarantee future success because the organization's relevant environment may change and thus require adaptations in the organization's culture characteristics.

[1] ROI: Return on Investment.

9.11.2 Multidimensional Orientation

An organization's multidimensional orientation represents another quality criterion and thus an additional indicator for viability- and performance-enhancing organizational culture. A study investigating company failures that led to a loss in firm value of up to 40 percent or bankruptcy revealed that one major reason was a one-dimensional orientation towards excessive growth or maintaining the status quo (Probst & Raisch, 2005). To stay competitive and viable, organizations ideally focus on all dimensions discussed in this chapter and check them regularly. The qualitative studies of the cultural characteristics of seven high-performing companies within their respective industries showed that all of them considered the ten dimensions discussed above. Furthermore, the seven companies did not emphasize some characteristics over others; instead, they observed these ten cultural characteristics overall at a high level and kept them in balance (Sackmann, 2005; Sackmann & Bertelsmann Foundation, 2006). Analyses of data collected with the DOCS Denison Organizational Culture Survey also showed that successful companies score higher on all twelve dimensions of the DOCS than less successful companies (Denison, 2005).

9.11.3 Congruence Between Normative Expectations and Practiced Behavior

The level of congruence between an organization's normative expectations and the actual organizational practices is the third indicator for the quality of a given organizational culture. Congruence implies that the organization's self-image in terms of identity, purpose, values, and priorities is both documented on paper and observable in organizational members' behavior and daily work practices. The importance of congruence is supported by a study that found that the degree of congruence between the practiced organizational culture and the desired culture strongly correlated with organization success and explained 46 percent of the variance of the companies' EBIT (Flamholtz, 2005).[2] As mentioned above, consistency between normative expectations and practiced behavior requires that the organization's culture supports implementing the strategic (goal-) orientation in line with the organization's relevant environment.

The discrepancy between postulated values and priorities and lived organization culture can serve as a quality measure for the respective organizational culture. High consistency between the proclaimed and actual organization culture, however, does not guarantee an organization's success. Besides consistency between normative

[2]EBIT: Earnings Before Interest and Taxes.

aspirations and actual behavior, the content-related characteristics of culture also matter.

9.12 Concluding Comments

The above discussion and related research suggest that several content-related culture characteristics exist linked to the success and the viability of organizations operating in a turbulent environment. The meta-analysis results of Hartnell et al. (2019) indicate that organizational culture dimensions explain a unique variance of 75 percent of the relationships with organizational performance. Based on the existing knowledge, organizations need to focus on all of the ten discussed dimensions in combination and a balanced way for an organization to stay competitive and viable. In turn, these ten content-related dimensions and the three quality criteria can help to assess an organization's culture regarding its contribution to an organization's viability. The discussion also supports the notion that culture is a multifaceted, complex, and dynamic phenomenon requiring conscious and regular attention.

For organizations to stay competitive and viable, it is essential that key decision-makers timely recognize relevant environmental changes and act accordingly. Such actions may include adapting the organization's strategy, design, and culture in an aligned way. In addition, their efforts need to consider all relevant stakeholders, which may also change over time, including their concerns. Furthermore, organizations should avoid a crisis and the related revolutionary culture changes whenever possible. Instead, regular attention to the external challenges and their potential impact on the organization and its culture allows developmental activities, thus helping prevent a crisis. Such attention to culture requires culture-sensitive and culture-mindful leaders and managers—the subject of Chap. 10.

References

Amran, N. A. (2012). Mission statement and company performance: Evidence from Malaysia. *International Journal of Business and Behavioral Sciences.*, *2*(4), 98–107.

Barney, J. (1986). Organizational culture: Can it be a source of sustained competitive advantage? *Academy of Management Review.*, *11*(3), 656–665. https://doi.org/10.2307/258317

Barney, J. (1991). Firm resources and sustained competitive advantage. *Journal of Management.*, *17*(1), 99–120. https://doi.org/10.1177/014920639101700108

Benner, M. J., & Tushman, M. L. (2003). Exploitation, exploration and process management: The productivity dilemma revisited. *Academy of Management Review, 28*(2), 238–256. https://doi.org/10.2307/30040711

Benner, M. J., & Tushman, M. L. (2015). Reflections on the 2013 decade award–"exploitation, exploration, and process management: The productivity dilemma revisited" ten years later. *Academy of Management Review, 40*(4), 497–514. https://doi.org/10.5465/amr.2015.0042

Bogdanowicz, M. (2014). Organizational culture as a source of competitive advantage: A case study of a telecommunication organization in Poland. *International Journal of Contemporary Management, 13*(3), 53–66.

Chan, L. L. M., Shaffer, M. A., & Snape, E. (2004). In search of sustained competitive advantage: The impact of organizational culture, competitive strategy and human resource management practices [HPHRP] on firm performance. *International Journal of Human Resource Management, 15*(1), 17–35. https://doi.org/10.1080/0958519032000157320

Collins, J. C. (2001). *Good to great. Why some companies make the leap … and others don't.* Harper Business Essentials.

Cooke, R. A. (1997). *Organizational culture inventory*. Human Synergistics.

Den Hartog, D. N., & Verburg, R. (2004). High performance work systems, organizational culture and firm effectiveness. *Human Resource Management Journal, 14*(1), 55–79. https://doi.org/10.1111/j.1748-8583.2004.tb00112.x

Denison, D. R. (1990). *Organization culture and organizational effectiveness*. Wiley.

Denison, D. R. (2005). *Discussion during the 3*. Workshop of the International Organization Culture Network in Basel, Switzerland, October 2005.

Denison, D. R., & Mishra, A. K. (1995). Toward a theory of organizational culture and effectiveness. *Organization Science, 6*(2), 204–223. https://doi.org/10.1287/orsc.6.2.204

Desphandé, R., Farley, J. U., & Webster, F. E., Jr. (1993). Organization culture, customer orientation, and innovativeness in Japanese firms: A quadrad analysis. *Journal of Marketing, 57*(1), 23–37. https://doi.org/10.2307/1252055

Dutton, J. (1993). The making of organizational opportunities: An interpretive pathway to organizational change. In B. Staw & L. L. Cummings (Eds.), *Research in organization behavior* (pp. 195–226). JAI.

Ellsworth, R. R. (2002). *Leading with purpose: The new organization realities*. Stanford University Press.

Ernst, H. (2003). Unternehmenskultur und Innovationserfolg: Eine empirische analyse. *Zeitschrift für Betriebswirtschaftliche Forschung, 55*(2), 23–44. https://doi.org/10.1007/BF03372697

Fey, C. F., & Denison, D. R. (2003). Organizational culture and effectiveness: Can American theory be applied in Russia? *Organization Science, 14*(6), 686–706. https://doi.org/10.1287/orsc.14.6.686.24868

Flamholtz, E. (2005). Conceptualizing and measuring the economic value of human capital of the third kind organization culture. *Journal of Human Resource Costing & Accounting, 9*(2), 78–93. https://doi.org/10.1108/14013380510645360

Flamholtz, E., & Kannan-Narasimhan, R. (2005). Differential impact of cultural elements on financial performance. *European Management Journal, 23*(1), 50–64. https://doi.org/10.1016/j.emj.2004.12.009

Gast, A., Probst, N., & Simpson, B. (2020, December 3). Purpose, not platitudes: Personal challenge for top executives. *McKinsey & Company Online*. Accessed Sep 23, 2021, from www.mckinsey.com/business-functions/organization/our-insights/purpose-notplatitudes-a-personal-challenge-for-top-executives

Hartnell, C. A., Ou, A. Y., Kinicki, A. J., Choi, D., & Karam, E. P. (2019). A meta-analytic test of organizational culture's association with elements of an organization's system and its relative predictive validity on organizational outcomes. *Journal of Applied Psychology, 104*(6), 832–850. https://doi.org/10.1037/apl0000380

Herrmann, A., Schönborn, G., & Peetz, S. (2004). Von den Besten lernen: Der Einfluss der Wertekultur auf den Unternehmenserfolg. In G. Bentele, M. Piwinger, & G. Schönborn (Eds.), *Kommunikationsmanagement. Strategien, Wissen, Lösungen* (pp. 1–27). Luchterhand. (loose leaf edition: contribution 1.23).

Hunsdiek, D. (2005). *Messbarkeit von Unternehmenskultur anhand der internationalen Mitarbeiterbefragung von Bertelsmann*. Presentation given at the 1st meeting of the International Network Organization Culture, Gütersloh, March 2, 2005.

Koene, A. S. (1996). *Organizational culture, leadership and performance in context: Trust and rationality in organizations*. Datawyse.

Kotter, J. P., & Heskett, J. L. (1992). *Organization culture and performance*. Free Press.

Netta, F. (2009). Gezielte Schwachstellenanalyse bis auf die untersten Führungsebenen. *HR Today, 5*, 25–28. Accessed Sep 23, 2021, from www.hrtoday.ch/de/article/gezielte-schwachstellenanalyse-bis-auf-die-untersten-fuehrungsebenen

Ogbonna, E., & Harris, L. C. (2000). Leadership style, organizational culture and performance: Empirical evidence from U.K. companies. *International Journal of Human Resource Management, 11*(4), 766–788. https://doi.org/10.1080/09585190050075114

Ouchi, W. G., & Jaeger, A. M. (1978). Type Z organization: Stability in the midst of mobility. *Academy of Management Review, 3*(2), 305–314. https://doi.org/10.2307/257670

Petty, M. M., Beadles, N. A., Lowery, C. M., Chapman, D. F., & Connell, D. W. (1995). Relationship between organizational culture and organizational performance. *Psychological Reports, 76*(2), 483–492. https://doi.org/10.2466/pr0.1995.76.2.483

Pfeffer, J., & Sutton, R. I. (2000). *The knowing-doing gap: How smart companies turn knowledge into action*. Harvard Business School Press.

Probst, G., & Raisch, S. (2005). Organizational crisis: The logic of failure. *The Academy of Management Executive, 19*(1), 90–105. https://doi.org/10.5465/ame.2005.15841958

Sackmann, S. A. (1991). *Cultural knowledge in organizations. Exploring the collective mind*. Sage.

Sackmann, S. A. (2005). In Bertelsmann Foundation (Ed.), *Toyota Motor Corporation. Eine Fallstudie aus unternehmenskultureller Perspektive*. Bertelsmann Stiftung.

Sackmann, S. A. (2006). In Bertelsmann Foundation (Ed.), *Assessment, evaluation, improvement: Success through organization culture*. Bertelsmann Stiftung.

Sackmann, S. A., & Bertelsmann Foundation. (2006). *Success factor: Corporate culture. Developing a corporate culture for high performance and long-term competitiveness*. Bertelsmann Stiftung.

Simpson, B. (2020, June 18). Leading with purpose and humanity: A conversation with Hubert Joly. *McKinsey & Company Online*. Accessed Sep 23, 2021, from www.mckinsey.com/business-functions/strategy-and-corporate-finance/our-insights/leadingwith-purpose-and-humanity-a-conversation-with-hubert-joly

Sørensen, J. (2002). The strength of organization culture and the reliability of firm performance. *Administrative Science Quarterly, 47*(1), 70–91. https://doi.org/10.2307/3094891

Starbuck, W. H., Greve, A., & Hedberg, B. (1978). Responding to crisis. Journal of Business Administration, 9(2), 111–137. Available at SSRN: https://ssrn.com/abstract=2708264.

Van der Post, W. Z., de Coning, T. J., & Smit, E. V. D. M. (1998). The relationship between organizational culture and financial performance: Some south African evidence. *South African Journal of Business Management, 29*(1), 30–40. https://doi.org/10.4102/sajbm.v29i1.768

Wilderom, C. P. M., & Berg, P. T. van den. (1998). *A test of the leadership-culture-performance model within a large Dutch financial organization.* Discussion Paper #2000–03. Tilburg: Tilburg University, Center for Economic Research. Accessed May 24, 2021, from https://research.tilburguniversity.edu/en/publications/a-test-of-the-leadership-culture-performance-model-within-a-large-3

Chapter 10
Culture-Mindful Management, Leadership, and Leaders

The previous chapters addressed why culture is essential for the competitiveness and viability of organizations. I discussed the characteristics and potential functions of organizational culture, its assessment, further development or change, including the characteristics of a culture that enable an organization's competitiveness and viability in a volatile environment. Paying attention to culture, taking it seriously, and developing or changing it requires those in power positions. Hence, managers and leaders play an essential role in consciously developing, and mindfully maintaining an organization's culture and initiating related measures. Even though all organizational members are culture carriers, taking deliberate care of an organization's culture cannot be delegated. It has to be part of the attention and decision-making processes of the top executive group, as demonstrated by those organizations that take their culture seriously (c.f., Sackmann & Bertelsmann Foundation, 2006). Good managers and leaders need to have culture on their agenda and deal with it in terms of culture-sensitive and culture-mindful management and leadership.

This chapter addresses culture-mindful management and leadership characteristics and the characteristics and behaviors of culture-mindful managers and leaders. The term leader is used in the broadest sense and refers to formal and informal leaders attributed to power by other organizational members. Hence, the term leader may also refer to key decision-makers, and managers whose role requires leadership skills, including cultural sensitivity. The term manager is used when referring to the role of managers having organizational members reporting to them directly.

S. A. Sackmann, *Culture in Organizations*, Contributions to Management Science,
https://doi.org/10.1007/978-3-030-86080-6_10

10.1 The Role of Managers and Leaders in Culture-Mindful Management and Leadership

As discussed in Chap. 2, every member of an organization can be considered a culture carrier with the potential to influence the existing culture. However, people in key positions, such as managers and leaders at different levels, play an essential role in maintaining and shaping an organization's culture due to their visible role. If they are culturally mindful and act accordingly, they can avoid an unintended culture drift (see, e.g., Sackmann, 1991; Schein, 1986, 1995). Work organizations are conditional systems. They hire people under certain conditions specified in a contract. Consequently, the work contract defines the exchange between employer and organizational member (Williamson, 1996). No matter how flat an organization is, some kind of hierarchy always exists in which managers represent the employing organization towards their organizational members. Managers' hierarchical position gives them legitimate power that allows them to apply sanctions and distribute rewards. In addition, the position of a manager has a leverage effect. Their influence is multiplied by the number of employees directly reporting to them. This number depends on the span of control, as illustrated in Fig. 10.1.

Given the exposed position of managers and leaders, it is critical to regularly check whether people in these positions behave according to the desired organizational culture. If they want it or not, managers and leaders represent role models for the people directly reporting to them and thus personifying an organization's culture. Hence, their position and role come at least with four interrelated functions regarding organizational culture—no matter how aware managers and leaders are of the existing culture and how consciously they deal with it. They

- personify an organization's culture,
- are role models,
- demonstrate priorities,
- set standards.

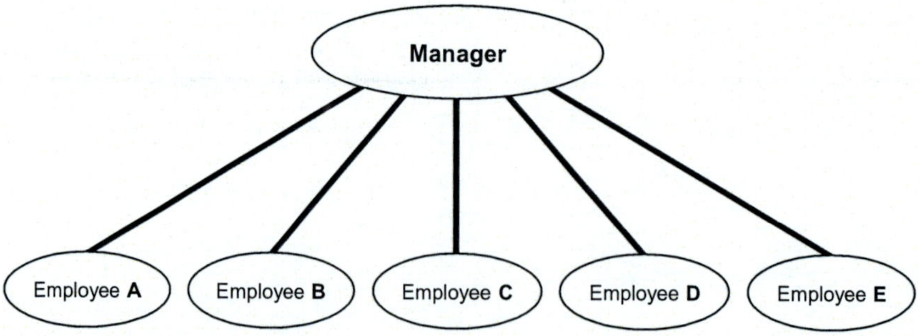

Fig. 10.1 The leverage of managers

10.1.1 Managers and Leaders Personify an Organization's Culture

Organizational culture as such is an abstract concept challenging to grasp for its members because it essentially refers to the invisible basic beliefs that guide their thoughts, feelings, and actions. This mindset serves as a cognitive map and becomes visible in the daily work behavior of those people that represent the organization. For organizational members, these are the leaders, key decision-makers, and especially their direct managers. The behavior of managers and leaders expresses and symbolizes culture and makes it tangible for organizational members. Their actions demonstrate what kind of behavior is considered appropriate and thus culturally expected. The basic beliefs of an organization's culture become manifest in the way leaders work, communicate, act and interact in their day-to-day work activities. These refer to managers and leaders' interactions with their people, colleagues, and their superiors. How do they handle contacts with customers and demanding situations? How do they make decisions? Thus, the concrete behavior of managers and leaders demonstrates the organization's culture and makes it visible and understandable for its members.

This personification of culture implies that managers and leaders are not only holders of a particular position or function. Besides the specific tasks associated with their position and organizational function, their managerial and leadership roles also entail a symbolic function. As leaders, they represent, symbolize, and embody the current corporate culture. *Heinz Dürr*, former CEO and Chairman of the Board of Deutsche Bahn AG describes this as follows:

> Leaders exert great influence on the company's culture because a corporate culture consists of people, of their attitudes, demeanor, and behavior. Corporate culture becomes tangible for every individual once role models live it. In successful companies, the managers' behavior is congruent with the guidelines for leadership and cooperation. (Dürr, 1990, p. 134).

Leaders at all levels of an organization play an important role in embodying organizational culture since their behavior is visible to all members. However, for every employee, their direct managers' behavior is most important since managers decide about the current and future situation of those directly reporting to them. Managers decide about their subordinates' tasks, responsibilities, degree of freedom at work, salaries and bonuses, sanctions and rewards, and the next promotion. Hence, if organizational members want to survive and advance in an organization, they behave to meet or excel their managers' expectations.

The symbolic function of managerial and leadership roles has important implications for maintaining and developing an organization's culture and, hence, leaders' selection. In addition to professional skills, organizations need to critically examine candidates for a leadership position regarding their fit with the desired culture. Can the potential managers or leaders live the desired culture in their daily work practices? Do they personify those things that are important to the organization and its culture? Are the candidates able to act as authentic role models of the organization's culture? Jack Welch, long-time CEO and Chairman of the Board at General Electric (GE), used two dimensions in assessing leaders:

(a) their performance and
(b) their adherence to the organization's values.

For Jack Welch, leaders had to live up to both criteria. He did not consider a person suitable for a leadership position at GE who did not adhere to and live by the organization's values as expressed in the GE leadership principles.

Jack Welch on Assessing Leaders
GE Leaders . . . Always with unyielding integrity . . .

- Are **passionately focused** on driving customer success.
- Live Six Sigma Quality . . . ensure that the customer **is always its first beneficiary** . . . and use it to accelerate growth.
- Insist on **excellence** and are intolerant of bureaucracy
- Act in a boundaryless fashion . . . always search for and apply the **best ideas** regardless of their source.
- Prize **global intellectual capital** and the people that provide it . . . **build teams** to maximize it.
- See change for the growth opportunities it brings . . . i.e., **»e-Business«.**
- Create a clear, simple, **customer-centred vision** . . . and continually renew and refresh its execution.
- Create an environment of **»stretch« excitement**, informality and **trust** . . . reward improvements and celebrate results.
- Demonstrate . . . always with infectious enthusiasm for the customer . . . **the »4 E's « of GE leadership:** the personal **Energy** to welcome and deal with the speed of change . . ., the ability to create an atmosphere that **Energizes** others . . ., the **Edge** to make difficult decisions . . . and the ability to consistently **Execute**.

Organizations whose leaders consider their culture a critical success factor pay careful attention to organizational members' fit with their culture. Examples are W.L. Gore & Associates, Grundfos, Hilti, NovoNordisk and Toyota. People may make a mistake in handling specific business situations, but disregarding the values and basic beliefs of the organization's culture are not tolerated. As one executive from NovoNordisk explained, "you can always fail on the business side but never on the values side" (Sackmann & Bertelsmann Foundation, 2006). Furthermore, representatives of every company mentioned above recalled instances when they parted with a manager who had performed well but had violated organizational culture values or norms.

The following example illustrates what may happen when people do not live the basic beliefs of an organization's culture:

An organization had a culture characterized by informal, cooperative, unpretentious, and direct interactions among its members—also across hierarchical levels. They hired a new head of finance who had the best professional credentials and excellent references regarding his professional skills. However, it became soon apparent that he did not live the company's central beliefs. He had difficulties dealing with others in an informal, cooperative way, and status was important to him. He had his office door mostly closed. Furthermore, the size of his company car, a personal parking space, the location of this office, and his external contacts seemed more important to him than the people in the current organization, especially his subordinates.

The Chairman of the Board had a long talk with him about his behavior and its negative influence on the organization's culture. Being the head of finance, he had a key position, and his behavior was visible to many organizational members. A second and the third conversation about his attitude and behavior followed. Since these conversations did not lead to a visible change in his behavior, the board decided to part with him despite his outstanding qualifications. They did not want to compromise on their culture. The board members considered adhering to and living the organization's culture in daily work practices as important as professional qualifications.

(Personal talk between the Chairman of the Board and the author)

The results of a study of 32 CEOs linking their personality characteristics to the cultural values of their organization indicated that several of their personal values were related to their organization's cultural values (Giberson et al., 2009). Furthermore, in a recent study of 1,348 North American executives, 85 percent of them believed that a poorly implemented culture increases the chance that an employee might act unethically or even illegally (Graham et al., 2021).

10.1.2 Leaders Are Role Models

Over time, organizational members start imitating the behavior of their direct manager if they want to stay in the organization and succeed. Managers have the legitimate power to sanction and reward their subordinates and regulate access to attractive resources. Organizational members observe their managers' behavior to learn about the organization's expectations regarding their behavior. Their manager's behavior conveys what is considered important and what is unimportant, what kind of priorities they should set, what to do to count as a *good* or excellent organizational member, and what not to do to avoid sanctions. Thus, the managers' behavior provides orientation for how to survive and advance in the organization.

Being a role model implies that those organizational members imitate the leaders' behavior who identify with the role model or aspire to the same kind of rewards that seem to come with the position of the role model (see also Bandura, 1994). Hence, over time, organizational members are likely to show the same behaviors they observe in their managers. Vice versa, leaders tend to characterize their successful employees as a mirror image of themselves. When asked about the qualities of people promoted in their organization, 50 CEOs characterized those successful people in terms of their own behavior. Some of them even concluding "those who are and act like me!" (Pelton et al., 1990).

Leaders do not have a choice, whether they want to communicate their organization's culture—they always do with all of their verbal and non-verbal behavior. They can only decide how and to what extent they want to influence whatever they are trying to communicate (Schein, 1986). One of the leadership lessons of Eric Yuan, the founder, and CEO of the video communications company Zoom, is.

> Lead by example when creating a company culture. … and we lead by example. (Nazar, 2021).

When in doubt about the meaning of a verbal message, people will always refer to observable behavior since they know that one can control words better than non-verbal behavior. For this reason, the way leaders practice their leadership daily has a strong influence on their employees. As Robert Bosch, the founder of Robert Bosch AG, allegedly once said:

> I prefer losing money over losing trust. The inviolability of my promises, the belief in the value of my products, and the value of my word have always been more important to me than a quick profit.

Hence, the extent to which leaders and people in key positions are authentic role models of the desired culture is critical for maintaining, developing, or changing a given culture. If the leaders' behavior is counterproductive, the organization will have difficulties maintaining its culture or moving toward the desired culture. Due to leaders' role modeling function, organizations must carefully select potential leaders and familiarize them with their culture. Organizations know the attitudes and behaviors of internal candidates, while they need to carefully examine external candidates regarding their fit with the current or desired organization's culture. Do the potential leaders merely use the expected rhetoric, or do they live according to the organization's basic beliefs? The probation period allows evaluating if the internally promoted or externally hired leaders are also cultural role models or only pretended to live the desired culture.

Several measures exist for socializing new leaders into their roles and functions. Mentors are helpful who live the desired culture. They can explain the expectations toward leaders, give feedback, and set an example with their leadership behavior. In addition, leadership development programs, including leadership instruments, need regular examination if they convey the beliefs, attitudes, and values of the desired culture in their content, structure, and delivery. These include on-the-job as well as off-the-job development initiatives. An organization's leadership principles and guidelines serve current leaders and potential leaders as orientation for their behavior. For example, Daimler AG developed new leadership principles in its initiated culture change project *Leadership 2020*. Among others, the company expects leaders to involve their direct reports more in their decision-making processes to utilize their knowledge better and increase their motivation. The specific way they developed *Leadership 2020* served as an example of this new kind of leadership: They included many organizational members in the development process (Pallenberg, 2018). In addition, decisions making processes should be faster. For example, they reduced the signatures needed to approve business travel to one single one by the immediate manager. They implemented a 360°-feedback process in which direct reports, colleagues, and managers assess the behavior of all leaders to ensure that the new leadership principles are also practiced (WirtschaftsWoche, 2016).

10.1.3 Leaders Demonstrate the Cultural Priorities

As representatives of the organization, leaders set an example with their specific behavior regarding cultural priorities and posteriorities. The leaders' daily work behavior signals to their organizational members what is very important, important, less important, and unimportant. In the example mentioned above of Daimler AG, the company prioritized participatory leadership and quick decisions. The above-mentioned leadership principles at General Electric signaled the following priorities, including their specific meaning to their organizational members:

- have complete integrity,
- see the customer as the first beneficiary and, thus, support the organization's growth at the same time,
- insist on excellence,
- always implement the best idea—no matter where it originated,
- build diverse teams to utilize as much intellectual capital as possible,
- view change for the growth possibilities it brings about,
- develop, adjust, and realize a clear and simple customer-oriented vision,
- design a work environment supporting challenges, stimuli, informality, and trust, rewarding improvement and celebrating results, and
- practice the GE leadership "4 Es" for customers with enthusiasm:
  - **energy** to cope with the speed of change,
  - the ability to design an atmosphere **energizing** others,
  - the **edge** to make tough decisions,
  - the ability to permanently **execute** and implement.

At W.L. Gore & Associates, leaders are partly elected by the organizational members, and a group of people assesses their leadership performance. Furthermore, leadership positions are temporarily assigned without any negative implications. Consequently, a person may work in a leadership role for some time and then continue as a regular team member under someone else's leadership. In addition to leaders with responsibilities in a line or project management function, the role of mentors exists. Organizational members elect their mentors. The election has positive implications for the mentor since it signals that the person has desirable leadership qualities.

10.1.4 Leaders Set Standards

The behavior of leaders signals to their organizational members the standards they should observe in their work processes. In the example of General Electric, the slogans *have perfect integrity*, *insist on excellence*, or *implement the best idea* require further specifications for organizational members. What does *perfect, excellence,* or *best* mean? These qualifiers, including official norms such as DIN or the European Quality model EFQM, leave room for interpretation. Suppose an organization has introduced, for example, *total quality* management. In that case, organizational members will ask themselves in their particular function what *total quality* means and what it may imply for their daily work, as illustrated in the following example:

The Meaning of *Total Quality*
A university hospital implemented the concept of *Total Quality Management.* The administrative director of the hospital was very proud of having initiated its implementation. However, nobody in the organization had thought about the concept's specific meaning for nurses' daily work. Were they supposed to fulfill every wish of each patient? Or did they need to ensure that the patient was not going to die? A wide range of nursing behavior exists between these two extremes, and it was left to every nurse how to interpret total quality on their job.

When in doubt, organizational members turn to their manager for help in trying to understand the culturally specific and thus correct interpretation of an ambiguous or vague term relevant for their particular work processes. Managers may verbally explain the concrete meaning of total quality management and discuss the implications for their specific tasks with their subordinates. In addition, managers' behavior will illustrate the meaning of total quality to their people. Hence, leaders set standards with their behavior by the way they prepare for meetings, conduct them and follow them up, and how they make decisions. Their daily practices implicitly and explicitly communicate the culture-specific meaning of concepts such as customer orientation, quality, innovation, fast decision-making, or employee involvement. For this reason, the existing leadership guidelines and leadership practices need to be explicitly reflected, discussed, and regularly evaluated regarding the desired culture.

The research results by Kotter and Heskett (1992, p. 143) show the importance of a specific kind of leadership behavior for an organization's adaptability. In adaptive cultures, managers cared about customers, stockholders, and employees and paid close attention to their constituencies in their daily work behavior. In addition, they initiated change when needed to serve their stakeholders' needs better. In unadaptive organizational cultures, managers tended to care mainly about themselves, their immediate workgroup, or some product or technology associated with their workgroup. Hence, they behaved somewhat isolated, political, and bureaucratic and did not or rather slowly adjust to changes in their business environment.

Since leaders and managers act within an existing organizational culture's framework, the question arises of who defines the organization's culture with its scope. Such a definition is one of the central tasks of top management.

10.2 The Role of the Founder and Leaders at the Top in Culture-Mindful Leadership

All the above also applies to founders and top-level leaders. Nevertheless, founders and top-level leaders have additional roles in culture-mindful leadership. In a start-up, the founders or founding team have a business idea associated with a mission and purpose that they want to pursue. They gather people around them with whom they can get along, who share their ideas and how to implement them.

As organizations grow, leaders at the top of an organization need to critically reflect and potentially adjust the fundamental decisions about the organization's cultural reality. These include

- decisions about core cultural beliefs and the appropriate indicators for reviewing them regularly,
- communicating these basic beliefs verbally and nonverbally in an authentic way, and
- enforcing these fundamental beliefs and their associated practices consistently and regularly.

10.2.1 Deciding on the Core Cultural Beliefs and Reviewing them Regularly

In practicing culture-mindful leadership, the role of the founders and top leaders entails deciding on the basic commonly-held beliefs of an organization's culture. These decisions also include the scope and specific meaning of these core beliefs. Hence, founders and the group of top-level leaders define the cultural reality of an organization, the degrees of freedom for its organizational members, and its boundaries. As discussed in Chap. 2, this cultural reality is defined by:

- the organization's strategy, i.e., the direction and positioning of the organization in its relevant market (see General Electric: Jack Welch's philosophy: "If you're not No. 1 or 2 in your field, get out."),
- the basic parameters of the organization's design, such as its structure and processes (see Bell Industries or W.L. Gore & Associates),
- the type of person who fits with the organization's cultural orientation and who can practice this orientation in their daily work behavior,
- the key performance indicators and measures used for regularly checking the organization's culture state,
- guidelines for conduct such as organizational principles, leadership guidelines, etc., and
- if necessary, introducing adequate measures for adjusting or improving the existing culture to avoid unintended culture drifts.

The business case of the multinational Hilti Corporation illustrates these steps in deliberately developing and maintaining an organization's culture (Sackmann and Bertelsmann Foundation, 2006). The following case of W.L.Gore & Associates explains the interrelated set of conscious choices required to develop specific organizational culture and maintain it.

Deciding on and Implementing Core Cultural Beliefs

When Bill Gore and his wife Genevieve (Vieve) founded W.L. Gore & Associates, the two had more in mind than pursuing new market opportunities for fluorocarbon polymers. They discussed "the kind of work environment they wanted to create: one that would foster innovation and business success. In particular, Bill was heavily influenced by his work experiences, as well as by the writings of psychologist Abraham Maslow and author Douglas McGregor:

"...I dreamed of an Enterprise with great opportunity for all who would join in it, of a virile organization that would foster self-fulfillment and which would multiply the capabilities of the individuals comprising it beyond their mere sum."– Bill Gore, Co-Founder (W.L. Gore & Associates, 2020, p. 1).

These core beliefs about the culture-to-be became reflected in the company name. Bill and Vieve did not want to have employees; they wanted to have engaged organizational members who took ownership of their work and organization. Hence, they chose the term *associates* and developed a stock ownership plan for associates with several years of tenure with GORE. They were cautious in selecting new people who would fit into their entrepreneurial, performance-oriented culture. To maintain associates' entrepreneurial spirit and commitment, Bill chose a grid design with small organizational units so that everybody could know and communicate with each other. One premise was *no ranks-no titles*, and once organizational units grew beyond a specific size, they split them like a cell.

Four basic principles guide all associates their behavior: freedom, waterline, commitment, and fairness. The waterline limits every individual's freedom to act. Hence, no decision should be so risky that it could cause the company (boat) to sink due to a hole beneath the surface. In addition to their work-related goals, associates commit to one self-initiated goal that they drive and implement to contribute to the company's success. All interactions with internal organizational members and outsiders such as customers or suppliers need to be fair. GORE uses several indicators to regularly check the extent to which associates live its cultural reality with its different facets to prevent an unintended culture drift.

Organizations that take their culture seriously regularly evaluate their managers' and leaders' behavior and the extent to which they act within the framework of the desired culture. If leaders do not practice what they preach, an organization needs to make appropriate decisions to prevent its culture and its leaders from losing their credibility.

10.2.2 Authentic Communication of the Core Beliefs

To maintain an organization's culture, it does not suffice to decide on the core beliefs, preach them once a year, and distribute glossy brochures. To implement the set of core cultural beliefs, translate them into appropriate actions, keep a given culture alive throughout the organization and avoid an unintended drift, authentic communication is vital. In authentic, credible communication, verbal and nonverbal behaviors match. A principle of interpersonal communication states that nonverbal behavior is more honest and trustworthy than spoken words in a mismatch. To come across as convincible, reliable, and credible, the observable behavior of leaders has to reflect their verbal communication manifested in conversations and official speeches as well as chats, emails, written documents, brochures, announcements, or memos. Leaders have to walk their talk and do as they say. Suppose speeches, conversations, emails, or brochures tell a different story than their observable behavior. In that case, organizational members will believe the message of the observed non-verbal behavior since they intuitively know that non-verbal behavior is more trustworthy than spoken words. The following examples illustrate this principle.

Examples of Inconsistent Communication

1. One of the leadership principles of an organization was an open dialogue between managers and their employees. Business unit manager Stuart Brown regularly emphasized the importance of his employees reporting to him. When conducting annual performance reviews, Stuart Brown always reserved one hour for each of his employees. During the annual review with his direct report Kevin, Stuart looked at his watch several times and answered the phone twice, talking to the person on the phone for several minutes each time.
2. An organization advertised special career paths for women and emphasized the importance of work-life balance in its brochures. Ninety-five percent of its management positions held men. A closer analysis revealed that women earned 10–20 percent less than their male colleagues in similar positions with comparable responsibilities. During a leadership development program, a female high-potential asked the Vice-President of Human Resources whether the organization would consider offering management positions on a part-time basis. The Vice-President of Human Resources denied.
3. An organization emphasized the importance of innovative behavior for its future success. It documented the importance of innovation in its organizational guidelines, its leadership principles, and the CEO regularly mentioned it during his annual New Year's speeches. At the same time, the top manager criticized the lack of proactive initiatives and willingness to try out new things. When making an improvement suggestion, four different decision-making groups need to approve the proposals, and they rejected most of them. In addition, organizational members told stories about how the organization had forgotten the contributions of initiators of new ideas in the past.
4. With a smile on his face, a CEO announced that he, unfortunately, had to terminate several hundred organizational members in the course of a restructuring process.

These examples show how important it is that leaders preach the basic beliefs and live them in their daily behavior so that words and actions, verbal and nonverbal behavior are congruent and consistent. Hence, all cultural manifestations regarding artifacts and collective behavior depicted in Fig. 2.6 require a check regarding their consistency with the proclaimed culture. This check includes decision-making processes, communication, interactions, and problem-solving behavior. Leaders also need to be aware of the symbolic meaning of their decisions and behaviors, such as the kind of message they convey when filling leadership positions with specific people. All these verbal and nonverbal behaviors make the underlying basic beliefs visible and send particular signals to organizational members about what is important and counts in the respective organization. Especially in situations of change and, hence, uncertainty, leaders need to send clear messages as illustrated in the following examples:

Examples of Clear Messages in Culture Change Situations

SAS exchanged its whole management during a *cultural revolution* initiated due to an entirely new market situation. As a result, SAS became new management with new management philosophy and new goals. The focus changed from the organization, technology, and product to a customer and market orientation (Carlzon, 1989, p. 149).

MTU, one of the world leaders in producing driving systems, had undergone a considerable change process at the end of the 1990s that encompassed a culture change. As part of the culture change process, top managers had to re-apply for their current position or another position for which they felt qualified. When choosing the new leaders, one of the critical criteria was the extent to which the applicants were good examples and role models of the desired organizational culture.

Embracing change and implementing change processes more effectively was one of an organization-wide culture change process goals. In the past, organizational members actively engaged in a change process tended to disappear somewhere in the organization after the change. However, in line with the culture change process, people involved in implementing the change now had high priority when staffing new positions.

The new CEO of a multinational firm wanted to change its culture. The change included three primary goals: (1) moving from a more directive leadership behavior to participatory leadership and better use people's potentials; (2) allow making mistakes in innovation processes; (3) more open, direct communication within and between different organizational units.

Instead of using the restaurant reserved for top executive members and essential customers, he decided to eat lunch in the firm's cafeteria. Standing in line while waiting for his food, the new CEO chatted with organizational members across hierarchies and functions. He also extended the top executive decision-making group with leaders from the next level. In their weekly meetings, he invited the respective experts to join the group and share their expertise when discussing topics in their field of knowledge. Since his predecessor had not allowed any mistakes to happen, he used one of his speeches to a large group of organizational members to demonstrate that he was willing to accept mistakes in innovation processes. He shared one of his prior mistakes, how he had felt about it, and how he had dealt with it. This story spread immediately through the company and stayed alive for many months.

10.2.3 Consistent Reinforcement of the Cultural Beliefs

Leaders at the top play an essential role in maintaining an existing culture. Due to their exposed position, their behavior is visible to organizational members. They carefully observe their top leaders' behavior and try to interpret its potential meanings. To avoid misinterpretations, leaders know about their important role in providing consistent cultural orientation to organizational members. They are aware of the symbolic meaning of their verbal and nonverbal behavior, its influence on organizational members, and they act accordingly. They convey the specific cultural meanings of decisions, situations, or events to employees by explicitly providing culturally appropriate interpretations, explanations, and reasons. These explanations help organizational members in their culturally appropriate sense-making, be it their daily work, decisions, or actions (Panda & Gupta, 2001).

For maintaining a given culture, leaders need to repeat these messages consistently over time. It does not suffice to preach important culture-related messages once a year. Instead, leaders need to address them verbally and nonverbally congruent throughout the year. If organizational members discover inconsistencies in conveyed culture-related statements, leaders lose their trustworthiness. Their messages, as well as the proclaimed culture, become incredible. Potential discrepancies may exist in different speeches over time, between verbal and nonverbal behavior, or between spoken and printed language.

Unfortunately, many managers and leaders are not aware of their position's symbolic role. Therefore, leaders must examine their verbal and non-verbal behavior regarding the potential meanings to organizational members. To be believable and trustworthy, they need to communicate their messages consistently what they consider essential. In addition, they also need to walk their talk and act upon their spoken words. Suppose organizational members discover discrepancies between words and actions. They tend to believe the message of the observed behavior rather than that of the verbal behavior or brochures since they know intuitively that nonverbal behavior is more honest than words because people control nonverbal behavior less consciously.

The following example illustrates the adverse effects of inconsistent reinforcement.

> Many organizations have an *open door policy*. An organizational member (Ben) once had a problem with his immediate boss and finally decided to use the organization's open-door policy. He took all his courage to skip hierarchies and walk directly to the CEO's offices. When Ben arrived, the door was indeed open, but the CEO was not in his office. Ben came back a second and a third time. The door was always open, but the CEO wasn't there. For Ben, the open door policy became meaningless even though that the door was open.

Such an incongruency in policy and lived behavior may eventually negatively influence an organization's culture.

10.3 Characteristics of Culture-Mindful Management and Leadership

Culture-mindful management and leadership imply that an organization's key decision-makers in managerial and leadership positions across hierarchical levels and functions are aware of their impact on culture and their influence in maintaining and developing its culture. They know and accept that this is an ongoing responsibility and a permanent task. Culture-mindful management and leadership at the team- and organizational level can be characterized as follows:

- knowledge exists about the meaning of an organization's culture and its impact,
- cultural sensitivity exists,
- the past is valued while being open for necessary adjustments,
- when faced with challenges or a crisis: cultural beliefs are critically examined and adjusted if necessary
- the team or organization can effectively deal with cultural dynamics,
- the team or organization manages the cultural network, and
- socialization processes are deliberately designed for newcomers to learn the desired culture.

The previous chapters have addressed all these aspects in detail. The following represent a summary of the most critical issues.

10.3.1 Knowledge about the Meaning of Organizational Culture and its Impact

Culture-mindful leaders know about the role and importance of culture for their organization, including its effects on organizational members, teams, and the entire organization (see Chap. 2). A culture's importance depends on the organization's societal environment, while its impact depends on its size, specific design, and life-cycle stage (see Chap. 4). If an organization originates and operates in a homogenous society and recruits its members from that society, attention to an organization's culture may not be so crucial since the societal culture offers guidelines for orientation that tend to be congruent with the basic cultural beliefs of the organization. However, in a heterogeneous, pluralistic society such as the U.S., and for multinationals, organizational culture becomes very important. When operating in diverse, heterogeneous societies, organizations need to provide their members a common framework for their cognitive and behavioral orientation. The same principle applies to inter-and multinational organizations operating in different countries with different subcultures from which they recruit their organizational members. Hence, a study found that employees of two companies with rather ethnocentric-oriented management considered corporate culture less important for internal coordination than those of two geocentric companies. In the latter case, the perceived importance significantly increased during five years, especially regarding vertical coordination (Ruigrok & Achtenhagen, 1999).

10.3.2 Cultural Sensitivity

Managers and leaders have developed a level of sensitivity that allows them to detect even weak signals regarding the condition of their organization's culture. In this endeavor, they can use informal measures such as regular walks through their organization, informal conversations, regular visits to business units or subsidiaries, and conversations with customers or vendors. In addition, regular culture checks may be helpful to detect unintended changes at an early stage. A culture assessment (see Chap. 7) may shed light on an organization's specifics using data based on a combination of surveys, culture assessment workshops, interviews with organizational members across hierarchical levels and units, and with selected customers and suppliers. The former CEO and Chairman of the Board of a large U.S. based bank regularly used external help to learn about the organization's strengths and weaknesses:

> We bring in people on a regular basis—at the moment, there is a group of consultants here, although I don't actually need consultants. I don't want these consultants to tell me what to do. In fact, I want them to tell us what we are doing wrong. I want relentless criticism. If their arguments are correct and make sense, we work hard to improve. We want an additional external opinion on what we do.
>
> *(Personal conversation with the author.)*

Organizational cultures are dynamic and further evolve in the daily interactions of their members. Hence, an organization needs to check its culture regularly to avoiding unintended drifts. The obtained information will also help to enforce a culture in the desired way. The multinational Hilti Corporation, received the Carl-Bertelsmann-Prize for its culture and leadership, annually reviews its culture using several measures. If the results identify an unintended development, they design and implement actions for maintaining their desired culture (Sackmann & Bertelsmann Foundation, 2006).

10.3.3 Valuing the Past while Being Open for Necessary Adjustments and Changes

Culture constitutes the collective memory of an organization. Founders introduced the core set of collectively-held basic beliefs translated into collective behavior in organizational members' interactions. Over time, cultural knowledge developed, including the cultural network with its collective routines and practices, recipes for success and failure, stories, and legends (see Chap. 3, Fig. 3.2). Hence, culture and its manifestations are rooted in the past. These historical roots may lead to inertia. Organizations can counterbalance this inertia if their culture entails the ability to learn and adjust. Learning and adapting to changes in its relevant business environment is vital for an organization's survival.

If an organization defines and interprets cultural norms and beliefs relatively narrowly, and if it does not periodically reflect its collectively-held fundamental beliefs regarding their appropriateness, the organization's viability can become endangered. The demise of the Appenzeller Reading Society is such an example. Their top leaders did not acknowledge their customers' changing reading tastes and interests. Hence, they only provided what they considered proper literature and refused to offer the new genre of magazines they evaluated as trashy literature. Eventually, they lost their customers and their entire business (Eberle, 1997).

In an adaptive and learning-oriented culture, leaders and organizational members can deal with the inherent dualities of maintaining valuable aspects of their culture from the past while embracing and developing new ideas and practices needed for the future. This duality is similar to an ambidextrous organization combining efficiency and innovation (c.f., O'Reilly & Tushman, 2011, 2013, 2016). When introducing and implementing necessary changes, culture-mindful leaders need to value the organization's past and embrace the future. They need to both appreciate those practices of the past that enabled the organization's success. At the same time, They need to explain why these practices will no longer support the organization's future success given the changes in the external environment. New challenges will require new approaches, routines, and methods. Such an appreciation of the past and a conscious parting with the cherished history help organizational members become open to trying new ideas and practices. It also helps them in implementing changes that are necessary to sustain the organization's viability.

10.3.4 Adjusting Cultural Beliefs when Faced with a Crisis

Evolutionary changes as discussed in Chap. 8 usually affects the cultural network shown in Fig. 3.2 (Chap. 3). The culture core, with its collectively-held basic beliefs, is not affected by evolutionary changes. However, when faced with a crisis such as a turnaround, an organization requires revolutionary change. In the course of a revolutionary change, the culture core—its set of cultural beliefs—need to be critically examined and assessed if these beliefs are still appropriate for the future. For example, in the case of SAS's revolutionary change (see Sect. 10.2.2), SAS had to change its culture core to better fit the new requirements of their business environment. A critical evaluation of the culture core may result in a new or adjusted interpretation of existing cultural beliefs and new related practices (c.f., Sackmann & Bertelsmann Foundation, 2006).

However, organizations should avoid revolutionary change processes if possible. The best way to prevent a crisis and the associated revolutionary changes is by being and staying aware of an organization's culture, regularly checking its status, and introducing adjustments if necessary. If culture-mindful leaders early detect unintended drifts and implement appropriate measures, they may prevent self-initiated crises situations and associated revolutionary changes.

10.3.5 Dealing Effectively with the Cultural Dynamics

Culture-mindful management and leadership entail effectively handling the existing cultural dynamics that emerge from the interplay of existing subcultures. Subcultures tend to emerge as organizations grow (see Chap. 3). Subcultures may develop whenever the group members interact more frequently with each other and differentiate themselves from other groups. Hence, organizational subcultures may form, for example, based on departments, functions, professions, hierarchy, tenure, gender, or ethnicity. Organization design parameters facilitate the emergence of specific subcultures. For example, a functional design promotes functional subcultures, while a divisional structure encourages the emergence of divisional subcultures.

Dealing effectively with cultural dynamics implies that existing subcultures operate constructively and have no adverse effects on the organization's overall functioning. The latter may happen if interdependent groups work independently of each other or even against each other. Hence, culture-mindful leaders recognize existing subcultures and regularly observe their development and impact on the organization. If they discover inefficiencies or counterproductive effects of how subcultures operate, they take appropriate measures to improve their interactions.

The following two general rules exist regarding the emergence of subcultures. They can serve as guidelines in observing and dealing with the cultural dynamics:

- The more intensively the group members work together, the greater the likelihood of developing its specific subculture.
- The more groups work separately and do not interact with each other, the higher the probability of developing their specific subcultures.

In the latter case, culture-mindful leaders create opportunities for contact between the groups so that their members communicate with each other and coordinate their work activities across subcultural boundaries.

10.3.6 Handling the Cultural Network

It is also essential for culture-mindful management and leadership to know and utilize the various components of the cultural network. These include rites, rituals, stories, celebrations, etc. (see Chap. 3, Fig. 3.2). These components of the cultural network preserve, maintain and enforce the existing cultural reality with its social structure and underlying collectively-held beliefs. Hence, they need mangers´ and leaders´ regular attention.

Rites (see Chap. 2) include, for example, rites of rejuvenation, rites for conflict reduction, as well as rites of passage (see also Trice & Beyer, 1993). Rites of rejuvenation cherish and enhance existing social structures. Implementing new programs such as quality improvements and many change programs are often rites of rejuvenation. Even though these initiatives happen under the label *change*, they tend to enforce the existing cultural reality, including the existing power structures, rather than changing them.

Rites for conflict reduction exist primarily to reduce conflicts and aggressive potential not to threaten the status quo. Many special taskforces and some meetings serve to reduce conflicting interests (e.g., Hickson, 1987). For example, research on meetings suggests that their primary function is maintaining the current status and confirming the current social structure. Hence, they sustain the existing order rather than introducing change (Schwartzmann, 1981).

Rites of passage are celebrations of a significant move, such as moving to a higher hierarchical level or achieving more organizational status. One example is the successful passing of an assessment center before being accepted to the next management level. Another example is the passing of a set of interviews, tests, and procedures before being hired. The successful completion of an assessment center or the hiring procedure has a symbolic message for both the newcomer and the group. It signals the newcomer that it is a privilege to join this elite group, and it enforces the group's elite status to existing group members.

Rituals (see Chap. 2) also sustain the existing social and power structures and the cultural reality with its subcultures. Regularly held meetings, various leadership- and human resource management practices may have the character of a ritual. Rituals are periodically recurring events, and their form is more important than their content. For example, annual shareholder meetings may be rituals. Regularly scheduled management meetings may have become rituals if they follow a predictable pattern with predefined roles and procedures. For example, the same people attend, the same person opens the meeting, the sequence of contributions stays the same, including their contributions. Even some board meetings may have turned into rituals when the board members no longer critically question the decisions of their executives.

Celebrations (Chap. 2) offer an opportunity for controlled emotional outbursts within the organization's existing framework and without endangering the current social and power structures. Celebrations also reinforce existing power structures and the dominant cultural reality. They provide the opportunity to reduce potentially accumulated aggression and disruptive energy at a set date and occasion. Examples are Christmas celebrations or annual events such as award ceremonies or annual celebrations for rewarding organizational members' best performance.

The **stories** told throughout an organization serve as orientation for organizational members, especially in critical situations such as being transferred to another position or a different location. As discussed in Chap. 2, each story contains a moral that serves as an orientation for organizational members. The underlying moral of the stories explains to them what they can expect from the organization in this critical situation and whatnot.

Culture-mindful managers and leaders know the meaning, function, and effect of the cultural network's components so that they can use them purposefully. Thus, they can use, design, stage, implement and communicate these components in effect enhancing ways. Leaders also need to address them in times of culture change and development when they cherish the past, reinterpret the collectively-held basic beliefs, and communicate and explain the new meanings.

10.3.7 Designing Culture Appropriate Socialization Processes

In addition to the careful selection of new organizational members, one of the core tasks of culture-mindful management and leadership is the appropriate design and socialization practices for newcomers. Several human resource management practices exist to conveying an organization's culture to new organizational members. These on-the-job, near-the-job, and off-the-job practices (see Sect. 8.6.1) communicate, mediate and enforce core components of an organization's culture. Hence, an organization needs to regularly examine them to ensure that they still convey the desired cultural reality with the appropriate meanings.

Off-the-job measures are workshops, training, seminars, and all kinds of development programs. In designing off-the-job training and development programs, their underlying philosophy and content should reflect the spirit of the desired cultural reality. In addition, it is also essential when choosing external experts, trainers, facilitators, or institutions that they are informed about the desired cultural reality and can deliver their programs with the appropriate spirit and message.

When developing near-the-job measures such as a rotation or stay in another organizational unit, it is crucial to select units that live the desired corporate culture. In addition, a mentor may help the newcomers in their orientation.

It is also advisable to check on-the-job socialization processes regularly whether they still communicate and enforce the desired organizational culture. Since managers and leaders act as role models, their specific behavior is essential since it conveys the priorities and standards that need to express the desired organizational culture. Hence, managers and leaders need to be culturally mindful.

10.4 Characteristics of Culture-Mindful Managers and Leaders

Ultimately, an organization's cultural context defines the characteristics of culture-mindful managers and leaders. Nevertheless, a few general guidelines exist that may serve as orientation for culture-mindful managers and leaders.

The following aspects can characterize the behavior of a culture-mindful manager and leader.

Culture-mindful managers and leaders

- radiate commitment to the organization and its organizational culture,
- set clear and high expectations for their people,
- repeat important things regularly and consistently,
- think positively and search for opportunities,
- explain situations and their interrelationships,
- set examples and live the (new) organization's culture,
- take time for their people,
- pay attention to small things, and
- continue to learn and develop themselves.

10.4.1 Culture-Mindful Managers and Leaders Radiate Commitment

Culture-mindful managers' and leaders' daily behavior expresses the organizational culture's basic beliefs and radiates commitment and dedication to the organization and its culture. Their identification with the organization's culture is noticeable in their verbal and non-verbal behavior. They believe in what they say and do. Culture-mindful leaders and managers come across to their people as being trustworthy and authentic. If leaders only pretend their commitment or enthusiasm for their work and the organization with its culture, people will quickly notice. Such a disguise has adverse effects on organizational members' identification with their employer and their performance. It also negatively impacts the organization, its performance, and its culture. Hence, managers and leaders need to be carefully selected and socialized into their new role and the organization's culture.

10.4.2 Culture-Mindful Managers and Leaders Set Clear and High Expectations for their People

Since organizational members were carefully selected, culture-mindful managers and leaders set high expectations for their people and communicate them. Hence, culture-mindful managers and leaders have high expectations for their organizational member's contribution and performance and express them. Even though this is an essential leadership task, providing the work context for achieving high expectations is frequently missing. Walter Wriston, a former CEO and Chairman of the Board of Citicorp, once explained that his impression was that organizations merely use about 30 percent of organizational members' potential (Pelton et al., 1990). This untapped potential may be partially due to their managers and leaders as well as the organization's rules, regulations, and bureaucracy that may go in the way of performing at a higher level. Several publications address potential reasons for motivational blocks to high performance (e.g., Herzberg et al., 1959; Pinder, 2008; Sprenger, 2002) and supported by research on the bore-out Syndrom (c.f., Costas & Kärreman, 2016; Özsungur, 2020). A worldwide survey of 11.238 employees revealed that in Europe, 32 percent of respondents felt very underemployed in their current job (StepStone Deutschland, 2012). Culture-mindful leaders tap into the potential of their people and mobilize it by setting high expectations and communicating them appropriately.

When culture-mindful leaders have high expectations in their employees and express them clearly, employees know what the organization and its culture expect from them regarding performance and work behavior. Hence, culture-mindful managers and leaders trust their people and dare to entrust them with *big* jobs (Malik, 2015). In addition, they support them in accomplishing their work. They provide the appropriate work context with the necessary resources, coach them or act as their sparring partner. In turn, organizational members do not want to disappoint their leaders, who have instilled them with trust and confidence for doing a good job.

10.4.3 Culture-Mindful Managers and Leaders Repeat Important Things Regularly and Consistently

Culture-mindful managers and leaders do not rely on their New Year's speech or another yearly event to communicate essential issues such as goals and priorities. Instead, they repeat important topics regularly in a consistent, comprehensible, and understandable way. They provide the necessary context information for organizational members to understand the meaning of their message. In addition to annual meetings, culture-mindful leaders and managers use every opportunity for communicating culturally essential issues—be it during a regular meeting, a visit in the organizational unit, management- or leadership meeting, a fireside chat with junior leaders, an organization visit or informal conversations with employees. In doing so, they take their conversation partners' perspectives and illustrate their message with appropriate examples that fit their work experience and work-life situation.

10.4.4 Culture-Mindful Managers and Leaders Think Positively and Search for Opportunities

One can look at every situation from at least two different perspectives: positive and negative. A glass half-filled with water is a typical example for illustrating these two perspectives of the same situation. Some may focus on the glass still being half full, while others focus on it already being half empty.

Culture-mindful managers and leaders know about the impact of a positive message and being realistic about situations. No matter how difficult a situation is, they will focus on and communicate the positive aspects of a given case and the inherent opportunities while carefully observing the development of potentially harmful elements. Even though the facts remain the same, the positive emphasis can unleash energy and motivation to move forward, especially in difficult times. To give an example of positive thinking:

> Roy Ash, co-founder, and former CEO and Chairman of Litton Industries, was recruited as turnaround manager for another company. After getting more familiar with the details of the organization's situation, he realized that the problems were much worse than he had assumed based on his initial conversations with board members and all the information he had gathered before accepting the job offer. Despite this highly critical situation, he focused on the positive side, keeping his energy and motivation: The firm was still alive!
>
> *(Personal conversation with the author)*

A positive attitude and positive thinking may help discover options that are still available even in the most challenging and messy situations. Furthermore, positive thinking and a positive approach mobilize the energy needed for tackling upcoming challenges. At the same time, culture-mindful managers and leaders are open to and listen to their organizational members' concerns. They create an atmosphere in which their people dare to bring up potential or emerging problems early. Early addressing issues allows them to discuss these issues openly and search together for possible solutions. Thus their positive thinking allows tackling challenges early before they become big problems.

10.4.5 Culture-Mindful Managers and Leaders Explain Situations and their Interrelationships

Due to their inherent role model function, manager and leader symbolize, represent and communicate an organization's culture both verbally and nonverbally. Hence, culture-mindful managers and leaders provide clear, unequivocal, consistent, and congruent messages in their communication. They explain situations in a way that organizational members can understand their intended meanings. Hence, culture-mindful managers and leaders can take their employees' perspectives, describe and discuss issues and events from their perspective in a language they understand. They also use and give examples their people can relate to.

Culture-mindful managers and leaders do not only convey information. They also point out and explain relevant connections and interrelationships between constituencies involved in the situation at hand. In addition, they provide contextually relevant information. Such information helps organizational members to understand the reasons behind certain decisions or actions better. In a change process, culture-mindful managers and leaders do not only communicate the goal of the change. They also share the reasons for the change, the options they explored, and the reasons behind the final decisions. They explain why the chosen path seems the most promising one and what kind of outcomes they expect. They also explain what might happen if they don't change. This contextual information and underlying reasons help organizational members to support even uncomfortable and unpleasant decisions and take the necessary actions for their implementation.

10.4.6 Culture-Mindful Managers and Leaders Set Examples and Live the Desired Culture

Culture-mindful managers and leaders take their role of symbolizing an organization's culture seriously. They pay close attention to the message their verbal and nonverbal behavior may convey to their people. They communicate carefully and intentionally set examples with their behavior, as illustrated in the following three examples.

1. The manager, Betty wanted to promote creativity, innovation, and open communication in her area of responsibility. She allowed her people to make mistakes as long as they were not jeopardizing the entire unit, and they used them as an opportunity to learn. In addition, Betty discussed with her people their range of freedom. In critical situations, she explored antecedents with them, reflected on the impact of actions taken, and gave them appropriate feedback. To provide a specific example of her way of communicating: "Good work, Henry! Now we know that the system can also lead to problems. Please, summarize for your colleagues what kind of conditions led to these problems and how you and your team could solve them." She rewarded her organizational members for experimenting with new behavior and work methods. In case of sustained performance improvements, those involved in developing and implementing them participated in the respective savings.

(continued)

2. A restaurant manager intentionally looked away when waiters dropped a glass or a plate. Knowing that the situation was awkward and uncomfortable for them, he did not want to make it worse by criticizing them.
3. A manager valued the physical presence of his people in the office and considered controls necessary. When he noticed that one of his people was getting ready to leave a few minutes before the end of the workday, he ostentatiously looked at his watch and made comments such as "you are leaving early today?" At the same time, he positively commented on the remarkable dedication of people who worked long hours. He rewarded the latter by giving them attractive tasks, placing them on desirable projects, and openly praising them in meetings in the presence of their colleagues.

Culture-mindful managers and leaders critically question their behavior regarding the message it may convey. They live the desired culture in their daily conduct and act as living examples of the organization's culture.

10.4.7 Culture-Mindful Managers and Leaders Take Time for their People

Culture-mindful managers and leaders are aware of their role and responsibility regarding their employees. They make and take time for one of their core tasks—leading the people who directly report to them. Their leadership behavior includes taking time for the annual meeting in which they agree on goals, appraise their performance, and give them feedback. However, this annual meeting does not entail surprises since it summarizes issues that were addressed over the year. Their employees can always approach culture-mindful managers and leaders. They are available for providing information, dialogue, and discussions. They regularly give feedback. They act as sparring partners, coaches, and mentors. They make time to discuss their employees' problems and concerns and share their success stories with them. To summarize, culture-mindful managers and leaders consider their employees their customers and try to serve them well.

10.4.8 Culture-Mindful Managers and Leaders Pay Attention to Small Things

Culture-mindful managers and leaders know about the impact that small things—from their perspective—may have on their people. In daily work, small attentions may count, such as remembering their employee's birthday or acknowledging them when completing a difficult task or project successfully. They make an effort to have a conversation with their people when they return from a long vacation and appreciate it when they work overtime to meet the deadline of a project. Even though these events may appear small in the eyes of a manager or leader, they are important to organizational members. Hence, culture-mindful managers and leaders recognize these things and accomplishments and express their appreciation to their employees.

10.4.9 Culture-Mindful Managers and Leaders Continue to Learn and Develop Themselves

Culture-mindful managers and leaders live and work by the principles that one can always learn and improve. They also apply these principles to themselves. They regularly reflect on their actions and try to learn from their experience and the results of their efforts. They periodically question their behavior and efficacy, critically reflecting and exploring more efficient and effective behavior modes if necessary. They regularly ask for feedback from their organizational members, colleagues, and managers to assess the effects of their behavior on various stakeholders better. They experiment with new behavior and actively seek out new situations—not for the sake of change or being different. Instead, they have a genuine interest in learning, improving, and further developing.

I hope you will enjoy your culture-sensitive and culture-mindful management and leadership and its impact!

References

Bandura, A. (1994). *Lernen am Modell*. Klett-Cotta.

Carlzon, J. (1989). *Moments of truth*. Harper Business.

Costas, J., & Kärreman, D. (2016). Bored selves in knowledge work. *Human Relations, 69*(1), 61–83. https://doi.org/10.1177/0018726715579736

Dürr, H. (1990). Kann man eine Unternehmenskultur ändern? In H. Simon (Ed.), *Herausforderung Unternehmenskultur* (pp. 131–135). Schäffer.

Eberle, T. S. (1997). Cultural contrasts in a democratic nonprofit organization: The case of a Swiss reading society. In S. A. Sackmann (Ed.), *Cultural complexity in organizations: Inherent contrasts and contradictions* (pp. 133–159).

Giberson, T. R., Resick, C. J., Dickson, M. W., Mitchelson, J. K., Randall, K. R., & Clark, M. A. (2009). Leadership and organizational culture: Linking CEO characteristics to cultural values. *Journal of Business Psychology, 24*(2), 123–137. https://doi.org/10.1007/s10869-009-9109-1

Gore, W. L., & Associates, Inc. (2020). *GORE enterprise culture*. Accessed Sep 24, 2021, from www.gore.com/system/files/2021-04/Gore-Culture-Press-Kit-February2021.pdf

Graham, J. R., Grennan, N. J., Harvey, C. R., & Rajgopal, N. S. (2021). *Corporate culture: Evidence from the field*. 27th Annual Conference on Financial Economics and Accounting Paper. Columbia Business School Research Paper No. 16–49; Duke I&E Research Paper No. 2016–33. Accessed Jun 8, 2021, from SSRN-id2805602.pdf.

Herzberg, F. I., Mausner, B., & Snyderman, B. B. (1959). *The motivation to work*. Wiley.

Hickson, D. J. (1987). Decision making at the top of organizations. *Annual Review of Sociology, 13* (1), 165–192. https://doi.org/10.1146/annurev.so.13.080187.001121

Kotter, J. P., & Heskett, J. L. (1992). *Organizational culture and performance*. Free Press.

Malik, F. (2015). *Managing performing living: Effective management for a new world* (2nd ed.). Campus.

Nazar, J. (2021, April 21). 13 leadership lessons from zoom founder and CEO Eric yuan. *Entrepreneur Online*. Accessed Sep Jun 24, 2021, from www.entrepreneur.com/article/368550

O'Reilly, C. A. I. I. I., & Tushman, M. L. (2011). Organizational ambidexterity in action: How managers explore and exploit. *California Management Review, 53*(4), 5–21. https://doi.org/10.1525/cmr.2011.53.4.5

O'Reilly, C. A. I. I. I., & Tushman, M. L. (2013). Organizational ambidexterity: Past, present, and future. *Academy of Management Perspectives, 27*(4), 324–338. https://doi.org/10.2139/ssrn.2285704

O'Reilly, C. A. I. I. I., & Tushman, M. L. (2016). *Lead and disrupt: How to solve the innovator's dilemma*. Stanford University Books.

Özsungur, F. (2020). The effects of boreout on stress, depression and anxiety in the workplace. *Business and Management Studies, 8*(2), 1391–1423. https://doi.org/10.15295/bmij.v8i2.1460

Pallenberg, S. (2018, June 18). How the Daimler Leadership 2020 initiative drives cultural change. *LinkedIn Online*. Accessed Sep 24, 2021, from www.linkedin.com/pulse/how-daimler-leadership-2020-initiative-drives-change-pallenberg

Panda, A., & Gupta, R. K. (2001). Understanding organizational culture: A perspective on roles for leaders. *Vikalpa, 26*(4), 3–19. https://doi.org/10.1177/0256090920010402

Pelton, W., Sackmann, S. A., & Boguslaw, R. (1990). *Tough choices. The decision making styles of America's top 50 CEO's*. Dow Jones-Irwin.

Pinder, C. C. (2008). *Work motivation in organizational behavior*. Psychology Press.

Ruigrok, W., & Achtenhagen, L. (1999). Organisational culture and the transformation to innovative forms of organising. *European Journal of Work and Occupational Psychology, 8*(4), 521–536. Accessed Sep 24, 2021, from www.alexandria.unisg.ch/publications/8367

Sackmann, S. A. (1991). *Cultural knowledge in organizations. Exploring the collective mind*. Sage.

Sackmann, S. A., & Bertelsmann Foundation. (2006). *Success factor: Corporate culture. Developing a corporate culture for high performance and long-term competitiveness*. Bertelsmann Stiftung.

Schein, E. H. (1986). Wie Führungskräfte Kultur prägen und vermitteln. *GDI-Impuls, 4*(2), 23–36. Accessed Sep 24, 2021, from www.gdi.ch/de/publikationen/gdi-impuls-archiv

Schein, E. H. (1995). *Unternehmenskultur: Ein Handbuch für Führungskräfte*. Frankfurt/Main: Campus.

Schwartzmann, J. (1981). Play, epistemology and change. In A. T. Cheska (Ed.), *Play as context* (pp. 52–59). Leisure.

Sprenger, R. K. (2002). *Mythos Motivation. Wege aus einer Sackgasse* (17th ed.). Frankfurt/Main: Campus.

StepStone Deutschland AG. (2012). Weltweite Befragung "Do you feel underemployed in your job sometimes?". *StepStone Online-jobmarket*. Accessed Sep 24, 2021, from www.stepstone.de

Trice, H. M., & Beyer, J. M. (1993). *The cultures of work organizations*. Prentice-Hall.

Williamson, O. E. (1996). Vergleichende ökonomische Organisationstheorie: Die Analyse diskreter Strukturalternativen. In P. Kenis & V. Schneider (Eds.), *Organisation und Netzwerk: Institutionelle Steuerung in Wirtschaft und Politik* (pp. 167–212). Frankfurt/Main: Campus.

WirtschaftsWoche Online. (2016, November 1). *Daimler stößt Kulturwandel an*. Accessed Sep 24, 2021, from www.wiwo.de/unternehmen/auto/daimler-daimler-stoesst-kulturwandel-an/14766332.html